Internet Site Security

Erik Schetina

Ken Green

Jacob Carlson

✦Addison-Wesley

Boston • San Francisco • New York • Toronto • Montreal
London • Munich • Paris • Madrid
Capetown • Sydney • Tokyo • Singapore • Mexico City

The publisher offers discounts on this book when ordered in quantity for special sales.

For more information, please contact:

Pearson Education Corporate Sales Division

201 W. 103rd Street

Indianapolis, IN 46290

(800) 428-5331

corpsales@pearsoned.com

Visit AW on the Web: www.awl.com/cseng/

ISBN 0-672-32306-0

05   04   03   02   4   3   2   1

First printing, March 2002

ASSOCIATE PUBLISHER
Jeff Koch

ACQUISITIONS EDITORS
William C. Brown
Kim Spilker

DEVELOPMENT EDITORS
Mark Renfrow
Nancy E. Sixsmith

MANAGING EDITOR
Matt Purcell

PROJECT EDITOR
Andy Beaster

COPY EDITOR
Krista Hansing

INDEXER
Angie Bess

PROOFREADER
Linda Seifert

TECHNICAL EDITOR
Shon Harris

TEAM COORDINATOR
Amy Patton

INTERIOR DESIGNER
Anne Jones

COVER DESIGNER
Aren Howell

PAGE LAYOUT
Brad Lenser

Contents at a Glance

Table of Contents

About the Authors

Erik Schetina is the chief technology officer for TrustWave Corporation, a Maryland-based Internet security firm. Mr. Schetina began his career in the information security field in 1985, when he joined the U.S. Department of Defense (DoD) as an electronic engineer. Over the next 13 years, he was heavily involved in the DoD's development of key signals intelligence and information security systems, including cryptographic tokens, public-key cryptosystems, and signal-processing systems. Mr. Schetina holds a master's degree in electrical engineering from The Johns Hopkins University and has a bachelor's degree in electrical engineering from Columbia University. He is a member of the Information Security Consortium and a Certified Information Systems Security Professional (CISSP). He is the author of two technical reference books: *The Compact Disc* (Prentice-Hall, 1989) and *Digital Audio Tape Recorders* (Prentice-Hall, 1993).

Ken Green is a senior security engineer for TrustWave Corporation. Before joining TrustWave, he served as a technical director and senior electronic engineer at the U.S. Department of Defense, where he gained broad experience in many information security and network-analysis engineering and operations programs. Mr. Green is a recognized expert across the intelligence community on telecommunications and data network analysis and protocols, including TCP/IP, IPSec, VPNs, ATM, SONET/SDH, Frame Relay, and SS7; he often has served as a consultant to other U.S. government agencies as well. His technical expertise includes protocol analysis, object-oriented software development, and large-scale data-processing system engineering. Mr. Green holds both bachelor's and master's degrees in electrical engineering from Purdue University, where he studied digital communications theory and signal processing. Post-graduate studies include work at The John Hopkins University, where he studied network theory, advanced signal processing, and wireless communications.

Jacob Carlson is a senior security engineer for TrustWave Corporation. He possesses deep experience in designing, developing, and implementing secure systems and network zones, as well as host and network penetration testing, incident response, and computer forensics, including data recovery. He has worked with, installed, and administered all manner of firewalls, host- and network-based intrusion-detection systems, and "honey pots." Additionally, he is well versed in encryption, authentication, cryptographic integrity mechanisms, and public-key infrastructure. A senior security consultant and penetration testing specialist at TrustWave, Mr. Carlson has conducted sessions on the subject of securing Windows NT, as well as buffer overrun techniques. He also has participated in an open panel discussion entitled "Update on the Hacker Scene," at which a number of noted security experts discussed the happenings at the DEFCON conference and new exploitation techniques that the hacker community is exploring. Mr. Carlson is also an experienced forensic analyst.

Dedication

It seems appropriate that a book published in the aftermath of September 11th be dedicated in memory of the victims of that day, both those who died and those who have gone on living.

Acknowledgments

The authors want to acknowledge the contributions of Phil Smith and Vizo Allman in the areas of forensics and Windows security, respectively. In addition, we want to thank William Brown for helping us to take this project from outline to reality. Finally, we could not have completed this book without the support and patience of those who are closest to us. Special thanks to our families for your encouragement over the past few months and the many years before that.

Mr. Carlson wants to extend special thanks: To Ms. Kelly O'Bannon (soon to be Ms. Kelly Carlson!) for unwavering support, understanding, and making me laugh so hard. To The Beard Cafe for offering an environment that made writing this book a possibility. To Dad, for always supporting me and being proud, regardless of how strange I seemed and how many scholarships I lost. And to Mom for, well, for everything.

Mr. Green wishes to thank his family, especially his parents, Kitty and Ralph, for all their love and support through the years.

Introduction

Before September 11, we probably would have started out this introduction talking about how nothing has made more of an impact in recent years than the growth of the Internet. In light of the events of that day, though, such a statement seems both ludicrous and disrespectful. What we can do is point out that networks of all kinds have always been media of change and instruments of progress, good or bad.

Networks don't have to be created from routers and cable. Networks can weld together individuals of similar purpose and allow them to pool their efforts to accomplish an end. Such ends, unfortunately, are not always principled. Every day we read and hear about terrorist networks and webs of terror. The newspapers report about organized crime networks and law enforcement's efforts to break them. Unfriendly governments run networks of spies and saboteurs. Such images cast the network as an instrument of malevolence, an infrastructure for evil. But networks are not always used to promote discord. There are networks of giving that collect funds for the needy. There are networks of caring that concern themselves with the welfare of the sick. In the business world, people network to improve their company's growth opportunities, while others network to find a mate.

The Internet, like any network, provides the same opportunities to individuals who would use it for the common good as it does to those who would abuse it. The intent of this book is to provide security professionals with a guide to the real-world implications of security, to allow them to build their networks and systems in ways that least expose them to risk. Many security books take an encyclopedic approach to security, dutifully going through the details of every protocol and operating system configuration parameter. Although this book does cover the technical details of many operating systems, networking components, applications, and protocols, and although the intended reader of this book is an in-the-trenches practitioner, you will not find it filled with the usual collection of dry explanations and theoretical vulnerabilities. Our intent in creating this book was to encapsulate the experiences that we have garnered during years of system development, cryptographic design, secure networking, and security consulting for scores of large and small clients in a book that takes the reader from security policy to security reality. To that end, you will find that we have included many examples of how security principles have been applied in real networks by real companies. You'll also see a few examples of what can happen when sound security principles are not followed.

Most books make the choice of either talking to an audience at the policy and principle level or neglecting these aspects of security and delving immediately into the technical details of such components as firewalls, operating systems, and applications. We believe that it is an injustice to talk about security without talking about the *process* of security as well. Like it or not, for security to be effective, the steps that an administrator takes to lock down a network have to be an extension of an overarching security policy. Security practitioners who do nothing but implement point solutions such as firewalls and VPNs without thinking about how they fit into an overall program and policy are doing themselves, their employers, and their budgets a disservice. A company that does not protect its critical assets, whether they are information, business processes, or services, will not be in business for long.

To protect an asset, you need to first identify it. To protect it adequately, you need to determine what threatens it. To protect it in an efficient manner, you need to weigh the cost and effort to protect it against its value. All of these factors come together in the development of a security policy and program. In the end, the IT department still gets to deploy its firewalls and intrusion-detection systems, but only through a thoughtful process can these systems be selected and put in place in ways that offer the best protection to the most critical assets. This mode of thinking has led us to include two chapters that deal exclusively with risk and policy. These are not the usual dry calls to develop a security policy by picking the appropriate statements from a book of templates. We believe that a meaningful policy must be developed to protect the specific aspects of the organization and that the security practitioner can and should be a valuable contributor in putting together a policy that works.

After all this talk about policy, we really need to speak to what the bulk of this book is about, and that's down-and-dirty security. In each chapter, we have attempted to cover aspects of security that build upon each other and ultimately lead to the creation of a "secure" infrastructure. We have taken great efforts to make certain that we talk not just about "ivory tower" security, but that we bring that discussion down to the real-world implementation level as well. For example, many technologists talk about how digital certificates are the silver bullet that can provide a ubiquitous basis for authenticating users on the Internet. They forget to tell you that of the 500 million users who are estimated to be citizens of the Net, about 99.99% of them still rely on a username and password to log on to their systems. Knowing about PKI is good, but knowing how to utilize the username/password in an effective and secure manner is *practical*.

The same holds true in discussions of system vulnerabilities. The classic man-in-the-middle attack, in which a nefarious character intercepts the communications between two network entities and then masquerades as one of the entities, is interesting from a technical standpoint but hardly ever possible from a practical standpoint. This doesn't mean that such an attack *can't* happen—it just means that, in our experience, it hardly ever *does*. The security practitioner will utilize his time better by keeping Web servers patched to prevent a 13-year-old hacker from crashing them than by implementing encryption among all the servers to block man-in-the-middle attacks. That's just reality, and that's what we think is one of the main differentiators of this book—and a good reason for you to read it.

In the end, security requires constant learning and adaptation, much like life itself. This book presents a philosophy of security, an explanation of the techniques and processes used to engineer and maintain a secure network, and examples of how others have used these principles to protect themselves without closing the door on productivity and utility. It is our sincere desire that this book will help to raise the general level of security awareness as well as arm security practitioners with the specific knowledge that they require to go about, as Elvis used to say, taking care of business.

Core Concepts: Risks, Threats, and Vulnerabilities

Most of this book is about the technical nature of security: how Web sites get hacked, what intrusion detection is all about, and how to write secure code and design secure network architectures. This chapter and the one that follows it are a bit off that track. The reason for this is that too many administrators, IT directors, and even CIOs believe that security is achieved solely through the implementation of point solutions.

You might ask, "What is a point solution?" A point solution is anything that addresses a particular aspect of security. For example, a firewall might address one aspect of access control. How do you know if you've fallen victim to the belief that if you add enough point solutions, you will end up with a secure environment? Ask yourself this question: "How do I know that my information is secure?" If you answer that your information is secure because you have a firewall or because you've installed an intrusion-detection system or you do virus scanning, then you're missing the boat.

First Steps

The first step in developing a secure environment isn't figuring out how to spend your security budget, nor is it drawing up a network diagram and determining where and how to protect your servers. Before you can take either of these steps (both of which are ultimately necessary, by the way), you need to ask yourself and your organization a few basic questions:

- What information assets do I have?
- How important are each of these assets?
- What are the threats to these assets?
- What are the assets' vulnerabilities?

The answers lead you to some simple conclusions:

- You can't protect your assets if you don't know what they are.
- You can't determine how best to protect them if you don't know what's threatening them.
- You can't determine what assets are worth protecting if you don't know how important they are.

A classic example of the "point solution" mind-set is the organization that runs its own Web server, DNS, and mail server. You might find that it has hardened and patched its operating systems so that they're not easily hacked, that it has great firewalls and intrusion-detection systems that are monitored 24 × 7, and that it does everything right when it comes to protecting its servers. All of this protection, however, means very little if the lifeblood of the company has nothing to do with its Web site or the availability of email, but has everything to do with its client database that resides on some internal server that hasn't been patched in six months. Does the company care if its Web site is defaced? Certainly. Will business come to a grinding halt if this happens? Probably not. Will the company survive if a dissatisfied employee throws the database server out a window, or if someone on the cleaning crew steals the backup tapes and sells them to a competitor? Perhaps not. The lesson here is that if you don't know what you're protecting and from whom, they you might build a great moat around the wrong castle.

Now, given the fact that this book is a fairly technical treatise on security, you might ask why we even need to cover such high-level concepts as risks, threats, and vulnerabilities. The reason is because we believe that it's everyone's job to understand and apply good security practices. Many times we come across system administrators who couldn't care less about whether their company has a security policy, or who can't see the value in worrying about backup tapes when implementing an intrusion-detection system is so much more fun.

Although these individuals are technically competent, they should be much more interested and involved in the overall security process. Business managers might have the best feel for what information assets are really critical to the continued success of the enterprise, but very often these "techies" understand where the critical assets actually are located and how they are or are not protected. This same group also can be invaluable in helping the policy wonks develop a meaningful security policy, who can best help management understand the threats to the business, and who can help plan and develop a meaningful security program that takes into account policy, architecture, and implementation. So, without further pontificating, let's begin by examining some core concepts in security.

Defining Your Assets

Step 1: Identify your business' assets. Taking this step does a few good things. First, it focuses you on what's important to your organization; second, it can help you justify your security budget (more on this in the next chapter). An asset can take many forms. It can be a business process, such as order taking from a client, or a data component, such as a business plan or a design document. Eventually, you should be able to draw a direct line between an information asset, such as a database of client information, and point solutions, such as these:

- The access-control and auditing features of the operating system of the server that the database resides on.
- The intrusion-detection system that looks for attempts to break into the server that houses the database.
- The high-availability firewall that keeps everyone on the Internet from connecting to the server that houses the database, while ensuring that the sales team can access it whenever needed.
- The authentication tokens and remote-access VPN that is used by the sales team to access the business plan from members' homes while keeping the data from prying eyes.

Some of the typical forms that assets take include those listed in the following sections.

Proprietary Information and Intellectual Property

These types of assets can include lists of client contact information, sales databases, business plans, product designs, company performance numbers, methodologies, source code, and other "hard" assets. Safeguarding proprietary information often leads to requirements for access control, encryption, and intrusion detection.

Company Reputation or Image

Companies whose livelihood depends in large part on their reputation or brand identity should value this somewhat intangible commodity as an asset worth protecting. What would happen to the confidence of clients if an investigative firm's Web site were defaced? What kind of negative publicity would that create? Would prospective clients worry about how private their cases would be kept? Imagine what would happen to a software company if a Web site running the company's server product was defaced because of poor application security? Well, maybe that last one's not a good example.

Business Processes

Any process that is critical to the operation of an organization should be listed as an important asset. For example, the capability of a telecommunications company to bill its clients is key to maintaining the cash flow and, hence, viability of the company. The capability of the same company to accept orders from its salespeople also might be a critical function if it can be done only electronically. Interestingly enough, the employee payroll function, which the average system administrator would consider vitally important, usually is ranked by management at the bottom of the business process importance list because most companies wouldn't go out of business if payroll were delayed.

Threats Agents

Now that you have developed a neat little list of the information assets of your organization, you can start to look at where the threats to these assets come from. The knee-jerk reaction when thinking about threats is to worry about the ubiquitous "hacker," to the exclusion of all else. As security consultants are happy to tell you, well over two-thirds of all security incidents are perpetrated by insiders, not hackers. This figure still comes as a surprise to many people, probably because about 90% of all security incidents that make front-page news have to do with the latest email virus from Slobovia or the most recent online retailer to have its Web site defaced or credit card data stolen. Perhaps justly, businesses don't want to advertise it when they have a security problem, especially when it comes from within.

What, then, are the typical "threat agents" that most organizations face? They include the hacker, of course, but a long list of other threats must be taken into consideration when protecting information assets.

Insider Threats

By far the greatest threat to an organization comes from insiders. If you give this some thought, you'll see that it makes complete sense. Insiders know what your critical assets are, where they reside, and how they're protected. Insiders typically are trusted more than outsiders. They have physical and often network access to your systems. They sit inside your firewall and might not be monitored by an intrusion-detection system. These are all attributes that an outside threat such as a criminal or a hacker would love to have. Often the only thing standing between an insider and your critical assets is the insider's scruples, and many times this is not enough. Furthermore, the same advantages that an insider with intent has to do harm amplify the damage that an insider can do by accident. One wrong click on an executable Trojan horse email attachment by an unwitting insider can provide both remote access and system degradations that might be impossible to achieve through a direct attack from the outside. A quick review of the insider threat follows.

Full-Time Employees

This group has physical access to your network and knows or can find out what the critical assets are, where they can be found, and who has access to them. These people usually have the ability to log onto your network, they sit behind your firewall, and they have all the time in the world to probe your systems for weaknesses if they choose to do so. An employee might be motivated by personal vendettas (disliking a manager) or monetary gain (selling a client list to a competitor), or he might be an unwitting accomplice to another intruder ("Gee, I wasn't supposed to share my security token with anyone?"). Administrators have all these abilities, plus they hold the "keys to the kingdom" in the form of root access to systems and the capability to install new systems or change system configurations at will.

Consultants

The consultant that's working for you today might be working for your competitor tomorrow—or might even *become* your competitor tomorrow. Many organizations do a poor job of keeping track of consultants, especially when it comes to getting rid of computer accounts when a consultant's job is finished. A consultant often utilizes his own laptop when on your premises, so you might not have control over what applications are run or what "tools" are wielded against you.

Partners

Many organizations are opening up their networks to business partners without contemplating the fact that they could very well inherit their partners' security risks in the deal. If you plug another company into your WAN without implementing the appropriate safeguards, then you take on all the security risks and vulnerabilities of your partner. A good example of this is the well-publicized case of a Russian company that purchased a feed to the Bloomberg financial service. This service provides financial quotes, among other things, to its subscribers and installs a dedicated connection at the subscriber's site. An employee of the subscriber company promptly hacked into the Bloomberg network through this feed and then attempted to extort Michael Bloomberg, threatening to go public with the hack unless he was paid off!

New Acquisitions

Many industries have consolidated in recent years, with one company merging with or acquiring others. In the rush to bring together these companies as rapidly as possible, the IT staff often is told to get the networks connected immediately. Unfortunately, the rush to complete the merger often means that neither of the parties gets an opportunity to compare security notes before the Frame Relay circuit or leased line is put in place between the two networks. This can result in one formerly secure network being opened up to the world by a connection to a very insecure network.

Miscellaneous

Other threats to your information assets can come in all types of forms. A typical threat comes from cleaning crews, who might have after-hours or unescorted access to your physical system. In many buildings, companies share Internet connectivity with a myriad of other tenants of the building, all of whom can be considered as a threat agent. You also might find that your CEO's 14-year-old child is a threat agent if he decides to hack into your network through the cable modem VPN connection. In short, just about anyone with inside access to your systems or network can and should be considered as a threat agent when it comes to information security.

Outsider Threats

Outsider threats can be the main source of aggravation for organizations with a significant Internet exposure, such as large commerce sites or exchanges. The methods that outsiders use are greatly limited compared to those available to the insider, and the profile of the outsider falls into several major categories.

Script Kiddies

Because so many automated tools have been written to search systems for vulnerabilities and then run exploits against them, it no longer takes a computer expert to break into a system. "Script kiddies" are so named because they largely utilize exploits written by others to break into networks or deface Web sites.

Elite Hackers

A much smaller group of hackers falls into the "elite" category. These are the folks who truly understand the inner workings of network protocols, applications, and operating systems, and spend untold hours poring over source code and reverse-engineering executable code to find arcane weaknesses in systems.

Criminals

The opportunity for monetary gain, either from extortion or from the sale and exploitation of information, motivates criminals to explore every method at their disposal, from robbery and break-ins to information theft and network penetration. When you combine the motivation of a criminal with the skill of an elite hacker, you end up with a person who might be described as a professional thief. This type of individual steals credit card numbers from an online retailer, extorts the retailer to keep the incident out of the press, and, in the end, sells the numbers to the highest bidder. Considering the value of assets such as bank accounts and credit card numbers that are accessible electronically, it is no wonder that electronic crime is a significant source of worry for connected businesses.

Philosophically Opposed Individuals and Organizations

Many organizations have felt the sting of individuals who are philosophically opposed to their business practices, politics, or morality. For example after the U.S. reconnaissance plane landed in China in 2001, Chinese hackers defaced hundreds of U.S. Web sites in protest. Although these defacements were mostly nuisances, other companies or individuals can find themselves at greater risk from extremists or fringe groups at all ends of the political and moral spectrum.

Terrorists

A few years ago, this category of threat really wasn't thought about by the corporate world. Since September 11, 2001, that has changed. The federal government has been sounding this alarm for some time—in fact, in 1998, under the Clinton Administration, the Commission for Critical Infrastructure determined that not only government entities, but also nearly 50,000 commercial companies, truly function as part of the U.S. critical infrastructure. The findings of this commission prompted the issuance of a Presidential Decision Directive, PDD-63, that called for commercial businesses to assess the state of their network infrastructures. This directive was renewed under the Bush Administration as PDD-1. Along with other governmental initiatives, it points out that the terrorist threat can be directed at commercial as well as government or military targets.

Determining Risk

Now that you have catalogued your organization's assets and you understand the threats to these assets, it's time to look at how vulnerable they are to attack. From this, you can determine the risk to each asset. This might sound like a lot of "policy-ese," but, in practice, it is a

very useful way to go about the task of securing a business. You sometimes might see a formula that looks like the following used to describe a risk equation: *Risk = Threat ×
Vulnerability × Asset Value*. In fact, many professional risk managers have developed programs
to mathematically rate the risk to an organization's assets based on assigning risks and threats
numerical weightings.

As an example, let's say that the only vulnerability that you've identified for a particular information database occurs if an attacker can get physical access to the server that houses the database. If the database holds weather data that is publicly available, then the only threat agent
could be a script kiddie who wants to put a notch on his belt for hacking your server. However,
the vulnerability dictates that the script kiddie will have to break into your facility to exploit
the vulnerability. In this case, you have a minimal vulnerability, a minimal threat, and a low
value on the information assets, which means that the risk to this asset is low. Now, let's
assume that the database houses information about the movement of terrorists. Suddenly the
threat agent becomes a terrorist, a "numerically large" threat value. Even though breaking into
your facility is a "numerically small" value, it is offset by the threat. The asset value is also
extremely high, perhaps invaluable. Now you find that spending a good bit money to protect
against this rather minimal vulnerability makes sense when seen in light of the threat and value
of the data.

Summary

In this chapter, we've outlined a key security concept: mitigating risk to critical information
assets. To mitigate risks to your information systems, you need to first understand what assets
your organization holds dear. When you know what's important, you can categorize the risk to
those assets by determining the threats that face them and the vulnerabilities that they present.
Given the value of the asset, its threats, and its vulnerabilities, you can determine risk and
make informed decisions about how to mitigate that risk.

The bulk of this book deals with understanding fundamental technical vulnerabilities and how
to address them. To make good use of this knowledge, you must constantly run through the
risk equation in your mind to determine whether you are putting your efforts and budget into
areas that will deliver the highest value. Installing a security device in a Web farm to track
hacker activities might be technically interesting and have a high "gee-wiz" appeal, but if that's
not where your company's critical assets are, then you're not doing your job as a security professional.

In Chapter 2, "Developing a Trusted Internet Infrastructure," we're going to take a closer look
at the entire process of security at a macro level. This will include everything from policy and
assessment through security devices and incident response. In the following chapters, we'll
delve into much greater detail in most of these areas.

Developing a Trusted Internet Infrastructure

IN THIS CHAPTER

The previous chapter discussed the various types of threats and agents that constitute the motivation for security. Ultimately, security is really about protecting those assets that are dear to your enterprise. These may be a company's image, its products, its distribution mechanism, intellectual property, or its ability to conduct business. At the technical level, we tend to think about protecting systems rather than assets. The UNIX or Windows administrator focuses on keeping the server operating systems patched, hardening their applications against attack, or monitoring log files for unusual activity. The typical administrator doesn't think about how they fit into the overall picture and function of security or how their actions are really the implementation of an overall security policy and program.

The Motivation for Security

The goal of this chapter is to show how the many parts, such as administration, systems, architecture, policy, and audit, fit into an overall security plan. The intent of this plan is to protect assets and business functions, and the implementation of this plan eventually translates into protecting systems such as Web and mail servers. For the security practitioner, understanding the bigger security picture is the key to transitioning from a good technical person to a true security professional. The bulk of this book deals with the technical specifics of security, such as how to lock down an IIS server or how to harden a Linux system. This chapter, unlike the others, presents a higher-level look at security. The intent is to raise the readers from a myopic view of security that looks at point solutions such as firewalls and access control lists, to a holistic view of security that recognizes the importance of every component, from policy to implementation.

As a simple example, let's look at a process that has nothing to do with technical security: terminating an employee's employment. From the standpoint of the Human Resources (HR) department, concern arises about getting back the person's ID badge, briefing him about ongoing health benefits, finding out where the final paychecks go to, and perhaps paying him out for any accrued vacation. One critical step that's often left out is notifying IT that a person is being let go and then determining what should happen to that person's account information and access. Should that person's email accounts be deleted immediately or archived off for a period of time? What about his laptop? Should it be wiped and given to another employee? Should the network files be kept or deleted? And, most importantly, what about network access? Many a business has let an employee go only to find out much later that the person's remote access account was never disabled and that he can still log in to the account or send and pickup email. How this type of event is handled is something that many times is left up to the discretion of the system administrator but should really be driven from a policy standpoint, and perhaps even a legal standpoint.

For example, if the employee is being let go because he had a propensity for sending unsavory email, then it's probably important that his email account be frozen and archived just in case it's needed in any future legal proceedings. This isn't the typical thought that crosses an administrator's mind when being told that someone has left the company and that his account no longer is needed.

To develop a truly trusted Internet infrastructure, it's imperative to look at all aspects of security. As anyone will tell you, a chain is only as strong as its weakest link. In this chapter, we're going to examine those links and look at how they interact with and interdepend upon each other. In doing so, we hope to show how everyone with a direct responsibility for security can labor toward the same goals.

What Constitutes Security?

Security means different things to different people. To the systems administrator, it might mean making sure that the Internet systems aren't getting hacked. To the developer, it can mean using SSL when collecting credit card information from Web users on an e-commerce site. To the CIO, CFO, or board of directors, security means that the business is reasonably protected from loss and that they've been diligent in making sure of that. The IT manager lives somewhere between these extremes and is worried about not only the technical aspects of security, but also such issues as consumer privacy, reasonable audit, and configuration management of systems and software.

Often these different levels of responsibility and function accompany a "don't care" attitude about the roles of their counterparts. The system administrator doesn't care about policy and process; the manager doesn't care about implementation. Because this book is intended for an audience with a mostly technical background such as IT managers, developers, and administrators, we thought that it was important to include a complete view of information security for the simple reason that technical people *do* need to care about policy and process. The following sections discuss the high-level concepts of information security from the perspective of the implementer, administrator, or technical manager to highlight the areas where they can and should make a difference—and hopefully to alert them to components of security that sometimes fall through the cracks.

The Security Process

Any book on security, whether it's a technical work on the vulnerabilities of TCP/IP or an auditor's guide to policy creation, should address the process of security, not just the specific details of a single practice. Throughout this book, we attempt to stress that security is a process, not a final goal that is achieved and then forgotten about. In this section, we discuss this process as well as its components and goals. The intent of this section is to introduce a broad overview of security practices. Regardless of your position or responsibility, you need to understand how you fit into the process, what you should be concerned about, and what other factors might impact your function and duties.

As stated before, security is a process, not a point in time. The process generally can be broken down into four major components:

- Assessment and policy
- Asset protection
- Monitoring and detection
- Response and recovery

These four components compromise what is often portrayed as the security wheel.

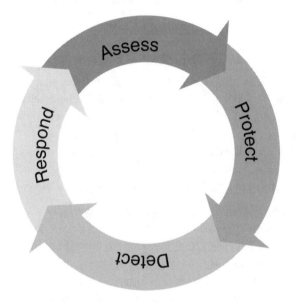

FIGURE 2.1
The process of security.

In the *assessment and policy* phase, organizations determine their security requirements and define organizational roles and responsibilities. They also might review the security mechanisms that are already in place and determine whether they are sufficient for the organization's needs. These finding then are translated into a security policy, which defines how the organization plans to protect its assets, whatever they might be.

When the policy has been defined, the organization transitions to the *asset protection* phase, during which it implements safeguards to address all the elements of the security policy. These could be procedural, such as regular reviews of system log files, or implementational, such as a firewall.

After safeguards have been put in place, the organization must monitor its effectiveness. This is accomplished in the *monitoring and detection* phase. For example, if you never look at the traffic passing through your firewall, then it's a good bet that you will never know whether it's really doing its job.

Finally, because no security measures can be expected to be 100% effective all the time, organizations must have a strategy for *response and recovery*. For example, what should be your response if you detect a denial-of-service (Dos) attack being perpetrated upon your network? Who would you call, and who within the organization would you alert? Or, if your Web server crashes, how will you know and what steps will you take to bring your Web site back into service?

After these four phases have been addressed, it's time to start over again and begin the assessment process once more. If your policy, safeguards, monitoring capabilities, and response mechanisms are not scrutinized on a regular basis, there's a good chance that they will soon become obsolete or be overtaken by new technology, new threats, or changes to your organization or network. For any security program to be effective, it must be supported by all groups within the organization, from the CEO and officers to end users, the Human Resources department, administrative staff, and IT staff. Each of these groups has a role in defining, implementing, and monitoring the organization's definition of and compliance with the security policy. Without buy-in from every group within an organization, especially senior management, the security program likely will not be effective.

Now let's dig into each of the phases of the security process to understand the specific tasks that comprise each of them.

Assessment and Policy

Assessment and policy seems to be the area that IT people tend to find the least interesting, probably because there's lots of interviews and paperwork involved and they don't get to build and administrator servers, write code, or design new architectures. Their general feeling is often that this area of security creates the least value, perhaps because security policies don't define the "how" of what's to be done—instead, they define only the "what."

For example, a security policy won't tell you that you need to implement a VPN, but it will tell you that you need to secure the data that travels between your home office and all the remote offices. This isn't exciting stuff for the average IT person. On the other hand, a small group of IT staff seems to like having defined policies because it tells them what's important and what's not. In general, it also helps them to define their goals and, more tactically, can be used to justify their budgets. If you say to your boss, "Hey, we need a new high-availability firewall and it's going to cost us $50,000," her first reaction might not be to immediately cut a purchase order for you. On the other hand, if you say, "Hey, our security policy dictates that our network connections are up 99.9% of the time, so we need a new HA firewall," then you'll probably get a more positive reaction. If you don't, point out that your board of directors runs the audit committee that reviews compliance to the security policy and that the next meeting is next month. You'll be amazed at how quickly these types of statements can free up money and resources.

Similarly, many system and network administrators tend to despise outside entities who conduct penetration testing against their networks. Their point of view is that such testing can only make them look bad if they turn up anything. Wait a second, though—if that penetration test shows that your network is Swiss cheese, then perhaps someone will start listening to your cries for an intrusion-detection system, some strong authentication, or another administrator to help keep patch levels current on your servers. Now perhaps you can see why it's important to get involved in the assessment and policy process: Ultimately, the results of this process will either help or hinder your efforts and budget.

IA Programs

The starting point for security is really at the organizational level, not the server or operating system levels. To use a well-worn analogy, you can't build a strong house on a weak foundation. An information assurance (IA) program is that foundation. By *information assurance*, we mean a program that incorporates all the aspects of security, from organizational responsibilities to individual roles, from chains of responsibility to audit mechanisms. IA is accomplished by first establishing an IA authority within a company and then empowering the authority to carry out a corporate IA program. The authority can be an individual or an office charged with this responsibility. This authority is responsible for applying comprehensive end-to-end security measures to the information assets and the systems used to process that information.

Typically, the IA program is headed by an IA director who reports directly to a company officer or board of directors. Within each organization, be it HR, IT, manufacturing, sales, or operations, someone carries the role of IA officer. This person is the point of contact for all information security issues within that organization, and in this role the person reports directly to the IA director. These roles could be full- or part-time, depending on the size of the organization and its IA needs. Each of these individuals has a hand in developing and monitoring compliance with the security policy, and this "virtual" organization is the skeleton of the IA program.

The overall goal of a properly implemented IA program is to apply the "security wheel" concept across the corporate enterprise. The specific step-by-step goals include these:

1. Assess the information infrastructure, determine the critical assets, and develop a document that outlines the critical assets and their vulnerabilities.

2. Develop a security policy to address issues documented in the previous step.

3. Establish organizational responsibilities and enforcement policies to implement the security policy.

4. Implement technical measures to enforce the policies in the security policy.

5. Implement administrative procedures to enforce the policies in the security policy.

6. Monitor and improve the IA program.

Understanding Assessments

We were recently called in to conduct a security assessment of a telecommunications organization. The first thing that we found was that nobody outside the IT group had been notified of the assessment or planned to be involved. In fact, the responsibility for security rested on someone within the Human Resources group, and this person had no authority over the manufacturing arm, the operations center, or any of the other company units.

When we explained what an assessment was all about, it triggered a reassessment of what the company really needed. Ultimately, we presented the project to the CEO, who tasked each organization's vice president with participating in the assessment process. In fact, the first task before even conducting the assessment was to help define the IA program and organizational structure. We ended up moving the IA responsibility to a VP level, and the person responsible for IA reported directly to the board of directors.

Whereas in the past, if someone reported a security concern to the HR security officer, that report could be squashed if it made somebody look bad (especially the HR person), now all security concerns could go from the IA director to the board of directors, if necessary. The assessment team also could gather much more information about the company structure and its critical assets by talking with business managers, VPs, and organizational heads than would have been possible by speaking with only the IT group.

The most important question that we asked was, "What type of loss or interruption could cause your business to fail?" After all, this is not something that your typical system administrator could answer. The business managers could. This engagement produced not only a security assessment of the organization, but also defined the company's IA program and produced the company's first security policy. The point of this story is that it's important to start at the beginning and to establish a framework for security, rather than just diving into the technical aspects or even assessments.

Organizational Assessment

Assuming that your company has defined some kind of IA program, or at least a role and a person responsible for security, the next step is to have an organizational assessment. The goal of this assessment is fairly simple: It's crafted to identify the information assets within your organization and rate them according to their level of criticality and the impact of their loss to the business.

This is very much a paper exercise, and the result of this assessment is not necessarily going to be a recommendation for a new firewall or a standard for password length and composition. One of the most important components that it will provide is something that at first might seem a bit far off from security and very much a "bean counter" result. This is a criticality matrix.

Now, before you decide to skip the rest of this chapter, take a moment to read about this matrix because it's quite important. The basic premise of developing a criticality matrix is that, until you know what the most valuable assets in your organization are, how they effect your business processes, and what would happen to your business if you lost them, it's difficult to determine what security measures to put into place to protect them. For example, as an administrator, you might spend all your time locking down your company's Web server to keep it from being defaced; in the meantime, a critical database might be left unprotected from pilfering by insiders. If there's just a small impact to the company if the Web site is defaced, but there's a catastrophic impact if the information in the critical database is lost or stolen, you've completely misdirected your efforts if you focus on only the obvious, which is the Web server. Unfortunately, as a member of the IT department, you might not know where all the jewels of the company are buried. This information often is known only to the business managers, officers, and other non-IT folk.

If they are doing their job correctly, the assessors will probe into every area that impacts security. The specific composition of these areas will change depending on the type of assessment being done and the nomenclature of the assessor. In general, however, they will cover the following topics:

- Policy
- Risk management
- Account management
- Configuration management
- Session controls
- Network security
- Remote access
- System administration

- Incident response
- Auditing
- Virus protection
- Contingency planning
- Backup and recovery
- Maintenance
- Media sanitization
- Physical security
- Personnel security
- Training and awareness
- Disaster recovery

An organizational assessment is intended to uncover all the critical information in the company so that you can build a security policy that addresses what's important to the business. The assessment process typically begins with the assessors briefing all the participants on how the engagement will be conducted. It's important to bring all the components of the organization in on this so that they know their roles and the importance of their participation in the process. The participants should include representatives from IT, Human Resources, sales and marketing, company officers, legal staff, operations staff, facilities staff, and any other critical components in the company. By participating in a kick-off meeting, all of these players can be brought into the process, can voice their concerns and (hopefully) have them allayed, and be made to understand the importance of the process.

Next, the assessment team will begin to learn about the company, what it does, and what processes and organizations are a part of it. This is done through a series of interviews geared toward identifying critical information assets. These interviews often spawn additional interviews because the interviewee often will identify new information assets or processes that didn't come out in the initial kick-off meeting. Eventually, the assessment team will develop a list of critical information assets and the criticality matrix discussed earlier.

The criticality matrix is worth exploring a bit because it will become the basis for the security policy. The matrix identifies each information asset, such as important databases, information sources, or processes, and ranks them according to three factors, called *impact attributes*. These are listed here:

- **Confidentiality**—What happens if this asset is disclosed to the wrong people?
- **Integrity**—What happens if this information is corrupted or modified inappropriately?
- **Availability**—What happens if this asset is temporarily unavailable for access?

A value is assigned to each of these impact attributes to determine the importance of each. These are called the *impact values*, and they often are rated as low, medium, and high. The definition of these values is really a function of the company and its business. For example, one set of definitions could be as follows:

- **Low**—Inconvenience to customers. Monetary loss due to service degradation is minimal. Threat of public relations damage is low.

- **Medium**—Company X cannot meet service-level agreements. Litigation is possible. Temporary loss of competitive edge results in this tight market.

- **High**—Lawsuits filed. High monetary loss occurs. Termination of customer contracts occurs. Permanent loss of competitive edge results.

The criticality identifies each asset and applies these criteria to them. For example, a simple criticality matrix might look like Table 2.1.

TABLE 2.1   Simple Criticality Matrix

Critical Asset	Confidentiality	Integrity	Availability
Client Database	H	H	L
Payroll	L	M	L

This identifies two assets, a client database and employee payroll information. The matrix says that if the client database is disclosed, such as to a competitor or even the public at large, there's going to be a very high impact (confidentiality). If the information is corrupted, there's also a high impact (integrity) because perhaps this is how the company makes its sales. If the database is temporarily unavailable, the impact to the business is low (availability) because the database isn't accessed continuously. This matrix can help the policy developers determine the appropriate level of protection for the company assets, and this translates directly into what IT eventually implements.

Read that last line again because this is how a little table in a document that you might not care about can directly impact your function. Access to the client database, for example, could warrant strong authentication using a token or a smart card, encryption using a VPN, frequent backups, or expensive RAID equipment to ensure integrity—but it won't support that triple redundant database cluster that you wanted because availability isn't a big concern. See, this stuff really is important!

Policy Development

So you've sweated it through an assessment, during which you gave your full support to those poor consultants, and they came up with a criticality matrix that truly addresses the assets of your organization. The next task is to develop a security policy that addresses how these assets should be protected. The important thing to remember about a security policy is that it's also a fairly high-level document. Like the assessment, though, its content very much dictates what gets implemented later.

A policy identifies what is to be protected, but not how. It might say that critical information should be protected using encryption, but it won't tell you whether this means that you use an algorithm such as TripleDES or IDEA, which product you should use, or even how the encryption should be implemented. Those details are left out because, if they were specified in the policy, its contents would need to change as technology changed. If someone finds a weakness in TripleDES that renders it useless, the security policy would be immediately obsoleted if it went to that level of detail. Generally, this is a good thing for IT because it leaves the implementation details to people who will be responsible for making it all work; hopefully, inappropriate solutions will not be imposed by nontechnical people who know security only at the policy level.

Developing a security policy should not entail cutting and pasting some canned policy statements into a document and calling it a day. If your policy doesn't address the specific needs of your organization, then it's nothing more than a showpiece, it won't be followed, and, worse, it won't lead to the adequate protection of your business. This book isn't intended to make you a policy-development guru; there are plenty of books, standards, and seminars tailored to that. However, like all the topics discussed in this chapter, you should know how a policy is developed so that you can help that process along, participate where you are needed, and influence the policy so that you ultimately can implement the solutions that truly are required.

The policy-development process takes up where the assessment left off. There are different ways to structure a policy. Sometimes policies are structured based on organizational responsibilities or functional areas. Our feeling is that, if the policy is initially broken down by organization—for example, what IT needs to do, what end users need to do, what HR needs to do, and so on— it's difficult to figure out where there are overlaps or gaps in responsibilities. On the other hand, if the policy is structured according to the type of categories listed in the assessment section (such as policy, risk management, account management, and so on), it's easy to make certain that each area is adequately addressed. The responsibility for each area can be assigned to a specific group or individual later.

Given the fact that most of your end users will not want to read the entire security policy, many organizations maintain a master policy with all the areas and responsibilities listed. Then they publish more concise versions for end users, executives, or the IT department, each of which addresses only its specific audience. In our experience, this type of policy works best. The type of policy that you develop will be largely driven by the needs of your organization.

It's worth mentioning that policy development should be a collaborative effort that includes everyone who eventually will need to bless the document. It's very important that entities such as legal staff are involved early in the process. You would be surprised how heavy-handed your chief council can be when you drop what you think is a completed security policy on their desks. Quite often legal concerns that the average employee doesn't even think about drastically can alter the content and style of the policy. The lesson here is to involve the appropriate people early, keep them apprised of how the policy is shaping up, and make them your friends so that you can resolve issues early rather than late. By nailing the security policy and doing it right, you'll find that adhering to it and implementing it will be many times easier than if you develop a policy that is just for show, thinking that security is really in the implementation.

The Real Cost of Security

Our company was called in to assist an organization that had just lost a senior IT person. The company, which did hundreds of millions of dollars in business a year, panicked when the IT person went to a competitor. The company's key information asset was a database that was used to generate a large portion of its revenue, and the company feared the worst: that this, along with the IT person, had made it to the competitor.

Our team conducted a forensic analysis and determined that the IT person not only had taken the database but also had developed software for the competitor on the company's own equipment, presumably during business hours. You would think that this would have had serious legal ramifications. There was one problem: The organization didn't have a security policy that prohibited any of this! So, even though this individual obviously had misused company resources and assets, there was little legal recourse that the company could take because it had not explicitly banned this in its policy. After licking it wounds, the company decided to do an assessment and subsequently developed a policy, but only after it had been burned and suffered what could have been a serious financial loss.

Operational Policies and Procedures Development

When the high-level policy is defined, there's still more documentation to be developed. These are the operational policies and procedures. This is where the "what" of the high-level policy is transformed into the "how" of specific processes, systems, and implementations. The security policy will tell you that critical information assets need to be backed up regularly; the operational documents will tell you what to implement and how to administer them.

For example, an operational document might identify a tape library as being appropriate for the level of integrity defined in the security policy. The operational document then might go on to address how and when the backups should take place, where and for how long the tapes should be archived, who has access to them, and how they are handled. It shouldn't be hard to figure out that the operational policies and procedures flow directly for the results of the organizational assessment, which is another reason that system administrators and IT managers should give their unbridled support to that pesky assessment team: They largely can determine your fate and the types of "toys" you end up playing with. The operational policies and procedures should be designed so that they are easily auditable, so that later when someone comes around to do another assessment, you can show that the policies are being followed and that you are implementing what was specified in the security policy. Depending on how mature your architecture and infrastructure is, these procedures can be developed during the asset protection phase or during the policy and assessment phase.

Technical Assessments

Policy and assessment—will it never end? Many types of assessments exist. Some, like the organizational assessment, are clearly higher-level exercises, while others, like those listed here, are done more at a tactical level and are geared toward digging into the guts of your IT infrastructure. These technical assessments include the all-familiar network penetration test during which tests are run to determine whether your systems can be compromised by outsiders (hackers) or insiders. A number of other technical assessments also target specific areas of your infrastructure. In this section, we'll quickly review these different types of assessments, how they are conducted, what the benefits are to the IT organization, and how to ensure that you're getting your money's worth.

Architecture Assessment

Many companies implement what would seem to be a good set of controls on their information, firewall, intrusion detection, and the like, only to find out that their architecture has been developed so that these protective mechanisms are largely ineffective. Later in this book, we will review some common network architectures and the specifics of how to do them correctly. For now, we need to stress the importance of having not only the effectiveness of specific controls assessed, but also the overall architecture of the network.

For example, we were engaged to assess the security of a large financial institution that was rolling out an e-commerce infrastructure to support Internet banking applications. The architecture had been largely designed by the company's equipment vendor, who, of course specified the brand of routers and switches, along with the firewall and intrusion-detection equipment.

The architecture was sound from the standpoint of availability, but the security architecture had some problems that were not related to the network components. For example, the Web servers, which were the front end to the system and were directly accessible by the clients, had a direct connection to the back-end database servers and mainframe that stored and processed all of the account requests. Although a firewall stood between the Web server and the back end, the applications required that it be set up to allow very open access between them. In effect, the firewall was physically in place but was functionally useless. A better solution was to place a proxy between the Web server and the back end so that the firewall could limit access to the back end and no direct connections ever were made between the Web server and the back end (see Figure 2.2). So, if someone did compromise the Web server, that person still could not get access to the critical information on the database servers, on the mainframe, and within the corporate network.

This example points out two lessons. First, never let your equipment vendor design your infrastructure without having a third party review it, preferably one that is vendor-neutral. Second, never assume that an infrastructure is functionally secure, even if it looks good from a topological standpoint. You need to probe the applications, data, and services before you declare an architecture secure.

Network Penetration Testing

Network penetration testing might easily be grouped in the "Monitoring and Detection" section of this chapter, but because it's typically required by the auditors, not the administrators, we'll leave it here in assessment. Network penetration testing, in a nutshell, consists of a team of security specialists trying to compromise the security mechanisms protecting your network, either through the Internet, by working from within your enterprise, through dial-in, through partner connects, or sometimes even using social engineering techniques. Now here's where it gets sticky: There are a few flavors of network penetration test, and the value of each is very much different.

Vulnerability Scans

The first type of penetration test is what we call a vulnerability scan. This type of test typically is run using an automated tool that scans for hosts on your network, checks them for a set of known vulnerabilities in well-known services or operating systems, and then reports these findings. The value of this type of scan is that it will find out whether someone has installed a new server without your knowledge or has opened up a service (such as telnet) that shouldn't have been opened. Plus, it will find glaring problems in your implementation, such as installing a Windows NT server in the out-of-the-box configuration and not applying any service packs. When run on a regular basis, such as monthly or quarterly, this type of test gives you a warm, fuzzy feeling that your network isn't wide open.

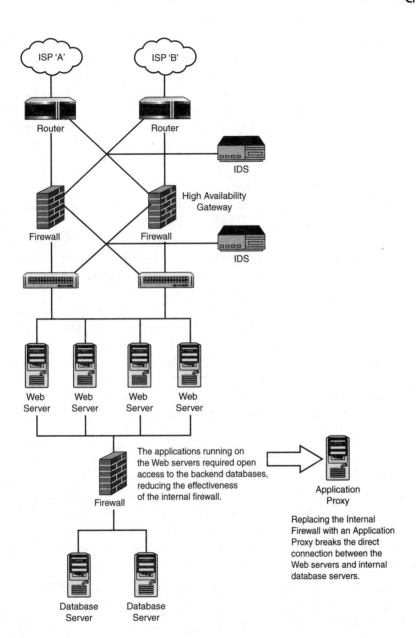

FIGURE 2.2

Operational requirements can limit the effectiveness of an internal firewall.

Vulnerability Testing

The next type of penetration test is a bit more heavy-duty that the typical network scan, and it's the type that most security firms out there are providing. This type of test utilizes a commercial vulnerability scanner that's a bit more thorough than those used for low-end scans. These scans are performed by some of the large accounting firms or security boutiques, and they utilize tools such as ISS Scanner or Network Associates' Cybercop Scanner. Unfortunately, many firms rely completely on these tools, and they don't do any manual investigation of the vulnerabilities they find.

Because running this tool doesn't take much more than punching in the IP addresses of the hosts that you want to test, the value that this type of vulnerability scanning provides is somewhat dubious, especially because it's just as easy for you as an IT professional to purchase and run the tools as it is for an outside consultant. Most often, this type of penetration test is done in response to a requirement levied by the auditors in the company, and having a respected firm perform the test is considered by many to be sufficient. Although these tests are of value, they have a few faults. For starters, the tools themselves are updated periodically, but certainly they don't keep up with the rate at which new vulnerabilities come out. So, when you have one of these scans, you're already behind the curve. Next, these scanners will find most of the vulnerabilities in your system, but certainly not all of them. If your intent is to protect yourself from the "script kiddies," hackers who download precanned attacks from the Internet rather than probing and prodding your network over weeks or months, then these types of tests are probably sufficient. However, if you believe that the assets that you're protecting are of high value, you need to move up to the next level in penetration testing.

Red-Team Penetration Testing

The most thorough form of penetration testing is the so-called "red-team" approach. With this approach, a team of skilled security practitioners attempts to exploit vulnerabilities in your network the same way that a determined and skilled hacker would. The red team gathers information about your network from all the open sources on the Internet and then runs through the automated scans to get a broad picture of your network and information assets. The team identifies specific servers or other hosts that provide the most likely path for exploitation and then attempts to manually exploit any vulnerabilities.

Let's take a very simple example of how the red-team approach can be more effective than the automated scanner. A scanner thinks that things operate as the standards (IETF RFCs) say they should. So, if a scanner finds a service on one of your servers that is listening on port 1433, it determines that the server is running a Windows operating system; then the scanner assumes that the service must be a SQL database (MSQL, specifically). So, the scanner throws all its MSQL exploits against the target server to see if it's vulnerable. The red team, however, can directly examine the server responses and determine, for example, that the traffic responses look an awful lot like Window Terminal Server (or Citrix WinFrame) rather than MSQL. The reason for this might be that the administrator changed the ports that the services listen on, in the hope of "hiding" the service from hackers. When the red team determines the true service running on the port, it can attempt to exploit that service instead of wasting its time trying to execute MSQL exploits that don't fit the true type of service running.

The drawback of the red-team approach is that it's tough to qualify the persons performing it. A red team comprised of inexperienced members isn't going to be effective, but because there's something of a "black art" to conducting such a test, it's hard to tell the quality of what you're getting. It's always a good idea to ask for sample reports when determining which firm to use for this type of test, and ask for and contact reference clients to see how good the firm's work product is. If you have some good technical people in your organization who really know their operating systems, routers, applications, and firewalls, ask for resumes of the red team members; if possible, interview them either in person or over the phone.

Security Scanner Versus the Red Team

Red teams are a bit like Marines: They adapt, improvise, and overcome. A scanner can only send packets to a host and see if a particular version of an exploit happens to work. The red team, on the other hand, is capable of cross-referencing all the information about a target to find less visible vulnerabilities. Here's an example of how a scanner missed an exploit that our red team found.

Some vulnerabilities can exist only if the set of core members of the vulnerability exist. For instance, the msadc.dll vulnerability can exist only if the following are true:

1. The target Web server is running a Windows operating system.
2. msadc.dll is present and accessible on the target server.
3. The target server is running IIS 4.0.
4. A set of file associations exists on the target server.
5. The appropriate data sources exist on the target server.

An automated scanner will declare a vulnerability if it matches on criteria 2 and only if msadc.dll is in its default (expected) location. So, a team using an automated scanner will report on one of two possible outcomes:

Outcome A: msadc.dll exists, so the server is vulnerable.

Outcome B: msadc.dll was not found in its default location, so the server is not vulnerable.

In actuality, these outcomes as defined by the scanner are not strictly true. In the case of Outcome A, the scanner believes that if the file msadc.dll exists, the server is vulnerable. In actuality, the server may be vulnerable, *unless*:

1. The target is not running a Windows operating system. Then the existence of that file most likely a honey pot, and the server is not vulnerable.

2. The target is running IIS 5.0 instead of IIS 4.0 so the server is not vulnerable.

3. There are no appropriate data stores on the target (required to take advantage of this particular hack), so the vulnerability cannot be exploited.

4. Certain file associations do not exist (also required to take advantage of this particular hack), so the vulnerability cannot be exploited.

So, if msadc.dll was in its default location, the scanner might report a vulnerability that was not actually exploitable. In this case, however, msadc.dll was not found in its default location, so the scanner would have dropped down to Outcome B, in which the server was not vulnerable.

The red team didn't stop there, however. It also looked at Outcome B, but with a twist. The red team knew that it was possible that msadc.dll might have been present in another location. This is called security through obscurity: The administrators of the system try to hide the location of the dll to fool the script kiddies. The red teamers (and determined hackers) were capable of overcoming this. They found this dll in another location, but they found that there were no appropriate data stores on the server that would allow them to take advantage of this hack (c), so they drilled down even further. They found that another vulnerability called newdsn.exe existed on the target. This vulnerability let the red team create its own data store on the server that allowed exploitation of the msadc.dll vulnerability. So, whereas the scanner completely missed this vulnerability (that would have left the server open to defacement), the red teamers caught it.

Application Penetration Testing

Let's assume that you've found a competent group to assess the security of your servers and infrastructure. The group has pointed out the vulnerabilities, and you've locked down your servers as tightly as possible. Are you done? Well, that depends. Many organizations that are on the Internet are there because they're doing some type of transaction processing. For example, online financial institutions let you access your bank account, buy and sell stocks, apply for credit cards, and do other such functions. The problem here is that, although the vulnerabilities of operating systems and networking equipment are fairly well known, the application that a company rolls out to, say, buy and sell stocks, probably was written by a bunch of programmers who were thrown into a dark room for six months and came out with a custom application.

The vulnerabilities of such an application, by definition, are almost completely unknown. What's worse, no automated scanner is going to detect them because they are not standard— that is, they are specific to that particular application. So, even though the operating systems have been locked down and have been considered, the application itself could be vulnerable. For example, it might be fooled into allowing one bank customer to access the funds of another bank customer when he shouldn't be able to.

Later in the book, we'll discuss the specifics of application vulnerabilities and how to check for them, but suffice it to say that penetration-testing your application is just as important as testing your network. For example, some applications allow users to query their account information by including the account number in the URL that talks to the back-end database. In a simple example, a poorly written application would let a crafty user create his own URL and replace his account number with that of someone else's. Now he could access someone else's account information through the Web browser, without ever touching the operating system or performing a traditional hack. These types of vulnerabilities currently are fully testable using only the red-team approach. Many institutions are beginning to embrace application penetration testing as an essential part of the infrastructure audit.

Source Code Reviews and Equipment Audits

Penetration testing is a great way to test your systems and applications in a live environment, but, ultimately, they are limited in effectiveness by the amount of time that can be devoted to them. A hacker might take weeks, months, or even years to break a system; a scanner or red team might have only days or weeks to perform the same function. For this reason, it's important to conduct a different kind of review: a hands-on audit in which the auditor can log on and access the system directly. Network infrastructures are generally comprised of several components, so it's important to be able to address all of these in the hands-on audit:

- Servers running specific operating systems and commercial applications
- Networking equipment
- Custom applications
- Other equipment, such as PBX and voice response systems

Once again, the later chapters of this book will delve into the specifics of each of these scenarios. The motivation for conducting such audits is simple. First, it's quite possible that, even if your server is running a vulnerable service—for example, a UNIX platform running a telnet service that doesn't require a password—the service might be blocked by the firewall and thus won't be revealed in a penetration test. Tomorrow, however, a firewall administrator might open up telnet through the firewall to accomplish some business need (for example, to allow a business partner to access his AS/400) and inadvertently would open up a serious vulnerability to your UNIX system in the process. A hands-on audit catches these types of vulnerabilities because the auditors have direct access to the system configurations, including the services that are running, patch levels, file permissions, and the like.

The second reason that a hands-on audit is worthwhile is that the auditors can help you develop a standard build for your systems, along with a system audit checklist. The standard build will tell you exactly how to configure your operating system, what services to turn on or off, how to set file permissions and other accounts, and so on. If you're running a Web farm and adding systems often, this standard build and checklist will allow you to deploy new servers that you know are secure and then audit them yourself against the checklist to make sure that they're up to specifications. Much like the red-team approach, it's important to know the capabilities of the audit team, interview them, get references, and check them out to make sure that they can deliver the goods.

Another type of hands-on audit is the code review, geared toward the custom applications developed for your site. We have a good bit of experience developing security gear for the Department of Defense, and we can tell you that every line of code that we wrote was scrutinized by a team of reviewers who knew their stuff when it came to software security. They looked for possible buffer-overflow conditions, asked themselves what would happen if a program or routine unexpectedly failed, and looked at the code from every angle to ensure that it couldn't be exploited.

Now, the commercial market typically can't justify this level of scrutiny, but code reviews still should be an essential part of the development process. One good strategy for performing a code review is to select those parts of the code that are client-facing or that interact directly with the back-end system components. So, for an electronic banking application, you would review all the Web components that interact with the end user, that query the database servers, and that access account information. However, you might not choose to do a code review of your report-generation code because it's likely not an avenue that could be exploited by an unscrupulous user. A benefit of code review is that it gives the developers a chance to hear their work critiqued from the standpoint of security rather than functionality. Most developers welcome the chance to learn how to code better, and many times what begins as a code review eventually leads to the development of a set of coding standards that help developers put together more secure applications.

Asset Protection

Okay, so now you've put together the mother of all security policies, and you have either had your existing systems audited and been told where the weak points are or are ready to deploy the protective devices that will implement your security policy. If you're at the technical level to understand and appreciate the bulk of what's going to be discussed in this book, then chances are good that you know what a firewall does, how a router works, and what the difference is between a switch and a hub. Later we'll discuss many specific security concerns that arise when any of these devices are used, but, for now, we'll restrict ourselves to some high-level discussions about the place and function of each of these components. Again, remember that the goal of this chapter is not to turn you into a security policy guru or a router expert, but rather to provide an overview of security as a holistic process and let you see how you fit into the process so that you can better understand and support the security efforts throughout your organization.

Implementing the Security Policy

It's key to remember that every protective measure that's implemented, from determining the length and composition of passwords to implementing a high-availability firewall, should be driven by the security policy. Of course, the implementations aren't defined by the policy; they can be determined only by people who know and understand the threats. However, it's a grave mistake to ignore the policy when deciding on what measures to put in place. Ultimately, you will be audited and judged on how well your implementations satisfy the policy statements.

As stated before, by using the policy wisely, you should be able to justify those systems that you feel are necessary to satisfy the policy's requirements. For example, if the need for the availability of your Web site was rated high in the criticality matrix, then you've got a pretty good justification for developing an infrastructure that's high availability. Your dream of multiple ISP feeds into a fully meshed set of routers, firewalls, load balancers, and Web servers might actually be realized. However, if Web site availability is rated low, perhaps because it's a fairly static, informational site, then you'll have a tough time justifying this type of expense.

The lesson for the IT group is to pick the projects that you can deploy and the fights that you can win based on how well the policy backs up your arguments. And if you believe that the policy is wrong, then either you weren't giving your support when it was being developed or you need to change it to implement the protective measures that you think are necessary. It's much easier to get your voice heard when the policy is being created than after it has been approved by 10 different VPs, the chief council, and the CFO. Our advice is to vote early and often.

Protective Devices

Each element in the security model presented here can be thought of as a layer protecting the information assets of an organization. Policy and assessment lead to decisions about what to protect, and this protection is realized partially in the form of software and systems. Because this book focuses on the technical aspects of security, we won't discuss certain security areas such as physical security or security awareness, we'll focus instead on the network-specific components. The most important piece of advice that you can get about security controls is to plan and implement them as a system, not piecemeal. Implementing as a system doesn't mean that if you use Cisco routers and switches, you should necessarily utilize a Cisco firewall. It means that every component should perform a function that augments or complements the other components. As a whole, the system should protect the assets that are called out in the security policy and should provide protection that is in line with the criticality of those assets.

A good example of a component that does not stand by itself but that is complementary is an intrusion-detection system. An IDS complements other security devices, such as a firewall. A firewall can't by itself keep your network safe from every attack, so IDS complements the firewall by helping you catch those attacks that make it through. You wouldn't want to ditch your firewall just because you have an IDS, and you shouldn't discount the value of an IDS because you have decided to rely solely on the protective capabilities of the firewall. This seems like a simple concept, but many IT professionals out there are putting steel doors on cardboard boxes and calling them secure. For example, you can put the most expensive, fastest, best-rated firewall in the world in front of an IIS 4.0 Web server on an unsecured Windows NT operating system and rest assured that your Web server will be defaced as soon as the first script kiddie tries an exploit against it. Unless all the security components work together, you're fooling yourself into an unwarranted sense of security.

Security Devices Do Not Equal Security

Here's a true story: A company with almost half a billion dollars a year in revenue hired an outside consultant to "lock down" its infrastructure with a firewall (we won't say what brand). During the American spy plane incident with China in 2001, the company's Web server was defaced, and the company called us in to respond to it.

We found that the company was running a completely unsecured IIS 4.0 Web server and that the firewall hadn't done a thing to stop the attack. When we investigated further, we found that the firewall was not set up to save any of its log file information, nor was the Web server. There wasn't much of a trail to follow, so we locked down the Web server, reinitialized the Web pages, and then did a cursory audit of the client's firewall configuration. During the course of the audit, we discovered that the company's most critical database was stored on a mainframe inside the network, and the firewall allowed it to be accessed from anywhere on the Internet!

The company's response was that the mainframe had unbreakable security, so it wasn't a concern. Of course, nobody in the company knew how the security on the mainframe had been implemented or why it was unbreakable, but it had been set up by an "expert," so that had satisfied everyone.

The scenario got worse the more we looked, but suffice it to say that the firewall might just as well have been a straight wire to the Internet. This was a classic example of putting too much faith in a single device without looking at how other components of the system played into the overall security profile of the organization. Why was the company so ill prepared? Among other things, it had no security policy.

Although we will dig into site architecture in depth in later sections, it is certainly worth reviewing a typical Internet infrastructure to understand its security architecture and set the stage for in-depth examination of each component. A typical Internet site is shown in Figure 2.3. It consists of an ISP connection to the Internet coming into a router. Behind the router is a firewall to protect the corporate network and a load balancer handling a Web farm. The Web servers talk to back-end database servers, and the site content is updated via a back-end connection to the corporate network. The site maintains its own mail and DNS servers, and it also has the capability of virtual private networking for remote users and remote offices.

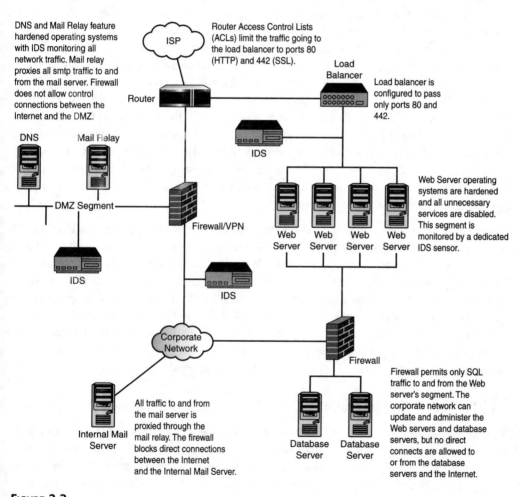

FIGURE 2.3

A "complete" security architecture.

Although it's not worth going into a deep discussion of this architecture (that will be done in Chapter 8, "Attack Scenarios"), it is worth noting that this architecture features layered levels of security, with protective devices positioned where they are most needed. For example, because this is an extremely high-volume site, the architect opted to forgo a firewall between the Web farm and the Internet, and instead dictated that the Web server operating systems be hardened and that the router and load balancer ACLs be set to allow the minimum number of services through (in this case, HTTP and SSL).

Because the site maintains its own name server (DNS), a DMZ segment is used off the main firewall to limit access from the Internet and also to prevent any traffic other than DNS or mail to flow into the corporate network—and then only from the DMZ. The architect also opted to locate the main mail server on the corporate network but, to minimize the risk of compromise, chose to install a mail relay on the DMZ that prevents direct connections between the Internal mail server and the Internet. In addition, the back-end database servers are connected via their own firewall to the Web servers. This allows the Web servers to query the database servers, without exposing the database servers to compromise if one of the Web servers falls victim to a malicious entity. This firewall also allows internal developers and system administrators on the corporate network to administer and update both the Web and database servers, without opening up a back door directly into the corporate network. IDS sensors are placed at strategic points on each segment to monitor the network traffic, look for attacks, and limit the chance of a system attack or compromise going undetected.

Of course, this is only one of many possible architectures, but what should be noted here is that each of the components plays a part in the overall security architecture of the site. Some operational concerns, such as throughput to the Web farm, outweigh the security concerns—that is, not having the Web servers behind a firewall. Some components, such as IDS, can take up the slack where needed, such as by monitoring the relatively unprotected Web farm, while the security features of other components, such as the ACLs on the router and load balancer, are utilized where they can be. This architecture should satisfy the requirements detailed in the security policy governing the site and corporate network, and it is a good example of how security features can be mixed to achieve an overall security goal.

Monitoring and Detection

At this point, we've developed an information assurance program and instituted IA responsibilities across the organization. The IA program office has worked with all the components within the company to list and categorize the critical assets of the company. Based on this, it has developed an information security policy. This policy has been approved by upper management and has led to the deployment of various security components, from firewalls and operating system security to a security awareness program. The administration of the security components has been documented in the operational procedures documentation, and all these components are humming along in perfect harmony. Now it's time to let the security stuff do its magic and work on what's interesting, rolling out new applications, servers, and services.

Hold on—that's not quite right. Sure, all the components of the security program are *supposed* to provide adequate protection to the critical assets of the company, but how do we know that they're doing their job? What if some new exploits are found in the server operating systems? What if someone circumvented the normal change request procedure and implemented an undocumented change on the firewall? What if a hacker or insider is slowly banging away at your firewall or probing your network for any vulnerability that he can find?

Security doesn't end with implementation. For the security measures to be effective, they must be constantly monitored, reassessed, and, when required, improved. This is the monitoring and detection component of the security wheel. In this phase, we make sure that all those great safeguards are working the way they're supposed to. This can be accomplished in a number of ways.

Log File Review

The easiest way to monitor your devices is to review the events that they produce. Routers, firewalls, Web servers, database servers, domain controllers, and other network devices have the capability to log just about anything you please—successful or failed connections, logons and logoffs, errors, file accesses, you name it. Part of the operational procedures that are carried out by the administrators should be to regularly review these log files for any security events.

Having said that, let's take a step back into reality. It's almost impossible to do a thorough job by manually reviewing log files. For one thing, it's boring; for another, you'll find that these devices can spew out much more information that a human can read, especially those high-volume sites. What's the answer? Well, there are, of course, many software packages that will review your log files for security events. They look for things such as multiple failed login attempts that could indicate that someone is trying to guess a password, or sequential port connections that indicate that someone is doing a sweep of your network with the intent of mapping out your topography.

You'll probably find that you need to strike a balance between the amount of information being logged, the level of data that you are willing to store, and the performance hit that you're willing to endure. Logging information takes both CPU cycles and disk access time, so for that reason, a minimal amount of logging often is performed by server-based applications. Other components such as routers and switches require an external log aggregator (such as a syslog server) to which they send their log information.

Because having such a server isn't required for networking equipment to operate, many organizations never get around to installing one. For those that do, the combined log file output can be both voluminous and cryptic. On the firewall side, heavy logging can bog down the devices' performance to the extent that the firewall can't handle the traffic that it's supposed to at the logging level imposed by the administrators. Obviously, every organization will have different requirements for logging. Again, this will be driven wholly by the security policy. If your policy says that you need to log and review all inbound and outbound connections and save the logs for six months, possibly for regulatory reasons, then that's what you're going to do. Such a requirement will drive your selection of hardware and software when you're planning the network. At the same time, such a requirement can be a justification for purchasing some heavy-duty log file parsers, or even having custom analysis and reporting capabilities developed if the business needs dictate it.

As a rule, you should at least log denied connections and failed events such as logons and file accesses. This is because many failed attempts will show up readily to both human and machine review, and it's likely that any attacker will fail a few times before succeeding in penetrating your network.

Intrusion-Detection Systems

Log file review is useful, but it does have its drawbacks. First, it's done after the fact, so if someone already has compromised your network, you won't find out about it until you get around to reviewing the logs. Second, logging takes up some of the processing power of your devices, which is often unacceptable in high-traffic applications. Finally, there are so many different devices on the network that reviewing each and every log file and event isn't always feasible—and you might have devices for which no automated log file parser is available. The first drawback is probably of most concern. If someone is hacking into your Web server, or if an insider is trying to access protected salary information, you don't want to find out about it a few hours or days later; you want to know it now, in real time, so that you can react before the intruder is successful. Intrusion-detection systems (IDS) answer some of these shortcomings.

IDS is much like the burglar alarm system that protects your physical facilities. Like its counterpart, which uses motion and infrared sensors, cameras, and sensors such as latch, pressure, and heat, the network IDS utilizes probes to watch for unusual or suspicious events on the network, such as someone attempting an exploit against your Web server or attempting to spoof an IP address on your network to fool a firewall. Like the burglar alarm, it alerts you to attacks in real time, as they happen.

In general, IDS systems monitor traffic on the network (network sensors) or run agents on each server and look for specific attacks against each system (host-based IDS). Each method has its strong points, but both share one commonality: An IDS works only if there's someone monitoring it when it goes off. Remember, hackers don't keep regular office hours. This is actually the downfall of many IDS implementations: It takes a seasoned security professional to sort out the real attacks from the false alarms and to react to an actual attack when one is uncovered. Remember, the IDS doesn't tell you what to do when it goes off; it only alerts you to something that is afoot. And unless you're planning on having a cadre of security engineers working around the clock (it takes roughly eight full time people to fill one 24/7 position), you won't be realizing the full benefit of the IDS. This is probably the best argument for outsourcing the monitoring of your IDS system because it's just not cost-effective to do it yourself unless you already have a sizeable security-savvy staff on hand. In Chapter 10, "Watching the Wire: Intrusion-Detection Systems," we'll go into excruciating detail on the pros and cons of IDS systems. For now, it will suffice to know that IDS is a useful and necessary tool in any robust security program.

Data Fusion

The strength of log file review is that you can look at all the data being produced by each system and then analyze the traffic in detail. The benefit of IDS is that it doesn't require you to necessarily monitor every device and log file, and it alerts you in real time when there's a possible attack. The most powerful way to monitor for attacks is actually a synthesis of these two methods— for lack of a better term, we call it data fusion.

Data fusion utilizes the attack signatures of an IDS and runs them against the log files of routers, firewalls, servers, and other equipment. This allows an entire chain of events to be examined rather than just one event at a time. For example, you might see a port scan being conducted in your router's log file, followed by an HTTP connection from the source of the port scan being made through your firewall, followed by a new process being spawned on your Web server. Separately, these events might not be a cause for alarm, but, together, they indicate that someone swept your network, connected to your Web server, and then was able to run a successful exploit against your Web server and possibly gain administrative control of the system. This is the power of data fusion. Some of the better IDS systems have the capability to do this sort of correlation, taking their data not only from network and host sensors, but also from a variety of networking equipment. This is currently the ultimate in network security monitoring, and it is your best defense against the wiles of the Internet.

Response and Recovery

Even if you've done everything right, from policy to implementation to monitoring, there's probably someone out there who is determined enough and smart enough to cause you some heartache. Even the best defenses can be compromised, sometimes by an insider, sometimes by a slip-up in security practices, and sometimes by finding a new exploit that nobody else has ever thought of before. Regardless of how robust your security program is, you always should plan for the worst. This is the last cycle in the security process: response and recovery.

Whole books have been written on disaster recovery planning, and this book won't attempt to compete. Because the goal of this chapter is to indoctrinate you into the process of security, it is important to talk about the importance of planning and preparedness. A good example will illustrate the importance of planning.

Two days after the Melissa virus incident, we happened to be visiting an agency that had fallen victim to the bug. We spoke with the head system administrator who was responsible for, among other things, virus protection. He informed us that he had detected the virus early in the morning because large volumes of email were queuing up in the mail server. About the same time, the head of the IT department heard about the virus and figured out that there was a problem on the network. The IT director called a meeting to determine how to handle the infection. This meeting lasted for one hour, during which time all the agency's employees came into work, logged onto their computers, and themselves were hit by the virus. The administrator bemoaned the fact that he could have prevented most of the damage if he had been left alone to disable mail services before the bulk of the workforce showed up in the morning. However, the IT director was vehement in his desire to meet and discuss how to handle the problem.

The previous experience is a classic example of a lack of preparedness. Whether you are concerned about Web site defacements, viruses, or loss of Internet connectivity, it is imperative that you develop response and recovery plans before an incident occurs rather than during or afterward. These response plans might not always be completely technical in nature. For example, part of your response plan for a Web site defacement could be to notify the CEO and Public Relations department so that they won't be caught off guard if they are contacted by the press. It's also imperative that the response and recovery plan is tested on a regular basis. You might find that although the response plan tells you to notify the CEO of any Web site defacement, the CEO's home phone number, cellular phone number, and pager number aren't listed in the document.

Response and recovery are the last—and, hopefully, least-often utilized—components of the overall security process. Any time that there is an incident, the last step in recovery should be a reassessment of the security mechanisms and processes to determine how, if possible, to improve them so that the incident will not be repeated in the future.

Preparing for an Incident

While conducting some DoS testing against a large online institution, one goal was to launch DoS attacks against the company's infrastructure and slowly ramp up the intensity of the attacks to test the robustness of their infrastructure. Because it's hard to launch a distributed DoS attack unless you're willing to hack into a few thousand hosts on the Internet, we set up a laptop on a 100Mb segment in front of the routers.

Utilizing some custom-designed software, we slowly ratcheted up the intensity of the DoS attack while the system administrators determined whether they could detect the attack and then how best to respond to it. We changed router ACLs, turned on various router security features, reconfigured their load balancers, and, in general, tried to see how well the incident response plan worked. As it turned out, the client's team learned a lot about DoS attacks and how to react to them, and the company updated its incident response plan with the information learned during the drill.

As a side note, we actually were able to bring the entire infrastructure to a standstill using only a single laptop. The reason? During the course of testing, we uncovered a vulnerability in the core router's operating system. The manufacturer's team was called in and eventually issued a patch for the OS. The lesson here? Not all attacks can be prevented.

Summary

As we've stated repeatedly, the goal of this chapter has been to give you a picture of security that is wider than just servers and firewalls. As we've attempted to show, security begins at the top, at the organizational level. After the roles and responsibilities for IA have been defined, the organization should be assessed and the critical information assets should be identified and categorized. The relative importance of these assets with regard to confidentiality, integrity, and availability drives the creation of the security policy. The policy, in turn, is the master document that the network architects and engineers should consult when they develop the infrastructure and decide upon specific products, technologies, and processes to put in place.

The architecture should be designed to satisfy the security policy and business needs of the organization, and it should utilize the security features inherent in the servers, routers, switches, and other networking equipment, while using additional protective devices such as firewalls and proxies where appropriate and necessary. Finally, the system should be monitored utilizing appropriate measures such as IDS and log file analysis. In the event of a compromise, a team should be ready to respond based on the incident response plan and level of preparedness, and, if necessary, should recover from any incident. This entire infrastructure is validated periodically through penetration testing, hands-on auditing, and other forms of assessment. The security posture is improved when new vulnerabilities are detected. Now wasn't that a piece of cake?

Even if you never have to write a security policy, conduct an audit, or respond to a security incident, it's good to know where you fit into the overall security process and how all the pieces are meant to function as a whole. In the next chapter, we'll dive into the specifics of the Internet and begin to understand the specific vulnerabilities posed by the many protocols, services, and transports that make up this gigantic network.

Infrastructure Components: A 10,000-Foot View

IN THIS CHAPTER

To connect to and utilize the Internet in a secure manner, the security practitioner must understand not just the "what" of the Internet, but also the "how." It is certainly possible to build a secure network by simply refusing to connect it to any others. Many very useful private networks such as this exist today; however, the users of these networks are cut off from all of the information resources and communication options that the Internet provides. It is fair to say that almost all commercial and federal organizations have decided that some form of connectivity to the Internet is worth having, from the "ma and pa" store with a single email account to large stock exchanges with redundant high-speed connections into hardened data centers. Even very sensitive government organizations such as the Central Intelligence Agency and the National Security Agency can be found utilizing the Internet.

Before plunging into the technical details of the Internet—packet-layer protocols, application-layer protocols, operating systems, applications, and security devices—let's take a 10,0000-foot view of the most ubiquitous network on Earth. The Internet is the world's largest network based on the TCP/IP protocol; however, it is not merely a collection of routers and switches that move packets around the world at the speed of light (well, pretty fast, most of the time). This core set of transport and routing mechanisms is merely the glue that holds the rest of the Internet together. The "rest" is composed of the myriad of servers, such as Web, mail, file, DNS, application, and transaction servers, that serve up everything from transactional experiences to the latest music video.

The Internet and its predecessors have been around for quite a while now. Students, scientists, engineers, computer specialists, and others have been emailing, exchanging files, and even chatting for several decades. It was the development of the Hypertext Transfer Protocol (HTTP) and Web browsers such as Mosaic and Netscape that brought the Internet into the average person's life, spurring the real growth in Internet service providers and online companies such as America Online, as well as infrastructure companies such as Cisco Systems.

The Internet is really as much about applications and the personal computers that they run on as it is about routers and fiber-optic cable. This said, it's still vitally important to understand what makes the Internet work and how it functions to effectively secure the protocols and applications that utilize its services. To that end, this chapter provides a high-level overview of the major components of the Internet. When you've developed an understanding of how this online world is built and organized, you will be ready to proceed into the more explicit details needed to design and implement a secure Web infrastructure. Details of specific security components and secure network design will be addressed in forthcoming chapters of this book.

Understanding and Connecting to the Internet

What we now call the Internet began as a government-funded network called the ARPANET (named after ARPA, the Department of Defense's Advanced Research Project Agency, which is now known as DARPA). Actually, the government funded the original Internet "backbone," the core that connected all of the edge networks. The edge networks were owned and maintained by universities, research organizations, and government agencies, all interconnected by the ARPANET (and later the National Science Foundation–funded NSFnet) backbone. This inter-networking of many IP networks through a core backbone gave rise to the popular term *Internet*. The modern Internet is built from a collection of privately built and operated backbone networks that are interconnected at major demarcation points around the world. The companies that own and provide access to these networks are called Internet service providers, or ISPs.

Internet Service Providers

ISPs come in many sizes. The "big names" in the industry—AT&T, MCI/UUNET, and others—operate global high-speed backbones. Smaller, regional-based ISPs might serve individual countries or states. Although they are less common than they were in the mid-1990s, many small ISPs also provide dial-up or specialized access to the Internet. This hierarchy of ISPs is illustrated in Figure 3.1.

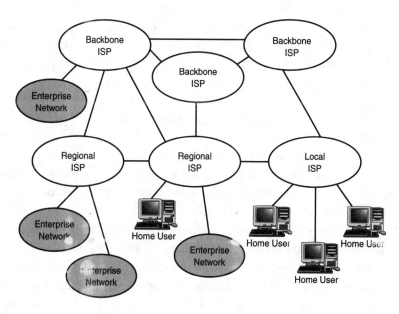

FIGURE 3.1

Internet service provider hierarchy.

To get "on the Internet," the first thing you must do is contract with an ISP that provides physical access to the Internet. Nowadays, physical Internet access comes in many forms, with examples including these:

- **Dial-up modem**—This access establishes low-speed connections (tens of kilobits per second, up to about 56Kbps) using an analog modem over a normal phone line.

- **ISDN**—Integrated Services Digital Networks, or ISDN, is a technology that never really caught on in the United States, although it had more success in some European countries. Narrowband ISDN provides two 64Kbps channels that can be used for voice, fax, or data. Some ISPs support ISDN and allow users to "strap" their two 64Kbps channels together to form a 128Kbps connection to the Internet.

- **DSL**—Digital Subscriber Loop is an always-on "broadband" connection that also uses normal phone lines. The advanced technology allows the phone line to be used for both normal telephone conversations and full-time Internet access. High-speed data flows from the Internet to the end user, while a lower-speed connection is provided for outbound traffic. This type of "asymmetric" service works on the assumption that the typical consumer user spends a lot of time downloading information and actually sends very little data.

- **Cable modem**—Cable television service providers have recently began offering their own "broadband" Internet access. Like DSL, cable modems offer asymmetrical connections to the Internet, providing a high-speed download capability.

- **Satellite modem**—Some satellite TV service providers offer "high-speed" downlink connections from the Internet. Like DSL and cable modem access, these connections are asymmetric and usually require that a dial-up modem be used for the client-to-provider uplink connection.

- **Frame Relay**—In the commercial world, businesses often contract with ISPs that offer higher levels of service than consumer-grade Internet connections. Frame Relay is one technology that is used for permanent Internet connections ranging from several hundred kilobits to over a megabit per second of access.

- **T1/T3**—The "T carriers" have been used within the telephone network for many years now and are convenient increments of bandwidth to sell to enterprise customers. A T1 runs at about 1.5Mbps, and a T3 runs at about 45Mbps.

- **OC3 and higher**—High-speed fiber-optic links starting at 155Mbps are available to really serious users. Although some enterprise networks use these connections, this type of link more commonly is found within ISP backbones and in connections between ISPs.

- **Ethernet**—Direct Ethernet connections, usually 100Mbps, are provided by ISPs that also provide server hosting. In these cases, a customer is provided physical "rack space" inside the provider's facilities in which to install things such as Web servers and database servers, and the ISP/hosting/colocation ("co-lo") company provides direct Ethernet connections into its backbone, along with high-availability power and a secure facility.

Regardless of the type of connection to the facility, an Internet connection provides a link into one of the ISP's local "points of presence" or POPs. For example, some dial-up providers have only a few POPs, all located within a small region to service a very local customer base. This means that you may "dial in" using only the local phone numbers that connect to the POPs in the local area. On the other hand, a larger ISP with national presence might have dial-up POPs in cities around the country or around the world. Because the POP ultimately connects to the ISP's backbone, it is possible for a customer to dial a local number wherever he travels to gain access to the ISP.

It also should be noted that many times the company that provides the physical connection to the network is not the same as the ISP. This is very common with DSL, in which one company (such as a phone carrier) provides the physical cable that runs into the facility, and another company provides the Internet connectivity. An example of this type of arrangement is illustrated in Figure 3.2. Similarly, most local cable companies partner with a national ISP to provide their cable modem service. The cable companies install the new equipment and fiber-optic lines in their system to handle the data connections to the end users, and the big ISP provides the high-speed IP backbone and connections to other backbones.

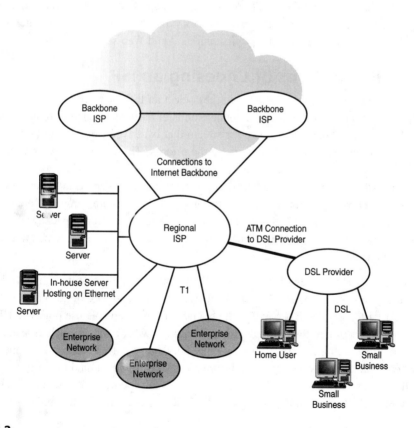

FIGURE 3.2

An example ISP.

What Does an ISP Provide?

The types of providers just described provide just a few simple things that are minimally required to "get on the Net":

- Physical access to the Internet
- An IP address (or set of addresses) that allows a device to send and receive packets
- The IP address of one or more domain name servers, which act as a sort of telephone book for the Internet (more detail on this in a few pages)

Depending on the service contract given to the end-user customer, the ISP also might provide one or more of the following:

- Email accounts (very common for consumer services)
- Disk space for Web pages (also common for consumer services)
- Security features, such as a firewall or intrusion monitoring

A home user is likely to want the email account and perhaps some space for a personal "vanity" Web page. On the other hand, an enterprise network might be more interested in getting highly reliable service with the intent of running its own mail and Web servers.

Security Implications of Choosing an ISP

The primary concerns for most people when they select an ISP are price and availability. The guaranteed "up time" of an Internet connection is of particular concern to many business customers, especially if they have a revenue stream that is derived from some online service. Security often comes up, but it is usually not a top priority. There is a good reason for this: Most ISPs provide little in the way of security services or guarantees. With most ISPs, you get a connection to the Internet—period. The exceptions to this statement usually are found in the server-hosting companies, which are geared toward providing a more complete Internet service solution. Clients of these providers often might choose a la carte security packages, such as firewalls or intrusion detection. We will describe both of these types of systems (and services) in subsequent chapters of this book.

ISPs often perform monitoring of their network, but that is usually to protect them from you, not to protect you from everyone else on the Internet. ISPs usually are quite concerned about whether their customers are living within the bounds of the acceptable use policy (AUP). For example, most ISPs geared toward home users do not allow for software such as Web, file, or news servers to be run on the user's systems. Basically, most consumer Internet connections are provided so that the customer can get information, not provide it, and the providers who cater to this market have engineered their infrastructures to support that. Note that this is similar to the way that telephone companies engineer their networks for residential and business phone lines differently, based on their experience on how these two different types of customers use the network. The ISP monitors the network to make sure that you are living up to your end of the contract. Sometimes it will actively probe systems to see if the customer is running an unauthorized server. If the ISP discovers that a customer is not living within the rules set out in the AUP, that customer usually will be asked to cease those activities or move up to a more expensive service package geared for commercial users.

Furthermore, an ISP's monitoring might provide insight into whether any of its client's systems are being used to hack others. The ISP might be capable of detecting unusually large volumes of traffic coming from a system, or the ISP might run a more sophisticated security monitor called an intrusion-detection system, or IDS. Sometimes the ISP simply might receive a call from another person, company, or ISP on the Internet complaining about attacks coming from a computer for which the ISP provides connectivity.

The fact to take out of the previous discussion is that most the security measures of most ISPs are geared toward protecting themselves and providing their core service reliably, not preventing their customers from getting hacked. Their responsiveness to your security problems will vary from offering a few suggestions to trying to help, to simply shutting off your connection until "you get your house in order." For example, if a customer is under a sustained denial-of-service attack, the ISP (perhaps working with other ISPs) could be the only entity that can track down the attacker(s). It also might be capable of filtering the offensive inbound traffic to reduce the severity of the attack. On the other hand, if the ISP discovers that your computer or network is the source of an attack (whether you purposefully are carrying out an attack or someone else has taken over your computer remotely), you might get a reaction ranging from a firm warning to a loss of your connection.

It is common for people to think that the type of connection they have offers some form of protection from the threats on the Internet. Most people seem to understand that if they have a 24 × 7 connection to the Internet, they are at some risk, while many dial-up users believe that because they are connected only for a little bit at a time, they are somehow less susceptible to attack.

The Threat on a Dial-Up Connection

We recently worked with a friend who owns a small law firm in the mid-Atlantic. He has a handful of employees whose computers are all configured as a Microsoft Windows Workgroup. One of these computers is used to dial out to an ISP and is online for several hours during the day. After being hit with a virus in the office, he started to wonder just how secure his network really was. As an experiment, we suggested that he load a free "personal firewall" program on his computer and let it collect logs of blocked activity for about a month. After a month, we looked at the log file and discovered several hundred probes from all over the world. He was

> surprised to find out that these probes came from not just the United States, but also countries such as Argentina, Australia, Belgium, China, France, Japan, Korea, Malaysia, Mexico, the Netherlands, Romania, Taiwan, and Turkey. A little more analysis revealed that these probes were designed to discover things such as the file sharing associated with his Windows network, any network applications he might be running that might be vulnerable to remote attack, and previously installed Trojan horse programs, such as Sub7.

To summarize, many factors go into selecting an ISP, including cost, reliability, *and security*. Commercial companies, in particular, should be sure to ask questions of their potential providers:

- Do you perform any security monitoring that protects me?
- If so, is it a standard feature or an option that costs more money?
- Is there a security "hotline" that I can call if I am being attacked?
- What services does the security staff provide?
- Will you be actively probing my network for any reason?

Transporting Information

In many ways, the Internet is very much like the postal service. The postal service delivers letters and postcards using various means of transportation and levels of reliability, such as postal carriers to carry local mail to its destination, trucks for moving mail locally or in bulk over long distances, and airplanes for moving mail over long distances quickly. It also offers different service levels and delivery time guarantees. Similarly, the Internet employs a number of technologies to move packets from place to place at various speeds and levels of reliability. The details of packet transport will be covered in Chapter 4, "Network and Application Protocols: TCP/IP," but it is worth reviewing a few of the general concepts.

The fundamental piece of data on the Internet is the Internet Protocol (IP) packet. IP packets can vary in size from the equivalent of a few dozen characters (such as letters and numbers) to a few thousands of characters. Emails, Web pages, music files, and movies are broken into packets of data and sent one at a time across the Internet (through the various ISPs that make of the Internet) from one device to another.

Some readers might confuse "the Internet" with "the Web." The Internet is simply the very large global IP network that transports many different types of application data, such as email, chat, and Web pages, between users and servers. The collection of Web servers that houses all the different cross-linked Web pages and e-commerce sites collectively commonly is known as the World Wide Web, or simply "the Web." Similarly, the Internet is the foundation for many other application networks, such as the EFNET and Undernet IRC chat networks, and file-sharing networks such as Gnutella.

The Internet moves all of this application data from place to place using some pretty simple techniques. Each computer on the Internet must have an address of some kind, and there must be a way to route the data from place to place until it gets to its final destination.

Addressing

Just like letters and postcards, a packet must have an address so that it can be routed across the network and delivered to the appropriate recipient. Where we use street addresses, cities, states, and ZIP codes to address letters, the Internet uses IP addresses. Every device on the Internet has an IP address, which is a number that takes on the now-famous "dotted-quad" format:

```
192.168.55.104
```

This is all that is needed to uniquely identify a computer on the Internet (the more experienced reader might take issue with that statement—we will defer the finer points of IP addressing until Chapter 4). Just like most letters, IP packets include a "return address" that provides the destination computer with a way of answering back. It should be noted that there is a limited supply of IP addresses. A total of about four billion possible addresses are available under the current version of the Internet Protocol. A planned upgrade to IP will dramatically increase this number.

Beyond physical access, the IP address is the most important thing that an ISP provides to its customers. Whenever a device is "on the Internet," it has one of these addresses. The address might not be the same one every time a customer logs onto an ISP, but the IP address is the key to being capable of exchanging data with any other system on the Internet.

Networks

The Internet is really a community of networks. The big ISP backbones connect to each other to form the core of the Internet. They also connect their own customers, including smaller ISPs and large enterprise networks, to the Internet. Smaller ISPs provide connections to other companies as well as to each other. At the end of the day, the Internet is a big mesh of both large and small networks. Without going into detail at this point, it is sufficient to say that the aforementioned IP address actually has two parts to it—a network and a host number. If you know how to read these numbers, you can fairly rapidly figure out which network the IP address "belongs" to.

The concept of the network can be taken to a very fine-grained level. We have already established that the Internet is a "network"—in fact, by definition, it is a network of networks. Each ISP runs its own "network" and provides Internet access to both home users (who might be running their own "home network") and commercial users, whose internal networks often are called "enterprise networks." Once inside an enterprise network, the local administrators might break their infrastructure into smaller networks associated with different parts of the organization. The HR group might have its own network, while the engineering group might have its own network. This network of networks is illustrated in Figure 3.3.

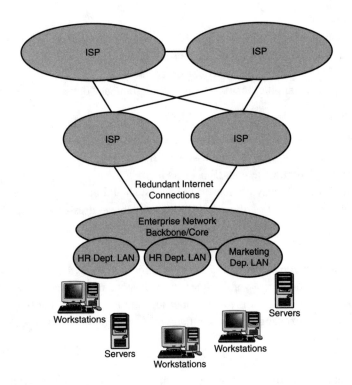

FIGURE 3.3
A network of networks.

Routing

Of course, the job of the Internet (or any other network built on the IP protocol) is to allow a computer from one network (for example, a personal computer connected to a small ISP in Cincinnati, Ohio, U.S.A.) to talk to another computer from another network (for example, a Web server at a big electronics company in Tokyo, Japan). This is where routers come into play. Each network is built from a collection of computers and routers; the job of the routers is to look at each IP packet that comes their way, figure out where the packet should go next, and send it on its way. If all goes well, the packet will go through anywhere from one to a few dozen appropriately selected routers, and the packet will end up at the server on the other side of the world.

The fact that the routers are capable of making smart decisions about how to pass on the packets is what makes the Internet work. Suffice it to say that at the same time all of the computers are talking to each other, exchanging emails and Web pages, the routers on the Internet also are talking to each other. They are exchanging information about things such as the speed of their links, what other routers or networks they can access, any congestion on the network, and so on. As a result of all of this router-to-router conversation, each router has a pretty good understanding of how to make decisions about what other routers to hand packets off to.

Overview of TCP/IP

The TCP/IP protocol family is the core technology that brings this all together. The term *TCP/IP* is used to refer to a number of individual protocols that collectively make the Internet work. Members of this family of protocols include:

- Internet Protocol (IP)
- Internet Control Message Protocol (ICMP)
- Transmission Control Protocol (TCP)
- User Datagram Protocol (UDP)
- Simple Mail Transfer Protocol (SMTP)
- File Transfer Protocol (FTP)
- Hypertext Transfer Protocol (HTTP, the protocol that makes the World Wide Web what it is)

Protocols are simply agreed-upon methods of communicating. In this case, they are specifications that tell software and electronic hardware developers how to organize numbers and words so that packets can be built that have meaning to every other computer, router, or switch on the Internet (or any other private network that is based on TCP/IP).

We will reserve our discussion of the details of these protocols for Chapter 4; however, it is important for you to grasp the importance of these standards. Communications standards are good because they enable many software and equipment vendors to develop products that interoperate—in this case, on the Internet. However, we will focus much of our attention in this book on the fact that these protocols were not developed with security as a top priority and that they are designed to facilitate communications between computers, not restrict it. This gives anyone who wants to communicate with any computer with connectivity to the Internet a big head start in his task.

Furthermore, we will place a great deal of focus on understanding some of the details of these protocols. The reason for this is that many "hacks" come from the ability to understand and take advantage of the finer points of a protocol or, as is often the case, to understand the details of the *implementations* of the protocols. Indeed, the title "hacker" used to be accepted proudly by developers who had enough insight into the operating systems and programs they had to work with that they could solve seemingly impossible problems. It was only when this kind of insight and skill was applied to less scrupulous activities that the term "hacker" got the malicious connotation that it has today.

For example, the TCP and IP protocols are described in two fairly lengthy technical documents. The hardware and software developers who build routers and write "protocol stacks" and Web browsers read these documents and design and build boxes or programs that implement the protocol. Unfortunately, they historically have assumed that everyone else who was working in their industry would read the same documents and develop products that would work cooperatively with theirs. Because of this, they do not always check for every twist or turn that someone with a more malicious intent might take to make an unsuspecting box or program do something the original developer never intended.

Consider a Web browser connecting to a Web server. Before it can even request a Web page from the server, it must exchange a few packets so that both sides of the connection are synchronized with each other (more on this in Chapter 4). At the end of the connection, after the Web page has been retrieved, one of the parties sends a packet that effectively says, "I'm done, let's disconnect." This sequence of events is analogous to making a phone call: One person calls another, the two talk, and then both people hang up. TCP/IP connections work the same way; however, with TCP/IP, it is actually possible to send a packet that is the equivalent of a "call" and a "hang-up" at the same time. There is no valid reason for this, but it can be (and is) done.

Because no developer ever expected that this might happen, the different software implementations of TCP/IP handle this differently. A few clever hackers figured this out in the late 1990s and used this knowledge to develop a method for remotely probing a computer with illegal packets and watching how it responded. It turns out that it is actually possible to learn a lot about a computer, such as what operating system it is running, simply by observing how it responds to these packets. Similarly, few developers considered that a packet might have the same source and destination IP addresses (TCP/IP actually provides a special address that allows a computer to "talk to itself"). As it turns out, some TCP/IP programs ended up handling the receipt of such a packet very poorly, and the computer ended up crashing, or "blue-screening," as it is said in the Microsoft world.

The Domain Name Service

Although the numeric "dotted-quad" IP addresses that are written in IP packet headers are quite easy for computers to process, humans need something a little friendlier to remember. Fortunately, the Internet provides the equivalent of a phone book in the form of the Domain Name System, or DNS. Suppose that a user would like to visit the online catalog maintained by a company called Acme. DNS allows the user to remember a simple name such as www.acme.com instead of the IP address that Acme's ISP happened to assign this server. This is the *domain name* of the Web server.

When Acme secures the right to use this domain name on the Internet, it can contract with any ISP that it likes to provide connectivity and an IP address for that server. The portability of the domain name comes from keeping an accurate mapping between the name and the current IP address in a DNS server, which is highly analogous to a phone book. If you want to know how to contact Acme's Web server, you simply "look up" the IP address by sending a request to a local DNS server. The reality is that few users actually ever do this; instead, their Internet applications do it for them. The domain name resolution process is illustrated in Figure 3.4. The user simply types www.acme.com into a Web browser (step 1), and suddenly Acme's home page is displayed. In the second or two that it took for the page to appear, the Web browser has sent a query to its DNS server on the Internet to find out exactly what IP address is currently assigned to the Acme Web server (step 2), the DNS server responded with the answer (step 3), and then it contacts that Acme Web server by sending packets to its IP address (step 4). This is analogous to the way that we locate people. A person knows someone's name, finds the phone number that currently is assigned to that person by the phone company, and uses this phone number to contact him. If the person moves, you simply look up the new phone number to contact him.

3

INFRASTRUCTURE
COMPONENTS: A
10,000 FOOT VIEW

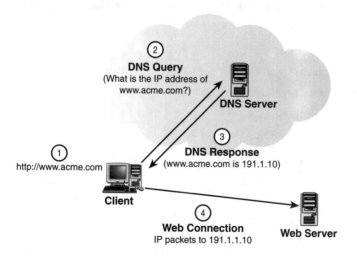

FIGURE 3.4

Resolving a domain name.

Given a high-level understanding of how DNS works, it now should be clear that most Internet applications rely on several things:

- The ability for everyone to get an IP address for their computers. This is one of the fundamental services that an ISP provides its customers. Inside an enterprise network, computers get their IP addresses through either manual configuration or an assignment protocol such as the Dynamic Host Configuration Protocol (DHCP).
- The ability for individuals or organizations to reserve a unique domain name. Unlike the phone book, there cannot be two acme.coms on the Internet.
- The ability to ask a DNS server to translate a domain name into an IP address. Recall that an ISP usually provides its customer (or the customer's computer) with the address of at least one DNS server that can answer these queries.

In theory, it is possible to function on the Internet without a DNS server, although things get a little more difficult. To do this, you would have to remember the IP addresses of every computer that you want to connect to, or you would have to maintain the equivalent of a personal phone list on your computer, in which you could keep a record of the computer names and their respective addresses. Because DNS servers do this for you, they're much more convenient to utilize. A more detailed description of the mechanics of DNS is reserved for the next chapter; for now, it is important to understand the basic roles of domain names, IP addresses, and the DNS servers on the Internet.

Top-Level Domains

Domain names are assigned in a hierarchical manner, with several "trees" of domains currently defined. One of the most widely known of the domains is .com—in fact, it is so widely known that a whole industry (the "dot com," may it rest in peace) was named after it. The top-level domains, or TLDs, are fairly self-explanatory:

- **.com**—Commercial entities
- **.net**—Entities associated with Internet networks
- **.org**—Noncommercial organizations
- **.edu**—Educational institutions
- **.gov**—U.S. government institutions
- **.mil**—U.S. military organizations

Given the popularity of the .com domain in the recent decade, several new TLDs have been proposed:

- **.aero**—Air-transport industry
- **.biz**—Businesses

- **.coop**—Cooperatives
- **.info**—Information sources
- **.museum**—Museums
- **.name**—Personal or individual sites
- **.pro**—Professional services

Of these, the .biz and .info TLDs began testing in July 2001, and the .name TLD was scheduled to be released in late 2001.

Furthermore, there is a whole series of "country code" TLDs, or ccTLDs, that are used to provide top-level domain trees in individual countries. Examples of the two-letter country domains include:

- **.uk**—United Kingdom
- **.au**—Australia
- **.ru**—Russia
- **.kr**—Korea

When an entity decides which domain(s) it wants to be a part of, it simply registers for the domain. Assuming that the registrant qualifies to join that domain (not just anyone can get a .edu domain name, for example) and no one else has obtained the domain name before it, the registrant simply pays the domain name registrar a small fee to make sure that the entry is inserted into the DNS servers so that others can find the entity's IP address(es). So, the IT staff for the aforementioned Acme company registers for the `acme.com` domain name. When it gets the second-level name (.com is the top-level domain, and acme is the second-level domain), it is free to add whatever additional members to the domain that it wants. Because Acme wants its customers to get to its Web and file servers easily, the company followed the now firmly entrenched convention of naming these systems `www.acme.com` and `ftp.acme.com`.

Management of the Internet

Back in the days of the ARPANET and NSFnet, the responsibility for management of things such as IP addresses, domain names, and core DNS servers (or hostname lists, if you go back far enough) was given to various organizations through federal contracts via DARPA and NSF. Several key organizations emerged through these activities, including these:

- Internet Network Information Center (InterNIC)
- Internet Engineering Task Force (IETF)
- Internet Assigned Numbers Authority (IANA)

Dr. Jon Postel, who was a graduate student at the University of California (UCLA) during the early ARPANET days, is fondly remembered as the person who maintained the early libraries of standards, pre-DNS hostname lists, and "magic numbers" lists. The InterNIC allocated IP addresses and domain names, while the IETF and IANA provided the mechanisms for setting protocol standards and defining official lists of important numbers associated with the protocols, respectively.

As the Internet became more commercialized, the U.S. government began the process of shifting management responsibilities away from federally funded companies and organizations and toward a collection of both nonprofit and for-profit entities.

Today, the last ties to the U.S. government have long since been broken, and the Internet is a totally commercial entity. As we already have stated, the physical infrastructure of the Internet is owned by many ISPs that have built and maintain numerous interconnected global and national backbones. A number of both nonprofit and for-profit organizations take care of day-to-day management issues such as these:

- The allocation of blocks of IP addresses to ISPs around the world
- The control over the domain name space (a new TLD cannot be created by anyone on the Internet—or, at least, it shouldn't be)
- The creation of new Internet protocols, such as the "next-generation" version of IP (IPv6) or a secure DNS query-and-response protocol

The various organizations that provide the "big-picture" management functions of the Internet are illustrated in Figure 3.5. Many of the policy organizations are staffed by volunteers who are elected from the public and private sector stakeholders. On the other hand, the efforts that require significant capitol investment, such as maintaining domain name databases, are for-profit enterprises, which compete with each other in the open market.

The ICANN

Many of the historical entities that handled the details of IP address allocation, domain name management, and other broad-ranging technical issues have been consolidated under a nonprofit organization called the Internet Corporation for Assigned Names and Numbers, or ICANN. The ICANN provides a structure for Internet-related businesses, researchers, and technology developers to come to consensus on high-level matters affecting the overall operation of the Internet. The ICANN primarily is concerned with four issues:

- IP address allocation
- Protocol development
- DNS management
- DNS root server management

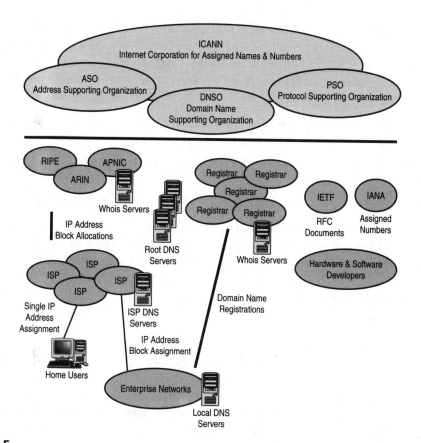

FIGURE 3.5

Internet management authorities.

The work of the ICANN is divided up among three principle support organizations: the DNSO, ASO, and PSO.

Domain Name Supporting Organization (DNSO)

The DNSO is responsible for setting the rules for assigning domain names and managing the top-level domains that we described previously (such as .com and .net). For example, the DNSO conducts the activities required to officially create new TLDs, such as the .biz, .info, and .name domains. Although the DNSO is not the place you go to get a domain name, it does retain the authority to accredit commercial domain name registrars.

In addition, the DNSO takes an active role in ensuring that a number of "root servers" maintained around the world act as the authoritative DNS servers for the .com, .edu, ,org, .gov, and .int TLDs. As of late 2001, there were 13 root servers, 10 in the United States, 2 in Europe, and 1 in Japan.

Address Supporting Organization (ASO)

The ASO is the ultimate authority for the allocation of IP addresses and a few other technical issues surrounding IP networks (such as autonomous system, or AS, numbers). The ASO principally deals with the *allocation* of large blocks of IP addresses to three regional Internet registries (RIRs):

- **ARIN**—American Registry for Internet Numbers, which covers North and South America, the Caribbean, and sub-Saharan Africa
- **RIPE**—Reseaux IP Europeens, which covers Europe, Russia, the Middle East, and parts of Africa
- **APNIC**—Asian Pacific Network Information Center, which covers the Asia-Pacific nations

The RIRs are then responsible for allocating smaller blocks of IP addresses to local Internet registries (LIRs), which are typically Internet service providers. The RIRs do not actually run any kind of backbone network; they simply manage the broad assignment of IP addresses across regions. For example, the smallest block of IP addresses that the APNIC will allocate is 4,096 addresses. An end user or small ISP can then go to one of the LIRs for an actual IP address assignment.

Protocol Supporting Organization (PSO)

The PSO coordinates the development of new Internet-related protocols. Its principle partners in this effort include the Internet Engineering Task Force (IETF) and the Internet Assigned Numbers Authority (IANA). At the end of the day, the fruits of these efforts are reflected in the Request for Comments documents (more commonly referred to as RFCs), which are the authoritative descriptions of things such as the TCP and IP packet protocols and the HTTP and SMTP application protocols. The IANA maintains a large collection of lists that describe the "magic numbers" associated with these protocols. For example, the detail-oriented reader might want to know what number is used in an IP header to indicate that TCP is being carried in the packet's payload, or which application protocol is associated with TCP port number 80. A quick check of the IANA references will reveal that the answers to these questions are 6 and HTTP, respectively. Any reader who is interested in Internet protocols should become familiar with the IETF and IANA Web sites:

- www.ietf.org
- www.iana.org

These are the sites where software and network equipment developers go to learn all about the details of putting together valid packets and application data so that one vendor's program or device can interoperate with another's. It is also the place where the more elite "hackers" go to look for opportunities to exploit systems that implement the standards.

The PSO also coordinates with other technical standards bodies, including the WWW Consortium (W3C), the International Telecommunications Union (ITU) and the European Telecommunications Standards Institute (ETSI).

Domain Name Registries

We have established that an ISP provides its customers with their IP address(es), as well as one or more DNS server addresses. After a user has obtained these two things, he is ready to surf the Internet. If a user wants other people to be able to surf to him, then that user needs to reserve a domain name of his own. To do this, the user must contact a commercial domain name registrar and ask whether the desired domain name is available. If it is, then, after the payment of a relatively small annual fee (remember, domain name registration is a competitive, for-profit enterprise nowadays), the registrar will take care of the formalities of assigning the name and entering it in the global system of DNS servers. Finding a domain name registrar is pretty easy—their advertisements can be found on many Web pages.

The first commercial domain name registrar was Network Solutions, Inc. This organization, along with any one of dozens of other registrars, will be happy to handle your request for a .com, .net, .org, .biz, .info, or .name domain name. These registrars also have put in place procedures for handling disputes over the use of copyrighted names—domain name hijacking has become a serious issue for companies that found that they were forced to pay large sums of money to cybersquatters who registered for popular commercial domain names.

A few of the top-level domains are controlled by specific entities. For example, .gov is reserved for U.S. government agencies, and .mil is reserved for the U.S. military. Similarly, the .edu TLD is reserved for educational institutions that meet certain qualifying criteria.

whois Databases

The various Regional Internet Registries, such as ARIN, RIPE, and APNIC, as well as the commercial domain name registrars, maintain "whois" databases that contain information about the people and organizations that register for addresses and domain names. Access to the whois databases is generally open and available through several means:

- Registry Web sites (for example, ARIN, RIPE, APNIC, Network Solutions)
- Web sites that provide interfaces to various online network tools (whois queries, DNS queries, and so on)
- Lookup tools that run on an end user's computer (for example, the whois command on UNIX systems)

These are good databases to get familiar with because they can be quite a useful source of information for performing any kind of investigation into suspicious IP addresses that might be associated with probes of or attacks on a network. Just as a phone number on a caller ID device is not very revealing without the name of a person or company next to it, an IP address on its own also is not very illuminating. Queries to the whois databases can reveal all sorts of interesting information, including the name and street address of the organization that is assigned the IP address, the ISP used, and the names and phone numbers of key IT staff. An example of a whois query and the database response is included in Figure 3.6.

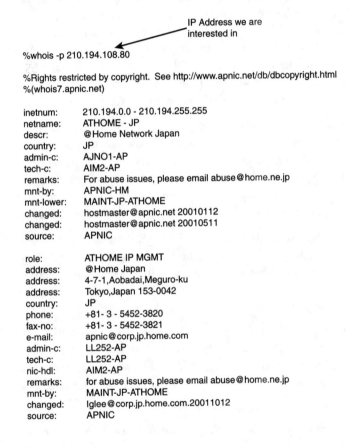

```
                                                IP Address we are
                                                interested in

%whois -p 210.194.108.80

%Rights restricted by copyright.  See http://www.apnic.net/db/dbcopyright.html
%(whois7.apnic.net)

inetnum:      210.194.0.0 - 210.194.255.255
netname:      ATHOME - JP
descr:        @Home Network Japan
country:      JP
admin-c:      AJNO1-AP
tech-c:       AIM2-AP
remarks:      For abuse issues, please email abuse@home.ne.jp
mnt-by:       APNIC-HM
mnt-lower:    MAINT-JP-ATHOME
changed:      hostmaster@apnic.net 20010112
changed:      hostmaster@apnic.net 20010511
source:       APNIC

role:         ATHOME IP MGMT
address:      @Home Japan
address:      4-7-1,Aobadai,Meguro-ku
address:      Tokyo,Japan 153-0042
country:      JP
phone:        +81- 3 - 5452-3820
fax-no:       +81- 3 - 5452-3821
e-mail:       apnic@corp.jp.home.com
admin-c:      LL252-AP
tech-c:       LL252-AP
nic-hdl:      AIM2-AP
remarks:      for abuse issues, please email abuse@home.ne.jp
mnt-by:       MAINT-JP-ATHOME
changed:      lglee@corp.jp.home.com.20011012
source:       APNIC
```

FIGURE 3.6

A whois *query.*

Finally, be aware that similar information about you and your domain is available from the whois databases. The whois database is a resource that many hackers use to find IP addresses associated with a network that they want to target. A combination of queries to DNS servers and whois database servers can provide would-be attackers with lists of IP addresses of both public and private servers, and even phone numbers and street addresses of particular individuals in the IT organization. This can come in quite handy for performing less technical hacking operations, such as "dumpster diving" for discarded documents and "social engineering," in which probing phone calls are made to unsuspecting users or employees in an attempt to gather information (or even asking someone at the help desk to reset a "forgotten" password).

What Makes the Internet (In)Secure?

Now that you have a basic understanding of the structure, support organizations, and rules of the electronic community that you have chosen to live in, you are in a position to assess the general security that it provides to its residents. Unfortunately, we must conclude that, without taking any kind of precautions of our own, the Internet is not an inherently safe place for you to be, especially if you have any kind of valuable information assets that you want to protect.

Inherent Insecurity of the Technology

The goal of the original funders and designers of the Internet (and its predecessor, the ARPANET) was to develop a technology that enabled computers of any type to communicate with other computers of any other type (today, this means that a Microsoft Windows XP workstation can communicate with a Sun Solaris Web server without any problems). On their own, the primary TCP/IP protocols provide this capability, allowing one system to reliably transmit a stream of data to another system on the Internet. The effort put into the development of the Internet and associated protocols was geared toward creating a high-speed, high-capacity infrastructure designed to get packets through to their destination in a reliable manner, and security was not a primary design goal. The result of this is that the Internet is a fairly trusting medium that puts the onus of security on its end users rather than embedding it as a core service.

Implicit Trust

One of the biggest issues in Internet security is that trust implicitly is assumed at many levels. Examples of this include the following:

- When an application receives an answer (in the form of an IP address) to a DNS query, it assumes that the answer is valid and will connect to the IP address that it was told to use.

- Most application programs will take any data that is handed to them and assume that the data is formatted properly by a valid source.

- Most TCP/IP protocol "stack" developers have taken into consideration problems that might arise in the Internet, such as packets getting lost, but they tend to assume that any packets that do arrive will follow the rules of the protocol standard that they are implementing.

The good-natured trust that is pervasive throughout the Internet comes directly from the philosophy of the original developers. The early Internet community was made up of researchers, students, and technologists who were looking for ways to share information and computing resources, not build critical infrastructures that would carry highly sensitive and private information. Credit card theft and denial-of-service attacks were simply not on the list of major concerns when the technology was developed.

Because of the recent attention that hacking and computer crime have received, many system and software developers are beginning to become more suspicious and less trusting in their work. As awareness improves, the security of new products will become stronger; however, it is important to remember that a lot of "legacy" code running on the Internet does very little error checking and makes a lot of assumptions about the source and the quality of the data it is processing.

Lack of Authentication

There is no provision for an authentication service at the lower layers of the protocol stack. This is part of the trust issue we have discussed. It is especially critical for management and address-assignment protocols such as DNS, which effectively directs traffic for the overwhelming majority of connections on the Internet. In effect, anyone can answer a DNS query; if a person gets an answer back to the requester first, he can masquerade as or redirect any network session desired. A solution to this problem in the form of public-key infrastructures and digital signatures has been developed and proposed; however, it could be some time before it is implemented.

Higher-layer protocols have done a somewhat better job or authentication. For example, the popular telnet and FTP protocols require usernames and passwords to gain access to systems, although these credentials are passed "in the clear" on the network, making them vulnerable to monitoring, or "sniffing."

Recent advances in security standards might begin to change some of this. A new authentication protocol (IEEE 802.1x) will allow enterprise network designers to require authentication to even transmit packets into a network. This is a promising development; however, it could be some time before other vendors provide support for the protocol and it is implemented in many networks.

Anonymity

There is a humorous cartoon of a dog surfing the Internet and saying to an onlooking cat, "On the Internet, nobody knows you're a dog." It is pretty easy to maintain your anonymity on the Internet. Online usernames often are picked by the users themselves, allowing anyone who wants to be j_doe to assume that identity. Mail anonymizers also can be used to relay email in such a way that the original source is hidden to the recipient. Without good record keeping by all of the computers on the Internet, it can be quite difficult to track down an attacker who has "hopped through" several systems before attacking his target.

Lack of Privacy

Many of the privacy issues raised in the debate over the Internet are really the result of business practices (such as selling client lists) or careless configurations of applications and operating systems. These are not so much weaknesses in the fundamental technology; this is simply a "nature of the beast" problem. Many companies do not respect the privacy of user data, or they have concentrated on getting their online services up and running, focusing on functionality first and figuring that they will get the security right "later." Unfortunately, when the day-to-day operations of their Internet site get underway, "later" never happens.

Some inherent privacy issues are associated with the Internet. The primary one is that most data is transported "in the clear," meaning that anyone who can gain access to the physical network can read the traffic. This is not always as easy as some people think; however, it is not impossible. The biggest threat here is that many of the operating system and application authentication mechanisms that do exist employ simple password schemes, with the password transmitted in the clear along with the subsequent data.

Lack of Centralized Security Management and Logging

Many products have security features built into them or are dedicated to a specific security function (such as a firewall). Unfortunately, the capability to centrally manage and monitor these systems is very limited. For example, many operating systems and applications maintain extensive logs that can tell an administrator if users or programs are doing things that they shouldn't be doing. The problem is, if the network is even moderate in size, it can be very difficult to review these logs in any useful way. Yes, there are solutions to these problems (such as log file analyzers and real-time log parsers), but relatively few IT administrators have implemented them.

Day-to-Day Security Is Hard!

Anyone who has ever tried to secure something—be it a building, a room, or a network—knows that, in the end, no matter how many locks and cameras and guards you deploy, the user community can make or break the security. Most people will tolerate only so much extraneous "stuff" that they need to do to use their computer. If an administrator insists that all users have a 15-character password with a mix of letters, numbers, and punctuation marks in them, it is highly likely that the passwords will end up being taped to the monitors and keyboards all over the building. So, perhaps it will make more sense to enforce "strong password" rules on power users and administrators, who have more online privileges than the typical user.

Similarly, if users are not educated about the dangers of opening unexpected email attachments, then the administrator might have to decide between rather draconian email-filtering systems or risking massive Trojan horse and virus infection.

Why Is the Internet Attractive to Businesses?

Given what we have just said about the lack of inherent security of the Internet, some people might ask why they should expose any of their really important information to these threats by connecting their systems to "the Net." For home users, the answer may be as simple as: "It is cool, and I can do really fun things," or, "It is the only way I can get my college kids to communicate with me." More commonly, home users have come to depend on the Internet for shopping (especially for hard-to-find and specialty items), staying in touch with loved ones, meeting new people, and conducting day-to-day activities such as paying bills, balancing the checkbook, buying movie tickets, and researching school papers. Many self-employed people and small businesses rely on the Internet to communicate with suppliers and customers.

Of course, the reason that they can do all of these things is that businesses also have chosen to join the Internet. Like all business decisions, this one is based on one of two possible outcomes:

- Saving money
- Making money

In the "saving money" department, the Internet can provide a significant reduction in communications costs. A connection to the Internet can be much cheaper than leasing a dedicated line between two campuses or branch offices, and it can even be made fairly secure from eavesdropping through the application of virtual private networking (VPN) technology. Similarly, the same technology can allow remote users, such as telecommuters and the sales force, to connect to the corporate computers without accumulating large long-distance bills every month.

It is the possibility of making lots of money that has really driven many enterprises to the Internet. Although many of the "dot coms" have closed shop, many of the traditional "brick-and-mortar" industries are finding that they can reach new customers and offer new services and products through the Internet. Alternatively, they might be capable of using data that they acquire through the Internet in a new product or service offering.

One other advantage of having a presence on the Internet is that it sometimes can level the playing field for small companies. It is not always easy to tell the difference between a company with 100 employees and a company with 10,000 employees by looking at a Web site. It might be possible for a small company that offers a product or service to a niche market to compete quite effectively, given the fact that, with a little bit of word of mouth and innovative marketing within the target market, the company can have global access to potential customers.

Although the types of services and products available on the Internet are fairly well known, it is worth our time to review the major categories with an eye on some of the security concerns that come into play with them.

Application Services

Application service providers (ASPs) offer enterprise customers an alternative to implementing and maintaining large applications and databases. By spreading out the day-to-day costs of maintaining these systems among many clients, the ASPs hope to achieve an economy of scale and realize a significant profit while allowing their clients to reduce operating costs.

Of course, the obvious issue here is that it is highly likely that these off-site application servers will contain private information. To make its product attractive, an ASP must be capable of guaranteeing that unauthorized users will not be able to gain access to the data that is contained in these systems. Furthermore, the ASP might have to ensure that the data is protected from eavesdropping as it moves between the ASP and the client's facility.

Media and Data Delivery

The tremendous popularity of file-sharing applications and protocols such as Napster and Gnutella "servants" has caused quite a bit of angst in the headquarters of the motion picture and music publishing industries; however, it is likely to lead the way to a new method of media product delivery. Although broadband access to the home is still in its infancy—cable modems and DSL do not fulfill the visions of the "fiber to the curb" crowd—it has enabled many people to download large volumes of music, television shows, and movies without paying any kind of fee beyond their monthly ISP bills. While most of the remedies to the industries' concerns have been on the legal front (for example, shutting down the directory servers of certain file-sharing systems), all of the major media companies are exploring similar methods of "safely" delivering their products to the consumer.

The security issues for this industry will involve antipiracy techniques. When the media is in the hands of the end user, it is simply a collection of bits. The publishing industry will never be happy as long as it is possible to simply transfer the data to a friend or, even worse, post it on a server that anyone in the world can get to.

Information Services

Many companies simply use their Internet presence as a means of publishing marketing information, either about a product or about a company itself. For example, just about every summer action movie has a Web site that comes up months before the movie is released, simply to generate "buzz" in the hopes of increasing those critical first-weekend box-office receipts.

The Internet provides not only an immense collection of raw information, but also an incredible array of customized information services. Today there are sites that will tell you the best (or, at least, a decent approximation of the best) way to drive from one building to another, across town, or across the country. Similarly, newspapers now produce customized news summaries, with the hopes of either collecting monthly subscription fees or advertising revenue.

Information sites have an obvious concern about ensuring that their information is presented accurately. An attacker who is able to change the content of these sites might be able to do anything from affect stock prices or "break" news before it should be released. One example of the latter involves the entertainment industry. For example, the developers of one high-profile "reality" TV show made the mistake of staging summaries about future episodes on their production Web server. The idea of hackers getting access to the "secrets" of next week's show might seem humorous to many people; however, the television networks' advertising revenue stream is directly tied to the number of people who tune in every week. Having the results of the series finale revealed halfway through the season could have cost the network millions of dollars. Once again, we see the value of knowing what your critical information assets really are.

Financial Services

Online banking and stock-trading Web sites have become very popular. These sites offer tremendous convenience to customers and cost-cutting (that is, profit-raising) opportunities for the financial institutions. They are also among the most obvious targets for penetration attacks. Not only do they have to protect their clients' personal financial information, but they also must ensure that no unauthorized transactions are performed. These kinds of security breaches result in direct financial loss, and, if made public, a serious erosion in customer confidence, which is critical to these types of services.

Products

Finally, both brick-and-mortar companies and new retail companies have adopted the Internet as the modern catalog. Although initial investments have been high and profit margins have been thin, Internet-based retail shopping has allowed vendors to rapidly change their product offerings and to tailor the view of their inventory to each customer.

These companies are faced with two major security issues: maintaining the integrity of their data (for example, the prices in the catalog should not be modified by anyone on the Internet) and keeping their client information private. Many of the product companies (as well as information-for-fee companies) have had the unpleasant experience of having customer credit cards numbers and personal information stolen—and learning about it through a blackmail message or angry phone calls from customers.

Summary

The goal of this chapter has been to give you an overview of the Internet, how it works, who administers it, and why it is inherently insecure. It should be clear that the Internet, although now a fully commercial entity, is still a community comprised of many ISPs, enterprise networks, and home users, all tied together by a collection of consensus-led management organizations, technical protocols, and a few large but critical services (such as domain name servers). Tremendous advances in technologies such as fiber optics, data storage systems, and desktop computing have allowed new and exciting applications such as e-shopping, chat, multimedia conferencing, streaming video, online gaming, and file sharing to touch the daily lives of the everyday person. However, in the end, all of these advances still utilize the same inherently insecure TCP/IP infrastructure developed in the late 1970s and early 1980s.

Fortunately, the same innovation (and desire to see the Internet be used commercially) has led to a whole industry whose purpose is to enable users to inhabit the electronic world of the Internet with a comfortable level of assurance that the information that they want to keep private can stay private. Technologies and products such as firewalls, virtual private networks, virus scanners, intrusion-detection systems, and authentication systems are all important tools that can be utilized by organizations to help secure their resources. However, security requires more than block boxes and new software. Users must be "street smart" and educated about the things they can do to prevent security compromises. Similarly, organizations should consider information security to be a critical issue and should ensure that it is considered in business planning and investments.

The remainder of this book focuses on providing you with three things:

- An appreciation for the kinds of threats that are prevalent on the Internet, with a focus on the mind-set and approach used by attackers rather than a laundry list of the exploits of the day
- Insight into the technical details of critical components in your network, and practical tips for securing those components
- An understanding of security-specific products that can be used to significantly increase the security posture of a network

Network and Application Protocols: TCP/IP

IN THIS CHAPTER

Introduction: The Importance of Knowing the Details

This book covers many aspects of network security. You will discover that many of the security "holes" that are exploited on a day-to-day basis result from implementers not always paying strict attention to the details in their work. This is not meant to be too strong of a criticism of hardworking software and hardware developers, who often must work under very challenging deadlines to get some product to market. In many cases, these people have done a great job writing code that implements the proper functions of a communications protocol standard; however, they have made the assumption that everyone will obey the rules defined in that standard. As you will learn in the following chapters, this is a critical mistake—one that the "hackers" of the world often depend on.

So, with this in mind, we will spend some time throughout this text reviewing some of the fundamentals of whatever part of a network we are trying to secure. In this chapter, we focus on the TCP/IP protocol stack, with a special eye on a few details and the assumptions that hardware and software developers have made that result in security vulnerabilities available to people who are not willing to "play by the rules."

We begin this chapter with a brief review of the history of the Internet and the TCP/IP protocol suite, to provide some perspective on how the Internet evolved and the early considerations for security. We then examine some of the details of the TCP/IP protocols, including basic header layout and protocol functionality.

We hope that this is not simply another regurgitation of TCP/IP headers and that all readers will find something new here. With that said, readers who are more experienced with IP networking concepts might want to skip this chapter and focus on later material that will get them immediately into the nitty gritty of network security.

A Brief History of Networking and Protocols

The Internet that we know today has a longer history than many people realize. Much of the research that lead to the development of the modern Internet began in the late 1950s, when researchers at institutions such as MIT worked on time-sharing computer systems that would allow several users to make use of the rare and expensive computers of the time.

At the same time that multiuser operating systems were being developed, several other researchers began exploring the concepts that would lead to practical packet networks. Key figures include Paul Baran at the Rand Corporation, who worked on the design of a robust, survivable communications network for the Department of Defense, and Leonard Kleinrock, who developed much of the mathematics surrounding queuing theory, required to optimize the performance of the early networks.

The actual development of what we now call the Internet has its direct roots in the ARPANET, a government-funded network designed and built in the 1960s and 1970s. The U.S. Department of Defense's Advanced Research Projects Agency (ARPA) sponsored many of the original computer science departments and research projects at universities across the United States. J.C.R. Licklider, the visionary head of ARPA's Information Processing Technology Office, was particularly interested in the application of computers to communications, not just computation. This focus led to the government's funding of the ARPANET project.

Many people assume that because much of the original work was funded by the DoD and ARPA, security must have been a major consideration in the design of the early packet networks. As you will see, the focus was more on facilitating communications between users, sharing computing resources, and ensuring basic packet network functionality. Serious considerations about security did not become an emphasis until the late 1980s.

The ARPANET

In the early 1960s, J.C.R. Licklider was selected to head the Advanced Research Project Agency's (ARPA) Information Processing Technology Office (IPTO). Dr. Licklider is considered by many to be the spiritual father of the Internet because of his vision that computers ultimately would be used for communication, not just computation. Under his leadership, ARPA provided funding for both the first computer science departments and the ARPANET.

In the summer of 1968, ARPA announced the Resource Sharing Computer Network program plan and its intentions to fund a computer network that would interconnect several ARPA research sites, including the University of California's Los Angeles and Santa Barbara campuses (UCLA and UCSB), SRI in California and the University of Utah in Salt Lake City. Each of these sites was running a different type of computer (for example, the SDS Sigma 7 and 940, the IBM 360, and DEC's PDP-10) and operating system (such as GENIE, SEX, OS/MTV, and TENEX). That same summer, the Network Working Group was formed, providing a venue for researchers and their graduate students at those sites to begin working out the technical details of the ARPA network.

Each node required two components: a common network interface and a specific hardware/software interface between each site's host computer/OS and the network device. Although each of the original ARPANET sites was left with the responsibility of developing the platform-specific interfaces for the respective systems, a contractor had to be selected to build a common component for the four sites. This component, known as the Interface Message Processor (IMP), would "speak" a common protocol that was independent of each of the sites' hardware platforms and operating systems, thereby allowing the different systems to communicate with each other. In early 1969, Bolt, Beranek, and Newman (BBN) was selected to design and construct the IMPs that would be deployed at each node in the ARPANET.

Throughout 1968 and 1969, the researchers at the ARPANET sites and BBN worked to develop the architecture that would allow the different computers and operating systems to communicate over a common network infrastructure. During this time, the minutes of the regular technical meetings were entitled "Request for Comment," or RFC. For example, RFC 1, which was entitled simply "Host Software," was released in April 1969. This practice caught on, and, to this day, these RFC documents are the means for documenting protocol standards, recommended practices, and general architectural thoughts within the Internet community. As of July 2001, there were more than 3,100 published RFCs. Refer to the Internet Engineering Task Force (IETF) home page (www.ietf.org) for a complete archive of the RFC documents.

In the fall of 1969, the first two IMPs, which were rack-size assemblies based on Honeywell computers, were delivered to UCLA and SRI. In November of that year, just a few months after the first moon landing, the first Telnet-like connection was established between the two computers.

The original protocol that the IMPs employed, the HOST_HOST Communication Protocol, is not the TCP/IP stack that we know and love today. It was not until 1974 that Vint Cerf and Bob Kahn published their paper entitled "A Protocol for Packet Network Interconnection" in the IEEE Transactions on Communications, marking the early development of TCP/IP. This paper discussed all the primary issues that would be faced in the design of a larger "internetwork"—that is, a packet network connecting many different smaller networks. Topics such as host addressing, process addressing, fragmentation, and connection establishment are directly addressed in this paper; although some of the details would change in the coming years, the heart of TCP/IP is clearly defined here. It would be almost 10 more years before the ARPANET officially switched over to the TCP/IP protocol suite in January 1983. Details on the inner workings of the HOST_HOST Communications Protocol and the associated Network Control Program (NCP) can be found in the early RFC documents on the IETF's Web site. Two excellent starting places for the reader interested in the technical history of the Internet are RFC 1000 ("The Request for Comments Reference Guide") and the Internet site www.livinginternet.com, which includes links to other reference sites.

How Big Would an "Internetwork" Be?

One interesting piece of trivia from the Cerf/Khan paper is that the packet "network identifier" originally was selected to be 8 bits in length, allowing for up to 256 networks that could be interconnected. At the time the authors felt that this size would be "sufficient for the foreseeable future." Of course, the eventual success of what we now call the Internet was probably unimaginable to the two researchers, just as the original developers of the PC's Disk Operating System (DOS) would have been pressed to come up with a reason why anyone would ever need more than 640KB of memory.

The ARPANET grew significantly in the 1970s and early 1980s. During this time, major milestones included the first satellite links connecting California to Hawaii and the first international connections to England and Norway. Key application developments in the early 1970s included the first forms of email (and the introduction of the user@network addressing), file transfer, and Telnet protocols. By 1983, when TCP/IP became the official protocol of the ARPANET, there were more than 4,000 nodes in the network.

The ARPANET, along with its military sister, the MILNET, continued in operation throughout the 1980s. The MILNET was largely spun off from the main ARPANET in the early 1980s for unclassified defense networking, and it later became the Defense Data Network. While the ARPANET continued to grow, a new government-sponsored network, this time funded by the National Science Foundation, was deployed. This network eventually replaced the ARPANET (which was decommissioned in 1990) and led to the Internet as we know it today.

NSFnet

In the mid-1980s, another government organization, the National Science Foundation (NSF), was faced with a problem: Funding supercomputer research at many universities was becoming an expensive endeavor. The NSF had either directly or indirectly purchased supercomputers for a number of research institutions and was facing growing demand for more. To address the need for wider access to supercomputing technology, the NSF decided to fund a backbone network that would interconnect several of the major supercomputer facilities across the nation. Regional networks that connected various campus networks then could connect to the backbone and gain remote access to the existing supercomputers.

The first NSF backbone, NSFnet, was built in 1986 and consisted of 56Kbps links that connected the following research facilities:

- San Diego Supercomputer Center (San Diego, California)
- National Center for Atmospheric Research (Boulder, Colorado)
- National Center for Supercomputer Applications (Champaign, Illinois)
- Pittsburgh Supercomputer Center (Pittsburgh, Pennsylvania)
- John Van Neumann Supercomputer Center (Princeton, New Jersey)
- Cornell Theory Center (Ithaca, New York)

Each NSFnet backbone site contained a router that was implemented on the DEC LSI-11 platform. The NSFnet was connected to the ARPANET at Carnegie-Mellon University.

The NSFnet proved to be an overwhelming success. In 1988, the backbone was expanded to 13 sites, and the primary communication links were upgraded to T1s, which run at 1.544Mbps. MCI and IBM were two of the primary contractors involved in the NSFnet upgrade, with MCI providing the T1 links and IBM providing the early routers, implemented on the company's RT platforms running Berkeley UNIX. Each backbone node was built from several IBM computers, was interconnected by a Token Ring network, and provided a bridge to the site's local Ethernet network.

A final upgrade to the NSFnet backbone was deployed in late 1991. The backbone was expanded to 16 sites and the primary links were upgraded to T3s (45Mbps). By the time the new backbone was made operational in early 1992, approximately 3,500 campus and regional networks were interconnected by the NSFnet backbone.

It should be noted that some of the major Internet "players" arose during this time. Cisco and UUNET are two examples of companies that were founded in the mid- to late 1980s. This is also the time when the first network security threats became known to the public. Robert Morris Jr. wrote the worm that brought the Internet to its knees in 1988, and the Computer Emergency Response Team (CERT) was established at Carnegie-Mellon University shortly after that incident. Finally, Tim Berners-Lee and other researchers began the work that led to "the Web," making the Internet the wildly commercial success it became in the mid-1990s.

The Morris Worm (November 1988)

Robert Morris Jr.'s worm was certainly not the first security incident involving the Internet, but it was definitely the one that resulted in the first real community focus on Internet security. Morris was a graduate student working on his doctorate at Cornell University in the late 1980s when he wrote what was labeled a "worm" that propagated across much of the Internet. One interesting piece of trivia involving this incident is that Morris's father (Robert Morris Sr.) served as the head of the National Security Agency's computer security group.

Although it appears that the worm was meant to be relatively harmless, it turned out to be quite efficient at spreading itself and consumed far more resources on infected systems than its author expected. Ultimately, it ended up infecting and incapacitating thousands of VAX and Sun systems before it was halted. In November 1988, "thousands of computers" represented a significant percentage of the systems connected to the Internet. One estimate of the success of the worm placed the number at 6,000 infected systems, or approximately 10% of the Internet.

The worm used several techniques to spread itself, including buffer overflows of the finger daemon, clever use of the sendmail daemon, trust relationships defined in the .rhosts and hosts.equiv UNIX system files, and automated password guessing. These techniques, which involved understanding the under-the-covers details of how the target operating systems worked, are used to this day to successfully compromise systems on the Internet.

The overwhelming success of the ARPANET and NSFnet eventually gave rise to the need for a more commercial network. As private industry became more involved, the U.S. government eventually decided to "pull out" of the Internet. By the time the NSFnet officially was decommissioned in 1995, more than 50,000 networks were interconnected by the backbone.

The Commercialization of the Internet

By the early 1990s, being "on the Internet" meant that you had some connection to the NSFnet backbone. As the Internet became more popular with commercial entities, the government's role in the network became a subject of debate.

- Did private industry have a right to use the network that originally was funded by the government to support research for commercial purposes? The NSF's "acceptable use policies" restricted the use of the network to educational and research activities.

- Was it appropriate for the government to "compete" with private telecommunication providers by giving away access to this now international network?

Faced with these issues, several private IP network providers got together and developed a site in which they could exchange network traffic. The Commercial Internet Exchange, or CIX, was built in San Jose, California, in 1993 and provided a means for several small network providers to trade traffic. This began to redefine the concept of the "backbone." Each provider maintained its own backbone network, and the combined networks formed an even larger network. A user on one of the networks was able to exchange data with a user on another network via the CIX, where the two providers connected to each other. The individual network providers eventually were labeled Internet service providers, or ISPs.

The National Science Foundation saw this model as a means of extricating itself from the continued construction and management of "the Internet." In 1994, the NSF announced that its last major act would be to fund the development of four network access points (NAPs), which would perform the same function as the CIX and would be used to launch an entirely commercial Internet (see Figure 4.1). The four NAPs were situated in these locations:

- New York (run by SprintLink)
- Washington, D.C. (run by Metropolitan Fiber Systems)
- Chicago (run by Ameritech)
- San Francisco (run by PacBell)

With the NAPs in place, the various ISPs could interconnect and exchange traffic. These initial government-funded NAPs paved the way to many more NAPs around the world at which the many commercial ISPs were interconnected. Today, the combination of NAPs and private peering relationships, in which two ISPs decide to exchange packets over direct connections between their two networks, form the backbone of the Internet. If these ISPs did not exchange traffic at either the public or the private connection points, Internet users would not be able to send email or view Web pages hosted by other service providers. In effect, there would be many competing mini-internets instead of one Internet with competing access providers.

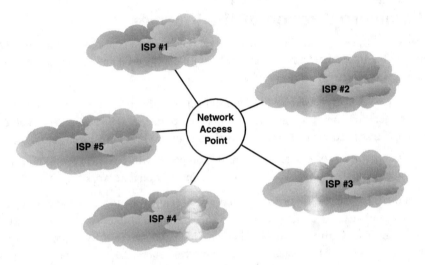

FIGURE 4.1
Network access points.

When the four NAPs were successfully deployed, the official NSFnet backbone was decommissioned on April 30, 1995. At that point, "the Internet" was composed of many privately run backbone providers that were interconnected at one or more NAPs. Today, many NAPs exist, including the more well-known facilities such as MAE-EAST and MAE-WEST. The Internet is a hierarchy of backbone networks that interconnect smaller regional and local Internet service providers (ISPs). Throughout the late 1990s, the various government-run Internet services, such as domain name registration, were privatized, leading to a purely commercial network.

The OSI Model and Relevance to TCP/IP

The point of the earlier section is that, with the evolution of the Internet, the TCP/IP protocol suite has emerged as the dominant networking technology of the new century. Given that fact, the rest of this chapter is devoted to providing an understanding of the various protocols that make up the TCP/IP family, with special attention paid to the details affecting the security, or lack thereof, of an IP network. In discussing the various protocols, we use terms from the common OSI model to describe each protocol's role within the family. Note that the ISO's Open Systems Interconnection (OSI) model and its seven layers (physical, data link, network, transport, session, presentation, and application) really was developed *after* TCP/IP was deployed and reflects the natural evolution of the modern networking protocols more than it actually serves as the basis of design for those protocols. In fact, the ISO designed a family of standard communication protocols that conformed to the seven-layer model and was intended to replace TCP/IP and a variety of other protocols that had been developed in the 1970s and 1980s. Although history has shown that the ISO protocol suite was not commercially successful, the OSI model has been widely accepted as the basic framework for developers and vendors to work from.

Data-Link Layers: Moving Data Across a Single Link

Complex packet networks, such as the IP-based Internet, actually are built from a series of individual links. For an IP packet (or, more accurately, "datagram") to get across the Internet or any other private IP network, it must get across a number of individual links that comprise the network. As indicated in the previous section, the Internet actually consists of numerous IP-based backbone networks assembled and maintained by different Internet service providers, each of which may choose to use different types of technologies to build the infrastructure. In the core, an ISP might use ATM, packet over SONET/SDH, or some of the newer "packet over light" technologies. At the edge, where the providers' clients connect into the network, the ISPs may offer dial-up, cable modem, DSL, or satellite technologies.

In a typical enterprise environment, a user's computer might be connected to an Ethernet switch. When the user opens her Web browser and types in the URL for her favorite Web site, the packets leave her computer, go across the Ethernet cable, and move through a few routers and switches that are all connected by Ethernet. Finally, the packets get to a gateway router, which employs a serial line to connect to an upstream ISP. When the packets leave the company's network, they might cross several ISPs, each of which could be using a number of the aforementioned technologies. Finally, the packets end up at the company that is hosting the desired Web site. Many handy programs can give you a feel for the number of links, or hops, that a packet takes to get to its destination. The most popular is the `traceroute` command, which is commonly available on both UNIX and Windows systems. (On older Windows systems, this command might be called `tracert`.)

An Analog to the Internet: The Postal Service
Part I: The Data Link Layer

Suppose that your Aunt Betty does not yet have an email account, and you still want to be able to stay in touch. You decide to write her a postcard every few months. How does the postcard get to your aunt? The "snail mail" postal service is another global network that employs different technologies to move items from place to place. In the core of the postal network, we find airplanes and trains. Nearer the edge, trucks might be used in between post offices and air/rail nodes. Finally, the edge user is serviced by either a postal agent in a small van or, more uncommonly today, by a postal agent on foot. The postcard from you to your aunt stays the same as it traverses each of the different links in the postal network between you.

The data link layer of the OSI model embodies functions that are required to get packets across a single link in a larger network. A "link" could include the following:

- An Ethernet cable (twisted-pair, fiber-optic cable or coaxial cable)
- An FDDI ring (fiber-optic cable)
- An analog modem connecting a computer to an Internet service provider
- A cable modem connection between a computer and the cable service provider
- A serial line connecting two routers
- A spread-spectrum radio-frequency (RF) link, as used in wireless LANs

Although a communications link simply might be a wire connecting two devices (a point-to-point link), it is important to remember that a "link" actually can have many devices connected to it. The most common example of that today is Ethernet. When Ethernet originally was released, it was deployed with coax cables that each station "tapped" into. These links often are referred to as broadcast media because they allow one device to talk to many other devices at the same time. A network comprised of both point-to-point links and broadcast links is illustrated in Figure 4.2.

FM Radios and Broadcast Networks

The FM radio network is an example of a well-known broadcast network. Although this network carries music instead of packets, the concept is still the same. The devices in the network include the transmitting station and all the receiving radios. In this case, the "link" is the radio waves in the air between the antennas in the system. One device can transmit and all the other devices can receive the data at the same time.

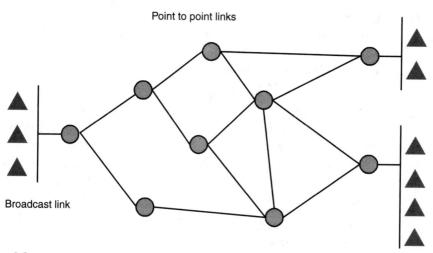

Point to point links

Broadcast link

FIGURE 4.2

A network and its links.

Many protocols provide the functions necessary to move a packet from one device, across some communications link, to the next device. Data link–layer protocols must provide several functions:

- A means to differentiate one packet from another and to fill up the link when there are no packets to send (often called framing)

- A means to detect whether the packet was delivered without error (often through checksums of cyclic-redundancy checks)

- In broadcast networks, a means to identify which device the packet is to and from (called addressing)

In the modern wide area network (WAN), common data link–layer protocols include Frame Relay, the Point-to-Point Protocol (PPP), ATM, and Cisco's proprietary Serial Line Encoding protocol (documented in various Internet newsgroups). In the local area network, the most common protocol by far is Ethernet; however, you still might run into ATM, FDDI, and Token Ring networks, with the latter still common in industries that employ IBM's SNA networking. Although ATM has failed to capture the local area network the way its developers had hoped, it is still found in the core of the Internet backbone networks, as well as at the edge, where it often runs "under the hood of" commercial DSL technologies.

Although we have established the need for and basic functions of the data link–layer protocols, we will defer any additional details about this layer until after we have discussed IP.

The Physical Layer

Technically, we skipped a layer when we began our discussion on the OSI model. The first layer is actually the physical layer, not the data link layer; however, it is helpful to understand what a logical data link is before addressing the actual physical connection.

The data link layer (Layer 2) provides all the functions needed to package some block of data in a way that it can be sent to a neighboring node in the network (for example, a nearby computer, switch, router, and so on). It usually provides a way of specifying which node to send it to (for example, an Ethernet MAC address), adds some check bits to the block of data so that the receiving node can determine whether it received the block correctly, and performs other data-formatting functions. In the end, the data link layer produces a new block of bits (ones and zeroes) that can be sent to the destination node.

The typical system programmer is usually happy with this view of the data link because he is writing software that deals with blocks of ones and zeroes. In reality, the bits will have to be transmitted in some way to the receiving node. This is where the physical layer (Layer 1) comes into play. The block of bits, also known as a frame or a packet, must be converted into some format that is amenable to transmission. On a wire, the bits might be turned into different electrical voltages. Similarly, a fiber optic system would turn a laser diode on and off to represent the bits. Dial-up modems and wireless networks employ frequency and phase modulation. In a very simple system, the digital 1 would be transmitted as a high note and a digital 0 would be transmitted as a low note.

Most networking professionals do not usually think too much about the physical layer. For example, when you buy a box of Ethernet cards, a switch, and a bunch of Cat 5 cable, you just trust that it will physically work. Logically, you might be concerned with things such as Ethernet/MAC addresses, but that is a data link layer issue, not a physical link issue.

The different Layer 2 and Layer 1 technologies have been combined in many ways. You can buy Ethernet cards that use twisted-pair copper wire (the Category 5 cables with RJ-45 connectors), fiber-optic cables, wireless radios (IEEE 802.11), or even coaxial cable. From a security perspective, the main thing to consider here is unauthorized physical access to the network. Twisted-pair or fiber-optic cables require physical access to monitor a link, whereas wireless networks are easier to monitor remotely.

Network Layers: Moving Data Across a Series of Links with IP

We have now established that it is possible to move a packet from one host to the next using a number of data link–layer (Layer 2) protocols. So, how do you build a more interesting network that will let you move packets across a series, or network, of links from the source to the destination? This is the role of the network layer, or Layer 3, protocols. The Internet Protocol (IP) is certainly the most famous of the Layer 3 protocols today. Other network-layer protocols that you might have heard of include IPX and X.25.

IP's job in life is pretty simple. It really performs only two functions:

- It provides a logical addressing scheme that allows packets to be forwarded from one hop to another until they get to their destination.

- It provides a means for "chopping up" packets if a link along the way will not support a large packet. The more technical name for this is fragmentation.

IP packets—or, more accurately, datagrams—are passed across a network through devices called *routers*. A router has a very simple job, at least in concept: It looks at the destination address of the packet that it has just received and determines whether it is destined for a network directly connected to the router or whether the packet needs to be forwarded to a neighboring router.

One very important detail about IP routers is that they work on a "best effort" basis to deliver the datagrams to their intended destination—there is no guarantee that an IP packet will get to its destination. Many things can happen to result in a datagram being discarded by a router along the way:

- The router might detect that a transmission error has occurred through the checksums attached to the packet. In this case, because the router has no idea where the error occurred (it could be in the destination IP address), it simply discards the packet.

- The router might be very busy processing many packets from other routers. In this case, the router starts discarding the excess packets.

- The packet might be too old. IP packet headers contain a field called the Time to Live, or TTL, which indicates how many links through the network the datagram has traveled. If this counter reaches 255 hops, the packet is discarded.

In many cases, packets are discarded silently, meaning that the sender is never notified that there was a problem. For this reason, IP is considered to be a *connectionless protocol* and is deemed to be unreliable as far as datagram delivery is concerned.

> ## An Analog to the Internet: The Postal Service
> ## Part II: The Network Layer
>
> Recall your postcard to Aunt Betty. We have discussed that the card is likely to cross several different types of "links" in the global postal network. But how does the postal system know which links to send the postcard across to get it to Aunt Betty's house? First, the postal system has established a well-known protocol for encoding the source (return) and destination addresses. For purposes of routing the letter, the ZIP code is used for the route-selection process at the majority of the network nodes. When the postcard gets to Aunt Betty's local post office, the street address provides the final routing instruction for the postal agent.

IP Addresses

So, how does IP encode the source and destination addresses? This matter was documented in the early 1980s in RFC 791 (remember the Network Working Group and its meeting minutes?). A quick read of this document reveals that the header of an IP packet generally is 20 bytes long and is organized as in Figure 4.3.

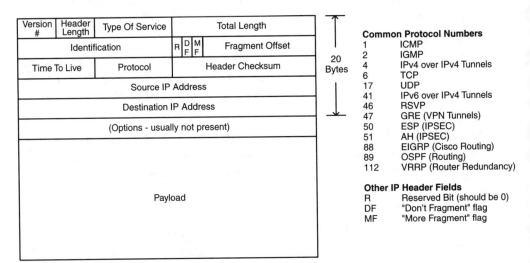

FIGURE 4.3

IP headers.

The IP header has a number of fields in it, including the well-known source and destination IP addresses. Technically, an IP address is simply a 32-bit number, meaning that more than four billion IP addresses are available for use on an IP network. However, the IP address space is not organized as a simple "flat" network. IP addresses are broken into two components: a network and a host. The network portion of the address is used by routers to direct a packet to the right local network, much like the way a ZIP code is used by the post office to direct a letter to the right neighborhood. The host address is used at the destination network to deliver the IP packet to the specific computer or device that it is intended for. This is analogous to the way that a postal delivery person would use the street address to get a letter to the correct addressee.

The dividing line between the network and the host address varies. The initial addressing plan for IP used a class-based concept in which the first few bits indicated which class of network the packet was destined for. A hundred or so large Class A networks were reserved and could accommodate more than 16 million hosts each. On the other end of the spectrum, the more plentiful Class C networks could accommodate approximately 250 hosts each. The details of classful addressing are illustrated in Figure 4.4.

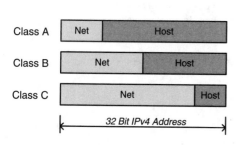
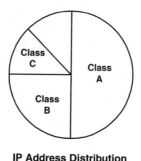

IP Address Distribution

Class A: 126 networks with 16,777,124 hosts
Class B: 16,384 networks with   65,534 hosts
Class C: 2,097,152 networks with   254 hosts
        2,113,662 Total IP Network Addresses

FIGURE 4.4
Classful IP addressing.

This system worked for a while; however, as the Internet became more popular, it soon became clear that an IP address crisis was coming down the road. This did not mean that all four billion IP addresses were even close to being allocated. The critical resource turned out to be *networks*, not hosts. A little math reveals that, although more than four billion possible IP addresses exist, only two million or so Class A, B, and C network blocks are available.

CIDR Blocks

Two primary solutions exist to the IP network space crunch. The first is the move to *classless* network addresses, in which the dividing line between the network and host portions of the IP address can be assigned arbitrarily instead of using the traditional Class A, B, and C dividing lines. The new Classless Interdomain Routing, or CIDR (pronounced "cider") scheme employs a new notation to designate how much of the network address is set aside for the network identification. For example, a /26 network uses the upper 26 bits of the IP address for the network number, leaving the lower 6 bits for the host space. Using traditional IP address assignments, this leaves space for 62 hosts. CIDR notation is illustrated further in Figure 4.5.

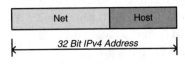

32 Bit IPv4 Address

/19 Network
19 bits are reserved for the network portion of an IP address
13 bits are reserved for the host portion of the IP address
(8,192 host addresses available in a /19 network)

/24	254 host addresses	Class C equivalent
/25	126	
/26	62	
/27	30	
/28	14	
/29	6	
/30	2	Router-to-router serial link

FIGURE 4.5
CIDR addressing.

CIDR allows ISPs to allocate reasonably sized blocks of IP addresses to end users. In the old classful system, the smallest block that could be assigned was a Class C network, meaning that 256 IP addresses were given away at a time. CIDR really provides a means for the ISPs to do what network administrators have done for a long time: break one block of addresses into smaller routable blocks by subnetting. The "slash" notation (as in /26) replaces the old subnet mask notation (as in 255.255.255.192) that has been used in the local area network.

Network Address Translation (NAT)

The second solution to the IP address shortage is Network Address Translation, or NAT. By employing an address translator in either a gateway router or a firewall, a number of host computers can be "hidden" behind a single IP address. The "internal" hosts typically are assigned IP addresses from one of several special blocks of reserved, "private" networks:

- 10.0.0.0/8: Equivalent of one Class A network
- 172.16.0.0/12: Equivalent of 16 Class B networks
- 192.168.0.0/16: Equivalent of 256 Class C networks

These addresses are set aside for private use and are not to be forwarded onto the Internet by gateway routers. If a host computer assigned with such an address wants to communicate with other users on the Internet, the packets must be passed through some NAT device (for example, a router or a firewall) that is capable of keeping track of all the outbound connections from the private network and swapping private IP addresses for public addresses. A typical NAT architecture is illustrated in Figure 4.6.

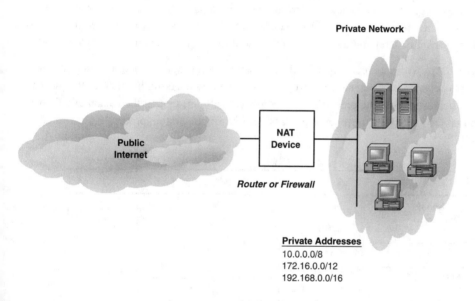

FIGURE 4.6

Network Address Translation and private networks.

Private addressing is a good solution to the IP address shortage because it allows networks to utilize much fewer public IP addresses. For example, our company has been allocated a /26 network space, which provides a block of 64 IP addresses. Most of the systems in the company's network have been assigned private IP addresses from the 172 block, and the main firewall performs the private-to-public translation when these computers need to access the Internet. This provides plenty of room for growth because hundreds of computers could be added to the internal network without any additional public IP addresses.

NAT also provides some security benefits. In the case of the aforementioned network, all of the internal desktop computers are NATed to a single public IP address by the company's firewall, so it is very difficult for an outsider to remotely scan the internal network and discover the actual layout of the protected network.

It is important for a network that utilizes NAT to be designed with equipment that supports the anticipated user base. For example, NATing firewalls usually are limited, either technically or by licensing, to supporting a certain number of NAT connections at a time.

IP Fragmentation

The second major issue that IP must deal with is that different data link technologies support different sizes of packets. An Ethernet network can handle packets of approximately 1500 bytes, while some serial links might limit packets to 512 bytes. What is a router to do if it has a 1500-byte packet to send and the best path to send it down supports only 512-byte packets?

Fortunately, IP provides a mechanism for dealing with this through a function called fragmentation. IP packets can be split into pieces by a router as needed. Assuming that all the pieces make it to the destination, the receiving host computer will defragment the packet and then send it on up the stack for higher-layer processing. The fragmentation process is illustrated in Figure 4.7.

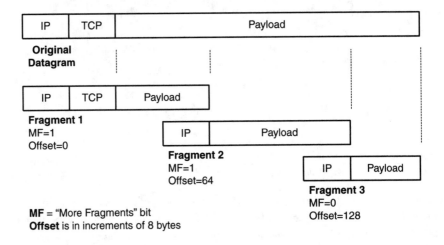

FIGURE 4.7

IP fragmentation.

Fragmentation is quite simple and actually is fairly rare in modern networks. The maximum transmissible unit (MTU) on most IP networks is set low enough that IP datagrams tend to make it to their destination intact. One practical use for fragmentation in data networks is to provide some measure of enhanced quality for streaming, "real-time" audio or video. These packets tend to be relatively small and can get stuck waiting behind larger packets in routers. Some systems employ fragmentation to break a big packet into smaller pieces so that the more time-critical media packets can "cut in line," so to speak. There are other techniques for dealing with this problem as well, such as simply discarding non–real-time data packets (remember, IP *is* unreliable).

Are there any security implications regarding fragmentation? You bet! Without giving away too much of what we will cover in our chapters dealing with firewalls and IDS, we again ask you to think about the implicit trust that most protocol stack developers have in the packets coming their way. How would you implement the code necessary to defragment the pieces of an IP datagram? The most logical approach would be simply to reverse the process that was used to break the original datagram into pieces. We don't have to be fancy here—the fragments come in contiguous blocks, and all we need to do is put them back together again. At least, that is the way it *should* work.

What should the defragmentation code do if fragments arrive with overlapping data space, as illustrated in Figure 4.8? The answer is really, "That is a good question—it isn't supposed to happen!" In many cases, the protocol implementers didn't even consider this. When we study firewalls and intrusion-detection systems, you will learn that this and other observations about proper protocol function can be used for less-than-honorable purposes.

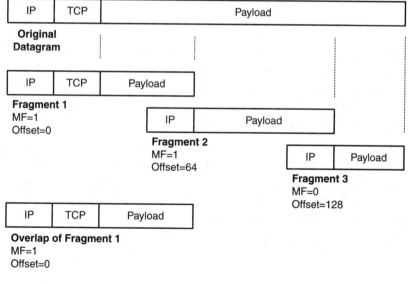

FIGURE 4.8

Overlapping IP fragments.

Routing Protocols

Now that you know the basic format of an IP datagram, it is reasonable to ask how all the routers between the sending computer and the destination know how to properly forward the packet through the network. It turns out that all those routers talk to each other, sharing information about which links are fast and which ones are slow, whether there are any problems in the network, and so on. To do this, they use protocols with names like Open Shortest Path First (OSPF), Routing Information Protocol (RIP), Interior Gateway Routing Protocol (IGRP), and Border Gateway Protocol (BGP).

Whole books have been written about these protocols, and we will not attempt to cover them in any detail here. We will simply make the point that all the routers are talking to each other and are always trying to figure out what is the fastest way to get from one place to another. Although most users are completely unaware of all this inter-router chatter, it should be clear that this is a critical part of keeping the Internet (or any other decent-size IP network) up and running.

Many of the routing protocols are actually somewhat vulnerable to corruption. If someone is able to change the routing tables in a router, that person can cause traffic to be re-directed in an unusual path. One technique for doing this is to effectively impersonate another router on the network and forge one of the router protocol update packets. Like many other protocols in the TCP/IP family, the early versions of the router protocols assumed much trust and did little or nothing to authenticate the source of routing information updates.

ICMP

The Internet Control Messaging Protocol, or ICMP, provides a means for the IP software on routers and hosts to communicate error information and very lightweight management information to each other. ICMP packets are carried within IP datagrams as protocol no. 1. The payload is usually very simple and includes a type and code to indicate which type of message is being communicated, as illustrated in Figure 4.9.

The most commonly used ICMP packets are the Echo Request and Echo Reply messages, popularly known as "pings." The Echo Request is simply a packet that asks the destination host to reply back, providing a means for checking whether a remote host is up. Other common ICMP messages include the Destination Unreachable and Time Expired messages, indicating that a router cannot deliver a packet to the specified IP address and that the IP Time to Live field has expired, respectively.

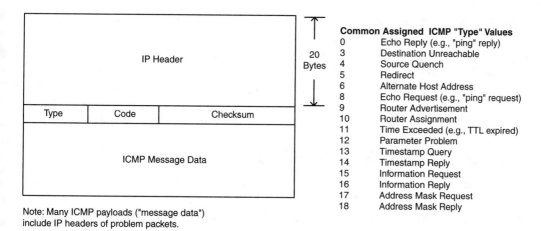

Common Assigned ICMP "Type" Values
0	Echo Reply (e.g., "ping" reply)
3	Destination Unreachable
4	Source Quench
5	Redirect
6	Alternate Host Address
8	Echo Request (e.g., "ping" request)
9	Router Advertisement
10	Router Assignment
11	Time Exceeded (e.g., TTL expired)
12	Parameter Problem
13	Timestamp Query
14	Timestamp Reply
15	Information Request
16	Information Reply
17	Address Mask Request
18	Address Mask Reply

Note: Many ICMP payloads ("message data") include IP headers of problem packets.

FIGURE 4.9

ICMP packets.

Historically, most networks allowed ICMP traffic to enter or leave freely because things such as ping were so useful for network monitoring (for instance, "Are my servers all up and running?"). Many hackers have taken advantage of this and have developed network-reconnaissance tools and covert command and control techniques that employ various ICMP message types. Although it can be frustrating to legitimate users, many network administrators are beginning to enforce strict rules on the passage of ICMP traffic in and out of their networks.

The traceroute Command

One very useful program that makes use of ICMP messages is traceroute (or tracert on some older Windows systems). This command can be used to find the approximate path between a host computer and a destination IP address. It does this by playing games with the IP Time to Live (TTL) field in a series of specially crafted packets. How does this work? Suppose that you want to find out the IP addresses of the routers that a packet will go through to get to 192.168.20.245. The traceroute program begins sending packets to that address, but it starts by setting IP's TTL value to 1. This causes the first router to return an error message via ICMP to your host, indicating that the TTL has expired. Next, the program sends a packet with a TTL value of 2. This time, the packet makes it to the second router before the TTL value expires. This process continues, with the traceroute program collecting all the ICMP error messages from the routers along the way until a packet finally makes it to its intended destination.

When using traceroute, you should be aware that the answer really reflects the current condition of the network. Packets can take different paths over the course of time, especially through the core of the Internet. On the other hand, the path that a packet follows as it leaves your

4

PROTOCOLS: TCP/IP
APPLICATION
NETWORK AND

computer and arrives at its destination could be fairly well fixed. The `traceroute` command is often useful for identifying an upstream ISP or router for a suspect computer or for diagnosing network problems. For example, if you cannot connect to a remote server, the `traceroute` command can be used to help determine whether there is a network outage somewhere between your computer and the remote server. When performing security analysis, the results from the `traceroute` command might reveal some information, such as the name of an ISP, about the network that is hosting a computer that has been attacking your network.

The Domain Name System (DNS)

You now know that IP provides an unreliable, "best-effort" means of moving a packet of data from one computer to another. All you have to do is put the right IP address into the packet header, and the packet is ready to go. Easy, right? The only question is, how do you know what the IP address of the intended receiver is?

Let's start by looking at your own network. Somewhere along the way, all the computers in your network probably were assigned a name. Most likely, these names have something in common: They are all characters from *The Simpsons*, starships from *Star Trek*, your favorite martinis, or some other theme that appealed to you or your system administrator. Instead of remembering the IP addresses that you assigned to each computer, you probably could use some kind of lookup table, just like a phone book, that lists computer names and their corresponding IP addresses—for example:

bart	192.168.1.10
lisa	192.168.1.11
maggie	192.168.1.12

In fact, such a table exists in your computer. In a UNIX environment, the /etc/hosts file is a simple listing of computer names and IP addresses. That works great for a small local network, but what about the Internet? Who is responsible for keeping track of all the computers that are accessible on the Internet and their IP addresses? Every network administrator could send her list to everyone else, but that would get out of hand quickly. First, the list would probably get big very fast, and distribution would become a serious chore and a bandwidth hog. Second, it is highly probable that one of your peers likes *The Simpsons* or *Star Trek*, too, and used the same names that you did.

DNS Concepts

The answer to this problem is found in the Domain Name System, or DNS. This is a second logical addressing scheme that was developed to assist us poor humans with the task of keeping track of IP addresses. We are all familiar with domain names such as `www.microsoft.com`, `www.sun.com`, and `www.acme.com`. These names are easy for people to remember, but they mean nothing to the IP protocol. They must be *resolved* to IP addresses. DNS is actually a distributed database. The work of maintaining the database is divided among all the network owners. In the previous example, Microsoft is expected to keep a list of its computers, and Sun is expected to do the same. The lists are maintained in DNS servers, which anyone can query. So, Acme might maintain publicly accessible servers for Web, mail, and file transfers, and name them as follows:

```
www.acme.com
ftp.acme.com
    mail.acme.com
```

Acme's DNS database would contain the IP addresses of each of these servers. If a home user wanted to view the Acme product catalog on the home page, she would simply type the (usually) intuitive URL into her Web browser. The browser then would contact the closest DNS server, which, in this case, would be run by her ISP. If her ISP's DNS server didn't know the answer, it would ask the .com DNS root server to tell it how to get to the Acme DNS server. The Internet's root DNS servers provide the master list for each of the top-level domains. These are critical components of the Internet and are maintained in redundant high-availability configurations. For example, the .com root servers know the IP addresses of the second-tier (for example, acme.com) domain name servers. Ultimately, the response would be returned to the ISP's DNS server, which would pass the answer on to the Web browser.

This usually happens rather quickly. To speed things up for the next user, the ISP's DNS server might make note of the answer in its cache so that it will know the answer if anyone else asks for the same information in the near future. This process is illustrated in Figure 4.10.

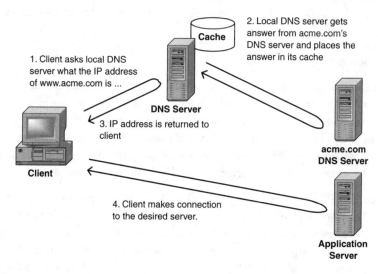

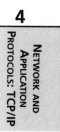

FIGURE 4.10

Looking up an IP address in the Domain Name System.

DNS Protocol Details

DNS servers are assigned the well-known TCP/UDP port 53, and all domain name queries should be directed to UDP port 53. If that doesn't make sense now, it will by the time you finish reading this chapter. A typical DNS query is a single packet that contains a question such as "What is the address of www.acme.com?"

The packet is forwarded to the DNS server that the host computer has been told to use in its configuration files. In a UNIX system, this address is stored in the file /etc/resolv.conf. The response that comes back contains several fields:

- The "answer" is a list of one or more IP addresses and a "time to live." This time-to-live value tells the cache on your local DNS server how long it can hang on to that answer before it must send a query back to Acme's name server. To speed up future queries, the local DNS server places the answer in a temporary local list (the cache) for as long as the TTL value indicates that the answer will be valid.

- An "authority" list identifies the DNS servers responsible for that zone (for example, ns1.acme.com).

- A matching list of "additional" records specifies the IP addresses of the authoritative DNS server(s).

In many cases, a DNS response will contain several answers. This indicates that multiple host computers are capable of responding to that domain name, providing a method for an organization to both balance the load coming into their servers and provide a "hot backup" in case a server goes down. For example, Acme might get so much traffic to its Web site that it must run multiple physical Web servers to handle the load. These servers might actually be named:

```
www1.acme.com
www2.acme.com
      www3.acme.com
```

The DNS server might respond to all queries for the IP address of www.acme.com with a list of all three servers and their respective IP addresses. Getting multiple answers provides some fault tolerance because the Web browser now has alternatives that it can try if the first server fails to respond. Many larger Web sites employ dedicated load balancers based on DNS server technology to direct customer Web browsers to one of many physical server sites distributed around the world, or to one of many servers co-located in the same site.

DNS servers contain other specialized records. One of the most important is the Mail Exchanger (MX) record, which is the IP address of the mail server(s) serving that domain. For example, we showed previously that Acme ran three network servers—Web, mail, and FTP. The mail server was conveniently named mail.acme.com. If a customer wanted to send a message to support@acme.com, his mail relay would have to know the IP address of the Acme mail server. It might guess that the mail server is named mail.acme.com, but no rule says that it must be named in such an obvious manner. This is where the MX record comes into play. Mail relays know that they should be able to get the exact name and IP address of a domain's mail server by performing an MX request of that destination domain's DNS server.

DNS servers are a critical component in the Internet and in most private networks. For this reason, DNS servers almost always are deployed in a high-availability configuration. There are at least two servers, and hosts on the network are configured with both DNS servers' IP addresses. Generally, one server is the primary server and the other is the backup. The servers stay in sync with each other via DNS zone transfers. Zone transfers are used to replicate the domain name database in one server onto another server. Zone transfers employ TCP port 53 because the DNS tables usually will not fit in a single UDP datagram.

Using the `nslookup` Tool

The vast majority of DNS lookups are performed automatically, when applications make calls to C language functions such as `get_host_by_name()`. Examples of applications requesting name resolution include these:

- A Web browser going to a home page, such as `http://www.acme.com`. Similarly, any link on that page with a new domain name will require a DNS query.

- Any command-line program that takes a domain name as a parameter (for example, `ftp ftp.acme.com` or `ping homer.acme.com`).

It turns out that most modern operating systems provide a command-line interface to the DNS database as well through the `nslookup` command. This tool can be used either as a simple query engine or interactively. The normal operation is to look up the IP address associated with a domain name, using the following syntax:

```
        $ nslookup homer.acme.com
Name:    homer.acme.com
Address: 192.168.200.204
```

More useful in investigations is to perform an inverse query, using the tool to map an IP address back to a domain name:

```
        $ nslookup 192.168.200.204
```

Finally, the tool can be used in interactive mode to discover other information contained in the DNS database. For instance, suppose that you want to know the IP address of Acme's mail server. This is something that your mail system will need if you ever send email to anyone@acme.com; it is a query that can be performed manually by starting `nslookup` in its interactive mode and changing the query type to perform a mail exchanger (MX) lookup:

```
        $ nslookup
> set querytype=mx
> acme.com
        mail addr = mail.acme.com
```

DNS Security Issues

By now, you should be convinced that DNS is a critical piece of the Internet infrastructure; therefore, it is worthy of a few extra minutes of our time as we consider security issues in networks.

First, DNS is ubiquitous. All IP networks of any size run DNS servers, so any vulnerabilities discovered in the popular server implementations (such as named in the UNIX world) translate into widespread opportunities for hackers. It is very important that administrators maintain the patch level of their DNS servers.

Aside from program vulnerabilities, the DNS protocol itself is not secure. The answers to queries implicitly are trusted by host computers. This means that anyone who can answer a query first can redirect a client program to an invalid server, presenting an opportunity for "man-in-the-middle" attacks, in which an unintended receiver acts as a middle man, reading and perhaps modifying packets on the way to their proper destination. Note that security extensions have been developed under the name DNSSEC (DNS Security); however, these extensions were not operationally deployed at the time that this text was written, primarily because this would require a trusted public-key infrastructure (PKI).

In the case of DNS poisoning, the intercepting system would reply to the requesting system before the legitimate DNS server could. It might even be able to block the valid answer from reaching the querying system. If this attack were successful, the attacking computer could trick the querying system into going to another system. For example, if the attacker wanted to collect account numbers and passwords for an online banking portal, he could easily duplicate the look and feel of the bank's main Web page and then redirect the bank's customers to the fake site. The bogus Web site could be rigged to store the information that the unsuspecting customer enters at the login screen and then either return an error message or redirect the information to the valid server.

Man-in-the-middle attacks require that the attacking computer be able to either observe or intercept packets on the way to their intended destinations. Note that this is not typically very easy in most modern switched Ethernet networks. We will discuss the details of network monitoring in Chapter 10, "Watching the Wire: Intrusion-Detection Systems."

Additionally, it is usually easy for an outsider to request a zone transfer from your DNS servers. In general, the information in a DNS server is intended to be made available to the public; however, some administrators like to know when outsiders perform the relatively unusual step of downloading their entire DNS database instead of making normal queries. Also, some networks might run several logical servers: one for the public to use to access the servers intended for them, and the other for intranet users, which contains information about internal servers. Of course, there are ways to protect the internal network; that is a subject for future chapters of this book.

Finally, and perhaps most importantly, because DNS servers play such an important role in the day-to-day functions of the Internet, they are obvious targets of denial-of-service attacks. If an attacker can either crash a DNS server or block access to the server, he effectively can prevent most Internet traffic from flowing because none of the common desktop applications will be able to determine the IP addresses they need to communicate with other servers. We will discuss a number of general denial of service attacks which could be used to disable a DNS server in Chapter 8, "Attack Scenarios."

All-in-One Network Tools

Many of the command-line utilities discussed in this chapter can be found embedded in friendlier tools. Neotrace is a handy Windows-based tool that combines traceroute and whois information. Sam Spade is another Windows application that provides traceroute, whois, DNS lookups, finger, and other query tools. Some Web sites, such as www.network-tools.com, provide useful investigative resources as well.

Revisiting the Data Link Layer: Ethernet and IP

Ethernet has become the de facto standard in the local area network (LAN), and understanding its relationship to IP is important to understanding how most real-world networks are built today.

A Brief History of Ethernet

Like TCP/IP, Ethernet has its roots in the early 1970s, with the work performed by Robert Metcalfe and David Boggs at the Xerox Palo Alto Research Center (PARC). Xerox PARC was responsible for many of the advances in computing that we take for granted today, including bitmapped displays, the mouse, and the laser printer. Metcalfe and Boggs developed a technology that they called Ethernet for connecting PARC's Alto computers to each other. Their coax-based Ethernet was an enhancement of the broadcast radio packet network developed at the University of Hawaii, called the Aloha Network. By adding the carrier sense ("listen to see if anyone else is talking before you do") and collision detection ("notice if anyone starts talking before you are finished") features of the CSMA/CD algorithm, Metcalfe and Boggs significantly increased the efficiency of the broadcast networking. Interested readers are referred to their original article in the July 1976 issue of *The Communications of the ACM*.

In 1980, two groups got together to market and further develop the Ethernet protocol. DEC, Intel, and Xerox developed the DIX standard, while the IEEE formed the 802 committee (named after the date of its inception, February 1980) to develop the IEEE

802.3 CSMA/CD standard. For those who worry that technology inventors don't always enjoy the fruits of their labor, it should be noted that Bruce Metcalfe formed the 3Com Corporation around the same time and that 3Com sold its first EtherLink network adapters for just less than $1,000 a piece.

Two events that further enhanced the market position of Ethernet include the development of the twisted-pair technology by SynOptics in 1987, which led to the 10Base-T standard in 1990, and the decision by Novell to license its NE2000 interface design to other manufacturers (recall that Novell was a leading networking operating system vendor at the time, and cheap networks were good for its business!). These developments resulted in significant reductions in the cost of deploying and maintaining Ethernet infrastructures.

First, although it is not critical from a security perspective, it is important to understand that three "flavors" of Ethernet can be found in a network today. The three header types are illustrated in Figure 4.11.

- **Ethernet DIX**—This is the DEC/Intel/Xerox standard. It includes an EtherType value that indicates the type of network-layer packet being carried. For example, the value for IP is 0x0800—note that this is hexadecimal, the common format used in Ethernet documentation.

- **IEEE 802.3 CSMA/CD**—This is the IEEE standard, in which the DIX EtherType is replaced with the length of the packet. IEEE 802.3 headers are followed by an IEEE 802.2 header and sometimes a SNAP header, which effectively perform the same function as the DIX EtherType.

- **Novell's "Raw"**—This is another version of Ethernet in which the EtherType is replaced by the length, as in IEEE 802.3. However, the payload is always an IPX frame.

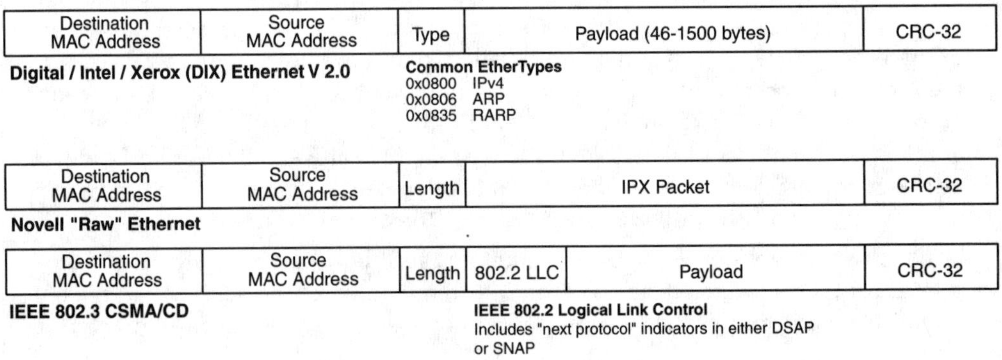

FIGURE 4.11

Ethernet protocol headers.

We will use the term *Ethernet* generically throughout this text, although in practice we could be dealing with either DIX or 802.3 frames. The type of Ethernet framing used often is related to the vendor of the network device or software. In fact, in an environment with mixed operating systems, all three types of Ethernet packets might be found on a network at the same time. Bear this in mind in case you find yourself looking at raw packet dumps through a packet-capture system such as a protocol analyzer (such as Network General's Sniffer, Microsoft's Network Monitor, or Net X-Ray), UNIX utilities such as tcpdump and snoop, or intrusion-detection systems.

Within an Ethernet network, packets are really delivered to the appropriate device via its MAC or Ethernet address, a 48-bit number that should be unique to each physical Ethernet interface. In fact, the MAC address actually is comprised of two 24-bit parts: a vendor ID and a unit (serial number) ID. Furthermore, just as in IP, Ethernet includes an "all ones" broadcast address (in which all 48 bits are set to the value 1) that typically is written as FF:FF:FF:FF:FF:FF. Each network interface (a network adapter in a computer or server) listens for frames either that are addressed to it or that have the broadcast address as their destination.

So, there are two obvious questions with respect to Ethernet and IP:

- When an Internet application has figured out the IP address that it wants to talk to (for example, through a DNS lookup), how does that IP address get mapped to the appropriate MAC address? This is important because, although the IP address is the logical network address, the packets must actually be sent over the Ethernet network, in which the MAC address has meaning, not the IP address.

- Which MAC address should it use if the destination at the IP level is not in the local Ethernet network?

The answer to both of these questions lies in the Address Resolution Protocol, or ARP. ARP has a very simple function. When a host computer needs to deliver a packet to a new IP address (for example, 192.168.1.15), it sends out an Ethernet broadcast packet called an *ARP Request*, which basically says, "Which Ethernet device has an IP address of 192.168.1.15?" All the Ethernet devices on the LAN hear this, and the correct device answers back with an *ARP Reply*, which says, "I do, and here is my MAC address so that you can get the packet to me." The host computer then uses that address for forwarding packets to the intended destination. It also tucks that address away in its *ARP cache*, a local table of IP-to-MAC conversions, so that it doesn't have to ask again for the next packet that it has to send to a packet to that IP address. You can check the contents of your ARP cache via the arp command at both the UNIX and Windows command prompts.

In many cases, the destination IP address might not be in the local network. What happens then? In this case, the gateway router should "proxy ARP" for the destination device—it answers back saying, "Send the packet to me" so that it can forward it on to the appropriate IP subnetwork. Note that, in some cases, the host or server might know that the IP address is not local (based on the local subnet mask) and do a direct ARP query for the gateway router.

By now, if you have your security hat on, you should be thinking to yourself, "Aha! Another address lookup table! If I could affect that table, I could redirect traffic to an unintended receiver."

A quick review of the ARP header (see Figure 4.12) reveals that the protocol is indeed very simple. There is nothing to prove that the answer is coming from the right Ethernet device. Again, you can see that the IP infrastructure is built on a strong foundation of implied trust. If someone else on your network so desired, he could potentially transmit fake responses to your broadcast ARP Requests and reroute all traffic to his computer as a man-in-the-middle attack. This is known as ARP cache poisoning.

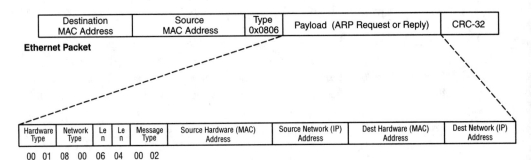

FIGURE 4.12

The ARP header.

Configuring a Host to Work on an IP Network

So, given what you now know, what does a host computer need to know to interact productively with the Internet? The basic configuration requirements include these:

- An IP address
- A netmask (or CIDR mask) so that it knows what is local

- A means of getting to its gateway router so that it can talk to computers beyond the local network

- The IP address of at least one DNS server

IP configuration information is loaded into a host in several ways:

1. **Manual configuration**—An administrator edits by hand the correct configuration file(s) or graphical interfaces.

2. **DHCP**—The Dynamic Host Configuration Protocol commonly is used in LANs, including cable modem and DSL services. When the computer powers up, it sends out a query asking for its network-configuration information. A DHCP server responds with a packet that contains the required data. These usually are issued as "leases," in that an expiration data is included with the IP configuration information.

3. **PPP**—In dial-up connections, the PPP protocol includes an IP Configuration Protocol (IPCP) packet, which contains the basic network-configuration information.

Again, note the implied trust present with the automatic-configuration techniques. With PPP, this isn't a serious issue because the user generally selects the ISP being dialed into. For DHCP, there is some danger that an unscrupulous user on the local network could hijack the initial DHCP request and provide bogus configuration information. For example, by changing the gateway router address, someone could trick the host computer into sending all outbound traffic to itself. Similarly, by changing the IP address for DNS queries, the hijacker selectively could forward traffic to himself by falsely answering any domain name query desired.

Transport Layers: Moving Data Reliably with TCP (and Not So Reliably with UDP)

We now have established that we can use IP to move a packet of data from a source to a destination computer in an *unreliable* manner. This is a mildly useful capability, but it is hardly the infrastructure on which you would want to send email, exchange programs, browse the Web, or shop electronically. This is where OSI Layer 4, or transport-layer, protocols come into play.

We will examine two common Layer 4 protocols from the IP family: UDP and TCP. UDP provides the basic capability of allowing multiple applications running on a single host to send data over an IP network. TCP enhances this by adding all of the overhead necessary to make an IP network reliable, guaranteeing that every byte sent is delivered, in order and without error, to the destination program.

Multiplexing with UDP

IP, which operates at OSI Layer 3 (the network layer), provides all the mechanisms necessary to (hopefully) get a packet from one computer to another. Which applications on the computer are communicating? IP addresses identify an interface on a host computer, but without additional information, you would have to "hard-wire" the network data to a specific application or process running on that computer. That is, without additional information, the packet can be delivered to only one application. The User Datagram Protocol, or UDP, adds a small amount of additional header information to an IP packet so that the packet can be addressed to a specific process/service/application on the host computer.

UDP headers, as defined in RFC 768 and illustrated in Figure 4.13, contain four fields: source and destination *ports*, the length of the UDP payload, and a checksum, which might or might not be used. The ports are the new and interesting part of the UDP header and are implemented as 16-bit integers, meaning that they can take on a value ranging from 0 to 65,535. The source port identifies the process or application on the source host that the packet's data came from, and the destination port identifies the intended receiving process or application on the destination host. So, when a UDP/IP packet arrives at a computer, the protocol software looks at the destination port number and delivers the data to the appropriate program running on the system. If the program needs to send any data back to the source, it has the IP address and port number of the application running on the sending computer. This ability to combine the data from multiple applications is called multiplexing.

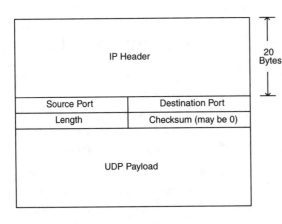

Common UDP Port Values

53	Domain Name System (DNS)
67	Dynamic Host Configuration Protocol (DHCP)
68	Dynamic Host Configuration Protocol (DHCP)
111	Remote Procedure Call (RPC)
161	Simple Network Mgmt Protocol (SNMP)
162	Simple Network Mgmt Protocol Trap (SNMP)

FIGURE 4.13
The UDP header.

Note that all UDP does is add a multiplexing capability to an IP network: Many processes on a host computer now can share the host's IP interface and have an opportunity to send packets over this inherently unreliable network. What is the value in that? As you will discover in the next section, making IP a reliable network is a critical step in developing useful packet networks, but the reliability comes with a price that is paid in complexity and setup time. Some applications can tolerate the unreliability of the basic UDP/IP protocol combination. For example, many simple "lookup" protocols, such as DNS queries, use UDP. If either the query or the response packet gets dropped in the network, the host that issued the original domain name query simply gets tired of waiting (that is, a timeout counter expires) and asks again. The advantage of DNS using UDP is that the vast majority of the domain name queries are completed quite quickly. We will revisit the question of when to use UDP after the next section.

So, how are port numbers assigned? How does the source know what port on the destination host to send packets to? To understand the answer to these questions, we must introduce the concept of *clients* and *servers*. For now, we will define these terms as follows:

- A *server* provides some kind of service on the network that applications or processes might want to take advantage of. For example, a DNS server provides the domain name–to–IP address lookup that is required by most applications. Likewise, a Web server provides access to Web pages.

- A *client* is an application that "calls" a server in an attempt to make use of its services. Common DNS clients include the resolver in a UNIX system or the command-line nslookup tool. Similarly, Netscape Navigator and Microsoft Explorer are two common examples of clients for Web servers.

Servers are processes that "listen" for network connections on certain ports. In theory, a server could listen on any old port, but that would leave all the potential clients having to guess where it was. Two potential solutions exist: Either provide a port lookup service or give common servers a standard port number to listen to. It turns out that both techniques are used; however, the former is the most common and is addressed in this section.

Well-known ports are assigned by the Internet Assigned Numbers Authority (IANA), which is now managed by the ICANN. For example, DNS servers traditionally are found listening on port 53. A complete list of the current well-known ports can be found at the IANA Web site (www.iana.org).

Adding Reliability with TCP

UDP has added a little bit of extra capability to the IP network: Now you can have more than one program using this unreliable network. Still, this is not something that we would expect to cause a revolution in personal and business communication.

The Transmission Control Protocol, or TCP, is the key to completing the Internet infrastructure. Defined in RFC 793, TCP includes the same port numbers that we introduced with UDP. It then adds state flags and sequence numbers so that reliability can be introduced to an IP network. The TCP header is illustrated in Figure 4.14.

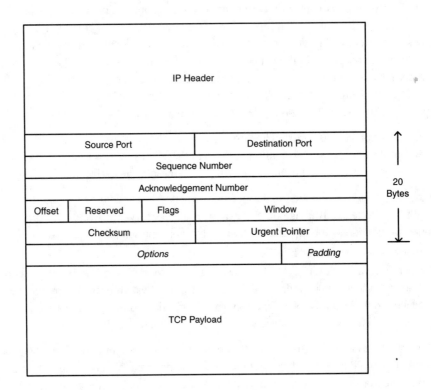

FIGURE 4.14

The TCP header.

TCP's reliability is the direct result of adding sequence and acknowledgement numbers, as well as a few other control fields, to the TCP headers. Every TCP segment includes the TCP header, which is *usually* 20 bytes in length, and the application layer payload that it is carrying. The payloads represent a continuous *stream* of data. Indeed, the interface that is presented to the higher-layer application is a generic byte stream interface, meaning that TCP simply guarantees that the stream of data bytes will be delivered in order. As a general rule, the application does not know how its data will be broken up into packets in the network; it simply sends blocks of data to the TCP protocol, and TCP decides when is the best time to save up, or buffer data or send data down the line. This allows TCP to make efficient use of packets because it optimally should save up enough data to fill up the maximum-size packet allowed on the network. Of course, this wouldn't make sense if the higher-layer application was something like Telnet and the TCP connection was carrying the user's keystrokes. Those should be delivered in short order, so the Telnet application can use a special "push" function to tell the TCP protocol to send whatever it has ready to go.

Each TCP header contains a *sequence number*, which keeps track of which byte in the stream is at the beginning of the payload. This number is used by the receiving TCP protocol software to make sure that any bytes that arrive out of order are resequenced before they are delivered to the higher-layer application. Each TCP header also contains an *acknowledgement number*, which is used to tell the remote TCP protocol software how much of the stream has been successfully received at the local side. If too much time goes by without a block of data being acknowledged (that is, another timeout counter is running in TCP), then the originating host retransmits that block of data. Ultimately, if the receiving side has to wait too long for a part of the byte stream, it reports an error condition to the application program.

An Analog to the Internet: The Postal Service
Part III: The Transport Layer

Again, let's revisit your postcard to Aunt Betty. Suppose that you are starting to get a little long-winded, and you want to send more than you can fit on a single postcard. Of course, you could send a letter, but that would break the analogy. Instead, let's suppose that you have lots of postcards ready to drop in the mail. You write as much as you can on each postcard, and then continue the message on a new postcard, using as many postcards as you need to. So as not to confuse Aunt Betty, you write a number on the corner of each postcard so that she can put the cards back in order before reading them. If one of the postcards gets lost in the mail, she can always write you back, asking you to fill her in on what she missed.

The concept of sequence numbering is very important to building reliability into a packet network.

One unusual aspect of TCP sequencing is that the sequence numbers do not start at 0 or 1 at the beginning of the connection. Because of this, some method for agreeing on each side's starting number is necessary to begin the transmission of the byte stream. This is where the state flags come into play.

Controlling TCP Connections

The *state flags* mentioned previously are used to control the reliable TCP connection. In many ways, TCP connections are just like a phone call. The client places a call to the server, the server answers, a conversation between the two takes place, and then one of the two parties hangs up. Because of the importance of this concept to many of our discussions regarding security issues, we will spend a little extra time on the details of the mechanics of TCP connections.

Several single-bit flags contained in the TCP header that are used to control which phase of the connection the two host computers are in:

- The SYN (synchronize) flag is set to a value of 1 in the first packet of a connection from both the client and the server. This flag indicates that the packet's source is indicating the sequence number of the first byte of the byte stream that will be transmitted. The first sequence number is known as the initial sequence number (ISN).

- The ACK (acknowledge) flag indicates that the acknowledgement number in the header is valid and should be examined by the receiver. The only time that the ACK flag is set to 0 is in the first packet from the calling client because it has not received anything to acknowledge yet.

- The FIN (finish) flag indicates that either the client or the server is ready to hang up and end the connection. This is the polite way of hanging up, akin to saying "goodbye" and waiting for the other person to say "goodbye" as well.

- The RST (reset) flag is a less graceful indicator that someone has hung up. Think of it as slamming down the phone on someone.

The process for establishing a TCP connection is illustrated in Figure 4.15. To call the server, the client sends a packet with the SYN bit set to 1 and the ACK bit set to 0. This is like dialing a phone number and saying "hello." The server responds with both its SYN and ACK bits set to 1, indicating that it has answered the call and received the client's initial sequence number (ISN) successfully. Finally, the server acknowledges the server's ISN with one more packet, this time with the SYN set to 0 and the ACK set to 1, effectively saying, "Great! Now we can talk!" From this point on, the sequence numbers in each direction go up as more bytes from the stream are sent, and each side continuously acknowledges how much of the other side's stream it has received. Ultimately, one of the sides will be ready to end the conversation and will hang up, preferably using the FIN flag as described previously.

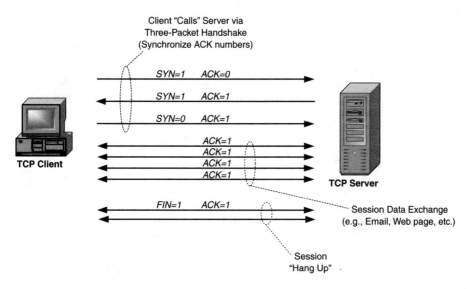

FIGURE 4.15

The TCP connection handshake sequence.

Understanding this sequence of events, often called the three-way handshake, is very important to understanding the subtleties of some of the network attacks that we will describe in the coming chapters. Again, it is important to put yourself in the mind-set of an attacker and consider how a firm knowledge of the TCP/IP mechanics can be used in ways that were not considered by the original protocol implementers. For example, what would happen if a packet were sent to a host with the SYN and FIN bits set to 1 at the same time? This is like calling and hanging up at the same time. It is certainly not normal behavior, and unless the person who wrote a particular TCP/IP protocol stack was being very careful, this eventuality probably is not handled explicitly.

Two common command-line tools can be used to check on the status of the TCP connections on a given host. The `netstat` command is commonly found in UNIX and Windows systems and displays the details of any active network connections, including the source and destination socket information and the "state" of the connection (that is, whether it is just starting, is in the normal connection phase, or is ending). An example of the output of the `netstat` command is contained in Figure 4.16. On some BSD systems, the `sockstat` command indicates the connection between network connections and the running processes that they are associated with.

4

NETWORK AND
APPLICATION
PROTOCOLS: TCP/IP

```
$ netstat -a
Active Internet connections (including servers)
Proto Recv-Q Send-Q  Local Address          Foreign Address         (state)
tcp4      0      2    soddus.telnet          192.168.1.100.1580      ESTABLISHED
tcp4      0      0    soddus.telnet          win98.1742              ESTABLISHED
tcp4      0      0    soddus.9000            soddus.1051             ESTABLISHED
tcp4      0      0    soddus.1051            soddus.9000             ESTABLISHED
tcp4      0      0    *.9000                 *.*                     LISTEN
tcp4      0      0    *.3306                 *.*                     LISTEN
tcp4      0      0    *.http                 *.*                     LISTEN
tcp4      0      0    *.ssh                  *.*                     LISTEN
tcp46     0      0    *.ssh                  *.*                     LISTEN
tcp6      0      0    *.finger               *.*                     LISTEN
tcp6      0      0    *.login                *.*                     LISTEN
tcp6      0      0    *.shell                *.*                     LISTEN
tcp6      0      0    *.telnet               *.*                     LISTEN
tcp6      0      0    *.ftp                  *.*                     LISTEN
tcp4      0      0    *.telnet               *.*                     LISTEN
tcp4      0      0    *.ftp                  *.*                     LISTEN
udp4      0      0    *.syslog               *.*
```

FIGURE 4.16

Checking network connections with netstat.

Common Well-Known Ports

Just as with UDP, TCP servers often are associated with well-known ports. A short list of some common servers and their standard ports is included in Figure 4.17. The port assignments on a particular host typically are managed in one of two ways:

- Standalone services often have their port number assigned in a configuration file. For example, the Apache Web server's configuration file httpd.conf includes a directive that sets the server's port.

- On UNIX systems, a process called inetd can be used to act as a traffic cop of sorts, looking at incoming TCP connections and starting the right process based on the destination port number. The inetd process uses a pair of configuration files called services and inetd.conf to map port numbers to applications.

Again, nothing says that a mail server *must* be run on port 25; however, if you want anyone to be able to connect to your mail server, it is probably a good idea to run it on the well-known port. If you were running a private network and wanted to apply a little "security through obscurity," you could configure your server to listen on a different port. Although this is not exactly robust security, it would mean that mail relays that wanted to connect to your mail server would have to be reconfigured to send packets to the nonstandard port. Note that there are only 65,536 possible ports, so it would not take that long for an automated port scan to discover this "hidden" server.

Common TCP and UDP Ports

7	Echo		500	ISAKMP (IPSEC Key Negotiation)
11	Sysstat		1080	SOCKS
19	Chargen		1701	L2TP (VPN Tunnel and Control)
20	FTP Data		1720	H.323 Host Call
21	FTP Control		1723	Microsoft PPTP (VPN Control)
22	Secure Shell (SSH)		5632	PC Anywhere
23	Telnet		12345	NetBus (Trojan Horse)
25	SMTP (mail)		27374	Sub-7 (Trojan Horse)
53	DNS		31337	Back Orifice & Other Trojan Horses
67	BOOTP/DHCP			
68	BOOTP/DHCP		32770-32990	Sun RPC Programs
69	Trivial FTP (TFTP)			
79	Finger			
80	HTTP (Web)			
110	POP3			
111	Sun RPC Portmapper			
113	Authenitcation Service (auth/ident)			
119	NNTP (news)			
135	Microsoft/DCE RPC Portmapper			
137	NetBIOS Name Service			
138	NetBIOS Datagram Service			
139	NetBIOS Session Service			
143	Internet Message Access Protocol (IMAP)			

FIGURE 4.17

Well-known TCP ports.

Port reassignment is probably done most commonly with Web servers. Although most servers run on port 80, it is not unheard of to see proxy servers listening on port 8080 or 8000. In fact, if a Web server is running on a port other than the default port 80, you can specify the port that you want to try to connect to in the standard URL that is typed in a Web browser, as follows:

```
http://www.somesite.com:8000/
```

Similarly, the `telnet` command provides a way of connecting to a port other than the well-known port 23. For example, if you wanted to Telnet to port 80, you could use the following command on either a Windows or a UNIX system:

```
telnet 192.168.1.110 80
```

You will see in Chapter 8 that this can be used for all sorts of interesting reasons. Although someone *might* run a Telnet server at a different port, this command more likely could be used to see what kind of banner information a specific port presents upon a connection. This turns out to be a handy tool for "banner grabbing" as a means of network reconnaissance.

4

NETWORK AND
APPLICATION
PROTOCOLS: TCP/IP

Common Application-Layer Protocols

If the 1970s was the decade when packet networking technologies were proven and the 1980s marked the emergence of TCP/IP, then the 1990s was the decade when the Internet applications achieved commercial success. Although email, newsgroups and chat all existed in early years of the Internet, it was the advent of the graphical Web browser that really triggered the explosive growth in the Internet and e-commerce. And although many of the first round of dot coms have fallen, it is clear that the Internet has become a critical component in modern business and personal communications and that more critical and personal information is carried and maintained by the many new Web applications. Because of this, we believe that the first decade of the 21st century will be the period when IP security and network ubiquity will be the dominant issues in enterprise networking.

Common Internet Applications

Many application-layer protocols exist on the Internet today, including these:

- Simple Mail Transfer Protocol (SMTP)
- Post Office Protocol version 3 (POP3)
- Hypertext Transfer Protocol (HTTP—"the Web")
- File Transfer Protocol (FTP)
- Internet Relay Chat (IRC)
- Telnet, for remote login access

Just as the developers and implementers of the IP and TCP protocols could not anticipate every possible misuse of their standards, neither could application developers. Many vulnerabilities involving these protocols have been documented in recent years. We will discuss some of these issues in forthcoming chapters of this book.

UNIX Remote Procedure Calls

One twist on the client/server model—one that has important security ramifications—is the Remote Procedure Call programming (RPC) paradigm. In this model, the client and server components are actually parts of a single application that have been separated by a packet network. "What does that mean?" you might ask. To understand RPC, you need just a little bit of familiarity with general programming languages, such as the C language. Consider the following function call:

```
result = do_something(a,b,c);
```

In this example, the function do_something() takes three parameters, called a, b, and c; performs some computation or lookup; and returns a value called result. In normal application environments, all of this code executes on a single host. In an RPC environment, the actual executable code for do_something() is running on another machine (the server) somewhere on the network, and the calling function is running on the client. The only thing that exists on the client is a stub for do_something() that accepts the three parameters, packages them in a packet, and ships them to the server for processing. The result value subsequently is packaged in another packet by the server and sent back to the client, where it is returned to the calling software. As far as the client knows, everything happened locally.

In the Unix environment, a very common application that employs RPCs is the Network File System, or NFS. Remote disks are "mounted" to a host via a Unix command such as this one:

```
mount -t nfs fileserver:/old-stuff /archives
```

This command makes the /old-stuff file system, which is physically located on the computer named fileserver, accessible on the local computer as a file system called /archives.

What is happening on the network, then? The RPC system developed by Sun is based on the Open Network Computing RPC specification and is documented in RFCs 1831–1833. In this model, the remote application code can be found running on some dynamically assigned port that is associated with the RPC application (that is, it is not a well-known port that everyone knows). Because the port is not well known, how does the client know which port to connect to so that it can pass the arguments to the remote procedure? In this case, it first connects to a portmapper service that *is* running on a well-known port (port 111, in this case). The client connects to the portmapper and tells it which RPC program it wants to execute functions from, and the portmapper reports back to the client which port it can call to find the desired program. When the client has the program's port number, it sends a packet to the new port number that contains a reference to the function that it wants to call, along with the arguments for that function. When the results are ready, the server returns the output information back to the client over the same port. The protocol stack associated with these RPC transactions is illustrated in Figure 4.18.

So, in the case of NFS, the actual code that performs file functions on the remote system (for example, the code to open a file) is an RPC service running on a dynamically assigned port. When the local system wants to access the remote file system, it connects to the remote server's portmapper and asks where (that is, which port) it can find the NFS program. When the answer is returned, it can start executing remote NFS procedure calls.

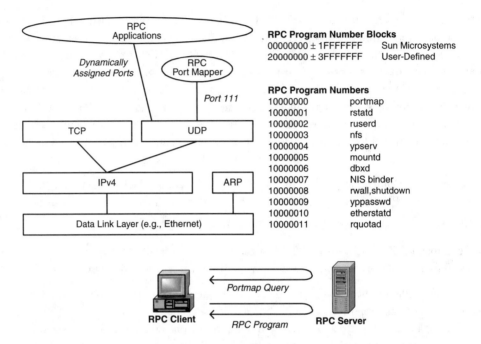

FIGURE 4.18

Remote Procedure Calls.

What does all of this mean to us from a security point of view? First, there is a service running on a well-known port (111) that will tell anyone who cares to ask which remote functions are available on that host computer. This leads to many serious vulnerabilities associated with the remotely executable functions, especially those involving buffer overflows (we will talk about this in Chapter 8).

SNMP

Throughout the 1990s, IP networks grew dramatically in both size and complexity, resulting in significant management problems for network and server administrators. The Simple Network Management Protocol (SNMP) was developed to facilitate remote monitoring and management of an entire enterprise network infrastructure, including routers, switches, and servers.

Using an SNMP-based network-management system, an administrator or engineer can check (GET) or modify (SET) the configuration parameters of a switch. For example, if it is necessary to change the IP address of a single port on a 48-port switch installed in a building across a corporate campus, the engineer simply would enter the command and an SNMP packet would be transmitted to the switch with the appropriate instructions.

One other feature of SNMP is the ability to set traps, which are simply SNMP alarms that a managed device can be configured to send back to a network-management station under certain conditions. One common use of SNMP traps is to monitor temperature within a chassis and to provide automatic notification if the system gets too hot.

SNMP is a powerful protocol and is critical to the operation of any enterprise network. Unfortunately, the security of the most widely deployed version of the SNMP protocol (SNMPv2) is embarrassingly weak. A clear-text password known as the *community string* must be included in the packet. The fact that the password is sent "in the clear" is bad enough; however, the problem is even worse because *many* networking professionals fail to change the community strings from their default values of public and private.

Although it is powerful from a network-management perspective, SNMP introduces a serious vulnerability when no inbound filtering is performed on traffic from the Internet. If SNMP traffic is allowed to wander in and out of a network, it is highly likely that anyone outside of the network will be able to issue GETs and SETs to any SNMP-capable device. In fact, free "security tools" available on the Internet mimic the network-discovery capabilities of expensive network-management systems and allow anyone to download the entire management information base (MIB) from all of the devices in a network. Not only can an outsider gain a strong knowledge of a network's topology, but he also might be able to reconfigure that topology by bringing switch or router interfaces administratively "down" or by modifying VLAN configurations.

SNMPv3 has addressed many of the vulnerabilities associated with SNMP; however, the new version of the protocol has not been widely deployed. Until a network's entire infrastructure has been upgraded, including both the management station and all of the SNMP-managed systems, the entire network is at risk. At a minimum, strict packet filtering rules should be enforced at either gateway routers (via access control lists) or firewalls (via the security policy set) to prohibit SNMP traffic (ports 161 and 162) from coming or going.

Microsoft Networking Protocols and TCP/IP

After TCP/IP, the most common protocol family running in most enterprise networks today are those associated with Microsoft networking. We will discuss the security model for the Windows NT and Windows 2000 operating systems in Chapter 7, "Operating System and Server Software Issues"; however, this is an appropriate time to provide a brief overview of the underlying protocols required to implement Microsoft networking features such as file and print sharing.

A Brief History of IBM and Microsoft Networks

The "Microsoft protocols" have their roots in the IBM networking interfaces developed in the early 1980s. At the time, IBM wanted to develop an extension to the BIOS calls that would support networking between PCs. The Network Basic Input/Output System (NetBIOS) programming interface was developed for IBM by Sytec in 1983.

Just like the BIOS in a PC, NetBIOS is actually a fairly low-level programming interface, not a packet protocol standard. A set of functions that an application could call were defined (including, for example, Send Datagram or Call for a session-oriented service). These functions were implemented by setting certain registers with pointers to a control data structure called the Network Control Block and then causing a specific system interrupt (interrupt 0x5C, for the detail-oriented reader). At that point, a proprietary packet protocol was used to perform whatever network action was required. In 1985, the interface was enhanced and renamed the NetBIOS Expanded User Interface (NetBEUI), and the underlying protocol was called NetBIOS Frames (NBF).

Finally, in 1987, with the emerging popularity of TCP/IP becoming apparent, an interface between NetBIOS networks and TCP/IP was developed and documented in RFCs 1001 and 1002. NetBIOS over TCP, or NBT, can be found in just about any modern network employing Microsoft platforms. The remainder of this section is dedicated to the fundamentals of this protocol standard.

NetBIOS Names

The first thing that must be understood about NetBIOS networks is the addressing convention that is used. Unlike IP, which uses a numerical address, NetBIOS employs an ASCII naming format. A NetBIOS network is a flat network in which all of the services on the various hosts are given a 16-character name. What do we mean by "flat"? NetBIOS networks originally were developed for relatively small local area networks. No consideration was given to large, multi-site networks, so there is no "network address" that a router could use to shuffle packets in between many networks.

NetBIOS over TCP (NBT)

Just like TCP and UDP, NetBIOS provides connection-oriented "sessions" and connectionless "datagram" network services. So, mapping the NetBIOS services to TCP/IP does not seem like an overwhelming task. The main issues involved in this effort are to do the following:

- Define an encapsulation technique in which NetBIOS packets can be carried in TCP/IP packets
- Define a mechanism for associating NetBIOS names with IP addresses

The NBT specification reserves three ports for communicating with Microsoft services over TCP/IP:

- Port 137 (UDP): Name service
- Port 138 (UDP): Datagram service
- Port 139 (TCP): Session service

NetBIOS name resolution employs a protocol that is a simple extension of the DNS protocol that was introduced earlier in this chapter. The NBT specification in RFCs 1001 and 1002 define an entity called the NetBIOS Name Server (NBNS), which is responsible for resolving NetBIOS names to IP addresses so that NetBIOS applications can find their required resources in an IP environment. Microsoft's implementation of an NBNS is the Windows Internet Name Service, or WINS.

So, if a NetBIOS application wants to communicate with some other NetBIOS resource in a TCP/IP network via either datagrams or a connection-oriented session, it first must resolve the IP address of the host that the remote NetBIOS resource resides on. Just as with domain name resolution in a traditional IP network, it can do this either via a local hosts table, which, in the NetBIOS world, is called LMHOSTS, or through a query to a name-resolution server (such as WINS).

NetBIOS Names and Scope ID

Although we have stated that NetBIOS employs a flat naming space, you should be aware of one twist. Microsoft introduced the Scope ID with its WINS server. The Scope ID in a Windows network is used to define the NetBIOS namespace where the various resources "live." In concept, it is like a network address; however, it is used to group NetBIOS names, not IP hosts. Under the Windows domain model of networking, the full NBT name of a computer is NBTname@ScopeIP.

The NBTname is simply a translated version of the 16-character NetBIOS name (see the next section). Most administrators do not change the Scope ID from its default null value.

It should be noted that the Scope ID is not used for routing but is used to simply identify the context of the NetBIOS names. Another way to think of the Scope ID is that it identifies a universe for a group of NetBIOS names.

Encoding NetBIOS Names in NBT

Under NBT, NetBIOS names are translated from a 16-character format to a 32-character format. The translation is performed as follows:

1. Each of the 16 characters in the NetBIOS name is split into two parts consisting of the upper 4 bits (known as a nibble) and the lower 4 bits.

2. Each of the 4 bits becomes the basis for two characters and occupies the lower nibble of each character.

3. A hexadecimal value of 0x41 (binary: 01000001) is added to each of the two new characters.

SMB and File Sharing

The most common feature of Microsoft networking that most users are aware of is the file- and printer-sharing capabilities. Under the hood, these features are implemented using the Server Message Block (SMB) protocol. SMB provides functions for opening and closing files, transferring files, printing documents, and so on. The SMB protocol also is known by the name Common Internet File System, or CIFS.

SMB typically is seen running over NBT encapsulation in a TCP/IP network. However, it is important to remember that SMB also has been implemented over Novell's IPX and a protocol known as NetBIOS Frames. A non-Windows implementation of SMB over TCP/IP is Samba, which provides file- and print-sharing services in a UNIX environment, allowing UNIX platforms to "share" their file systems and printing resources with Windows platforms.

The Network Neighborhood and the Browser Protocol

To make maximum use of the file-sharing capability in a network of Microsoft platforms, most users use the Network Neighborhood application on their Windows desktop. This tool provides a view of all of the networked computers in each accessible domain, as well as the file and printer resources available on each computer.

For this tool to function, each computer must have a logical map of all the network's resources. This information is shared through the Browser Protocol. Note that this protocol has nothing to do with Web browsers such as Netscape of Internet Explorer. The Browser Protocol runs over SMB, which is encapsulated in NBT frames for transport over the local TCP/IP network.

One host in a Microsoft network is designated the master browser, and all other workstations and servers report their shared resources to the master browser as they join the network. In an NT domain model, the master browser is typically the same as the primary domain controller. Similarly, backup master browsers can be deployed on backup domain controllers.

Microsoft Remote Procedure Calls

Microsoft has implemented its own version of the Remote Procedure Call paradigm, modeled after the DCE/RPC standard. Just as with the Sun/UNIX model, client programs connect to an endpoint mapping service, this time run on port 135, to find the dynamically assigned port for a particular remote program. Many of Microsoft's enterprise applications, such as Exchange Server, employ RPC between its components.

General Configuration Tips for Home Networks

As more consumers delve into home networking, the subject of Microsoft networking configuration becomes a big issue. Most cable modem and DSL Internet service providers recommend that users do not activate file and print sharing on any computers directly connected to the Internet. This advice is easy to follow if the end user has only one computer.

If a home user does want to use Microsoft networking, several steps should be considered to provide a secure networking environment:

- A firewall of some kind should be used so that undesired connections from the Internet are blocked. We will discuss firewalls in much greater detail in Chapter 9, "Protecting Your Infrastructure."

- If WINS name resolution is being used, the NetBIOS Scope ID can be changed so that NetBIOS probes using the default null Scope ID are rejected on the hosts.

- The Microsoft services can be bound to NetBEUI instead of TCP/IP so that all of the Microsoft services run over a non-IP infrastructure, effectively preventing external parties from injecting any NBT.

Summary of Microsoft Networking Protocols

The NetBIOS over TCP/IP protocols are important components of many modern enterprise networks. Although there is a large body of Microsoft certified networking professionals, many people still do not receive even basic instruction on how these networking applications and managements tools actually function. Although our coverage has been rather high level, it should be sufficient to provide an introduction to the underlying networking aspects surrounding Microsoft NT infrastructures. A summary of the Microsoft-related protocols is provided in Figure 4.19.

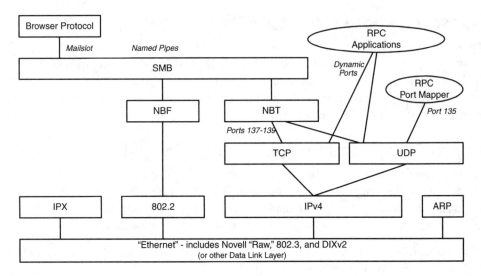

FIGURE 4.19

Microsoft networking protocols.

A Brief Overview of Other Networking Protocols

Several other networking protocols are still in use today, primarily in legacy networks. They include these:

- Novell's IPX/SPX and NCP
- AppleTalk protocols
- Banyan VINES
- DECnet
- IBM's SNA/APPN

Many networking infrastructure companies support these protocols, especially in the lower end of their product lines (has anyone ever heard of an OC-3 IPX network?). Although the interoperability issues with these protocols are a severe detriment, many people make the argument that at least they are relatively secure. This perspective is really a derivative of the philosophy of "security through obscurity" because relatively few people understand the details of Novel's Netware Core Protocol (NCP) or the SNA suite. As a result, there is not much of a hacking community with enough background to develop attacks. Furthermore, these protocols, especially SNA, tend to run in a fairly closed environment; therefore, the opportunity for remote attacks is almost nonexistent. If these protocols were as popular as TCP/IP and ran on publicly connected systems, this supposed security benefit would disappear very quickly.

These comments are not meant to be a slight to these protocols. Apple did a fantastic job of developing a protocol family that allowed for easy networking of its product line. Similarly, before anyone ever heard of Network Neighborhood, Novell brought powerful networking capabilities to the PC, and IBM's SNA was an enabling technology for corporate computing in the 1970s and 1980s. However, for a discussion of modern network security issues, these systems are simply not relevant.

Summary

The purpose of this chapter was twofold. First, we wanted to provide a general TCP/IP refresher to those readers who might not have spent much time with this subject recently. More importantly, we wanted to examine the fundamentals with our eyes open to security issues. We have saved the details of many of the attack techniques for a subsequent chapter; however, we have endeavored to point out some of the details that will be required to understand the forthcoming material.

At this point, you should be comfortable with basic concepts such as IP addresses and netblocks, domain names, ports, TCP functionality, and IP/Ethernet networking. This also might have been your first opportunity to tie in the Microsoft networking principles that we covered in this chapter.

If you knew all of the fundamentals of TCP/IP before you started reading this chapter, you should at least have gained a new perspective on the material. The critical lesson here is that an enormous amount of assumed trust is built into the protocols, especially when it comes to the underlying management protocols that are key to making the Internet as we know it today work.

- DNS, the "phone book of the Internet," currently provides no assurance that the returned IP address that is associated with a domain name is the correct one.

- ARP provides no assurance that the returned Ethernet address that is associated with an IP address is the correct one.

- DHCP provides no assurance that the returned configuration information is valid. This is another means by which a local user could assign someone invalid gateway or DNS server addresses.

In both cases, an opportunity exists for an unscrupulous entity on the network to redirect traffic to a bogus site, either to perform some kind of a man-in-the-middle attack or to impersonate some service on the network.

Finally, we have shown that a number of vulnerabilities arise when software and hardware implementers fail to anticipate every incorrect packet that might come their way. This is another case of implied trust, in which the developers trust that everyone will follow the rules as put forth in the protocol standards.

The lesson of this chapter is really that, to successfully attack or defend a network, you must understand what is really going on within the network infrastructure. We will explore the details of both the attack and the defense in the following chapters.

In-Depth with Protocols and
Building Blocks

IN THIS CHAPTER

If the underlying level of security afforded by the basic Internet protocols such as TCP/IP and HTTP can be measured by the number of additional security protocols designed to ride on top of them, then we can probably conclude that the native Internet isn't a very secure place. The basic network- and application-layer protocols were intended to provide generic means of communication for Internet-based applications and services. However, many of these protocols were developed in a time and environment that was naive with regard to what the Internet would eventually become: a medium used for stock trading, online purchasing, and the exchange of corporate secrets, among others.

To address the shortcomings and insufficiencies of these generic protocols, many new "standards" have been developed with the intent of layering security on top of them. These standards provide either replacements for or additions to existing protocols. For example, the Secure Socket Layer (SSL) provides an encrypted channel through which the ordinary (and insecure) HTTP protocol can be tunneled. HTTPS, conversely, is an augmented version of HTTP that attempts to add security functionality into the "old" HTTP protocol.

In this chapter, we discuss the most common security-centric protocols and review their idiosyncrasies, as well as the pros and cons of using them. This chapter does not provide a full explanation of the inner workings of each protocol. You can find these details in the relevant Request for Comments (RFCs) and other standards documents. Although this chapter reviews each of the protocols at a high level, it concentrates on the security implications, risks, and vulnerabilities associated with each of them.

Secure Protocols

As discussed in the previous chapter, generic IP Version 4 provides no concept of data security within the protocol itself. Thus, new protocols have been designed to be layered upon or tunneled within generic Internet traffic. These protocols aim to address one or more of the following issues:

- **The confidentiality of data in transit**—This can include not only the data itself, but also the source and destination addresses involved in the conversation.
- **Strong authentication**—This allows the source and destination systems to determine each other's identity with a high degree of certainty.
- **Data integrity**—This provides a mechanism to ensure that the data being transported by the protocol has not been altered while in transit.

These issues might have been addressed in different ways and to different degrees and ends by secure protocols, starting as low as the transport layer and extending up to the application layer.

Implementing Secure Protocols

Protocols, by definition, work only when each network component implements and utilizes the same or compatible protocols. At first glance, you might assume that upgrading from an insecure network to a secure network would require an upgrade of each component within it. For many reasons, this is a not a viable method because legacy systems will continue to exist that administrators are reluctant to upgrade or that users are not willing to part with. In addition, not every system *needs* to implement a secure protocol. For instance, a Web server that acts simply as an advertisement for a company or the external DNS server for an Internet domain is, by definition, a source of public information. Implementing secure protocols on this type of system would only add unnecessary overhead. For these and other reasons, secure protocols can be implemented in a number of ways:

- **Host-to-host**—In this implementation, hosts establish secure connections with each other. They utilize the underlying (and insecure) transport mechanism provided to them and add in their own security functions that only they need to have in common. This implementation makes sense for hosts that must operate through a medium over which they have no control, such as two email users who want to encrypt their email to each other but nobody else.

- **Gateway-to-gateway**—Here, routing devices (which could be routers, switches, firewalls, bridges, or any other systems responsible for forwarding packets from one network to another) are used as the endpoints for the security "upgrade." The benefit of utilizing gateway-to-gateway security is that the networks behind each gateway automatically inherit many of the security functions provided by the gateway. For example, if two routers encrypt all traffic between them, then each host on the routers' networks automatically benefits from the confidentiality that encryption provides.

- **Host-to-gateway**—This configuration is the hybrid of the first two: It lets a host securely access a remote network by establishing a secure session with a gateway to the network. The hosts behind the gateway do not have to be aware that encryption is taking place; they simply leave it up to the gateway. A typical scenario for host-to-gateway communication is allowing home or traveling users to access the resources of an internal corporate network (file servers, email, and so on) over the Internet.

These configurations are illustrated in Figure 5.1.

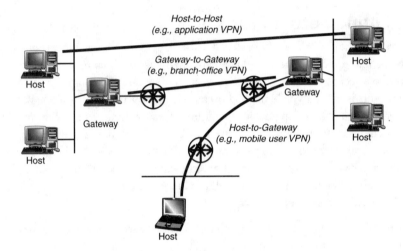

FIGURE 5.1
Security connections.

Network-Layer Implementations

Security can be introduced at various layers of the protocol stack. For example, a generic link encryptor can be used to provide privacy on an arbitrary communications system, whether or not it is carrying TCP/IP packets or a telco-standard bit stream such as a T1. This works well on a hop-by-hop basis, but it can be challenging to implement across a network of nodes. For TCP/IP, it is convenient to introduce security at the network (that is, IP) layer because that will be the constant protocol across a network.

Implementing confidentiality, authentication, and integrity functions at the IP layer is a special challenge. Because IP is a sessionless protocol, each datagram must be encrypted and (optionally) digitally signed on its own, independent of every other datagram transmitted on the network. This is in contrast to an application-layer encryption system, such as Pretty Good Privacy (PGP) or Secure Socket Layer (SSL), in which the session information is encrypted prior to transmission through a TCP/IP network. Additionally, any attempts to layer a session-oriented encryption mechanism on top of a protocol that is inherently unreliable would be extremely expensive in both time and computation and would, of course, defeat the original purpose of IP.

The security protocol also *must not break* the existing protocol. Although this might seem obvious it also implies that the protocol must be capable of supporting issues such as data arriving out of order, data being arbitrarily fragmented along the way, packets never arriving, and so on.

The advantages of encryption at the network layer, however, make it a very attractive proposition. First of all, by encrypting at the network layer, the packets involved are automatically routable (and can take advantage of the numerous dynamic routing protocols in existence), which is not normally possible at the data link layer. Second, implementation at a higher layer (transport or session layers) would require the vast majority of network-aware applications to be rewritten. We will delve more deeply into network-layer encryption mechanisms in our discussion of IPSec.

Virtual Private Network Protocols and Encapsulation

Several protocols have been defined by the IETF that address the problem of encrypting network-layer packets—that is, to encrypting IP. These protocols include the following:

- IP Security (IPSec)
- Point-to-Point Tunneling Protocol (PPTP)
- Layer 2 Forwarding (L2F—originally developed by Cisco but now effectively obsolete)
- Layer 2 Tunneling Protocol (L2TP, the IETF merge of L2F and PPTP)

Although these protocols vary in their details, they all provide means of transporting one IP network's packets across another IP network. In the vast majority of cases, VPNs are used to transport a private IP network over the public Internet. This offers two significant operational advantages to a network designer. First, a VPN can be used as a replacement for a dedicated leased line or other wide area network service, such as Frame Relay, often dramatically reducing the cost of recurring intersite communications expenses. Second, VPNs allow remote users to access their "home network" as if they were physically inside the network.

The various VPN protocols all have several features in common:

- **Tunneling**—The packets from the IP network are "picked up" and placed in the payload of another IP packet. At the other end of the VPN connection, the original IP packet is "unwrapped" and dropped into the remote private network. This is equivalent to putting internal departmental mail envelopes into a new envelope and sending them through the public mail system.

- **Encryption**—If the internal IP packets that are being tunneled across the Internet contain confidential information, then the "wrapped" packets also can be encrypted. When most people think of VPNs, they assume that the traffic is encrypted; however, that is not necessarily true. All of the remote access benefits offered by tunneling can be enjoyed without encrypting any packets.

- **Payload authentication**—Sometimes the integrity of the data might be more important than the confidentiality of the data. Public-key cryptographic algorithms also can be used to append nonreputable mathematic hashes of the packets, providing the receiver with good assurance that they are receiving valid data. This is essentially a per-packet digital signature.

- **Connection authentication**—Before tunnels are established between two computers, the connection usually is authenticated. This process ensures that the two ends of the tunnel know who each other is. Connection authentication usually is closely associated with a user's authentication.

IPSec

IPSec, which also commonly is written as IPSEC, will likely become the de facto network-layer security protocol. IPSec principally is defined in a dozen RFCs (numbers 2401–2412) published by the Internet Engineering Task Force (IETF). It is already supported by a wide variety of systems, including routers, switches, firewalls, servers, and desktops. It is also the default security extension for IP Version 6. IPSec may be employed in host-to-host, host-to-gateway or gateway-to-gateway configurations (refer to Figure 5.1).

IPSec is actually both an architecture and a family of protocols that are designed to provide security on all three aspects: confidentiality, integrity, and authenticity. IPSec introduces two new protocols and two new acronyms for administrators to throw around: the IP Authentication Header (AH) and the Encapsulating Security Payload (ironically abbreviated ESP). AH offers (predictably) the data authentication portion of the protocol, as well as a high level of data integrity. It accomplishes this by cryptographically signing the entire packet, from source address to the end of the payload. Additionally, the AH can offer protection against replay attacks by using time-based signature methods, in which the signing key is valid for only a short period of time. The ESP provides the data confidentiality (that is, encryption), which, in most instances, also means data integrity. Both the AH and ESP protocols offer a concept of access control by cryptographic measures (more on this in a bit). The two protocols can be implemented either in tandem or alone, depending on the operational needs of the system.

The option to employ one or both of these protocols has a decided advantage: Not all data requires encryption, and encryption is computationally expensive. For instance, normal DNS data involving host resolution does not contain sensitive data, and thus it is not generally necessary to encrypt each request and response. However, because DNS runs on top of UDP (which, by its nature is trivial to spoof), it would be nice to be able to verify that responses arrive from trusted DNS servers and that the data was not tainted while in transit. Additionally, in environments in which encryption is not allowed (by law or otherwise), IPSec still can be employed with the AH protocol only, providing strong authentication and data integrity without actually encrypting the payload. The placement of the AH and ESP headers is shown in Figure 5.2.

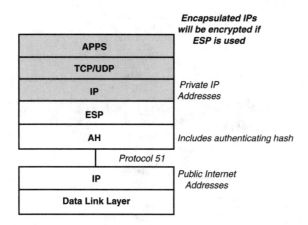

FIGURE 5.2

AH and ESP headers.

IPSec Security Associations

At the core of IPSec communication is yet another acronym, SA, for the Security Association. SAs, like most concepts in networking, seem daunting and overly complex until you make sense of them, so we will try to make liberal use of diagrams to help speed up this effort. This will be a worthwhile expenditure of your time because many VPN products provide powerful configuration interfaces, most of which are associated with the definition of security associations.

Before going into the details of SAs, let's put all of this in some context. Most IPSec products require that an administrator do three things in the process of defining IPSec connections:

- Define the potential endpoint of the tunnels (for example, the IP addresses of the IPSec-compliant gateways at each branch office of an enterprise network).

- Define the parameters of the tunnel(s) between each pair of endpoints. Usually each tunnel is given a name or identifier, and it is configured to use AH, ESP, or both security protocols. The tunnel configuration also will require algorithms to be selected for the AH and ESP protocols (for example, which encryption algorithm to use and how to manage key exchange).

- Define what kind of traffic should be encapsulated and sent down the tunnel.

For example, consider a company with a headquarters and three branch offices, as shown in Figure 5.3. IPSec provides a great deal of flexibility in designing a VPN. The VPN will be configured in a "star" network, with each branch office connected to the headquarters through at least one tunnel. Many IPSec products actually support multiple tunnels between two locations. For example, an AH tunnel and an ESP tunnel could be configured in parallel with each other.

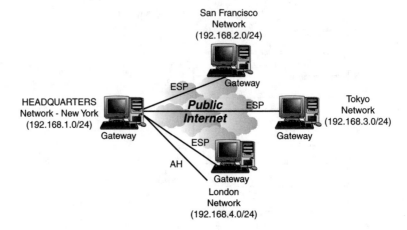

FIGURE 5.3

An IPSec network.

An SA defines one half of a secure connection, so, for secure two-way communication, there is an SA defining each direction of communication (and because setting up a connection that is secure in only one direction is relatively pointless, you can safely assume that each real-world connection will have two SAs associated with it). Not only is an SA defined by a specific end of the conversation, but it also is defined by the combination of a Security Parameter Index (SPI—more in this later), a security protocol (either AH or ESP, but not both), and the destination address. An example of a real-world IPSec implementation is illustrated in Figure 5.4.

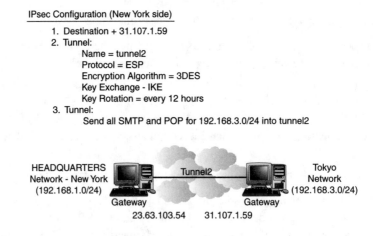

FIGURE 5.4

An example IPSec implementation.

An SA cannot specify both an AH and an ESP; therefore, for a connection to make use of both the AH and ESP protocols, *two* SAs are required for each endpoint in the actual network connection. So, for a single connection in which both ends are making use of both the AH and the ESP, there are *four* SAs that, in conjunction, uniquely identify that conversation.

But we're not done yet. An SA can be defined as being in either transport mode or tunnel mode. Transport-mode SAs generally are used for host-to-host communications or whenever the packet header information is not considered sensitive (because transport mode encrypts only the payload). Tunnel-mode SAs are used generally in host-to-gateway and gateway-to-gateway communications, or when the packet header information *is* considered sensitive (in tunnel mode, the headers are part of the encrypted payload).

In Figure 5.5, section A shows two SAs that make up a host-to-host (transport-mode) connection using only the AH. Section B shows two SAs that make up a gateway-to-gateway (tunnel-mode) connection using only the ESP. Section C shows four SAs that make up a host-to-gateway connection (tunnel mode) using ESP and AH.

The SAs normally are kept in a database on each system. For instance, the FreeBSD `setkey` command with the `-D` option will print out all current SAs. On a commercial VPN appliance or software package, a graphical user interface might be provided for defining SAs. The fact that the user is defining an SA might be hidden in the interface; however, it is important that a security-conscious administrator understand what is actually going on "under the hood" of these products.

Each security association will have an algorithm associated with it. For AH, the MD5 and SHA1 hashes are the most widely supported options for integrity checksums. For ESP, there are actually many choices for data encryption algorithms including DES, Triple DES, Blowfish, CAST, and RC5. The actual algorithms supported by each IPSec product can vary, so it's important for an administrator to standardize on a given algorithm during the planning phase to ensure maximum interoperability. The selection of an algorithm could be affected by licensing issues and export restrictions. For example, if one end of a tunnel is in the United States and the other end is in another country, it will not be legal to ship a product with a high-grade encryption algorithm to the remote site. When two systems begin their IPSec conversation, a handshaking process takes place in which they settle on the authentication and encryption methods to use. During this process, the systems run through their list of the administrator-defined methods until they find a suitable match.

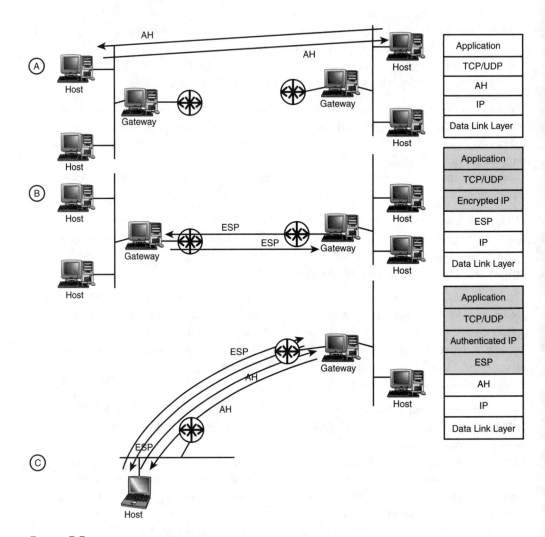

FIGURE 5.5
Several SA configurations.

The final step in configuring an SA is to select a key exchange mechanism. All of this encryption and authentication is great, but if the secret cryptographic keys are not exchanged securely, then all of the effort that has been expended in purchasing and implementing a VPN solution is wasted. How does each side of the conversation receive the session key in a reliable and private manner? Technically, IPSec has no built-in support whatsoever for key exchange. IPSec simply defines a protocol for encryption and authentication. Key exchange and management are left up to other protocols. Two common methods exist for distributing keys in an IPSec system:

- **Manual**—A shared secret phrase or key string is configured at each end of the tunnel, usually into a configuration file or through a graphical interface.
- **Automatic/dynamic**—A key exchange protocol is used to securely pass encryption keys over the network.

The most common key exchange protocol is the Internet Key Exchange (IKE) protocol. It was designed from the beginning to interoperate with IPSec, though it could feasibly support other encryption protocols as well. IKE is responsible for performing the initial SA negotiation between hosts automatically, including the secure transfer of the initial session keys. Additionally, it supports the changing of session keys during the conversation, with key life-times being defined by the administrator. This feature allows an administrator to configure an IPSec system to exchange new cryptographic keys after either a specified time (such as every hour or every day) or traffic volume (such as every 2MB). Most implementations of IKE also have built-in support for public key infrastructures (PKI) as well.

IPSec Policies

After a tunnel between two nodes is defined through security associations, the final step is to configure policies that will determine which traffic should be transported through the tunnel. For example, consider a laptop user connected to the Internet through a hotel-room Ethernet connection who wants to use a VPN to check her email back at the office. This is a common "remote user" VPN application and is illustrated in Figure 5.6. As this user opens her Web browser and mail client, how does the computer know which packets to encapsulate and forward over the tunnel, and which ones to pass directly to the Internet? This is where IPSec "policies" come into play. These policies, which look very similar to firewall rules, simply tell the IPSec software how to route packets. If this user's normal internal network was 172.16.1.0/24, then a simple policy set for the IPSec VPN might be as follows:

DestAddress	DestService	Route
172.16.1.0/24	—	Tunnel1

In the earlier example of a branch office VPN scenario, the VPN might simply be configured to tunnel internal mail traffic to each branch's email server:

DestAddress	DestService	Route
192.168.1.0/24	SMTP	Tunnel1
192.168.2.0/24	SMTP	Tunnel2
192.168.3.0/24	SMTP	Tunnel3

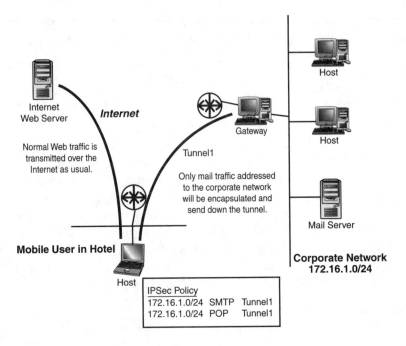

FIGURE 5.6

IPSec policies.

The reader should note from the preceding example that network address planning is very important when rolling out an IPSec VPN. Most products require that the networks on each end of a tunnel be logically distinct. This requires coordination between sites to ensure that every branch office or campus isn't using the same IP address space (such as 192.168.1.0/24).

IP Address Problems with IPSec

We recently ran into a frustrating problem associated with a hotel Internet connection. Our company issues authentication tokens and VPN client software to its employees so that we can telecommute or connect to the corporate network while we are on the road. The normal internal network employs the 172.18.1.0/24 private IP address block. Whenever the laptops determine that they are not on the internal network, a VPN login screen is presented so that we may perform our two-factor authentication and establish a secure, encrypted tunnel back to the corporate network.

It turns out that this particular hotel happened to use the exact same IP address block when assigning IP addresses to the guest rooms. So, the laptop thought that it was in the local network and refused to even present the VPN login screen.

Network administrators should be aware of the protocol and port numbers associated with IPSec traffic because it might be necessary to reconfigure router access control lists and firewall rule sets to allow this traffic to flow freely.

- ESP uses IP protocol number 50.
- AH uses IP protocol number 51.
- ISAKMP/IKE uses UDP port number 500.

This information is especially critical in applications in which IPSec client software is running on internal workstations or servers. Alternatively, IPSec gateways are often placed on the edge of a network as a peer to the border firewall, completely bypassing the security policy enforcement provided by the firewall.

Point-to-Point Tunneling Protocol (PPTP)

PPTP is defined in RFC 2637 and generally is associated with the Microsoft implementation of the protocol within Windows 9x/NT workstations and Remote Access Service (RAS) products. PPTP tunneling is accomplished through the encapsulation of Point-to-Point Protocol (PPP) packets within IP datagrams. PPP is a very popular data-link layer (Layer 2) protocol that is used in just about all dial-up modem connections to ISPs. It also can be found encapsulated in Ethernet frames using the PPP Over Ethernet (PPPoE) standards.

PPTP employs a client/server model that is very similar to a dial-up user calling an ISP. In this case, client software running on a computer establishes a control connection to a PPTP server over TCP port 1723. When the client and the server can communicate, the client usually authenticates with the server and then requests that a tunnel be created so that PPP frames can be forwarded to the server over the Internet. Assuming that the server successfully authenticates the user, the tunnel is created. This tunneled PPP layer is actually independent of the data link layer used to connect to the Internet. The client computer can be connected via a dial-up connection, which will likely also use PPP, or through an Ethernet LAN connection.

You should note that PPP can be used to carry many network-layer protocols, not just IP. For example, PPP can carry IPX, NetBIOS, AppleTalk and SNA traffic, hypothetically all at the same time. So, although most people think of VPN connections as providing IP-over-IP tunnels, this is not strictly true. Because PPP allows for multiprotocol encapsulation, and because PPTP tunnels PPP, just about any network-layer protocol can be tunneled across the Internet using this protocol. This multilayered tunneling is illustrated in Figure 5.7.

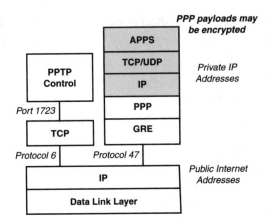

FIGURE 5.7

PPTP encapsulation.

Although TCP is used for the control channel, the actual tunnel is carried within a different protocol called the Generic Router Encapsulation (GRE) protocol. GRE is a peer of TCP, UDP, and ICMP in the protocol hierarchy, and it is referenced as IP "protocol" number 47 (just like TCP and UDP are protocols 6 and 17, respectively). This might sound like trivia, but it can be a quite handy fact to know if there is a firewall or router access control list in your network that might not be configured to pass this protocol.

Confidentiality can be added to PPTP's capability to encapsulate and tunnel PPP (and, therefore, just about any network protocol in use) via PPP's native encryption functions. The PPP standard provides a means for negotiating the use of many encryption and session-authentication protocols; however, under the Microsoft implementation, Microsoft Point-to-Point Encryption (MPPE) and Microsoft's Challenge Authentication Protocol (MS-CHAP) are used.

Security Problems with Microsoft PPTP

The original version of MS-CHAP (MS-CHAPv1) was shown to have serious security problems in a paper published by Bruce Schneier and Mudge (Peiter Zatko) in 1998. Their analysis revealed that user passwords could be cracked by "sniffing" the authentication exchange and that the MPPE encryption keys could then be derived, essentially allowing a mildly sophisticated third party to decrypt the confidential data. Microsoft addressed most of the issues in an update to the Dial-Up Networking (DUN) modules of the Windows operating systems; however, a follow-up paper published in 1999 concluded that there were still weaknesses in the authentication mechanism. For this reason, many network administrators have migrated to IPSec-based VPNs.

Layer 2 Forwarding

Details concerning Layer 2 (L2F) forwarding are relevant only to users of legacy VPN systems. This early VPN protocol was developed by Cisco Systems and is not generally available anymore. L2F tunneling, as defined in RFC 2341, is performed using UDP port 1701 and is intended to transport PPP or Serial Line IP (SLIP) packets across an IP network (such as the Internet). Like PPTP, L2F has both a control channel and an encapsulated data channel; however, in this case, both are carried on a common UDP port, with control messages and encapsulated data differentiated by a special value in the L2F header. The typical L2F protocol stack is illustrated in Figure 5.8.

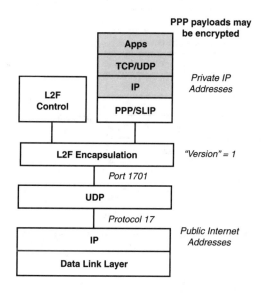

FIGURE 5.8

L2F encapsulation.

Because L2F tunnels PPP over an Internet connection, it actually can be used to carry any (or many) network-layer protocols. On the other hand, the simpler SLIP, which is rarely used anymore, is capable of carrying only a single Layer 3 protocol, which is almost always IP.

Layer 2 Tunneling Protocol (L2TP)

L2TP is the IETF merger of the PPTP and L2F protocols, and it is specified in RFC 2661. Like L2F, L2TP employs UDP port 1701 for both control and tunneled data packets. Because the same UDP port number is used for two different encapsulation systems, L2TP headers contain a version number, with "version 1" meaning L2F and "version 2" meaning L2TP. The RFC document discusses alternate methods of transporting L2TP frames, including ATM and Frame

Relay connections; however, because this book is concerned with using the Internet, we shall focus our attention on tunneling over TCP/IP. The L2TP protocol stack is illustrated in Figure 5.9.

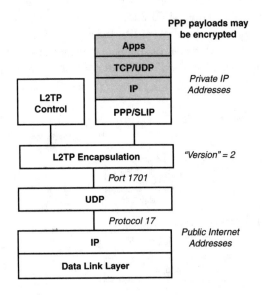

FIGURE 5.9

L2TP encapsulation.

Because L2TP carries PPP packets, it can use any of the encryption and compression facilities offered by PPP.

Secure Socket Layer (SSL)

Moving up the OSI model to the nether-regions between the transport and application layers, we have the Secure Socket Layer, or SSL. SSL is a protocol that makes use of a reliable transport layer (such as TCP) to offer nearly seamless encryption support for arbitrary application protocols. Functionally, its goals are the same as those of IPSec: to offer confidentiality, integrity, and authentication to applications using existing network protocols. It simply does so at a higher layer.

SSL makes use of certificates for authentication. Certificates under SSL generally follow the x.509 specification and can be used to authenticate both the client and server, although most implementations for secured Web sites perform only authentication of the server. The certificates make up the public-key authentication mechanism and also enable the protected transmission of the session key. Because public-key encryption is expensive from a resource standpoint, this session key is used as a symmetric key to encrypt the session. Thus, the certificates are used only for authentication and for the transmission of session keys. This initial setup is a defined subprotocol of SSL known as the *SSL handshake*.

The SSL handshake must occur when a client initially requests the services of an SSL server. This handshake is responsible for authenticating the server (and optionally the client), settling on an encryption method to use, and establishing the symmetric session keys that will be used to encrypt the session as a whole. The first step in the handshake is for the client to send its SSL version number, the ciphers that it supports, and other sundry housekeeping information. The server responds in kind with its version number and supported ciphers as well as its certificate. If the server requires client authentication, it also asks for the client's certificate at this time. Next, using the information in the server's certificate, the client verifies the authenticity of the server. It does so by checking the expiration date of the certificate, verifying that the CA (the certificate authority that verifies that the certificate does indeed belong to the party that it claims to belong to) is trusted by the client, and checking the signature of the CA. In most instances (particularly in Web browsers), the client also verifies that the domain name in the certificate matches the domain name of the server itself. If all this information matches up with what is expected, the client relents and believes that the server is who it claims to be.

Armed with the server's public key, the client now generates what is called a *premaster secret* and encrypts it with the server's public key. The premaster secret is used to derive the *master secret*, which, in turn, is used to generate the session keys. So, the client now sends the premaster key to the server, and if the server asked for it, the client also sends the client certificate. The server verifies the client certificate in much the same way that the client verified the server certificate and decrypts the premaster key. At this point, if all went well, both sides believe that they are talking to the correct computers, and both sides use the master secret to generate the session keys. From here to the end of the conversation, the session keys are used to encrypt and verify all data passed between the client and the server.

Because lots of people have written implementations of SSL in many different ways, most administrators will not have to burden themselves with intricacies of setting up an SSL connection. The previous overview of the SSL handshake protocol is offered to help administrators learn *how* things work so that they can better understand *why* something isn't working. And the main two facets of the handshake that can cause problems for administrators come from the certificates and lists of supported ciphers.

On the server side, self-signed certificates are adequate for use in internal applications. In general, you like to think that you can trust the company for which you work; if the company's CA says that the certificate is valid, the clients should agree with this. However, if you are hoping to offer SSL-ized services to the greater world at large, you most likely will need to rely on a third party to sign your certificates. A large number of these "top-level" CAs in the world will gladly sign your certificates for a fee. This issue is not so much that anyone in particular signs your key, but simply that the CA is trusted by the users who will be the clients of your server. For instance, if you are a Web vendor who accepts payment over the Internet, you must have your certificate signed by one of the major CAs that are automatically considered trusted by the major Web browsers. If not, your potential customers will receive scary-sounding messages from their browsers talking about how insecure your site is, and they likely will take their business elsewhere.

Potentially more important to administrators is client certificate signing. If you are implementing client authentication with SSL, you must provide a method for verifying that client certificates are valid and signing them with the key of some CA. This could be done by making use of one of the third-party companies that sign server certificates, but this would quite quickly become cost-prohibitive. The most common solution is to have an internal CA that can sign and issue the client certificates. Maintaining an internal CA can be quite a chore, and maintaining the security of the CA's private key is of the utmost importance. However, the added effort of establishing an internal PKI greatly increases the ease of offering strong authentication and encryption within internal applications.

Defining the list of accepted ciphers can create enormous administrative headaches. What makes sense from a security standpoint might not make sense from a usability standpoint. For instance, if as an administrator you decide that the only acceptable encryption cipher is 128-bit Triple-DES and the only acceptable authentication algorithm is SHA-1, you likely will run into trouble when the clients are configured to accept only 56-bit DES and MD5. Incompatible cipher lists can range from annoying (when an internal user can't access mail) to costly (when users from a country not allowed to use strong encryption algorithms aren't allowed to shop at your site). As with the rest of security, it is your job as an administrator to balance security with operability.

Wired Equivalent Privacy (WEP)

Although it is not technically a VPN protocol, the Wired Equivalent Privacy (WEP) algorithm is used extensively in products compliant with the IEEE 802.11b wireless LAN standard. Although this text is not intended to describe every possible encryption algorithm, it is important for you to be aware of critical implementation issues concerning specific algorithms. Three researchers (Nikita Borisov, Ian Goldberg, and David Wagner) have shown that the WEP algorithm is vulnerable to a number of passive and active attacks. In this particular case, this means that if enough data is collected, it is possible to break the encryption and read the traffic. Because wireless LAN traffic is relatively easy to intercept, and because the software required to perform the passive attack is now widely available in the form of programs such as AirSnort, the use of IEEE 802.11 wireless LANs should be carefully considered when confidential information is at stake.

Several solutions to this problem exist. Vendors now offer modifications called "dynamic WEP," which essentially force regular changes in the keys. Because the WEP attack requires that a significant amount of data that has been encrypted with the same key be collected, this can reduce the chances that wireless data can be successfully decrypted. Another option is to run a VPN (such as IPSec) over the wireless interface. Depending on the client devices, this might or might not be a practical solution.

Secure Shell (SSH)

Secure shell (SSH) began its existence as a secure replacement for the terribly insecure r* commands (rsh, rcp, and so on). However, it has evolved into a suite of tools that secures options to traditional remote access applications, as well as a method for tunneling other protocols. On its own, the ssh UNIX command and other SSH client applications are indispensable tools for remote administration, offering strong authentication and encryption. When used as a tunnel, SSH also can provide a secure mechanism for accessing normally insecure services such as the X Window system, or even as an ad-hoc VPN of sorts. The OpenSSH project has brought a free, open-source, and highly portable SSH implementation to the Internet.

SSH Authentication

A variety of authentication options are built into SSH, and a virtually unlimited number when it is used with PAM (pluggable authentication modules). It supports generic password authentication (although clear-text passwords are never sent over the network—all communication is performed over an encrypted channel), plain .rhosts-style authentication (whose use is not recommended), and RSA or DSA authentication (possibly in conjunction with an .rhosts file). The RSA/DSA authentication mechanism is the core of ssh's security (DSA replaced RSA in ssh Version 2 as the public key algorithm due to patent restrictions associated with RSA).

Each user on a system is expected to generate a public and a private key. If the user wants to take advantage of the public-key authentication mechanism, he needs to place a copy of his public key in a file called authorized_keys on each remote system that will be accessed. When the user tries to connect to a system that has his public key on it, the ssh daemon on the remote system will encrypt a random number with the user's public key and send it to the user. The client side then decrypts the random number challenge and sends it back to the server. Sufficiently convinced that the user is, in fact, who he claims to be, access to the system is granted. If this challenge fails, however (or if no public key for the user exists in the authorized_keys file), by default, the user is challenged for a password. It is possible to configure the ssh daemon to require RSA/DSA authentication, and doing so on critical systems is highly recommended.

SSH Server Authentication

Hosts running the ssh daemon also have public keys associated with them. Anytime a user connects to a system via ssh, it receives a copy of this key. These keys are kept in a file called known_hosts. If an entry in known_hosts already exists for the remote host, ssh challenges the remote system much in the way that the server challenges the user logging in with RSA/DSA authentication. If the server fails this challenge, the user is warned. This check is performed to detect man-in-the-middle attacks and attempts by nefarious users to steal passwords.

Tunneling with SSH

One of the great advantages of ssh is that any TCP connection can be tunneled through an ssh connection—and in either direction. When initiating a connection, the client can specify one of two option: -L, which specifies that local ports should be forwarded to the remote machine, or –R, which specifies that remote ports should be forwarded to the local machine. For instance, the following command specifies that all traffic from port 8000 on the system switchstance should be forwarded to port 8001 on the local system:

```
ssh –L 8000:switchstance:8001 switchstance
```

When doing port forwarding, the ssh client on the local host allocates and binds the port on the local side, and the ssh daemon on the remote host allocates and binds the port on the server side. In the previous example, after successful authentication, all traffic destined for port 8000 on the local host automatically will be forwarded over the ssh connection and will be delivered to port 8001 on the other side. Likewise, to have all traffic on a remote system tunneled to the local system, the user would issue the following command:

```
ssh –L 8001:switchstance:8000 switchstance
```

This command would do the opposite of the previous example: All traffic destined for port 8001 on switchstance would be forwarded to port 8000 on the local host.

The ports that are specified can be any TCP port, although on UNIX systems only root may forward privileged ports. Using port forwarding in this way is most useful when accessing insecure services over a public network or when firewall rules prohibit the desired services.

Using SSH Port Forwarding

We recently installed an intrusion-detection system in a client's facilities to demonstrate the system's capabilities. This particular product employed a Web interface for management and configuration of the sensors. In normal circumstances, we would have installed the management server in our local facility and then used the IDS product's native encrypted TCP/IP connection to manage the remote sensors. In this particular case, the client wanted to have local access to the management server, so we were asked to install everything at the client's site. The client also wanted to minimize its firewall rule set changes and asked if we could perform our tests with only an SSH connection between the two sites.

SSH's port-forwarding feature came in quite handy in this case. We were able to configure our Windows SSH client so that we could both securely log on to the remote UNIX systems *and* forward the Web browser traffic over the SSH connection to the Apache server running on the management platform.

Authentication Systems

Providing data confidentiality through encryption is certainly important on the Internet, but, from a practical standpoint, it is harder to "sniff" network traffic than most texts assume. The idea that any information that traverses the Internet can be easily monitored by ever-present hackers is simply not the case. On the other hand, the level of authentication provided by the "raw" Internet is atrocious, and the ability of one person to masquerade as someone else is an altogether trivial undertaking. Ask bob_23567@hotmail.com if he's ever been mistaken for bob_32567@hotmail.com, and you'll get the idea. It also turns out that positively identifying a person's identity on the Internet is one of the toughest things to do well.

The problem of data confidentiality largely has been solved through the use of protocols such as SSL that are invisible to the average Internet surfer and that require little, if any, effort to utilize. Conversely, the problem of authentication traditionally has been solved by means that require significant effort on the part of the user, such as by using digital certificates, smart cards, or tokens (all of which we are about to discuss). To date, very few technologies such as these have been deployed in any significant numbers when compared to the number of users of the Internet. Now, before all the vendors get up in arms and start emailing the publisher about the huge number of devices they've deployed, divide that number by 513 million (the estimated number of Internet users as of late 2001) and you'll see the significance.

To date, the most prevalent form of authentication on the Internet is the username/password combination. The next closest authentication mechanism is probably orders of magnitude behind. The runners-up, along with the leader, will be discussed in the following sections; they include a mix of protocols, standards, and devices including these:

- Tokens such as one-time password generators, dongles (yes, dongles), smart cards, and soft tokens
- Digital certificates
- One-time pads
- Challenge/response mechanisms

Passwords

Not much of the username/password paradigm requires explanation. From a security standpoint, a username/password combination is a perfectly viable solution as long as the following criteria are met:

- The password is not trivial to guess, such as happens when the password is the same as the username (that covers about 25% of the passwords that we have audited), a birthday, or a simple word or other easily guessable combination.
- The password is kept secret. This means not taping the password to your keyboard or sharing it with a coworker.
- The password is not used across many systems. If the password is compromised, many systems become vulnerable.
- The password is changed on a regular basis and is not reused. Even super-secret government agencies change their encryption keys on a regular basis because they recognize that they have shelf-lives.

Unfortunately, most username/password combinations will fail at least one and probably all of these criteria. For example, Internet banking has become popular in recent years. Banks do a good job of getting you a password that is secret (sent in the mail), requiring you to change it when you first log onto the system. They even enforce good criteria for how the password is created, requiring number-letter combinations of significant length. They also utilize encryption, usually SSL, to keep the password from being "sniffed" during the logon process. However, few, if any, banks require users to change their password ever—and the fact that they require a strongly constructed password means that many users probably write them down or tape them to their monitors.

In short, effectively using a password to authenticate a user requires a good amount of discipline on the part of the password holder in creating, changing, and secreting the password, and this has historically been the downfall of passwords.

Authentication Versus Identity

Although the username/password is a good way to authenticate a user, it requires a pre-existing relationship between the user and the system that the user is logging into. For example, a system administrator must assign a user an initial password. If the administrator really wants to tie the user's *identity* to this username/password, then there must be some relationship between them, such as Human Resources authorizing the account for new employee Jane Doe. After that, if the account of Jane Doe is used for some illicit purpose, Jane Doe can be held responsible because her identity is tied to the account. Now contrast this with the username/password used for most free Web email accounts. When a person signs up for such an account, that person can put *any* information into the identity section, such as a bogus first and last name, residence, even gender. For example, so as not to create any problems for bob_23567@hotmail.com (used previously), we created this account at hotmail using the first name e, the last name b, and the first state and ZIP code that came to mind. In this case, the username/password that was created for this account is a decent way to authenticate to get access to the bob_23567@hotmail.com mail account, but it in no way links the true *identity* of the author (you really do have three guesses, in this case) to the bob_23567@hotmail.com account.

Good Rules for Password Generation

If you do plan on using password authentication, and chances are in the 99.44% range that you are, here are some guidelines for creating and keeping strong passwords. Keep in mind that the type of password that your system requires is very dependant upon the criticality of the account and system data, as well as the type of password attacks that can be expected.

- Don't use dictionary words or names. Most password-guessing programs will run through all these possibilities. And please don't use your username!

- Try for at least seven to nine digits for the length of your password—more is usually better. Note that some operating systems, such as Solaris, have a maximum password length of eight.

- Use a combination of letters, numbers, and nonalphanumerics, such as punctuation marks and spaces.

- Choose something that you won't have to write down. Making #$%^2$jkdf_232 your password might keep people from guessing it, but it will end up on a yellow sticky on your monitor for sure.

- Consider a passphrase. For example, "My car is a '68 Mustang" is a 22-digit password that uses letters, numbers, caps, and punctuation marks; is easy to remember (if your car is indeed a '68 Mustang); and is fun to type.

- Never write down or share your password, and don't store it in an easily accessible place such as in a file on your computer. Administrative passwords often need to be physically recorded so that they can be retrieved in the case of an emergency. In these situations, they should kept in a locked vault or an encrypted file.

- Change your password regularly. The change frequency will depend upon how stringently you enforce password-generation rules and how important the account is that is protected by the password. For example, system administrators and nuclear missile silo operators should change their passwords more often than Yahoo! chat room users.

- Crack your password files often. System administrators should run password-cracking programs such as Crack and L0phtcrack against their password files to ensure that system users are creating strong passwords. In one engagement, the authors found that 90% of system passwords, including the administrator passwords, were compromised by a password-cracking program after only a few minutes.

- Enforce password-creation and aging requirements. Most systems allow the administrator to specify the minimum requirements in length and complexity for passwords. Operating systems also can be set to require passwords to be changed after a set period, and they can keep track of previously used passwords so that users can't repeatedly flip-flop between the same set of passwords.

Well, that was certainly a lot of talk about passwords, but considering that they're the basis for Internet authentication, it's well worth the effort.

One-Time Passwords

Although we have been giving passwords a hard time, there actually is an implementation of this form of authentication that is quite strong: one-time passwords. One-time passwords, as the name might suggest, are single-serving passwords, good for one session only. Because manual implementation of such a system would be more than a little challenging, these systems generally are implemented by making use of hardware devices known as tokens that are time-synchronized with an authentication server. After the devices have been synchronized, both the token and the server generate a new, identical password at specific time intervals, generally every minute. The password is good only for one use or until it is automatically changed at the next time interval, whichever comes first. When a user wants to authenticate to a system, such as a firewall or a VPN, he uses the password that is displayed on his token (sometimes appending a PIN to the token's password). The system then passes this authentication information to the authentication server, which checks that the password matches the one that is current for that user.

The security of such one-time password tokens relies on the difficulty of predicting the password generation sequence and the capability of the token and authentication server to stay in sync over long periods of time. These are both significant and complex tasks, but several successful implementations of one-time password generators have been brought to market and found reasonable acceptance in organizations that require this level of security.

One-time password systems usually are implemented as one-factor or two-factor. In a two-factor implementation, a secret such as a PIN number is combined with the token's currently generated password. This is generally the recommended type of implementation because, even if the user loses the token, it cannot be activated without the PIN. It also fulfills the general security principle of "something you have (the token), something you know (the PIN)," which generally is accepted as a very secure way to enforce user authentication.

Challenge/Response Mechanisms

In its simplest form, the challenge/response mechanism is one in which a user is presented with a question that he must answer to be authenticated. For example, in the NT challenge/response mechanism, the user's computer is given a "challenge" that is a 16- or 24-byte number. The user's system encrypts this challenge using an encryption key based on the user's password. This encrypted challenge is sent back to the server as the "response." The server, knowing the user's password, performs the same function on the challenge and checks its result against the response sent by the client. If they match, then the user is authenticated.

In a simpler form, the challenge/response mechanism can be used to allow users who have forgotten their password to still log onto a system. Most often, this is done by asking the user a question to which only he knows the answer. Obviously, the strength of this system is dependent on how "hard" the question is and whether the user really is the only one who knows the answer. For instance, the oft-used question "What is your mother's maiden name?" is a fairly weak method. By combining several simple questions, this system can be significantly strengthened. For example, posing this series of questions to a user makes it extremely difficult for an attacker to guess the correct responses:

- What is your mother's maiden name?
- What is your favorite color?
- What make of car do you drive?

In fact, such systems are extremely useful for enrolling new users into an online system. Suppose that a utility company wants to allow its customers to move to an online billing and payment system, but it does not want to go to the expense of sending out millions of letters that contain usernames and passwords for their accounts. By directing customers to its site and using the following information, the utility company can authenticate new users and assign them an account with a high degree of confidence in their identity:

- Your name exactly as it appears on your bill
- Your address exactly as it appears on your bill
- Your account number exactly as it appears on your bill
- The billing date and exact amount due as printed on your last bill

After the customer has answered these questions correctly, he can create a normal username and password to access the system in the future. Note that such a system should never tell the user what questions he has answered wrong because this allows an attacker to "brute force" each question; it also severely dilutes the strength of using a series of questions. Given the fact that viewing and paying someone else's utility bill is not high on the list of hacker to-do's, this initial authentication method is perfectly satisfactory for low-risk accounts.

Implementations of two-factor challenge/response mechanism generally take the form of small devices. When a user wants to authenticate to a system, he is prompted with a challenge such as a series of numbers. The user enters the challenge into the device along with a second factor such as a PIN. The device then generates the correct response. The user utilizes this response to authenticate back to the system, which checks the response and then grants access if correct.

Biometric Mechanisms

Biometric systems appeared mostly in James Bond and sci-fi films just a few years ago, but they have since begun to be more commonplace. Biometric systems make use of physical characteristics of an individual as their authentication credentials. Retina patterns, fingerprints, hand geometry, voice recognition, and others all can be used with a great amount of certainty to identify an individual to a system. These authentication systems can be one-factor (in this case, the something you have is "you"), although multiple physical characteristics can be used in combination, such as hand geometry fingerprint. For instance, one commercial vendor offers an authentication product that combines facial structure, voice, and lip movement while speaking to authenticate a user.

Biometric systems in use today include these:

- Fingerprint recognition, usually used as part of a challenge-response mechanism to reduce the chance of a replay attack. Such systems can also check for body heat, skin galvanization, and a pulse to ensure that a live finger is doing the authenticating.

- Hand geometry recognition, which takes specific measurements such as the curve of fingers and spatial relationship between the joints. Although hand geometry is not truly unique between individuals, it does allow for a simple, nonintrusive biometric scan that does not carry the paranoia associated with giving up your fingerprint to log onto a network.

- Retinal scans, which are highly accurate but somewhat invasive. That is, you need to allow someone to probe your retina with a laser.

Others include facial recognition, voice recognition, and even weight (as a secondary factor). Here's a little-known fact: Facial recognition was used by law enforcement at the 2001 Super Bowl to check for wanted individuals as they entered the gates.

Digital Certificates

The problem with all of the authentication mechanisms that have been examined so far is that they don't provide a portable way to identify yourself to a system on which you do not have some type of association. Passwords and challenge/response mechanisms require that you be assigned a password by an administrator, while biometrics usually require an enrollment period during which the system learns your biometric pattern and associates it with your username. Given that the Internet provides simple mechanisms for surfing to new locations, such as retail sites, it would be nice if you could present some kind of "digital driver's license" to identify yourself to a site when you wanted to perform a transaction. Imagine for a moment that to write a check at a store, you first had to be enrolled by the store's manager, or that every time you wanted to buy a beer you had to preregister with the bar owner. This is essentially what the aforementioned authentication mechanisms make you do every time you go to a new site on the Internet.

Digital certificates tackle the problem of providing a portable identification mechanism for use on the Internet (or for any electronic transaction, really). A digital certificate is nothing more than a data file that can include information that identifies you as a person rather than an account on a computer system. For example, Figure 5.10 shows a certificate generated for Bob Public at his email address of bob_23567@hotmail.com. This digital credential is digitally signed by the issuer—in this case, VeriSign Corporation. The certificate is analogous to a driver's license. The driver's license has absolutely nothing to do with your ability to write a check, but it is accepted by merchants as positive identification and allows you to conduct a transaction with an entity (the store) with which you have had no previous associations.

FIGURE 5.10

A digital certificate.

A driver's license is issued by a trusted source (the DMV) and is "signed" by using a special seal, such as hologram, to ensure that it has not been tampered with. A digital certificate is issued by a trusted source called a Certificate Authority (CA) and is signed by utilizing public key cryptography. The specifics of a CA are not worth going into in this forum, but suffice to say that a digital signature is nearly impossible to forge. The key to generating a digital certificate that has *valid* information about the user lies in the enrollment processes. Yes, just like getting a driver's license, getting a digital certificate requires that you prove your identity to the issuer. For example, to get a certificate that can be used on a Web server for SSL, a company needs to provide a myriad of information to the issuer, such as its Dun and Bradstreet number (used to reference business information, such as financial statements), street address, a confirmation letter on company letterhead, the company's phone number, and other identifying tidbits that are checked and reviewed by a person before issuing the certificate.

Certificate Classes

Certificates come in different classes that require different levels of checks during the enrollment process. The certificate shown for Bob Public is a Class 1 Individual Subscriber "Persona not verified," meaning that the issuer did nothing to validate Bob's true identity before issuing "him" the certificate. The different classes of a certificate have the following meanings:

- Class 1 certificates are issued only to individuals and provide very little in the way of true identification of the bearer.

- Class 2 certificates are issued to business or individuals. Businesses must send in authentication information such as company letterhead and Dun and Bradstreet number, which can be verified by the issuer. Individuals might have to fax copies of identity cards or send in a signed request for a certificate.

- Class 3 certificates have all the requirements of Class 2, plus companies might have to present notarized documentation. In addition, a representative of the company must show up in person at an agent of the issuer to complete the issuance process.

- Class 4 certificates are issued only to organizations and also require that a representative of the organization authenticate in person at the issuing authority.

The standard for certificates is the X.509 digital certificate, which includes extensions for different formats such as lightweight (less data for faster transmission) certificates for use in wireless devices such as PDAs and cell phones, certificates for use in electronic commerce transactions, email transactions, you name it.

Shortcomings of Certificates

Given this great technology, it would seem that the authentication woes of the Internet would be history by now. Why isn't this the case? There are several roadblocks to the widespread usage of digital certificates:

- **Portability**—Try getting a certificate for your IE browser and then moving it into a Netscape browser, or even moving it to an IE browser on another computer. As of the publication of this book, it was an enormous headache to use a certificate the way you use a driver's license, by carrying it with you wherever you go. Smart cards were supposed to solve this problem (put your "cert" on a smart card and carry it in your wallet), but smart cards have yet to catch on in this country, and almost nobody has a smart card reader.

- **Application support**—Only in the last few years have applications been digital certificate–enabled. Email and browser applications such as Outlook, Eudora, IE, and Netscape now support certificates, but not many operating systems are easily certificate-enabled. In general, *seamless* certificate integration is still not a reality.

- **Deployment and complexity**—Certificates are part of what's known as a public key infrastructure (PKI), with the accent on the *infrastructure*. With only a few well-established CAs, corporations must invest large sums of money to implement certificate-based services, train their administrators and users, and then support the technology.

- **Lack of ubiquity**—Single sign-on, the capability to sign on once and then use a myriad of systems, has been the goal of corporations for years. Digital certificates would seem to be the "key" to providing single sign-on because they offer a portable means of identification. However, because many applications either are not certificate-enabled or work only with specific PKIs, this goal has not been reached.

- **Lack of additional security**—This one's going to get us in trouble, but most implementations of PKI don't offer a much better level of authentication than a traditional username and password. This is because the private keys associated with a digital certificate must be kept secret. The best solution is to store private keys on a hardware device such as a smart card, but smart cards are not yet in widespread use. Therefore, many vendors fall back on encrypting the private keys using a password that is kept by the user. Well, if the private keys are protected by a password, then the security of the certificate system is only as good as that password. This has been a major obstacle when it comes to defining the cost-benefit of PKI over traditional authentication methods.

Uses of Digital Certificates

Now that we've thoroughly examined the pros and cons of certificates, let's examine how and where they can be used. The major uses of certificates include these:

- Signing code that is distributed over the Web. This keeps attackers from inserting Trojans into programs or passing themselves off as trusted code developers.

- SSL server certificates for Web servers. Certificates identify that the machine the user is connecting to via SSL is indeed the site that they expect. Therefore, if a browser is redirected to another site by an attacker, the certificate will show that the user has been misdirected. Most browsers come with a preinstalled set of certificates from trusted CAs (click Tools, Internet Options, Content, Certificates, Trusted Root Certification Authorities to see the certificates that come with the IE browser). If an SSL certificate is not signed by an authority that is trusted by the browser, a warning message will pop up alerting the user. One mistake that some administrators make is to store the private keys that were used to generate the certificate on the Web server. Private keys must be safeguarded! If a private key is compromised, an attacker easily can spoof your site or sign software in your name.

A Final Word on Certificates

Import a certificate into your mail client, and you're off to the races: You can encrypt and digitally sign your email. The issue, of course, is, can anyone decrypt it or validate the signature? Unless a recipient has a digital certificate of his own for which the sender can obtain a copy, and unless the recipient has a copy of the sender's certificate, secure communications still can't be accomplished. Given the ease with which you can obtain a certificate via the Web, and the fact that both Sun and Microsoft are incorporating PKI support into their latest operating systems, the ubiquity of certificates might at last be poised to become a reality.

Summary

Some books have entire content that looks like it was cut and pasted directly from a bunch of IETC RFCs. This chapter has not taken that approach to educating you on secure network protocols. Although it is important to understand the underpinning of the various network and application security standards, that information is freely available from sources on the Internet. The goal of this chapter has been to discuss important and widely used standards with respect to security and, more directly, to point out those implementation and real-world considerations that can cause seemingly secure protocols, such as WEP, to become insecure.

This chapter began with a review of one of the most widely employed security "add-ons" in use: encryption and encapsulation protocols. The IPSec protocol, which initially suffered from a lack of compatible implementations, has caught on in the past two years to the point that it has become a ubiquitous method for Internet encryption in firewalls and VPN devices. We then explored other widely used encapsulation protocols such as PPTP and L2TP, each of which has been built into such operating systems as Windows 98, NT, and 2000. These "built-in" encryption capabilities allow end users to create VPNs into their corporate networks to support telecommuting from home or the office.

The next protocol that we reviewed, SSL, is probably the most mainstream security protocol of them all. It can be argued that SSL has brought encryption and digital certificates into the vocabulary of the public at large. WEP has the opportunity to do the same for the wireless market, although it currently has a broken security paradigm.

After hitting all of the encryption methods, we turned our attention to authentication systems. We saw how the least secure method of authentication, the username and password, also happens to be the most widespread. Finally, we looked at digital certificates, which, although they have made significant inroads to usage in the server market, still have not made much of a dent in the Internet user market.

All of these protocols and standards are being widely utilized to help secure the infrastructure of the Internet, and they are being extended daily into layers ranging from transport through application to provide ubiquitous security services to network users.

Example Network Architectures and Case Studies

IN THIS CHAPTER

This book has covered a lot of material and provided all sorts of advice on how to better provide a secure network infrastructure for your critical information assets. It should be clear by now that there is no panacea for security. The greatest firewall in the world will not provide 100% protection, nor will the most sophisticated intrusion-detection system catch every possible exploit from an external hacker or malicious act from a determined insider. However, this book has described in detail many of the components and practices that can be combined to provide a high level of practical information security. We will now put all of this information to use and examine several real-world network designs, drawn from our experiences working with organizations to secure their e-commerce and enterprise networks.

Bringing It All Together

We have endeavored to ensure that you emerge from this book with a strong appreciation for the fact that information security should be approached as a never-ending process of improvement, with a continuing evolution in an organization's assessment of its critical information assets, the development of policies designed to safeguard that information, and the implementation of procedures and technical means. Although the themes are the same for all networks, the operational requirements—and, therefore, the implementation details—can vary depending on the purpose of the network. We will focus on three general classes of network designs in this chapter:

- Enterprise networks
- Small office/home office (SOHO)
- Web sites and e-commerce

The Enterprise Network

The term *enterprise network* commonly is used to describe the technical infrastructure required to support a large organization. These organizations can include large corporations, educational institutions, government agencies, and health care organizations—basically any network that must support and provide services to many users. These networks usually have several (or all) of the following characteristics:

- Many users, all with different roles within the enterprise (such as sales, engineering, management, IT, HR, students, faculty, visitors, and so on)
- High availability requirements for access to the network and information services
- Many different information stores, often related to the roles that users fill within the enterprise (for example, customer data and internal HR resources information such as payroll)

- Remote users (such as the "road warrior" salesman, telecommuters, or the system administrator who must log in at midnight to fix a problem)
- Multiple sites (such as headquarters, local campuses, and branch offices)

These networks are often quite complex and require significant investments in both technology and skilled staff. As enterprises become more dependent on their IT infrastructures, they also become far more sensitive to information security issues than they might have been in the past. Companies that either derive direct revenue from their network, such as e-commerce or stock-trading companies, or depend on their network to be up and running for their employees to be productive have become painfully aware of the financial losses that can result from rampant virus propagation or denial-of-service attacks.

Larger enterprise networks face many information security challenges, including these:

- Many unsophisticated and untrained users
- Distributed management and design of networks, especially between interconnected branch offices or campuses
- Conflicting requirements from management that demand both easy access and impenetrable security
- Different entities competing for authority over information security (typically the "security group" versus the "network group")

We have worked with many enterprises that have put significant focus on their information security operations. In one example, a company in the financial world went through a formal assessment of its information assets, developed clear policies for its employees and network design, implemented a robust network and monitoring architecture, and put in place formal processes for continually improving its security posture. These processes include training of IT staff, all the way up through quarterly penetration testing and periodic denial-of-service attacks specifically crafted to try to bring down the network. After each test, the network and server infrastructures, as well as the Internet-facing applications, were enhanced to stand up to these attacks. This continuous cycle of assessment and improvement has resulted in an extremely robust infrastructure that features both high availability and formidable security.

On the other end of the spectrum, we have encountered surprisingly large companies that are just now beginning to consider the introduction of firewalls into their architectures. When asked about their information security practices, these companies often respond with statements such as, "I manufacture widgets; I don't have anything that anybody would want." After a little more discussion, it is slowly revealed that the company's entire supply chain is managed through its network connections and that a successful denial-of-service attack could seriously impact its ability to meet production schedules. Furthermore, the company's entire client list is sitting on a shared disk available to anyone in the company, as well as any outsider who happens to figure out the IP address block of the company.

A Typical Enterprise Network

Although the details change with each organization, the basic model for an enterprise network can be described in a simple diagram. The components of an enterprise network are illustrated in Figure 6.1. Typically, the enterprise infrastructure is built out in a number of locations, including the headquarters and branch offices. In some cases, the local sites actually might be campuses that span several buildings in relative proximity. Although the vast majority of the users of the network usually are located within these offices, the business needs of the enterprise might require that customers, business partners, and remote employees also have access to the network. As a final addition to this picture, you must remember the ill-minded outsiders whom we will refer to with the popular term *hackers*.

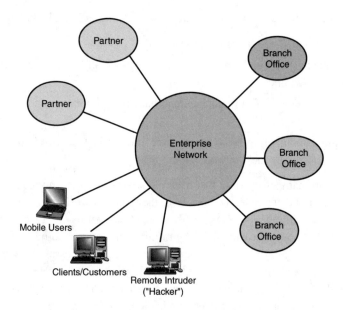

FIGURE 6.1
Components of an enterprise network.

External Threats

We will begin by focusing on the security of the intended connections into a site's network from the outside world. We have used the word *intended* here very purposefully because we will address some of the unintended connections from the outside world in the section on internal threats later in this chapter. After securing access from the outside, we will examine the security aspects of the design of the inside of the enterprise network.

Example Network Architectures and Case Studies

CHAPTER 6

157

6

EXAMPLE
NETWORK
ARCHITECTURES

The common points of access into a network are illustrated in Figure 6.2. A thorough understanding of all of these points of access into the network reveals just how complex the security issues of the enterprise can be:

- **The Internet**—Any system with an unprotected public IP address, including network devices such as routers and switches, as well as servers and workstations, can be reached from the Internet. This is typically how clients will connect to any network services that you want to provide. Just about every modern enterprise network has at least one connection to the Internet, typically at DSL, T1/E1, or T3/E3 rates (although the access rates are getting faster and cheaper with each passing month). Remote users can connect to your Internet-addressable hosts via any dial-up or broadband (such as DSL or cable modem) connection to their ISP.

- **Wide area networks (WANs)**—Branch offices and even some partners commonly have been connected to enterprise networks by some sort of wide area network. Privately leased lines are common; however, their popularity has been reduced with the introduction of affordable WAN services such as Frame Relay and, to a lesser degree, Asynchronous Transfer Mode (ATM). It should be noted that all of the physical circuits that these links employ are owned and managed by service providers, and they can be transported as different logical data streams on the same physical fiber, cable, or satellite link. So, although WAN links are logically secure (for example, packets from one Frame Relay channel do not cross over into other channels), they are not necessarily any more physically secure than the Internet if you are concerned about service provider staff observing your traffic.

- **Virtual private networks (site-to-site)**—The ubiquity of Internet connections has brought about the viability of significantly reducing recurring communications costs by employing VPN technology to tunnel private network traffic over the public Internet. VPN technologies provide two benefits: the capability to make remote networks a part of your local network by encapsulating internal IP packets in other IP packets, and the option of encrypting traffic so that it is kept private as it crosses the Internet. Note that site-to-site VPNs can be used to secure WAN connections, such as Frame Relay or leased lines.

- **Wireless links**—Another alternative to leased lines and WAN services is to use Radio Frequency (RF), or even optical link technologies to interconnect nearby buildings. Many wireless product vendors offer "point-to-point" options such as stronger transmitters and directional antennas to support links across campuses. An extreme case of this is to employ satellite terminals to connect remote locations via private links in leased satellite spectrum (for example, via Intelsat).

- **Dial-up connections**—Many companies have installed modems so that telecommuters, customers, or partners can dial directly into their networks. It is also very common for the IT staff to install modems for remote administrative access in case the primary connections or routers go down and they want to try to fix the problem immediately from their homes.

- **Virtual private networks (remote user)**—Just as site-to-site VPNs have replaced many WAN connections in the past few years, remote-user VPNs have become a very popular alternative to dial-up modem pools and remote access servers. In this case, remote users use third-party or OS-native VPN client software to establish an encrypted tunnel to the enterprise network through their Internet access of choice (dial-up, DSL, cable modem, and so on).

- **Physical media**—Last, but certainly not least, it is important not to forget that large volumes of data can come into and leave a network in the form of tapes, floppy disks, and CDs. Viruses still can be found in corrupted software installation media that arrive at your doorstep.

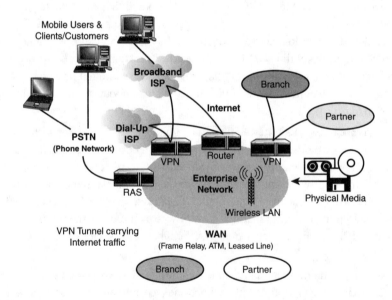

FIGURE 6.2
Connections to the enterprise.

Securing External Links

Now that you have a good feel for how data gets to the network, you can take a look at the edge of a typical site and examine a good approach to keeping the enterprise's border secure.

Example Network Architectures and Case Studies

CHAPTER 6

159

6

EXAMPLE
NETWORK
ARCHITECTURES

Consider a typical enterprise network, as illustrated in Figure 6.3, which consists of Internet access routers, VPN gateways, firewalls, DMZs for publicly accessible network services, and an internal private network. Although there are many variations on this theme, the overall architecture is fairly common.

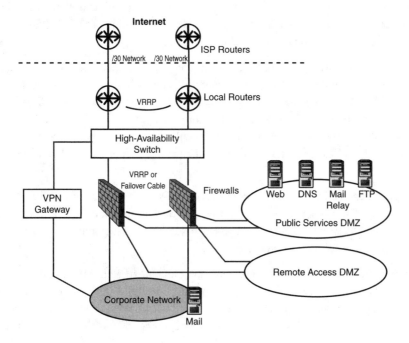

FIGURE 6.3
The edge of an enterprise site.

Internet Routers

The "front door" of the enterprise network is its connection to the Internet. In its simplest form, this consists of a serial link of some kind, such as Frame Relay, the Point-to-Point Protocol (PPP), PPP over Ethernet (PPPoE), ATM, or a proprietary protocol such as Cisco's Serial Line Encoding, which connects an ISP's router to the organization's border Internet router.

Many enterprise networks employ high-availability (HA) configurations in their Internet connections. Although HA is not technically an information security measure, HA configurations are an important component of *information assurance*—the capability to provide both secure and reliable access to information. We have worked with many network engineers to design secure Internet connections, and this issue almost always comes up.

HA router configurations are implemented using several techniques. First, the links themselves typically are provided either by different ISPs or by the same ISP from different points of presence (POPs). The goal here is to minimize the chance that both communication links will fail at the same time. Link failover is accomplished via Border Gateway Protocol (BGP) router configurations so that when the primary interface into your network is no longer reachable, traffic destined for your network is routed through the backup link by your ISP(s). Link failover configurations should be discussed with your ISP.

The next step in providing HA connectivity to the Internet is to guard against router failures. This is commonly accomplished by using routers that employ a failover protocol such as the IETF standard Virtual Router Redundancy Protocol (VRRP) or Cisco's proprietary Hot Standby Router Protocol (HSRP). Routers configured with this protocol send heartbeat messages to each other. If the backup router determines that the primary is no longer operational, it will assume the IP address and MAC address of the primary's interface and take over the routing job.

From a security perspective, the access control lists (ACLs) in routers commonly are used to implement several "best practice" screening rules, as well as any other bulk filtering that the network administrator wants to perform. The IETF's RFC 2827 recommends that all border routers implement the following screening rules:

- **Antispoofing rule**—Border routers know the block of IP addresses that they connect to the larger Internet (such as the CIDR block "sitting behind" the router). These routers should drop all outbound packets with source IP addresses that do not belong to the internal network because these are most likely spoofed, or forged, source addresses.

- **No broadcast forwarding rule**—Similarly, you should ensure that no packets with destination IP addresses that have broadcast significance be allowed to leave your network. This *should* be hard to do; however, the classic Smurf attack used just these types of packets to trick an entire network to transmit packets at a targeted computer by "pinging" a broadcast address instead of a specific host. In this particular case, the source address was spoofed to that of the targeted victim computer.

These rules are critical not only to securing your own site, but also for making you a "good citizen of the Internet." The antispoofing rule, in particular, is a great step toward reducing the number of hosts on the Internet that can act as distributed denial-of-service (DDoS) agents. It also keeps any would-be hackers in your employ from conducting any attacks against external servers using a spoofed source address. Because in many cases your company can be held financially responsible for attacks launched from your site, the antispoofing rules are a good way to ensure that you're doing due diligence with respect to security.

Other ACL rules can be added as you see fit. Many network administrators have adopted the practice of blocking all ICMP Echo Request and Echo Reply packets (that is, "pings") at their router. This rule can block many denial-of-service command and control channels and attacks, although it does have the effect of blocking legitimate ping traffic. Another common rule is to block all SNMP (network-management packets on UDP ports 161 and 162) traffic that originates from outside your local network, preventing outsiders from remotely reconfiguring your routers, switches, and server. If no firewall is present, many other rules often are added to the border router's ACL.

Note that if a denial-of-service attack is directed toward your network, your local router ACLs could be of limited use, for several reasons. First, many of the modern DDoS attacks employ random source IP address spoofing and randomized TCP/UDP ports (of course, if every router and home PC could implement the antispoofing rule we just described, these attacks would be less effective). This makes it very difficult to come up with a reasonable number of rules that can block out an attack in progress. Furthermore, even if you could successfully write the rules to stop the DDoS traffic from getting past your router and into your network, the link to your ISP still would be fairly well saturated with the attack packets. This is why it is always a good idea to know whom to call at your ISP(s) so that someone can work with you to either block the traffic upstream in the routers or help find the source of the attacks.

Firewalls, DMZs, and the Corporate Network

In most modern enterprise network architectures, the bulk of the security policy enforcement is performed by one or more firewalls. As we have previously discussed, these firewalls can be implemented in many ways; however, they generally behave as traffic cops on a network, regulating the flow of traffic between network segments based on rules that implement a security policy. Simple firewalls can have only two or three segments that they interface to, while larger enterprise firewalls can be more complex.

It is quite common to refer to three types of segments with respect to a firewall: external, internal, and DMZ. As illustrated in Figure 6.4, the external segment is usually the public Internet, and the internal segment is your private network that you want to protect.

A DMZ, or demilitarized zone, is simply a network segment that is used to house publicly accessible network services. These servers must have some visibility from the Internet and are therefore at higher risk than internal systems. There are several ways to configure a DMZ. In some cases, a DMZ is formed by simply placing public servers on a network segment between the border router and an internal router that serves as a gateway to the "internal" systems. In these cases, some kind of access control list on the gateway router further restricts traffic into the internal network.

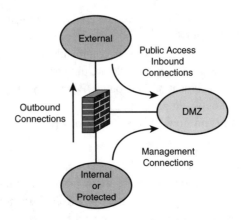

FIGURE 6.4

Firewalls and network segments.

It is now increasingly common to find that a firewall is used to separate the DMZ servers from the internal network. In one scenario, the DMZ servers are connected on a segment between the border router and the firewall. Additional security policy can be enforced by moving the DMZ servers to their own network segment "behind" the firewall. In this case, the DMZ segment is connected to a firewall that has been configured so that untrusted hosts on the external network (the Internet) can initiate at least limited types of connections to the DMZ systems. There is nothing physically different about a DMZ—the term *DMZ* simply indicates that the firewall rules will allow external users to connect in, as opposed to a more heavily protected internal network.

Because the firewall is a critical component in providing both internal users with access to the Internet and external users (such as clients or partners) with access to information services, these devices also commonly are deployed in a high-availability configuration. An HA router/firewall configuration (refer to Figure 6.3) is increasingly common in enterprise networks. We will examine the details of this configuration in the next section. For now, it is sufficient to understand that many enterprise-quality firewalls include failover support, using either the VRRP protocol or dedicated "failover cables" to pass heartbeat information between the primary and the backup.

With the firewall(s) in place, you now can begin to implement your security policies. The first step is to determine how the network will be broken up for the purposes of controlling flow. Most enterprise networks will maintain at least one DMZ. The traditional DMZ will be the home of several systems that provide public services:

Example Network Architectures and Case Studies

CHAPTER 6

163

6

ARCHITECTURES
NETWORK
EXAMPLE

- **Public DNS servers**—These allow the public to resolve names such as `www.acme.com` to the appropriate IP address. DNS servers also maintain special Mail Exchanger records that are required to get mail addressed to user@acme.com to the computer running the enterprise mail server.

- **Mail (SMTP) redirectors**—These are the publicly accessible mail servers. We recommend that this *not* be the server that internal users get their mail from. The public server should be responsible for forwarding incoming mail to an internal server.

- **Public Web (HTTP) servers**—All publicly accessible Web pages should be maintained in servers in a DMZ, including any corporate informational pages or Web-based services. We will look at several Web server DMZ configurations later in this chapter.

- **Public FTP servers**—Many sites are used to maintain public FTP servers; however, this is less common, given the amount of information that is available through HTTP servers.

When the publicly accessible services are placed in a DMZ segment, the firewall rules will be configured to restrict external traffic to these servers to that which is necessary. In our example, the following rules might be used:

Source	Destination	Service	Rule
Any	`mail.acme.com`	SMTP (25)	Allow
Any	`www.acme.com`	HTTP (80)	Allow
Any	`ftp.acme.com`	FTP (21)	Allow
Any	`ns.acme.com`	DNS (53)	Allow

You might want to allow some additional access to these servers from internal machines. For example, if you wanted to allow secure management and file transfer into these servers, you would add a rule allowing secure shell. Furthermore, you need to add a rule to allow the mail redirector to forward mail to the internal mail server:

Source	Destination	Service	Rule
Internal	DMZ	SSH (22)	Allow
mail.acme.com	mail	SMTP (25)	Allow

Of course, the "catchall" default rule for firewalls would take care of anything else:

Source	Destination	Service	Rule
Any	Any	Any	Deny

So far, we have not directly addressed the fact that the firewall also will probably be performing network address translation (NAT). NAT is useful for several purposes:

- Mapping many private addresses to a few public IP addresses helps conserve the Internet's address space.
- The enterprise network designer has considerable flexibility because he has large numbers of addresses to employ in his network design.
- From a security perspective, the number of workstations and servers that are deployed in the network are hidden from the outside world.

All of this is best illustrated by a real-world example. Figure 6.5 provides a high-level view of a small enterprise network. The firewall is used to regulate traffic in and out of four corporate network segments, as well as the public Internet. Two business units are each given their own network space. The "corporate" network houses the professional office staff and their internal Active Directory, Microsoft Exchange, and file servers. The "operations" network houses a number of servers, workstations and other systems that are used to support a 24/7 service for many customers on the Internet. Both of these network segments use blocks of addresses from the private 172.16.0.0/12 blocks.

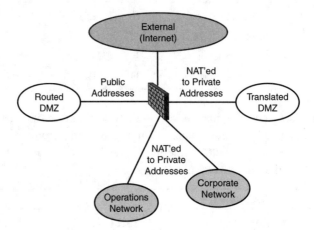

FIGURE 6.5
Multiple-DMZ configuration.

There are two DMZs in this network. The first is the "routed DMZ," which is the home of several servers that require that publicly routable IP addresses be assigned to their interfaces (this is primarily due to the applications that run on these systems). In this case, the servers all have normal, routable, public IP addresses, and the firewall simply provides fine-grained access policies.

Example Network Architectures and Case Studies

CHAPTER 6

165

6

EXAMPLE
NETWORK
ARCHITECTURES

The "translated DMZ" is used to house more publicly accessible servers; however, in this case, the servers are all assigned private, nonroutable IP addresses. In this particular case, the firewall is configured to perform network address translation, and each private address is "statically translated" to a corresponding public IP address. These servers all map to routable IP addresses when a DNS query is performed from the Internet; however, the interfaces on the servers all reside in a private 172.16.0.0/12 network block, and the firewall is configured to perform a one-to-one translation of the IP addresses as Internet clients attempt to connect to these servers. An alternative to this configuration would be to map specific services (in the form of TCP and UDP ports) to specific internal addresses. For example, the firewall could map all SMTP (TCP port 25) traffic to 172.16.1.5 and all HTTP (TCP port 80) to 172.16.1.8.

The reason for the translated DMZ borders slightly on the line of paranoia, but that is often the line that security professionals must walk. We generally prefer that all publicly accessible servers be translated to a private address as a precaution against firewall failure. Specifically, we are concerned about a firewall that "fails closed," meaning that if the firewall software crashes, all traffic can flow freely. The analogy here is to a closed circuit vs. an open circuit in electronics: If a circuit is "closed," electricity will flow; if it is "open," electricity will not flow.

This sounds like something that should never happen; however, it is actually possible with some vendors' firewall products. One very popular firewall vendor provides its product as software that can be installed in either a Solaris or a Windows NT environment. In the Windows installation, the native NT routing functions are used; if the firewall software fails, it "fails closed" and the platform becomes a simple router.

By forcing the firewall to perform the network address translation, the threat of this potential compromise is eliminated because there will be nothing left to convert the address from the public IP address to the private IP address. It should be noted that we do not use this particular version of the firewall and that our actual firewall should "fail open" if it ever does fail; however, just as a standard practice, we like to live by the "always translate publicly addressable servers" rule whenever we can.

Connectivity Devices and HA Configurations

When you simply have a router talking directly to a firewall, a simple Ethernet cable (UTP or fiber optic cable) can be used to connect the two devices. As we have discussed, many enterprise networks choose to employ a more robust configuration and opt to install routers and firewalls in high-availability configurations that employ protocols such as VRRP or failover cables to ensure that if one device goes down (due to a hardware failure or preventative maintenance), its backup will take over.

Actually several options exist for deploying HA configurations at the Internet access point:

- Cross-connecting the routers and firewalls with redundant cables and switches.
- Installing a single high-availability switch (one with redundant control modules and power supplies) between the two sets of devices. (Refer to Figure 6.3.)
- Installing redundant switches that each device plugs into.

Although true HA requires a fully meshed and redundant hardware infrastructure, our general preference is to install the single HA switch between the routers and the firewalls. This configuration provides a good balance between high availability and complexity. It provides for recovery from failures of the ISP links (not uncommon at all), the routers, and the firewalls, and it keeps the wiring complexity under control. It also facilitates the connection of other devices in the external segment, such as a VPN gateway (if that service is not embedded in the firewall) or a network IDS sensor.

One final option is to provide not just failover, but also load balancing to the Internet connection. If you are going to pay for multiple ISP links, you might want to take advantage of both of them. Several vendors offer products that support link load balancing and firewall load balancing.

Virtual Private Networks

We have discussed the fact that many network engineers have adopted VPN technology to accomplish two goals:

- To provide remote access to users, giving them the feel of being on the internal network while on the road or telecommuting
- To reduce recurring telecommunications costs for connectivity between sites (for example, replacing a leased line or Frame Relay circuit with a site-to-site VPN)

VPNs usually are implemented by installing either a firewall with VPN capability embedded in it or a dedicated VPN appliance. The option that you select will be based on factors such as whether you already have a firewall in place, how much of the firewall's CPU resources are available for the computing burden introduced by a VPN, how many users or sites you plan to support, and management issues. A third option is outsourcing your VPN requirements, in which a service provider handles all of the technical and administrative burden, and you simply get another connection coming into your network from the service provider's VPN gateway.

In all three cases, you will have to take a close look at exactly how security policy is really implemented with respect to the VPN traffic. In our enterprise network prototype, we have included a dedicated VPN gateway appliance, with an external interface connected after the border routers but before the firewalls. Tunneled traffic is routed to the VPN gateway's external interface, and the encapsulated IP packets are decrypted and dropped into the internal network. There is a (hopefully) obvious problem here: This traffic bypasses the firewall completely.

A little more detail of a typical VPN configuration is illustrated in Figure 6.6, which contains both a branch-office VPN and a remote-user VPN. VPN systems provide some policy control over what traffic *enters* a tunnel. The IPSec architecture includes this. In practice, it is required so that a remote client software or VPN gateway knows what traffic to forward through the tunnel. For example, the policy at the branch office might be as simple as this:

```
"Encrypt all packets destined to 192.168.1.0/24"
```

This instruction is really more of a routing instruction than anything else because it is telling the VPN gateway which traffic to transmit in the tunnel instead of sending it out on the Internet as normal traffic. Additional restrictions can be imposed on the traffic flow. For example, if the branch office users need access only to Web-based services at the headquarters, the VPN policy could be tightened up a little:

```
"Encrypt all TCP port 80 packets to 192.168.1.0/24"
```

This issue becomes critical when you do not have knowledge or control of the information and network security practices at the remote site. If you are going to set up a site-to-site VPN, you should be asking yourself questions such as, "Do I know the security posture of the network on the other end of the tunnel?" The other site's security posture includes the development of an overall information security policy, use of firewalls, virus scanners, and other security measures. If the answer is "No, I have no idea what they are doing for security over there" or "Yes, I do know their posture, and it is really scary," then the VPN could end up opening a really big back door into your network. This exact same question should pop into your head if you are told to get a leased line or Frame Relay connection in place with another network. This is an especially serious issue in the modern business world, where companies are acquired rapidly and management demands that everyone get connected immediately.

The same concern needs to be raised about remote users. It is probably a safe assumption that all of those telecommuters, traveling managers, and sales reps are using their computers to connect to the Internet when they are away from the corporate office. In fact, they probably need to in order to VPN into the office. Even if you require that they dial in directly to your network's remote access server or a VPN service to gain access to your internal systems, you still need to be concerned about the fact that these users probably are connecting their computers to the Internet while they are away. If these systems are compromised by a Trojan horse or some other exploit and then they connect into your internal system, you might have accidentally provided a totally open hole for further infection or some other malicious activity. Worse yet, most Windows machines, even those intended for home users, now can be configured to act as gateways into the company's internal network.

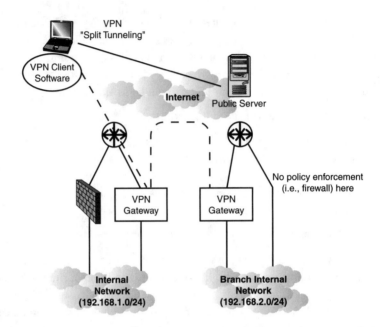

FIGURE 6.6
Bypassing firewall policy with VPNs.

As a general rule, we recommend that all of these access points be evaluated carefully with respect to their effect on your real security posture. It is a good idea to consider implementing a "remote access DMZ" that all of these pseudotrusted connections (VPNs, leased lines, Frame Relay circuits, and so on) must traverse before gaining access into your primary infrastructure. If firewalling this traffic is not feasible or desirable, then you should consider adopting the "trust, but verify" philosophy and employ a good network IDS to monitor this traffic.

The other important issue to consider when deploying a VPN is how to implement authentication. This is not so much an issue in site-to-site configurations because the VPN really is acting as a replacement for a permanent connection between two networks. That is not to say that an authentication mechanism will not be used; the problem is just fairly simple to solve. On the other hand, authentication is critical and more problematic in remote user configurations, where users outside your physical network generally will be granted highly privileged access to your internal systems.

VPN solutions commonly come with a native authentication facility so that you can specifically administer which users can access your network via the VPN. They also usually allow you to use some other authentication mechanism, such as a RADIUS server or Microsoft NT domain authentication. In most modern deployments, users still end up having to authenticate

Example Network Architectures and Case Studies

CHAPTER 6

169

6

EXAMPLE
NETWORK
ARCHITECTURES

twice to gain access remotely: once when they log onto their computers and again when they connect to the enterprise network over the VPN.

We also recommend the use of two-factor authentication for remote access. This has been described as needing two things—something you know and something you have—to be granted access. The "something you know" is usually a password or PIN, while the "something you have" is a smart card or token that is cryptographically synchronized to the corporate authentication system. So, all of our employees are issued small hardware tokens. Whenever we log into our corporate systems from home (or anywhere else outside the office), we need to type in our username, password, and the six-digit number from the token (which changes approximately once a minute).

Network IDS and Log Processing

Now that you have a good understanding of how to set up a pretty secure "front door" for Internet connections, you should consider installing some alarms, just to make sure that nothing gets through. Remember that firewalls don't stop all attacks; they simply apply rules to the traffic flow between network segments. So, installing some kind of network monitoring would be a prudent step. The monitoring functions that we will consider all fall under the category of intrusion-detection systems. At this point in your network design, there are four basic functions that IDS can perform:

- Looking at packets on the network to detect suspicious or malicious activity
- Monitoring file integrity and access of publicly accessible or critical internal servers
- Monitoring process/service activity on publicly accessible or critical internal servers
- Monitoring system log files from routers, firewalls, VPN gateways, publicly accessible servers, or any other log-generating device

Installing a network IDS (NIDS) on the outside of a firewall is analogous to putting cameras on the outside of a building. It provides the first opportunity to detect a threat to your network. You can see who is probing your network, and you usually can perform some useful trend analysis regarding potential threats to your network. For example, consider attacks such as Code Red and Nimda. Infected systems will scan nearby (in Internet address space terms) networks, looking for other Web servers to infect. An external NIDS can detect these scans of a network block.

On the downside, a NIDS placed on the outside of a firewall will see lots of "Internet noise" consisting of automated scanning activity from many amateur hackers and script kiddies, and it might become fairly demanding of your time if you decide to investigate every source. Deploying external sensors really becomes a choice that will be affected by your personal philosophy. Do you want to know about every remote system that knocks on your front door, or do you want to focus on detecting anything that breaches your defenses?

Although the usefulness of an external IDS can be debated, internal network sensors are clearly of value. As a general rule, we recommend that sensors be placed on the chokepoints introduced by connections to a firewall. Although these sensors still will generate false alarms, they provide an early indication that a security breach of some type has occurred. For example, most host and port scan traffic should be blocked by a properly configured firewall. If an internal network sensor detects scans of a protected server's TCP and UDP ports, the network administrator should quickly check to see whether the firewall rule set has been corrupted, either through some form of attack or, more likely, because someone has misconfigured the firewall.

Host-based IDS (HIDS) can be useful when deployed on DMZ platforms. Although the general function of network IDS sensors is fairly well understood by many networking professionals, the term *host sensor* could mean different things, depending on the product. As we discussed in the Chapter 10, "Watching the Wire: Intrusion-Detection Systems," HIDS products provide one or more of the following functions:

- Intercepts operating system calls to monitor specific user access to system resources
- Monitors the integrity of the file system, watching for modifications in attributes such as ownership and permissions to important system configuration or audit log files
- Checks for overall changes to key system files (such as the password file), usually through periodic checksum computations of the files' contents
- Parses log files for security-related events such as failed authentications

Each of these functions provides different security indicators, and which you use is, to some degree, a matter of choice. However, there are some things to consider in the selection process. For example, intercepting and analyzing every system call can have serious impacts on overall system performance. Similarly, computing a cryptographic hash of many files every second can drive CPU performance into the ground.

We have found that judicious monitoring of key configuration files and automatic parsing of system and application logs usually can be performed without significant impact on a server's performance. Log processing, in particular, can be a good supplement to a network IDS sensor when working in an encrypted environment (for example, with Web applications that employ SSL).

Similarly, log files from routers and firewalls can be monitored for security events using automated host-based parsing agents. This usually requires that a dedicated syslog server be installed in your network so that the network devices can export their logs to a platform that you can install additional software on.

Example Network Architectures and Case Studies

CHAPTER 6

171

6

EXAMPLE
NETWORK
ARCHITECTURES

You should note that our reference architecture does *not* include a logical path from any of the IDS components back to the router or firewall. Many IDS vendors will point to their capability to block suspicious traffic by automatically updating router ACLs or firewall rule sets. We strongly believe that this is not a wise feature to activate in your network because it effectively turns over control of your security policy to external forces. We already have discussed several denial-of-service attacks that can be enabled by this "feature," but the point is important enough to repeat. You should think very carefully about the potential benefits and drawbacks associated with allowing an IDS to take active measures against suspicious traffic.

Network-Management Issues

At this point, you are well on your way to building a secure interface to the Internet. The only big challenge left is managing what you have built.

On the technical side, care should be taken to limit who actually can modify the configuration of firewalls and routers. Access to these devices can be limited in several ways:

- Management can be enabled only through a physically attached console. Assuming that the network equipment is kept in a physically secure location, this is a pretty good way to limit access to management functions. The downside to this approach is that the administrator has to go to the device to modify it. This is not always feasible in a large enterprise network.

- A "back-rail" management network can be built that is dedicated to system-management traffic, such as telnet, SSH, and SNMP. Some network devices, such as routers, switches, load balancers, firewalls, and IDSs, supply Ethernet interfaces that are meant to be used solely for management. These interfaces could be plugged into a dedicated Ethernet switch with a management console so that only a few authorized users could configure to the devices. This can work well in a relatively small network, especially when all of the equipment is co-located within a few contiguous racks.

- A "management VLAN" can be configured in a modern switched infrastructure, providing the logical equivalent of the physical "back-rail." When properly configured, this solution can restrict both protocols and terminals that can be used to perform management functions. The primary drawbacks to this solution are the infrastructure requirements (you must have a VLAN-capable switched network) and the configuration complexity.

Although most workstations and servers now support the Secure Shell (SSH) protocol, this is still not a common feature on routers, switches, and other network devices. Although we always prefer SSH for remotely accessing any system, it is pretty common to have to use the telnet protocol to log onto a router.

Although SSH or telnet will be used to log onto the host platform for many UNIX-based firewalls, VPNs, and IDSs, the actual security applications might provide their own secure management protocol. Care should be taken to ensure that firewall rule sets allow the appropriate management protocols to be passed to the devices. These rules should be as restrictive as possible, allowing only authorized systems to access management interfaces.

Finally, the Simple Network Management Protocol (SNMP) very commonly is used in enterprise networks for both monitoring and configuring many devices in a campus. This is a very powerful capability and can be a requirement for large networks. We have worked with both ISPs and Web-hosting companies that have hundreds of routers and switches in their networks. It would be virtually impossible to maintain these infrastructures without the capabilities provided by SNMP. Unfortunately, the most widely deployed version of this protocol, SNMPv2, is not very secure at all, with authentication being simple, plain-text passwords. The problem only gets worse when you consider that many, many enterprises never change the default passwords associated with querying and configuring remote devices. The seemingly easy answer is to simply upgrade to the more secure SNMPv3. This can be quite problematic because, even if your management station "speaks" SNMPv3, many of your infrastructure devices might not. You should contact your vendors to check on the availability of firmware and software upgrades that add this capability. Even if your systems can be upgraded, this will not likely be a trivial rollout.

From a procedural perspective, we have found that the biggest threat for compromising the interface to the Internet is lack of process and configuration control mechanisms. Most enterprise-quality firewalls are pretty secure, in that vulnerabilities have been identified and patched; however, at the end of the day, the protection that the firewall provides is only as good as the rule set loaded into it.

Within the DMZs, it is critical that a process be in place to ensure that all systems are kept up-to-date on their OSes and application patches, especially those associated with security vulnerabilities. Furthermore, although the firewall *should* keep packets associated with unused services out of the DMZs, it is a very good idea to disable all unnecessary network services on these systems. For example, if you never intend to telnet into a system because you have decided to use SSH, then the telnet service should not be running on that system.

Internal Links and Threats

Now that you have locked down the access to the network from the Internet and the publicly accessible servers in tour DMZs are protected to the best of your ability, you can take a look at security architectures for the internal network. We will not attempt to cover every detail of UNIX and Microsoft network architectures (such as NT domain design) because many other texts cover these subjects. Instead, we will focus on a few key security concepts that should be considered in the design of the internal infrastructure.

Threats on the Inside

Many organizations focus their security architecture with the "hacker" threat in mind. Although this is a necessary consideration, it is not sufficient on its own to provide the security-in-depth that most enterprises really require. Again, the goal of a network design should be to protect critical information from whatever threats exist against it. Let's begin by reviewing some of the threats that can arise inside the network:

- **Password sniffers**—Any insider who wants to eavesdrop on network communications has an immediate advantage over the external hacker because he is given routine access to the internal infrastructure. Depending on the design of the network (for example, hubs vs. switched), it is easy for any user to turn his computer into a packet sniffer and capture other users' passwords or other information.

- **Information theft**—Insider access to information that there is no legitimate need for can be a big concern in an enterprise environment. For example, large financial institutions do a lot of mergers and acquisitions work. The details of these deals usually are held very private, and they can be very valuable to someone who wants to make a lot of money through insider trading on the stock market.

- **Information manipulation**—Similarly, an insider can profit through manipulation of corporate data. This is exemplified by the recent case in which several employees of a very well-known networking company were caught manipulating the stock option distributions, with the intent of making a considerable profit for themselves.

- **Accidental compromises**—Many statistics are thrown stating that a large percentage (50–90%) of compromises are from insiders. The numbers are hard to determine exactly, but we agree with the general statement. The main point that often does not get mentioned is that many of these compromises are unintentional. A major example of this is a Trojan horse infection, which occurs when uneducated users execute attachments with malicious code in them.

Security via Switched Infrastructure

Although many older Ethernet networks were built using either coaxial cable or with twisted-pair wire and hubs, most new networks are built using Layer 2 switches. The difference between these two implementations is very significant. Coax cable is, by nature, a broadcast medium. If one device transmits a packet, every other device gets to hear it. Hubs are not any different; they are simply repeaters that enable network designers to use a more convenient type of cabling. On the other hand, switches actually look at Ethernet addresses of packets and forward them to the intended recipient. This allows many pairs of computers to operate at the full capacity of the switch instead of having to compete for access to the shared bandwidth of coax cables or hubs. This is illustrated in Figure 6.7.

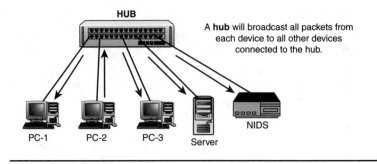

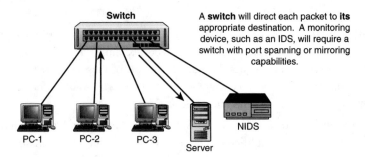

FIGURE 6.7

Switched networks.

Switching not only provides more efficient use of resources by providing much more effective bandwidth to users, but it also has an important security benefit. The capability to "sniff" a network is extremely limited in a switching environment because the only packets that any specific host can observe are those originating from and destined to the local interface, as well as any broadcast traffic. Although it still might be possible to extract some useful information from the network, the possibilities are significantly reduced.

As we discussed in Chapter 10, switched infrastructures do have one seminegative consequence: It is much more difficult for authorized monitoring to be performed. Fortunately, modern enterprise-quality switches usually provide a "spanning" or "mirroring" capability that allows for the packets of individual or multiple interfaces to be copied to another interface port for purposes of passive monitoring. This allows a network designer to use network analyzers, remote monitor (RMON) probes or IDSs as desired.

Example Network Architectures and Case Studies

CHAPTER 6

175

6

EXAMPLE
NETWORK
ARCHITECTURES

Many people raise the concern that it is seems tough to mirror multiple 100Mbps interfaces to another single 100Mbps interface. Although technically this is true, practically, it all depends on which interfaces are being monitored. Unless workstation users are running high-speed network applications (such as streaming video), the odds are good that few users are using anything near the actual capacity of their network links. On the other hand, combining all of the feeds from a big "server farm" into one monitoring port probably would be a bad idea. We highly recommend that you discuss your packet-mirroring requirements with your vendor (preferably an engineer from the company) and ask very specific questions concerning your operational needs.

Security via VLANs

Switching provides significant security from an eavesdropping perspective, but it does not in any way limit where a user can go on the network. Switches simply make more efficient use of the available bandwidth. In an Ethernet environment, the same basic rules still apply for defining a local area network. That is, the local network is defined by the Layer 2 broadcast domain, which typically is constrained to a physical network.

Virtual LANs remove the physical device restrictions and allow the administrator of a switch to distribute logical LANs across a larger infrastructure. For example, if the marketing group is spread between two buildings on a campus and you want to put them on the same logical LAN, you could configure the switches in the two buildings to talk to each other and treat specific interfaces on each device like they are on a common LAN. Broadcast packets from a computer in one building will be forwarded to the switch in the other building and transmitted to the interfaces that are a part of the virtual LAN, or VLAN. From a network perspective, these computers all appear to be on a single LAN. This VLAN now can be connected to other physical or virtual LANs through IP routers, and all the normal access-control mechanisms can be employed to restrict traffic in and out of the Marketing group.

VLAN identification is handled inside each vendor's switch however the vendors see fit; however, it would be nice if the various switches could interoperate and VLANs could be defined across a multivendor environment. The IEEE VLAN specification (IEEE 802.1Q) defines a new encapsulation protocol that is used between physical switches so that devices on a common VLAN can be connected to different physical systems. This encapsulation protocol adds a new header to a packet that identifies the packet's member VLAN. This is what allows VLANs to span multiple devices in an enterprise network. A simple VLAN architecture is illustrated in Figure 6.8.

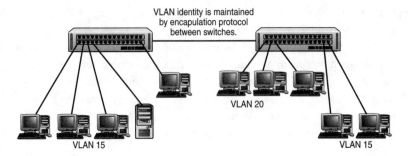

FIGURE 6.8

Virtual LANs (VLANs).

VLANs can be used to segment a large enterprise switch into independent LANs. For example, a large switch could be used to implement two LANs—one for the users and one to serve as a "back rail" for managing network devices. The network administrator would simply log onto the switch and tell it which ports were reserved for the "user LAN" and which ones were for the "management LAN." These two VLANs could be kept totally isolated from each other, or they could be allowed to communicate through a router. It should be noted that the isolation of these two VLANs is strictly due to the fact that the switch was configured to keep the two networks' broadcast packets away from each other. *It is certainly possible to make a mistake in the configuration and lose this isolation.*

Networking vendors have gotten pretty creative with VLANs in the past couple of years. Given the right switch, it is now possible to define VLANs based on several criteria:

- Physical interface on the switch
- Ethernet address (by host, no matter which physical port it is plugged into)
- IP address
- TCP/UDP port number

Furthermore, some products allow for the definition of access control lists (ACLs) on the switches. These ACLs are just like the packet filters that we have discussed in conjunction with routers, except that now they are associated with VLANs. Although they are not as powerful as a firewall, the switch-based ACLs can be used to limit the type of traffic that a user can inject into the network. For example, if you do not want casual users to have access to the payroll server, you could define an ACL that blocks traffic to that IP address at the switch.

So, given a modern VLAN-cable switch, the network engineer has quite a bit of freedom to assign systems (and the users on those systems) into logical groups and to apply specific security polices to those systems.

The most advanced security solutions involving VLANs that are coming onto the market today involve dynamic VLAN assignment based on user authentication or role-based network access. The general philosophy of this type of architecture is that most users have a role within an organization and that their need to access network services is based upon that role. Examples of roles in an organization might include these:

- System/network administrator
- Executive/management
- Sales
- HR
- Developer
- Visitor

Each of these types of users might have different needs from the network. Obviously, system and network administrators need access to management interfaces on routers and switches, but there is no legitimate reason for someone from the sales team to ever do this. On the other end of the spectrum, a visitor on the network might be allowed only to surf the Internet while logged onto your systems.

This capability is really more of an authentication and management problem than a technical VLAN problem. We have established that it is possible to define VLANs administratively, through either a console connection or some kind of graphical interface. The role-based security simply required the capability to automatically assign a user to the correct VLAN when he connects to your system. Recent IEEE activity that supports this function has resulted in the 802.1x standard, which defines an authentication protocol that can be used to authenticate with a switch.

An example of one vendor's solution is illustrated in Figure 6.9. In this solution, users log onto their local workstations. At this point, the workstation passes the credentials to the switch using the 802.1x protocol. Note that the switch initially is configured to pass no other traffic from the user. The switch then passes the user's credentials to an authentication server (RADIUS, Windows Domain Server, and so on) and waits for the reply, which will indicate whether the user is allowed onto the network, and, if so, that user's role within the network. The switch uses the role information to determine which VLAN the user should be placed in, meaning that any ACLs associated with that VLAN will be applied to the user's traffic as it enters the network infrastructure. The glue that ties all of this together is a management system that provides for the role and VLAN configuration.

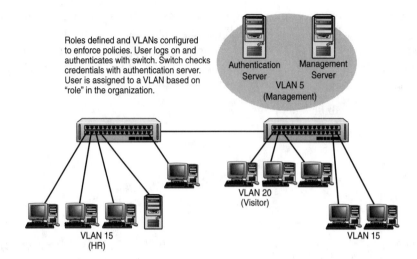

Roles defined and VLANs configured to enforce policies. User logs on and authenticates with switch. Switch checks credentials with authentication server. User is assigned to a VLAN based on "role" in the organization.

Authentication Server   Management Server
VLAN 5 (Management)

VLAN 20 (Visitor)

VLAN 15 (HR)

VLAN 15

FIGURE 6.9
Role-based VLAN assignment.

It should be noted that switches that support VLAN often allow you to configure VLAN mirrors. This enables you to place network analyzers, IDSs, or any other network-monitoring device on the logical networks. Of course, for this to work properly, you should have a feel for the average traffic loads on the VLAN because it might not be possible to squeeze the data from all the VLAN members into a single monitoring interface. A solution to this problem is to employ a higher-speed interface, such as a gigabit Ethernet card, for the monitoring device.

Security and Wireless Networks

One increasingly common technology that is being deployed in networks is wireless LANs. Wireless technologies are great for mobility but can be a nightmare for security, for two reasons:

- Without good encryption (and key management), just about anyone can "sniff" your network.

- Without robust authentication, it can be quite easy for an outsider to join your network.

It is actually quite easy to compromise an otherwise secure network that employs wireless in its internal infrastructure. We know of one informal test that was performed in the summer of 2001 in downtown San Francisco, in which a team drove around the city with a wireless system—a technique that recently has been dubbed "war driving." The team reported that it was able to pick up approximately 100 different networks, half of which were not using any form of encryption.

Example Network Architectures and Case Studies

Chapter 6

179

6

**EXAMPLE
NETWORK
ARCHITECTURES**

The problems only get worse: Even the networks that were using encryption might have had a bit too much of a false sense of security. The current industry standard for wireless encryption is a protocol called Wired Equivalent Privacy, or WEP, which is part of the IEEE 802.11 standard. Unfortunately, analysis has revealed that there is a fundamental vulnerability in the implementation of WEP: It does not take all that long for the same key stream to be used to encrypt data. Without going into the theory of cryptoanalysis and the details of the WEP attack, we will simply say that this is a bad thing and that the security industry has not just proven but also demonstrated that WEP-encrypted data can be broken. In fact, an open-source program called AirSnort is now available that allows a user with a wireless interface card to collect 802.11 wireless traffic. This program also includes the code necessary to "break" the traffic if it is encrypted and enough data is collected.

Although observation of traffic is bad, the capability to insert traffic into a network is even worse, especially if it is your internal network. This problem usually arises from the age-old problem of not changing default values, such as network names, in the system configuration.

In the end, each network designer will have to balance the benefits of a wireless infrastructure with the potential security problems. We are not trying to say that wireless is bad—it could be the perfect solution for your operational requirements. Until the security issues associated with the current generation of wireless products are resolved, you should consider several solutions and policies:

- Employ VPN technology in conjunction with your WLAN so that a more secure encryption and authentication algorithm (such as IPSec) can be used.

- Limit the use of WLANs to less critical user groups.

- Employ filtering or a firewall at the wireless access point (the connection from the wireless terminal into your wired infrastructure).

- Never allow system management traffic to be passed over the wireless LAN.

- Be sure that any default values required for a wireless device to connect to the access point are changed.

Security and Dial-Up Modems

One potential nightmare for network designers with any significant security requirements is the problem of uncontrolled dial-up modems in the internal network. These modems are commonly delivered as standard equipment in desktop and laptop computers, and it is very likely that your users will have them. Unfortunately, they represent many potential back doors into your private network that completely bypass all of your border safeguards.

If you are providing access to the Internet through corporate resources, there is really no reason for the vast majority of your users to be "dialing out." Furthermore, assuming that you have provided a dial-in capability for legitimate users, there is certainly no need for anyone to be allowing outsiders to call their computers.

Uncontrolled modems can be a tough problem. One seemingly easy solution is to simply purchase workstations without analog modems in them; however, this might not be a very practical plan. Alternatively, this could be a place where your security policy and awareness training comes into play. Users should understand that the use of personal modems in your network is prohibited and that they should contact the IT staff if their communication needs are not being satisfied by your current infrastructure.

Many enterprises conduct penetration testing of their networks, with the tests performed by internal security staff or a contracted security auditing company. These "pen tests" usually include all sorts of IP network scans and server-exploitation tests. This is a good time to look for unauthorized and misconfigured modems by employing a war-dialer that will exhaustively call every phone number in a specified range looking for answering modems.

Security Monitoring Inside the Network

The same intrusion-detection technologies that can be used to detect security breaches at your border with the Internet can be used to monitor your internal systems. However, IDS deployment issues can be a bit more challenging inside the network.

Network sensors can be installed in one of several places, depending on the design of the network. Obviously, if your network is still built with hubs, then network monitoring is easy—just plug the sensor into an open port. On the other hand, if you have a switched infrastructure, things can get a little complicated. If there are chokepoints between users and critical information servers, then a mirrored port or network tap can be configured so that traffic in and out of the servers can be monitored. For example, servers can be connected to a dedicated switch with a single interface connecting the server switch to a large workgroup switch. In this case, all of the user-to-server traffic could end up being transported over a single high-speed uplink connection that could be monitored. On the other hand, if the network is "flat," meaning that the workstations and servers all are configured as peers on the switch, monitoring can be a bit more problematic. When we discussed port and VLAN mirroring earlier in this chapter, we mentioned that, as long as the traffic loads "added up," many systems could be aggregated and monitored with one network sensor.

On the other hand, if you have a switched infrastructure that doesn't support any kind of native packet monitoring, your choices get a bit more difficult. One option is simply to not do any internal monitoring. If this is not acceptable, then a network tap can be inserted in the middle of Ethernet cables that carry critical information or act as chokepoints in the network.

Workstation-Management Issues

The final challenge in designing a secure internal network is more procedural than technical. Although this chapter focuses on network infrastructure, no secure architecture can be built without considering the implications in the choice of desktop operating systems. Most system administrators have processes in place to ensure that servers and other critical systems are updated regularly with operating system and application patches, especially those that are related to documented security vulnerabilities.

Keeping on top of workstation updates can be a bigger issue. The importance of this though can be illustrated by recalling the Nimda virus. Nimda propagated in several ways:

- Via Trojan'ed email attachments, with infection occurring if a user opened the attachment or if the message was "previewed" in a vulnerable version of Microsoft Outlook. The former infection mechanism actually relied on a vulnerability in Microsoft's Internet Explorer (MSIE) rendering library, which Outlook also used.

- Via a JavaScript embedded in the Web pages of infected Web servers. In this case, a vulnerable version of MSIE would allow the virus to be uploaded and executed on the browsing computer.

- Via common IIS Web server vulnerabilities (such as directory traversal and UNICODE attacks).

All of these vulnerabilities had been previously documented, and vendor patches had been available for some time. The important point here is that the first two propagation methods took advantage of unpatched user workstations, emphasizing the need to keep both servers and user systems patched at all times.

Given the fact that Microsoft is the dominant desktop operating system vendor, it is worth exploring the options that a system administrator has in this area. First, to be blunt, Windows 9x has no place in a secure network. Period. This operating system is intended for the home consumer and does not provide the management, security, and auditing functions required for a secure network. On the other hand, many of these security-oriented features are built into Windows NT, Windows 2000, and the UNIX variants.

Windows NT provides support for managing the application environment of user desktops through the System Management Services (SMS); however, in practice, this can require quite a bit of scripting or programming background, especially for non–Microsoft Installer Package (MSI) programs. Windows 2000 and Windows XP make full use of the Active Directory server, which supports the addition and removal of MSI programs. Other options include the use of start-up scripts for Windows 2000 and Windows XP or logon scripts, which also support Windows NT.

Small Office/Home Office (SOHO)

It is commonly said that small businesses are the lifeblood of the economy. Unfortunately, the small office/home office (SOHO) network community often is overlooked by the information security world. These companies and organizations tend to have very limited IT budgets and can afford neither large IT staffs nor significant expenses for "extras" such as IDS.

It also should be noted that the security of SOHO networks is important to many larger enterprise networks because these networks often are allowed to connect into enterprise networks through VPN connections, and these connections often bypass the primary security policy enforcement performed by firewalls. This is especially true of telecommuters, more of whom are building small home networks with permanent DSL or cable modem connections to the Internet. Therefore, the security posture of the SOHO network can directly impact the security of the remote enterprise network.

Fortunately, the operational requirements of the typical SOHO network are significantly less complex than those of a large enterprise network. The number of users is small, and there are not many connections into the network other that the Internet. A typical SOHO network is illustrated in Figure 6.10.

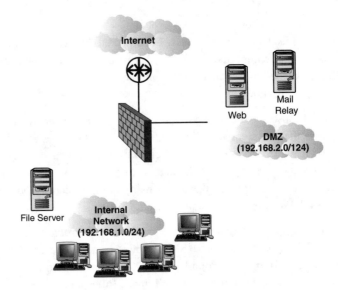

FIGURE 6.10

The SOHO network.

Example Network Architectures and Case Studies

CHAPTER 6

183

6

**EXAMPLE
NETWORK
ARCHITECTURES**

These networks might have a handful of computers on a small switch or hub infrastructure. There could be an internal file server or mail server and perhaps a Web server that is accessible to the outside world. In many cases, the ISP handles any DNS requirements. Given that most SOHO installations do not have the luxury of a dedicated system administrator and certainly do not have a dedicated security function, there are a few basic security recommendations for this type of network:

- Install a good low-cost appliance firewall with a default ruleset that implements address translation for the internal network, allows all outbound traffic, and has simple rules for any inbound traffic. Note that extremely low-cost appliances often suffer from reliability problems.

- Utilize commercial log file analysis software to review the firewall logs. Many packages can support both business analysis (to justify the cost of purchase) and security analysis. This will at least give you a basic view into the types of traffic that are flowing into and out of your network (and produce pretty pie charts for management).

- Install virus-scanning software on all desktops with an automatic virus signature update capability, and make sure that the signatures update without requirements for user intervention. If you have your own mail server or file server, install virus scanning on these platforms as well.

- Make sure that your users receive at least some basic education on good security practices, such as how to create a good password (don't use user names as passwords, for example), the dangers of opening unsolicited attachments, not always clicking Yes to every dialog box that's presented to them, and so on.

- Implement a basic security policy that addresses privacy and monitoring issues, user expectations, data backup, and other policy areas that affect the livelihood of your business and business processes.

By implementing a small set of high-value information security practices, a small or medium-sized business can dramatically reduce its exposure to risks (20% of the work gets you 80% of the coverage) without spending a lot of money or putting themselves under a huge administrative burden.

Web Sites

So far, we have glossed over the security architectures for Web sites, simply indicating that any publicly accessible servers, including Web servers, should be placed in a DMZ with tight firewall rules regulating access to the systems. Depending on the operational needs of the Web server, the architecture can get a bit more complex.

Outsourced Web Hosting

The first issue to consider is whether your public Web servers should even be maintained in your network. Many organizations choose to outsource their Web servers, deploying them in dedicated Web-hosting facilities that provide ample bandwidth and robust facilities (such as redundant power grids, backup diesel generators, laser smoke detectors, FM-200 fire suppression, and so on) and physical security.

In some cases, Web-hosting companies simply provide a local 100Mbps Ethernet connection that connects you to their high-speed Internet backbones and some rack space for your servers and any other equipment. Note that the 100Mbps connection could be rate-limited per your service-level agreement. This leaves you with the responsibility for security. This is a responsibility that you should take seriously, not only for the protection of your data, but also for the protection of your access to the Internet. We work closely with one particular ISP that is fairly representative of many service providers and Web-hosting companies. If the company detects that one of its clients is infected with any kind of aggressively spreading virus, it simply administratively disables that client's access to the Internet to protect other clients. This is particularly important to the provider because many of the more recent viruses (including Code Red and Nimda) focus their attention on finding "nearby" hosts to infect.

Other Web-hosting service providers might offer security services as part of their normal offerings or as a la carte features that you may choose from. Many service providers offer firewalls, intrusion detection, and periodic vulnerability scanning for additional fees. If you choose to outsource your Web site or host it in a commercial facility these services could be of value to you.

Content Delivery Sites

Many smaller organizations and most personal Web sites offer static content to remote users. In these cases, the network design is relatively straightforward. The server(s) should be placed behind a firewall capable of supporting controlled inbound connections to a DMZ. Any worthwhile enterprise firewall will support this feature. Although it is technically possible to use the cheapest of the consumer-grade firewalls, this is not recommended. Most of these devices provide a "DMZ" capability; however, this typically is implemented by simply allowing the administrator to designate an IP address in the protected network to be the "DMZ computer." The firewall then allows outside computers to connect to this host. Unfortunately, the DMZ computer is still in the same network as the other "protected" computers, so if it is compromised, there is nothing to stop the hacked machine from connecting to other computers in the network.

For content-delivery sites, the firewall should be configured to allow inbound connections on the HTTP port you are using. This is usually TCP port 80, although it is possible to change the listening port of most Web servers. If you do reassign the Web server port, your users will have to specify the new port in their URLs. For example, if the Acme Corporation decided to use port 8000, users in the know would type the following URL into their Web browsers: `http://www.acme.com:8000/`.

Similarly, if you want to add some confidentiality to your Web site, Secure Socket Layer (SSL) could be used to encrypt the Web traffic. The default port for SSL is TCP port 443. Web browsers will call this port if the URL specifies Secure HTTP (https) in the protocol field, as in the following example: `https://www.acme.com`.

After these rules are configured, anyone will be able to get to the Web pages on this server. Of course, more granular rules could be loaded into the firewall to narrow the IP addresses or networks that could connect to the site. If any other services are required, such as a DNS server for resolving `www.acme.com` into the host server's IP address, then the firewall would have to allow these services in as well.

Additional firewall rules will be required to allow for remote system management of the servers and updating of content from only trusted hosts. Whenever possible, Secure Shell (TCP port 22) should be used in lieu of telnet (TCP port 23) for both system administration and content updating.

Remember that installing the firewall does not relive the system administrator of his duties of patching the server's operating system or application code. Furthermore, a mechanism should be put in place for reviewing the audit logs produced by the Web server(s). The major HTTP servers (such as Apache and Microsoft IIS) produce logs that detail all of the legitimate connections and any errors that might have occurred. Although the connection logs might be very interesting from a business analysis perspective (for example, who is coming to your site and which content is most popular), the server failures will be the most interesting for security purposes. Attempts to access Web pages and CGI-BINs that don't exist on your system should be considered quite suspicious.

Attacks on the Web server can be detected in one of two ways. A good network sensor with a healthy inventory of Web attack signatures will detect documented attacks and suspicious formatting of HTTP traffic as it passes by the sensor on its way to the server. Similarly, a host sensor running on the server might detect attacks as it monitors the audit logs, looking for similar attack indicators in the logged URLs. The host sensor could be particularly valuable if the Web pages are served using SSL because the URLs will be encrypted on the network, rendering the network sensor quite ineffective. Sensors that can be customized for a specific site can be highly effective in detecting unusual requests from the outside world.

Sites that employ SSL extensively often use a dedicated SSL accelerator to handle the computationally intensive encryption and decryptions algorithms. This device logically sits "in front of" the Web servers. One additional advantage to this is that a network IDS sensor now has a place where it can view the plain-text Web traffic.

E-Commerce Sites

More advanced Web sites serve up dynamic data and have interaction with databases and other back-end applications. E-commerce sites are an obvious example of this. A typical e-commerce site provides a Web interface into a product or service catalog. These sites also must maintain client records, including personal information and credit card numbers, which are common targets for hackers (this data is great for blackmailing or embarrassing the site owners, or for profiteering from charging a few dollars to thousands of credit cards). Finally, some kind of "shopping cart" application is usually present to keep track of a client's product selection and handle the appropriate billing.

So, e-commerce sites require several new functions above and beyond those required for a simple content delivery site:

- Authentication software
- Relational databases
- Shopping cart software
- Advanced content management

You should follow several rules when building these kinds of sites. First, using private addresses in the DMZ is a good idea because it allows you to easily scale to higher capacity through the use of a site load-balancing system. Additionally, the database and any other processing systems that are required for the Web application can be assigned these nonroutable IP addresses so that they cannot be directly addressed from the Internet. Finally, the use of network address translation (NAT) protects you from any chance of a closed-circuit failure of the firewall.

Most serious Web applications with any kind of critical database system and high level of traffic will dual-home their Web servers and create a back rail on which the database and application servers sit. A common misconception shared by many Web administrators is that this dual-homed architecture provides a level of security for the database and application servers (which are the ones that typically have the credit card or privacy information). What they don't realize is that the Web server is the most likely server to be compromised by a hacker because it is exposed to the Internet. When the server is compromised, the back-rail interface becomes a direct conduit into the other back-end servers, thereby circumventing the security of the firewall. To truly secure your back-end systems, you need either a firewall or an application proxy between them and the Web servers! This type of network configuration is illustrated in Figure 6.11. The same holds true for the administrative connections to the Web servers and database

Example Network Architectures and Case Studies

CHAPTER 6

187

6

EXAMPLE
NETWORK
ARCHITECTURES

or application servers. You might have a back-end connection to allow your developers or third-party content providers to update information, or to let your administrators connect to the systems. These represent additional connections into your corporate network and so also should be regulated, by either a firewall or strict router ACLs.

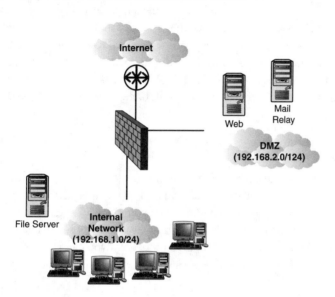

FIGURE 6.11

An e-commerce site.

Given the dynamic nature of Web server content and applications, the test environment should be installed on a separate DMZ to support configuration control and reduce security concerns. Many times, system security patches lag behind those of production systems, and application security settings and security procedures are fairly lax for these systems because of the access needs of developers. To reduce the chance of a production machine becoming a hacker's direct line into your network, always treat test environments as untrusted network with regard to your corporate infrastructure.

Another concern is that many e-commerce sites are built using a common physical-switching infrastructure that is segmented into VLANs. Many times, the Internet connection, DMZ, back rail, firewall interfaces, and development LAN all share the same physical switch, even though they are on different VLANs. This is big concern because it means that if the switch is compromised, the entire security infrastructure collapses. We often recommend that at least the router's internal interface and the firewall's external interfaces use a physically separate switch or hub to mitigate this concern. Other segments might warrant this level of separation as well, depending upon the criticality of the data being protected.

In a nutshell, the very nature of e-commerce sites means that they have significant exposure to everyone on the Internet, both legitimate users and hackers. Furthermore, they maintain information not just private to the corporation, but private to clients and customers, and this can offer significant monetary incentives to hackers to break into them. In many cases, e-commerce site information is stolen and then "sold" back to the site as blackmail or extortion (although the hackers like to call them "security consulting" fees). The prevalence of credit card and privacy information on these sites makes them prime targets. Given that new regulations such as HIPAA and Grahmm-Leach Bliley (for the health care and banking industries, respectively) will levy heavy fines upon organizations that don't sufficiently protect their infrastructure, it is a true responsibility of the IT professional and corporate management to address security in a substantial manner.

Summary

This book has delved into the details of many topics related to Internet security. In this chapter, we have attempted to bring together the pieces, tie them together with both wired and wireless infrastructures, and deliver a secure computing and communication environment connected to the Internet. Packet access control (firewalls and ACLs), network segmentation, secure remote access, and security monitoring are all important tools that you can use, but we also have shown how switched infrastructures with advanced VLAN management can provide significant security benefits.

It should be clear by now that security cannot be an afterthought in the design of a network. Assuming that there is anything of any value on a network, security must be addressed head on in the design phase.

If you are starting with a fresh piece of paper, then you should have some good ideas on how to use your operational business requirements to implement the appropriate technical and procedural mechanisms necessary to safeguard your information and operations. On the other hand, if your network has been running for years, you now should have some good ideas on how to notch up your security posture. A good place to start is locking down your connection to the Internet and then tracking down all the "hidden" connections to the outside world that you might not have considered in the past. When the front door, and any obvious back doors, are taken care of, you can move into the core of your network and supplement or transition your existing systems. At the end of the day, you have to remember that security is a process, and you have to start that process somewhere.

Operating System and Server Software Issues

IN THIS CHAPTER

The proper configuration of operating systems and software is arguably the most important aspect of Internet site security. Although access-point control mechanisms such as firewalls and router access control lists offer a level of protection against attack, these mechanisms are generally ignorant of server-side issues and can deny only specific types of network traffic. For instance, a firewall that blocks all but HTTP (port 80) traffic to a Web server still lets the entire Internet connect via this port and is hardly much of a security measure if the Web server's operating system and application isn't effectively secured.

Additionally, at some point, user-defined data will be processed by an individual system, and this is where everything could go horribly wrong. Using the previous example, the Web server will, by definition, parse the URLs presented to it. If such a URL contains "suspect" data the firewall, it will do little to eliminate it. At the operating system level, no firewall on the market can protect against a poorly configured operating system that allows a world-readable /etc/shadow (password) file, and it is unlikely that a router ACL will stop a locally exploited buffer overrun.

Without addressing the security of the underlying operating systems and applications, devices such as firewalls, IDS, and virus scanners are only postponing the inevitable. To address these issues, this chapter presents the technical security issues of operating systems and installed software. This will include not only the obvious, such as Web servers, but also remote administration, file transfer, and interface applications.

We will explain the ways in which Windows NT, Windows 2000, and Linux take security into consideration. Unfortunately, there is no "right way" to configure a system because each system must be set up for the environment in which it will operate. A service that might be unnecessary for a server running in a Web farm (such as the name service) might be critical in another environment (such as on a system that functions as a nameserver!). The goal of this chapter is to enable you, the administrator, to make informed decisions about what is acceptable risk and how to better tune your system for your environment. That being said, we also will provide suggestions and recommendations based on real-world experience and industry best practices, giving you some insight into the venerable question, "What is everyone else doing?"

Of course, there is a seemingly endless number of operating systems in use today, and discussing the security components of UNIX variants would result in an encyclopedic work. However, the general security concepts are similar for many operating system flavors, and because our space is limited, we have chosen to focus on just a few of the more popular operating systems in widespread use.

Even before we can present specific configuration examples for this limited set of operating systems, we first must establish a base understanding of operating system internals and vocabulary. This section provides an overview of the core concepts for a few of the popular operating systems, including Windows NT-based operating systems (including Windows 2000), the common Linux distributions, and Sun's Solaris operating system. Although that's hardly a superset of all the OSes in use today (not counting FreeBSD, OpenBSD, HPUX, AIX, to name just a few), we will introduce the core concepts that are common to most OSes.

Windows NT and 2000 Security Concepts

At the core of Windows NT and Windows 2000 internal security management is the security subsystem. The components of this system are responsible for permitting or denying access to operating system objects, such as files or applications, based on two factors: the credentials of the requesting process and the object's access control list. An example of the former is a user in the Administrator group, and an example of the latter is a file that is readable by everyone but modifiable only by administrators. Several components execute under the umbrella of the security subsystem (and execute as a part of lsass.exe, which you've likely seen and wondered about in the Task Manager), including logon authentication and management (both local system and network logons), local security policy enforcement, the Security Accounts Manager (or SAM), and, for some reason known only to Microsoft, the Secure Sockets Layer (SSL) implementation.

Many texts delve into the details of the security subsystem, but for our purposes, it will suffice to discuss the major aspects of how NT handles security and shed some light on the more arcane topics. The next few sections provide an overview of the mechanisms responsible for handling the NT concept of security.

Authentication, Access Tokens, and Security Identifiers

The first topic that we will review is that of authentication and how Windows NT uses authentication to allow or disallow access to particular objects. In Windows, user logons are authenticated based on either local system accounts (accounts that are specific to the local machine, such as a local workstations) or via a network's domain controller (which apply to all machines that are part of that domain). Logons do not have to be executed by a user sitting at a workstation (interactive logons), but they also can be accomplished by applications that log themselves on to execute with the permissions of a specific user (for example, a tape backup batch job or a service such as an ftp server). In the vast majority of Windows installations, authentication is password-based, although certificate-based (PKI) and smart-card based authentication also are available (but are far more rare).

After a successful logon, the user (or process) is granted an access token that then is supplied each time a process executing on the user's behalf requests system resources. This allows the user to start applications that access network resources without explicitly authenticating each time. Access tokens are composed of a security identifier (SID) that uniquely identifies the user, a SID identifying each group to which the user belongs (such as the Administrator group, the Everyone group, and so on), a list of privileges that the user has been granted, and a default discretionary access control list[1]. These three components are key to the Windows access-control mechanism because they uniquely identify a user, enumerate the group that the user belongs to, and define the privileges that the user can exercise. Whenever a user (or any thread within a process) attempts to access an object, his access token is checked to determine whether that user is allowed to perform a function on that object.

The token assigned at login is the user's primary access token. Depending on the local and domain security policy, a user (or process) might be capable of requesting an impersonation token. With an impersonation token, a process or thread can be executed with the credentials of whichever user is described by the token's user SID. Why allow a user (or, more specifically, a user's process) to pretend to be someone else? Ostensibly, this is to enable a server process to execute with the (presumably) lesser privileges of a client requesting services. However, there is no restriction forcing impersonation to happen only when downgrading the privilege level; whether a token is allowed to be duplicated (and thus impersonated) is determined only by the privileges assigned to that token. Tokens can be freely copied from RPC clients, named pipe clients, or logged-in users, all depending on the DACL associated with the token.

Object Access Control Lists

Each *protected* object within the operating system contains an ACL made up of two sections: the discretionary access control list (DACL) and the system access control list (SACL). A Windows "object" could be anything from a specific thread executing within a process to a file in the NT File System. The default DACL and SACL that are applied when new objects are created are inherited from the parent object. For instance, in the default Windows NT installation, the C:\ directory has neither a DACL nor a SACL assigned. So, any new files or directories created under C:\ will have no DACL or SACL, by default. When an object lacks a DACL, full access to Everyone is implicitly granted. When an object lacks a SACL, all audit functionality is disabled. This is no better than using the FAT file system, which offers neither DACLs nor SACLs. Our example talks about files and directories, but remember that the same methodology applies to any object.

When an object has been explicitly given a DACL, access control is enabled. Access control is defined by a list of access control entries (ACEs). ACEs are a combination of a "type" (either allow or deny), a "trustee" (a user or a group described by a SID) and a "right." Rights can be specified as one or more of the following:

- The right to read the data within the object in its entirety
- The right to write to the object
- The right to execute the object
- The right to delete the object

- The right to read the object's security descriptor, although not the object's SACL
- The right to read from or write to the object's SACL
- The right to use the object in synchronization
- The right to modify the object's DACL
- The right to change the owner of an object

Not all objects support all rights, and different objects respond differently to different rights. For example, if a file contains the execute right, that file can be executed as an application. If a directory has the execute right, it means that files within that directory can be executed (in case of a conflict in this situation, rights assigned to the directory win).

When a user attempts to access an object, the operating system checks sequentially through the ACE and then applies the first matching entry. If no matching entry is found, access is implicitly denied. (Consider Figure 7.1.)

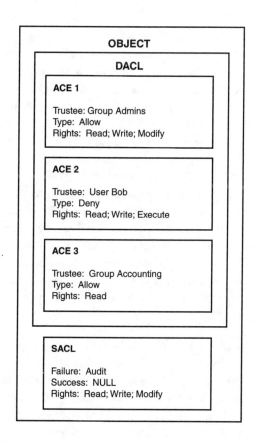

FIGURE 7.1

An example SACL and DACL attached to an object.

In this example, we see that the SACL defines the audit policy on the object, specifying how various events (successful or failed read attempts, successful or failed write attempts, and so on) are logged. In this way, it is necessary to explicitly deny access to a protected object only in cases such as allowing access to a particular group but denying access to a particular user within that group.

Remote Procedure Calls (RPC) and the Component Object Model (COM)

Computers work better as teams than they do on their own, so methods have been developed to let computers not only share their workload, but also dedicate certain systems to certain tasks. To facilitate this in the Windows environment, a couple of core technologies have been used: Remote Procedure Calls (RPC) and the Component Object Model (COM). The two are closely tied (well, COM relies on RPC, anyway). Each is described in the following sections.

RPC

RPC is a protocol that applications can use to offload some of their processing to some server. It's a way for an application developer to tell a program, "I'm not going to tell you how to do this, but I'll tell you how to talk to the server that does." Also note that when we say "server," this does not necessarily mean a physically separate system. An RPC server may reside on the same box as the "client" (the application that is offloading its work), or the RPC server may reside on some box halfway around the world. This is the advantage of RPC: The programmer doesn't have to know (or care) where the server software is; he just needs to know how to talk to it. The point of RPC is that an application can execute a procedure within the context of some other server and get back the results. This distributes the workload and lets certain systems be special-purposed. Windows software is becoming increasingly reliant on remote procedure calls, and it is necessary for administrators to become familiar with the concepts and ramifications of this service. For example, the Windows default interface, Explorer.exe, requires RPC for normal functionality. (To see just how reliant windows is on RPC, or if you want to cause someone a really bad day, stop the RPC service and observe the results.) Microsoft's implementation of RPC is quasicompliant with the OSF-DCE RPC standard. RPC can operate on a number of transport layers, including TCP, SPX, AppleTalk, and even HTTP.

COM/COM+

The Component Object Model is a system by which software and applications may expose their functionality to other software and applications. This is very similar to RPC, but it is a higher-level interface in which an application needs to know only about a specific object and the functionality that it exposes. This allows the functionality of one application to be utilized by another application so that the code does not need to be duplicated. COM is the backbone of Windows technologies such as ActiveX and Object Linking and Embedding (OLE). COM objects can be accessed either on the local machine or across the network. With Windows 2000, COM is so ingrained within the operating system that blindly disabling its features leaves the system in an almost useless state. The Windows Scripting Host (WSH) relies entirely on COM objects.

COM+ is the next iteration of COM that extends functionality and adds support for Microsoft Transaction Server (MTS), which allows for functionality to be easily spread across different systems. COM+ also has improved security features that allow for tighter access controls to be applied based on the user roles and the functionality that is requested by the client. For instance, a COM+ object might specify which users may request specific functionality based on that user's "role" (for example, a user defined as being Developer will be able to access certain functions that a user who has been given the role of Sales Associate cannot). For the sake of backward compatibility, however, these extensions must be manually implemented by the programmer, and security defaults are the same as for the original COM. For this reason, our discussions will focus on the original COM security model.

Security Mechanisms for RPC/COM

Because server applications need to know with whom they are speaking and also need to allow different access to different personalities or users, interfaces exist for the programs to define a "security level." When an RPC or COM server application starts up, it sets its security level to whatever it pleases (including no security mechanisms at all), based on how the developers predicted that the application will be used. However, Windows also provides default levels for those applications that choose not to do this. The default authentication mechanism for NT is the generic NTLMSSP service (that is, the normal Windows username and password). For Windows 2000, Kerberos is used if enabled; otherwise, NTLMSSP provides the authentication.

After a client (or process) has successfully authenticated, the client is granted an access token and given an authentication level that can be specified by the options Registry key HKEY_LOCAL_MACHINE\Software\Microsoft\OLE\LegacyAuthenticationLevel. The authentication level specifies how the operating system assesses whether the data that it receives really came from the authorized client. By default (that is, in the absence of this Registry key), connections within the local system are granted an RPC authentication level of Connect, meaning that after the initial connection is set up no further authentication is performed. For connections that occur across the network, this default value is Packet Level, meaning that each packet received from the client is checked by the server to ensure that it came from the expected client (normally based on IP address). This statement should sufficiently frighten most administrators because these packets might arrive via easily spoofed network protocols such as UDP. This type of attack can be remediated by setting the previous Registry key to a value of 6, specifying that all traffic should be encrypted in addition to authenticating client credentials every time a packet is received. By encrypting all traffic, not only do you protect yourself against a trivial spoofing attack, but you also hide all data in transit.

After these two phases of authentication (checking the access token and verifying the authentication level), each application exposing COM interfaces (that is, allowing other programs to access its functionality and data) should set an access permission level in the Registry that is associated with its application ID. The application ID is a 128-bit number that allows every application to identify itself uniquely. By *every*, we mean *every* application written—there are 2^{128} possible application IDs, which is ridiculously large (something like the number of atoms in the universe). The access permission level is a normal ACL that describes which users are allowed access to the object. Again, applications are not required to set their initial security level; if they choose not to do so, the value of yet another optional Registry value, HKEY_LOCAL_MACHINE\Software\Microsoft\OLE\DefaultAccessPermision, is used by default. If the value of this Registry entry is not found (it does not exist by default and must explicitly be created by an administrator). The application also does not set its initial security level; COM lets only the local system account access the exposed class.

Hardening Windows

The previous discussion of the Windows Security Subsystem, while hopefully interesting, probably leaves you wondering what all of that means to an administrator? It means that Windows NT and 2000 allow the execution of remote procedures and functions, which should be of concern to any administrator because that remote execution can be perpetrated by an unauthorized user. Turning off this functionality isn't really an option because COM and RPC are so tightly coupled with the normal operations of the system that they are not easily disabled. The good news, however, is that although administrators are largely stuck with RPC and COM whether they like it or not, Windows does provide fairly simple ways for an administrator to lock down the remote interfaces while still providing the necessary functionality.

It would be nice if there were a simple checklist for hardening the Windows operating system. Although some have attempted to develop just such a list, invariably there are some services that, although possibly insecure, are necessary for a particular deployment scenario. For this reason, this section provides suggestions from which administrators may pick and choose to secure their Windows NT and Windows 2000 installations. As always, there is a trade-off between usability and security, so our aim is to provide concise information about the security options available and the ramifications of enabling these features. Within each section, we also give examples of the types of systems that would benefit from these suggestions, as well as those that might suffer from a usability standpoint.

NetBIOS and SMB

Windows offers its own networking protocols to facilitate communication between systems in a more Windows-like manner. RPC, the services responsible for shared file systems, remote user authentication, and the like make, use of these protocols.

NetBIOS, on its own, is a network protocol that covers Layers 3–5 of the OSI model, although usually it piggy-backs on top of traditional network- and transport-layer protocols, such as TCP/IP. As a protocol, it is responsible for resolving the system names, session initiation and management, and data transmission. Before Windows 2000, NetBIOS was intimately involved with the Session Message Block (SMB). With Windows 2000 in native mode, the normal SMB services such as mapping network drives and domain logins can take place without NetBIOS. For our discussion, we will specifically talk about SMB, although, due to this tight entwinement within Windows NT, we sometimes talk about NetBIOS in an almost interchangeable way.

SMB was developed to enable several different hosts to act within the same functional *system*, authentication, sharing file systems and printers, and so on. RPC and COM also make heavy use of SMB when acting over the network. SMB provides a standard way to uniquely identify hosts and resources on those hosts, as well as users and groups. Additionally, a system cannot be part of a traditional Windows domain without SMB because that system will not be capable of providing credentials to the other SMB-savvy systems in the domain. Because so much of Windows functionality relies on SMB, it is not strictly possible to *disable* SMB entirely (and, really, there is no reason to do so). However, there are ways to restrict and disable its functionality over the network.

What are the risks associated with SMB and NetBIOS? Well, from the paranoid standpoint, SMB is fairly poorly documented. Although good documentation about it does exist, some of the internals are either "undocumented" or not explained completely. As a security administrator, you should have a healthy fear of any network services that are not entirely clear. From the traditional standpoint, SMB exposes some functionality that pose direct threats to a system's security.

At its core, SMB offers a lot of functionality. The unfortunate counterpart to functionality is vulnerability. For instance, when a user opens up the Network Neighborhood and is allowed to explore the various services offered by the systems around it, this information is usually available without supplying a username or password. Additionally, pretty much every Windows system is capable of sharing any of its resources to anyone else on the network. Although such functionality is great from a usability standpoint, administrators might not necessarily like the idea of their internal users sharing their C:\ drives, or the idea that anyone who cares to ask can retrieve the entire user list from a domain controller.

When a system wants to offer file systems or printers to arbitrary clients, the Server service performs these duties. This service is responsible for authenticating users, relaying data back and forth to the client, and controlling access to protected resources. The Workstation service (*Workstation* is synonymous with *Redirector*) handles the client side of things—for instance, making it look like a file system somewhere else on the network looks like it's just another drive (such as the F:\ drive).

We mentioned earlier that information such as usernames and shared file systems often is accessible without supplying a username or password. Windows has the concept of null sessions and Anonymous users. This is a "feature" built into Windows to ease administrative overhead, and it allows anyone to connect to a system as the Anonymous user, a special account that does not require either a username or password to authenticate. The Anonymous user has severely restricted access, but a wealth of information is accessible once establishing a connection with its credentials. Beyond the aforementioned username and share lists, network transport definitions, installed services, password policies, and more are all free for the asking over a null sessions. Unfortunately, simply disabling null sessions can be tricky. Although it is possible (under Windows NT a Registry value, HKEY_LOCAL_MACHINE\SYSTEM\ CurrentControlSet\Services\LanmanServer\Parameters, controls whether null sessions are allowed; under Windows 2000, the Anonymous user's rights can be explicitly controlled), doing so can break functionality of legacy application. However, upgrading an older application is a small price to pay for restricting access to such sensitive information.

So we've explained the functionality and touched on the risks associated with SMB and NetBIOS. Whether such functionality is useful on a given system can be broken down into the following questions:

- Does the system in question need to be capable of accessing file systems or printers over the network?
- Does the system itself need to be part of a domain?
- Does the system require COM or RPC across the network?
- What sort of application software relies on SMB for authentication or communication?

Unfortunately, these are hard questions without easy answers. With Windows 2000, we can address each of these questions more directly; with Windows NT, things are not so granular. And that last question is deadly: It's not always possible to determine exactly which applications need these services. Without good documentation, the only way to determine these dependencies is through experimentation. An administrator must weigh the pros and cons of each. We can, however, offer a couple of suggestions:

- If the system is a PDC, file server, or print server, SMB must be enabled.
- If the system is a user workstation, the Workstation service needs to be enabled, but the Server service does not.
- If the system is a mail server and is running Exchange, SMB must be enabled unless you are willing to spend a good amount of time tracking down problems and disabling what could be very useful functionality.
- If the system is a publicly accessible Web server, things get trickier. If Web-based authentication relies on Windows-style authentication, SMB must be enabled. If the Web server is mounting content across the network, SMB must be enabled.

SMB is a huge topic, and we have touched on only some of the highlights. However, we hopefully have provided you with enough information to let you know how to address common situations. Internal systems (servers and workstations) generally require many of the SMB services to perform their duties. Internet-accessible systems don't necessarily require SMB, although users might demand certain functionality (such as copying files across network drives rather than uploading files via FTP).

We always hate addressing a problem without offering clear-cut solution, but, in this case, it's unavoidable. However, we can give you the guidelines by which we approach these situations:

- Web servers have all SMB functionality disabled. Period.
- Mail servers that are accessible from the Internet have all SMB functionality disabled. We're a little more lenient on internal mail servers.
- Internal servers are allowed free reign with SMB, except for null sessions.
- Internal workstations are allowed free reign, except for the Server service and null sessions.

Disabling SMB

As we stated before, completely disabling SMB is impossible. Under NT, however, four basic steps must be taken to disable SMB access from the network. We have already discussed the Server and Workstation services, but two other configuration changes that can be made: the TCP/IP NetBIOS helper service and unbinding NetBIOS from network interfaces. Disabling the NetBIOS TCP/IP service prevents NetBIOS (and, thus, SMB) information from piggybacking on TCP/IP. Unbinding NetBIOS from a network interface prohibits NetBIOS information from being sent across the network. This doesn't mean that the SMB functionality doesn't exist, but simply that the network protocols required to exercise this functionality don't exist.

Under Windows 2000, things aren't so clear cut. Windows 2000 offers the administrator a greater level of granularity in what users and systems can do. With this greater level of granularity comes more administrative overhead (and freedom) in restricting who can do what. Additionally, in a pure Windows 2000 environment (that is, "native mode"), NetBIOS does not exist, and you can't rely on disabling a network protocol to disable functionality. However, you still can disable the Server and Workstation services. Then you must tighten down what users are allowed to do.

Tightening Windows User Rights

Both Windows NT and Windows 2000 allow administrators to restrict user rights in a fairly straightforward manner. Unfortunately, the default rights granted to users are not terribly restrictive. Here we present a table of the more critical rights that can be granted, who generally should and should not be granted these rights, and an explanation of what the security implications having that specific right are.

- **Log on locally**—Predictably, this grants a user the privilege of logging onto a machine locally. The only groups that would ever need this right would be administrators and perhaps power users. Normal users should not have this privilege.

- **Access this computer from the network**—This allows users to log in via the network. For systems that have network-accessible SMB disabled, this privilege is moot. For all other systems, almost all users need this privilege. The exception is the Administrators group, which should not be allowed to log in from the network. The reason for this is that because the Administrator account has nearly unlimited privileges, you don't want an attacker to be able to access this account across the network.

- **Act as part of the operating system**—No normal user accounts (including Administrator accounts) should ever be granted this right.

- **Bypass traverse checking**—This is an often misunderstood privilege. If granted, it lets a user access files based solely on the DACL of the file, ignoring the DACLs on any parent directories. So although a user might not be able to get a listing from a protected directory, if he knows the explicit path to a file for which he *does* have access, he can access that file. This can lead to an administrative headache and has no legitimate use. It should rarely, if ever, be granted to any users.

- **Debug programs**—By allowing a user to debug a program, access to protected memory, machine instructions, and elevated privileges is not only possible, but explicitly granted. No normal users should ever have this privilege. Developers will need such access, but only on their development workstations.

- **Increase scheduling priority**—This privilege could enable a user to purposely or accidentally deny processor time to legitimate programs. Only administrators should have this privilege.

- **Manage audit and security log**—Only administrators should be allowed to do this.

- **Shut down the system/force remote shutdown**—Only administrators and power users should be allowed to do this.

- **Log on as a batch job/log on as a service**—Both of these privileges allow users access to system resources that they should not normally have. The only users who should be granted this privilege are those created by applications that require such functionality. Any user granted these privileges should not be allowed to log in via the network.

Auditing Security Events

Without accurate logs, it is impossible to accurately respond to security events. Unfortunately, there is a fairly severe trade-off between enabling audits and system performance. The following list highlights the *minimum* events that should be audited; enabling the following will have a negligible effect on performance. Additional events should be monitored for systems in which performance is not as crucial as security:

- **Logon and logoff**—Both successes and failures should be audited.
- **File and object access**—Failures should be audited. Auditing success will very quickly bring a system to its knees due to successful object access occurring nonstop.
- **Use of user rights**—Failures should be tracked. Again, tracking success will drag down system performance drastically.
- **User and group management**—Successes and failures should be tracked.
- **Security policy changes**—Audit success and failure.
- **Restart, shutdown of system**—Audit success and failure.
- **Process tracking**—Only failures audits need to be enabled, although tracking successes will have a negligible effect on system performance.

Linux Security Concepts

After Windows (NT and 2000), the next most popular operating system on the Internet is UNIX, be it Solaris, BSD, Linux, or any of the many other flavors. In this section, we discuss the security mechanisms and configurations of a generic Linux distribution that is representative of most UNIX variants. We say "generic" because we will attempt to present information applicable across not only the different Linux distributions, but also for UNIX-esque operating systems in general. This is a slippery slope because, in its 25-plus year history "UNIX" has come to mean many different things (and, actually, to specify very little).

Internal Linux security is far more rudimentary than that of Windows NT. It, too, is based on the user and group IDs, but the permissions are less granular. Additionally, there is the superuser account (whose ID is 0) that is allowed to do anything. This is in contrast to the Windows Administrator account, which can, in fact, place limits on its own access rights.

We will start our study of Linux by explaining the basic file system permissions because the paradigm of "everything is a file," although not pervasive, plays a large role in the credential-checking mechanisms employed by the kernel.

Overview of the Linux Kernel

The Linux kernel is responsible for acting as a middleman between "normal" processes and the computer hardware. It arranges for processes to receive their fair share of the processor's time, handles requests to the hardware for sundry operations such as reading from a file or writing to the display, controls access to restricted objects, ensures that processes aren't allowed to do things that they shouldn't (such as modify another process's memory space), and performs all the other housekeeping that you would expect of an operating system. The Linux kernel is "monolithic" in nature—that is, the kernel is a single chunk of code loaded when the system boots. In addition, the kernel stays in memory the entire time that the system is running. However, Linux does support *loadable modules* (portions of kernel code), which then may be loaded and unloaded as needed, although the use of these modules is entirely optional.

Kernel space is a well-organized place where all operations and objects are segregated by process. The information describing a process is stored in a structure known as a "process tree" and contains information such as the user who started the process, what file handles the process is using, how long the process has been executing, and so on. Any requests that the process makes of the kernel ("Hey, open this file for me" or "Hey, send this signal to this other process") are subject to internal access control lists (somewhat like those described in the Windows section, although less granular). This ensures that users don't go mucking around where they shouldn't and that they are allowed to access only those objects to which they have been granted permission. In short, the kernel is everything about the system.

Overview of Linux User Space

Because the kernel controls access to everything on the system, the area where the kernel resides and runs, or "kernel space," is a highly sensitive and protected area. The majority of the system's functions execute in "user space," safely outside the realm of the kernel. It is here that shells, system daemons (more on daemons later), and user programs run, occasionally asking the kernel to perform some task on their behalf (such as opening a file or writing to the network).

All processes in user space have a "parent" process that spawns them and from which they inherit their privileges. Obviously, this cannot strictly be true because there must be at least *one* process without a parent (the prime mover, but let us not venture into the existential implications of pondering the opposite); this process is init, the mother of all processes. As the final stage of booting, the kernel starts init (whose process ID is, predictably, 1), which is responsible for performing the operations necessary to bring the system into a useable state, as well as basic system upkeep tasks such as monitoring system power levels. Although init does not run in kernel mode (which would give it access to the supervisor mode of the processor), it does run as root (which is almost as powerful).

Linux File System Permissions

In Linux, everything is a file, meaning that (at least from our standpoint) everything has permissions applied to it in the same manner, regardless of whether it is a file, a directory, or even hardware, such as a sound card or modem. File system objects have three main permissions that can be specified: read, write, and execute. These three permissions can be granted to three different types of users: a user (owner of the file), a group (the primary group of the owner of the file), and everyone (anyone else). In addition, two other bits can be set: the sticky bit and the setuid/setgid bits. Table 7.1 details the meaning of these permissions and the various types of file system objects:

TABLE 7.1 Linux File System Permissions

Permission	Normal File	Directory	Socket	Device
Read	User may read the file.	User may list the directory.	User may read from the socket.	User may read from the device.
Write	User may delete or append to the file.	User may create new objects in the directory.	User may write to the socket.	User may write to the device.
Execute	User may execute the file.	User may enter or change into that directory.	—	—
Sticky	—	User may create new files but can remove files only if he is the owner of the directory or has write permissions on both the file and the directory.	—	—
Setuid/Setgid	If executable, the process runs as the owner of the file.	All new files and subdirectories will be owned by the owner of this directory.	—	—

There are two types of "special" files in Table 7.1 that need a little explanation. A UNIX domain socket (simply labeled "socket" in the table) is a method for interprocess communication and is created on the file system. When this socket is created, multiple processes can read from and write to this socket, just as if it were a file. Note that the term *socket* also is used within the realm of network communication (specifically, an Internet domain socket) and should not be confused with the UNIX domain socket. Although both types of sockets are very similar from a programming standpoint, Internet domain sockets do not exist as objects on the file system and are controlled a little differently.

A "device file" provides a way to access hardware in a uniform manner from user space, allowing a process to read from and write to a device as if it were a normal file. We told you that everything was a file.

These permissions provide a baseline paradigm for the way in which the rest of the operating system handles object access. Each process is owned by a particular user and has a list of groups attached to it that may perform actions on that process (send signals, attach with a debugger, and so on). Any process running as the superuser (root, user ID 0) has free reign of the system; this is one of the inherent difficulties associated with Linux security.

Set-UID and Set-GID Concepts

In the section on Windows NT security identifiers and tokens, we spoke about the concept of impersonation. In the Linux world (and most of the UNIX world), there is a similar though simpler mechanism: the setuid(2) and setgid(2) class of functions, and the set-uid and set-gid file system permission bits. These mechanisms allow processes to execute in security contexts different from the process that spawned them. This can be done to allow temporary access to privileged files. For instance, for a user to change a default shell, the password database (usually /etc/shadow or /etc/master.passwd) must be modified. Because normal users cannot read from or write to this file, and because system administrators really don't need to be bothered every time a user needs to change a shell, the chsh (change shell) utility must perform the read and write operations as root. So, the chsh utility, which is executed by the user, actually is owned by root and has the set-uid bit set.

A process may explicitly call the setuid() function to drop privileges when it no longer needs the privileges that it started with. For example, only processes running as root are allowed to listen on TCP and UDP ports below 1024[2] (the "privileged" ports). Because most normal Web traffic is handled by processes listening on port 80, a Web server must have root privileges at least long enough to set up its listening socket to listen on port 80. However, after the socket has been set up, there is really no reason for the process to have these elevated privileges, so it sets its *effective user* ID to some unprivileged user, usually *nobody*. By dropping these elevated privileges, an attacker who takes advantage of a bug in the Web server software will be able only to execute commands as nobody instead of the all-powerful root.

The main issue with setuid and setgid processes is fairly straightforward: This allows a process to perform operations that normal access-control mechanisms would prohibit. In a perfect world, this would not be an issue because the application would execute exactly as intended and allow the elevated access for only a specific task or two. But this is not a perfect world, and software has bugs that malicious users can take advantage of to do their evil deeds. For instance, if there is unchecked buffer in some user-supplied data for chsh, an attacker might make use of buffer overflow techniques to execute a command with elevated privileges. In the case of chsh, these commands would execute as root. This might allow a malicious user to elevate his privilege to root and then use this elevated privilege to access and modify any aspect of the system.

Linux Authentication Mechanisms

The core of Linux user authentication is the Pluggable Authentication Modules, or PAM. Before PAM, unless a specific application had a built-in authentication mechanism, credential checking basically boiled down to "the username and password match what is in the password file." With PAM, however, administrators can define arbitrary authentication, management, and logging mechanisms based on individual applications. For instance, an administrator might want to require S/KEY authentication when a user telnets to a system, but require only a username and a password for ftp. PAM offers this flexibility. Although PAM was originally developed for Linux, it has since been adopted by many versions of UNIX-like operating systems, namely Solaris and FreeBSD.

How PAM Works

For any service that requires authentication (and has been written to support PAM), an administrator can instruct the PAM system to perform various operations associated with letting a user access that service. When you think of what is involved in a user attempting to access some application, there are a few points to consider:

- Is the user allowed to connect to this service?
- What is the authentication mechanism in use?
- Are the supplied credentials valid?
- What sort of logging needs to be done?
- What should the user be allowed to do during the session?

PAM allows administrators to define how all of these should be enforced and handled for any application. These definitions can be specified in one of two places: in /etc/pam.conf with all directives defined in one file, or by a group of files located in /etc/pam.d/ (if the latter is used, /etc/pam.conf is ignored).

The Structure of /etc/pam.conf

Each directive in pam.conf takes the following format, all on one line:

```
service    type    control    module-path    module-arguments
```

These directives can be "stacked" by service—that is, multiple directives can be defined for the same service. When a matching service is found, the directives are parsed in order starting from the beginning, but, depending upon the result, each step down the stack a "fatal" condition can be met and execution is aborted (this is explained in greater detail later). You should note that this is quite similar to the way that Windows NT checks the ACL for an object to find a matching access-control rule. The following sections define the meaning of each of the PAM directives.

The PAM Service Field

The Service field defines either the specific application that the user is attempting to access or the wildcard "other." Applications are specified simply by the name of the binary (as in telnetd, ftpd, su, and so on). The value of other matches any application/service that is not explicitly defined elsewhere in the file. So, if an administrator wants to define a directive for, say, the telnet application, he would start the directive with the service telnetd.

The PAM Type Field

The Type field specifies the type of management that this module is defining: account, auth, password, or session.

The account type performs checks based on the user's account. This could take the form of service-based access control lists, such as checking whether the user is even allowed to access the service that he is requesting (for example, user sally is allowed to log in via telnet, but user bob is not). The account type also could be used to specify housekeeping functionality for a user's account, such as whether the account has expired.

The auth type defines the type of authentication that should be used by the defined service, such as smart cards, passwords, challenge-response mechanisms, or others. For example, if an administrator wanted to make use of a RADIUS server for FTP authentication, he would include an auth line in the configuration file for the service ftpd and a path to a module that knows how to talk to a RADIUS server.

The password type is actually a misnomer because it handles issues associated with *maintaining* the authentication mechanisms. For example, a password entry could specify ways to ensure that anytime a user changes his password, it meets certain guidelines (for example, it is a certain length, it contains letters and numbers, it isn't a dictionary word, and so on). It also could be used check to see if a password has expired and to force a user to change it.

The session type allows an administrator to define actions to be taken just before and just after the service executes. This is most useful for custom logging but also could be used for setting up specific environments. For example, an administrator might want to enable extra logging mechanisms when a user logs in via FTP. Or, the administrator might want to give the user a restricted shell when logging in via telnet.

The PAM Control Field

The Control field lets the administrator define how to handle a failure in the specified module. The field can be one of four values: requisite, required, sufficient, or optional.

The `sufficient` value tells PAM that a successful return code from the module is enough to satisfy the authentication requirements. Thus, if the directive happened to be `auth`, the user would be successfully authenticated and no more stacked modules would be executed. If the module returns a failure code, though, this is not considered fatal by the application and the next module in this service's stack is checked. By stacking auth types, an administrator can define several different authentication mechanisms for the same service, which is useful when transitioning from, say, generic UNIX passwords to a token-based authentication system. So, if the first authentication mechanism isn't available (such as a smart card), the application tries the next one listed (perhaps a username and password). Only when all of the methods have been exhausted will the application fail.

By specifying `requisite`, the administrator instructs PAM to immediately cease the authentication process if the module returns a failure code. So, if you have an auth type and specify that it is requisite, failure means that the user is not logged in and any other stacked modules are ignored. If successful, however, the rest of the stacked modules are executed.

A value of `required` states that the PAM-API should return a code denoting failure but that any other stacked modules should go ahead and execute. While these modules are executed, it is not possible for a success in the subsequent modules to override the original failure. This is useful when you want to perform extra logging (a session type directive) even if authentication fails. For this, you would stack a `session` directive on top of a `required` auth directive. Thus, if a user fails authentication, the extra logging will still take place, but the user still won't be allowed to log in.

An `optional` control value is of little use because its return codes are ignored within the stack control. It can be used to specify extra logging when tracking down configuration errors or to test new modules without impacting the legacy modules. For example, an administrator could stack a new authentication module on top of a legacy module to see how the new authentication performed, without fear that the new module would lock legitimate users out of the system.

The Module-Path Field

The Module-path field is the path to the PAM module (the actual program) that contains the functionality that you want to use for directive. These modules take the form of shared libraries and are located under /usr/lib/security. Almost all Linux distributions contain modules for nearly every type of PAM directive that you can conceive. Additionally, a wealth of custom-written PAM modules are available across the Internet for specific situations such as checking password strength or for using SecureID. The two most common modules are pam_unix.so and pam_pwdb.so, which provide the normal UNIX /etc/shadow authentication mechanisms. To learn more about the more esoteric of the modules (such as pam_time, which allows for time-based authentication), consult the man pages.

The Module-Arguments Field

The Module-arguments field allows an administrator to define arguments that are to be passed to a module when it is called. The arguments are module-specific, with possible options (if any) described in the module's documentation. For example, the pam_unix.so module can be passed the debug option to send debugging information to syslog, or the nowarn option to turn off warning messages.

PAM Examples

Now that we've talked about the specifics of PAM, let's look at a few examples of how the pam.conf file might be configured in a typical Linux system.

```
login auth   sufficient   pam_skey.so
login auth   requisite    pam_cleartext_pass_ok.so
login auth   required pam_unix.so        try_first_pass

other  password required pam_unix.so try_first_pass
```

The previous lines define behavior for login and then uses the wildcard other as a cleanup rule. The definitions tell PAM to do the following:

- If someone is logging in via the login program, first prompt the user for an S/KEY one-time password. If this is successful, go ahead and let the user log in.
- If the S/KEY authentication for the login service fails, then prompt the user for a regular password (using module pam_cleartext_pass_ok.so). This module does not actually perform any authentication; it simply adds some integrity checks and asks the system whether clear-text passwords are okay. If clear-text passwords aren't allowed, authentication stops here. If they are okay, then go to the next line.
- If the service is login, prompt the user for the normal UNIX username and password. If the username and password are correct, grant access.
- If the service is anything other than login, then prompt the user for the normal UNIX username and password.

As you can see, pam.conf files can be a little tricky, but they are not overly complex. They just require a little forethought and knowledge (which are never bad things). However, due to the flexibility that PAM adds (not to mention its pervasiveness), it is important for administrators to become familiar with its configuration and inner workings.

UNIX Network Services and How to Secure Them

From the perspective of the Internet, computers are of relatively little use when not networked. Unfortunately, as soon as a system becomes network-accessible, it becomes a potential target for attackers. As always, administrators are caught between providing functionality and security, two diametrically opposed concepts. In this section, we discuss the best ways to provide system access from the network with as little exposure as possible. In addition, we include some examples of why the default Linux configurations are so vulnerable from a security standpoint. Although much of our discussion has centered on Linux thus far, this section is applicable to most UNIX environments.

Again (and this cannot be overstated), the golden rule of computer security is, "If it's not needed, disable it." In the UNIX world, this is a bit more straightforward than in the Windows world because UNIX has fewer interservice dependencies and clearer documentation (plus open source code so that you can actually see what the functions are doing). It is difficult to define a "baseline" configuration that will be applicable to arbitrary systems, so here we discuss the pros and cons of some of the more common services that users are likely to demand but that might negatively impact the security posture of a system. We also will list alternatives and ways to strengthen these services. Overall, we will review the following operating system areas from the standpoint of security:

- Remote access and file transfers
- Graphical user interfaces
- RPC
- NFS

Although this list is certainly not an all-inclusive list of what is required to secure an operating system, these are the most common areas of configuration errors that can hamper security. By using this information and these guidelines, you should be able to "port" your knowledge to the myriad services out there.

Remote Access/File Transfers

It is less than useful to have a networked system that you can't connect to remotely. Thus, myriad network services offer methods of logging in, getting a shell, and transferring files. Traditionally, these tasks have been performed by telnet and ftp, as well as with the Berkeley r* services (rsh, rcp, rlogin, and so on). The r* services are a nightmare from a security standpoint because they normally are configured to "trust" specific hosts and users, with authentication relying on IP addresses rather than usernames and passwords. In addition to having weak authentication, all data is transmitted in the clear (without encryption). Telnet and ftp are not much better. Although these services require that users specify a valid username/password combination or other authentication mechanism, the authentication and the rest of the session take place via plain text. The reason that this is a concern is that anyone that can view this network traffic (the term *sniffing* often is used) can "steal" the usernames and passwords and then later use them to gain access to the systems. Because the passwords used for file transfer are often the same used to log onto a networked system, remote file transfer is often the weakest link in a networked system's security. And not only can a user steal usernames and passwords, but he also can steal the content of files as they pass by.

It has been a constant struggle for administrators to wean users off of telnet and ftp, but wide support for the Secure Shell (ssh) has eased this tremendously. When properly implemented, ssh can replace telnet, ftp, and all of the r* services. It also supports strong authentication (and its authentication mechanisms are arbitrarily extensible through PAM) as well as encryption. The latter feature is key to the strength of ssh because, by encrypting the traffic between the ssh client and server, it is no longer possible for attackers to sniff passwords or intercept information in transit. Even better, arbitrary protocols such as X11 (the X Window System) can be "tunneled" through ssh, offering encryption and security to nearly any network service.

You may be asking yourself, "Well, there must be a downside." Although the answer to this question is "yes," the cons associated with ssh are far outweighed by the pros. The biggest hurdle in deploying ssh is training users to change the way they have been going about their business. However, at the time of this writing, there were ssh clients for nearly every flavor of UNIX under the sun, as well as Windows, MacOS, OS/2, BeOS, QNX...the list goes on. With such wide platform support, users' lives don't have to change too drastically. Additionally, implementing ssh might require some administrative overhead because the PAM files need to be updated and the actual ssh software must be installed. This, too, is not as terrible as it seems because the installation process is quite straightforward. In fact, most UNIX distributions (although, unfortunately, not Solaris) come with ssh ready to run, out of the box.

Graphical User Interfaces

Graphical user interfaces (GUIs) can take a number of forms under UNIX-like operating systems, ranging from the standard X Window system to the Common Desktop Environment (CDE), Gnome, and others. The intent of each is to provide a unified windowing environment to the user and to be accessible across the network. It is that last feature that is most troubling from a security standpoint.

GUIs (particularly network-aware GUIs) are very complex beasts. To perform their task, they rely on quite a number of services. As always, the more complex the system is, the greater opportunity there is for bugs. X on its own enables a number of network-accessible services by default: TCP ports 6000–6063 for the X protocol and UDP port 177 for the X Display Manger Control Protocol (XDMCP). XDMCP handles the authentication and distribution of displays within X (more on this in a bit). Additionally, CDE (the default interface under Solaris, AIX, HP/UX, and others) requires RPC to even function, requires inetd to perform as expected, and also enables TCP ports 6112 (CDE subprocess control) and 7100 (Font server), just for good measure. GUIs have long been a prime target for attackers, and a long list of GUI vulnerabilities are available on many hacker sites on the Internet. X has a particularly long list of well-documented vulnerabilities, so anytime such a GUI is used, it presents a potential avenue for attack. For instance, without proper access-control mechanisms, it is possible for an attacker to remotely record all keystrokes entered by the user of the GUI, or to remotely take a screen shot of the user's display. At the very least, unsecured X opens one up to information disclosure and might allow an attacker the information he needs to fully compromise a system.

Often there are legitimate requirements for a graphical interface, but these requirements are usually only within the domain of workstations. Servers should rarely, if ever, require a GUI, especially one accessible from the network. As a general rule, it is best never to allow X to run on a server; in fact, it's even better not to even install the associated software. This being said, in the environments where there is a legitimate need for a GUI, some measures can be taken to reduce exposure. We will restrict our conversation to the X Window System because it is the most prevalent and is the basis for nearly every other graphical interface.

X11 Authentication Mechanisms

First, let's say a word or two about the X11 protocol itself. X11 was designed to allow applications running on a remote system to be graphically presented to the user on his workstation. When a user is sitting at a workstation (we will call this system muffin) and also is logged into a remote system (we will call this system scone) and that user types "xterm," the xterm application executes on scone but is presented on the user's workstation. That is, the window shows up on muffin even though the process is running on scone. The presentation and the input take place on muffin's display, which is responsible for relaying this information to scone for processing. After processing, scone then lets muffin know what the output should look like. Access control (that is, which systems are allowed to read input from and send output to muffin's display) can be handled in a number of ways, the most common being Host Access, MIT-MAGIC-COOKIE-1, and XDM-AUTHORIZATION-1.

The Host Access mechanism is just that: an access control list of which hosts are allowed to talk to the display. Hosts are added and deleted via a utility named xhost. So, to allow scone to connect to muffin, the user would issue the following command on muffin:

```
[user@muffin]$ xhost scone
```

There is also the wildcard value +, which can be used to specify any host. At the time of this writing, the default Host Access policy on many Linux distributions was xhost +—that is, "let anyone read and write from my display." Under Solaris, the default is "don't let anyone read or write to the display."

The MIT-MAGIC-COOKIE-1 mechanism goes a little further, in that a host must not only be listed as authorized by the display, but also must provide a 128-bit identifier known as a *cookie*, which acts somewhat like a password. When a user wants to allow a remote system (in our case, scone) to be able to connect to her display (muffin), she places the cookie in a file (the .Xauthority file in the user's home directory) on the remote system via the xauth utility. Although it is admittedly difficult to guess a 128-bit value, this cookie is sent across the network in the clear and is susceptible to interception.

The XDM-AUTHORIZATION-1 mechanism is the most secure of the three but is rarely used. It is similar to the MIT-MAGIC-COOKIE-1 mechanism, in that a secret is placed on any system that a user wants to give control of the display to (so again, our user would take the secret from muffin and place it on scone). However, in this scenario, the shared secret is an encryption key. When an application on scone wants to start reading from and writing to muffin, it encrypts an identifier (a combination of system time and some network information) and ships it off to muffin. Muffin then cryptographically can ensure that scone really is allowed to control the display. Encryption, however, is used only during this authorization phase; the connection itself still takes place in the clear.

So why all this information about how X performs authentication? To illustrate just how insecure the default X installation can be, to show how easy it is to misconfigure X, and to point out that even in the face of relatively strong authentication mechanisms, potentially sensitive information is still sent over the wire unencrypted. Because the information is sent unencrypted, anyone who can "sniff" the network connection can intercept everything being transmitted. If this connection is taking place over the Internet, the dangers are particularly acute. As an administrator, you must seriously consider the ramifications of enabling such a service and weigh the risk against what users want. The consensus opinion is that if X must be enabled, it always should be tunneled through an encrypted protocol (ssh performs this duty quite nicely and was, in fact, designed to support just this).

But even then, let us leave you with one thought. We mentioned earlier that we do not even recommend having the GUI software installed on critical systems, even if it is not going to be enabled. Why is this? Let's say that scone is a Web server. The X server on scone has been disabled, but the /usr/X11R6 tree is still there. Because an X application can be displayed on any system willing to receive it, what if an attacker was able to make use of bug in a CGI, execute an xterm on scone, and have it display on his workstation? Even if the Web server wasn't running an X server, the attacker still has a nice, fully functional shell.

RPC

We talked about Remote Procedure Calls in the Windows environment and detailed some of the security considerations involved. Now let's turn to how UNIX systems make use of RPC and what you, as an administrator, can do to help mitigate some of the risks.

The "normal" RPC protocol used by Linux and Solaris is different from that used by Windows (remember, the Windows RPC protocol is a derivation of the DCE standard). The most common RPC implementation is one developed by Sun, unimaginatively called Sun RPC. It offers functionality much in the same way as DCE RPC, allowing client processes to execute procedures inside of server processes. Again, these processes can reside on the local machine or somewhere on the network.

Sun RPC connections generally are established by the client making a request to the RPC *portmapper* (TCP port 111). The client makes a request, such as, "I need to talk to the NFS server—what port is it on?" The portmapper keeps track of which processes run on which ports (because this could be arbitrary) and returns the answer to the client. The client then contacts the server process directly to request service. The actual communication could take place via either UDP or TCP (or actually an arbitrary network protocol). This initial connection setup seems a logical place to implement access control. Unfortunately, the generic portmapper application on most flavors of UNIX (most notably Solaris) does not have this functionality built in. However, Wieste Venema developed a replacement portmapper system with TCPWrappers-style host-based access control, in which an administrator defines which hosts are allowed to access which services. Whether you should implement the more secure portmapper should not even be a question. However, it should be noted that it is not strictly necessary to contact the portmapper before establishing an RPC connection; it's simply there for convenience. Nothing prohibits someone from manually determining which port a particular service is listening on (and there are a few programs out there to do this for you) and establishing the RPC connection directly.

Because Sun defined the standard, it makes heavy use of it within the Solaris operating environment. It seems that everything in Solaris makes use of RPC: the admintool GUI application, CDE, NFS, and Network Information Services (NIS). And although just the idea of executing processes on a remote system makes administrators uneasy, to compound things even more, RPC applications historically have been riddled with security-related bugs (and these bugs have not been restricted to just Solaris). Great care must be taken when considering whether RPC provides enough benefit to outweigh the risks.

Additionally, as always, by enabling various RPC services, you potentially are offering these services to anyone who can access your network, not just legitimate users. You have to ask yourself, "Is NIS really necessary on this system? Do I need to use the admintool application rather than performing the same tasks from the command line?" These are questions that only you can answer, but we can give you our opinion: No. We very rarely have seen the need for RPC outside of very large environments that require NIS. Any system that potentially could be accessed by untrusted sources should never have RPC enabled; it's just not worth the risk. And any system that is designed from the start to be publicly accessible should almost never have any RPC services enabled. We say "almost" because of one of the most difficult tasks of system administration: dealing with NFS. Also note the difference between RPC in the UNIX world and RPC in the Windows world. Under Windows, RPC is required for the system to function normally. In the UNIX world, RPC is more segregated from the rest of the system, and disabling it won't impact normal system operations.

NFS

The Network File System offers convenience that is hard to ignore. It allows remote file systems to be mounted locally, making it appear as if it's just another directory. For Internet-accessible systems, the main use is for Web servers. By mounting Web content from a remote file server, multiple Web servers can offer the same data without the need for replication. It also allows Web developers to publish to one single location, with updates taking place simultaneously across all servers. If you've ever been in charge of a large Web site, you know that these two advantages are hard to ignore.

Unfortunately, NFS has one of the worst records from a security standpoint than any other RPC service. It is relatively easy to configure insecurely and has a rich history of security-related bugs. NFS also relies on a number of RPC services: the status manager, statd; the lock manager, lockd (or, under Solaris, nlockmanger); the file system daemon itself, nfsd; and the mount manager, mountd. So just to enable the sharing or mounting of network file systems, five extra processes and network ports must be enabled (not to mention the portmapper). Every network-accessible service is another potential avenue of attack.

So here you are, with a rock on one side and a hard place on the other. You can make use of strict access control lists regarding which hosts are allowed to mount file systems and which hosts are allowed to talk to the portmapper. You can export only the bare minimum file systems, and so on. You can take all of the precautions that you can from an administrative standpoint, but there are still those five network-accessible services that you didn't write, and you don't know what bugs they might contain. If you decide that NFS is just too big of risk and disable it, you then have to figure out how to give secure access to the developers to your Web servers to update content, as well as figure out how to synchronize the content across multiple hosts. The solution that we usually recommend in this situation is to add a new *secure* network segment, known as a *secure back rail*. Figure 7.2 describes this mechanism.

This new network segment is responsible only for allowing access to an NFS server for the Web servers and the developers. This means that the Web servers must have *two* network interfaces: one that the general public uses to make requests to the Web server and one that mounts the content. The developer systems also can be multihomed, although static routes and severe network access control lists are a better approach. Routing *must* be disabled on the Web servers, and all NFS and RPC processes must be bound to the secure interface only.

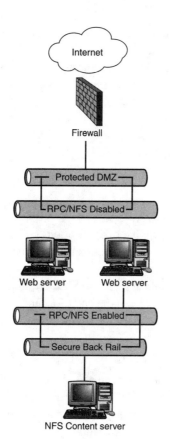

FIGURE 7.2

Multihomed Web servers and segmented NFS access.

Application Software Security

After you've secured your operating system, there's still the issue of securing the applications that run on top of the operating system, such as Web, ftp, or name servers. Tackling the vulnerabilities and security practices with regard to any one manufacturer's implementation of any one application, such as Microsoft's implementation of a Web server (Internet Information Server, or IIS), has consumed whole volumes. Given the nature of this book, it would be a gross omission not to talk about application software security, but, given the breadth of the subject, it's impossible to treat the subject completely in one section of one chapter.

The details of securing particular applications, such as securing Bind 8.9 on Solaris 7 or Microsoft IIS 5.0, are widely available from many sources, including books as well as manufacturers' Web sites, newsgroups, and dedicated security organizations. Rather than attempt to supercede this vast source of security tidbits, the goal of this section is to discuss the most prevalent classes of security vulnerabilities exhibited by the most prevalent Web applications, including these:

- Web servers
- FTP servers
- Mail servers
- Domain name servers

Although this is far from a complete list of applications (we've left out Web proxies, LDAP directories, databases, file servers, authentication servers, and others), it does include the core group of server applications that comprise the vast majority of Internet servers. Far from attempting to turn you into an application security expert, the goal of this chapter is to "pique your interest" in these areas and give you the basis for further research into the security vulnerabilities of your specific Internet applications.

Starting with a Secure OS

The first step in securing an application such as a Web, FTP, DNS, or mail server is to begin with a hardened operating system. Hopefully, you can apply the lessons in the first part of this chapter toward hardening your operating system of choice. The specific procedures are, of course, extremely dependant upon the application and operating system combination that you are working with. For this reason, you might notice that our dialogue is a bit obtuse with regard to specific vulnerabilities, and you're right. As we've stated before, security is a moving target, and what seems like a reasonable service today might become inadequate or risky tomorrow. Such is the life of a security administrator. However, you should take some general steps as part of this process:

- Never run an "out-of-the-box" operating system configuration.
- Install the latest supported version of the application, and apply all relevant application and OS security patches. This is a tricky topic because security fixes sometimes break legitimate functionality. All patches should be tested prior to implementation in production systems.
- Turn off any services that are not expressly required by the application. If possible, uninstall the service from the machine (including source code for UNIX machines). This is not limited to network-aware services. As we will show in future chapters, even local applications can be used for nefarious means.

- Remove any compilers or script interpreters from the system.
- Limit the trust relationships between the server and other network components. (For example, an IIS Web server should not be part of the same domain as corporate users.)
- When possible, remove guest accounts.
- Run the application at the least privilege level acceptable (don't let the application run as root).
- Tighten all system file permissions.
- Turn on available logging for security events, including all logons.
- Use a utility such as TripWire or L5 to create checksums on system and other critical files. This lets an administrator know when these files have been changed.
- Utilize an encrypted connection for remote administration. Examples include ssh and Kerberos.
- Subscribe to security newsgroups for your operating system and application, and review any new vulnerabilities on a daily basis to determine whether they are applicable to your configuration.
- Utilize appropriate banners on all systems to notify potential users of your site policy with regard to system accesses. Although this does not offer any increased security, it does offer increased legal options after an attack.
- Remove any application banners that identify the application's name and version number.

Although these are fairly common-sense guidelines, many servers are hacked because their administrators did not even put forth this level of effort when building and security their servers. Surprisingly (or perhaps not), following just these simple guidelines will put you ahead of the pack with respect to server security.

Web Server Security

Many of the well-publicized hacks against Web servers have been accomplished by hackers exploiting known security vulnerabilities in common Web server applications. Probably the number one thing that you can do to keep your Web server from becoming someone else's victim is to keep abreast of new vulnerabilities and apply the requisite patches or configuration updates when the effect your servers. The Code Red worm that infected scores of Web servers around the world took advantage of a well-known vulnerability for which a patch *already existed*. Had the bulk of system administrators simply applied the available fixes to their systems, Code Red might well have been a nonevent. A list of best practices for securing a "generic" Web server would include all of those mentioned in the earlier section "Starting with a Secure OS," plus these:

- Remove all unnecessary executables from all script directories, including demonstration scripts that come with the Web server.

- Require Web developers to do all testing on a development server rather than on a virtual address on your production server.

- Update Web content using a secure means rather than ftp with plain-text passwords. Utilize ACLs to limit the locations from which content updates can be performed.

- Lock down your directory permissions to prevent common directory-traversal attacks. Many Web servers traditionally have been vulnerable to these exploits that allowed attackers to utilize directory commands such as ../ to traverse the file system and read system files (such as the password file).

- If possible, run the Web server in a chroot'ed environment. Although chroot is not necessarily a security mechanism by design, it can prevent most types of directory traversal.

- Enable Web server logging and be sure to log the following for every connection: browser IP address, username (if applicable), method (such as GET or POST), URI stem, HTTP status, server IP address, and port.

Beware of UNICODE Attacks

Although there are many Web server–specific vulnerabilities, one broad class of attacks worth mentioning are the UNICODE attacks. UNICODE is an character set that supports non-Latin characters. Whereas the ASCII character set represents 256 English characters as 8-bit codes, the UNICODE character set attempts to provide codes for all languages through a mechanism known as code pages. A code page defines character mappings for the various character sets available under UNICODE. This has created an interesting problem in servers that can interpret the UNICODE character set because there is some overlap between code pages. For instance, most Web servers automatically strip any parent-directory path specifications in an HTTP request. However, the slash character (/)can be found in multiple code pages. If the stripping of ../ occurs *before* codepage conversion takes place, it will not be capable of stripping a parent path specification in a foreign character set. So, whereas a Web server might see and disallow a string such as ../../../ when embedded in a URL, it will allow the UNICODE version of this. For example, a / is encoded as %c0%af in UNICODE, and a ..%c0%af encodes the well-known exploit string ../. The best protection against UNICODE attacks is to stay up-to-date on server application patches and to lock down directory permissions.

The Chroot Mechanism

The chroot mechanism was first introduced in the 4.2BSD operating system and has since expanded to most variations of UNIX. Microsoft added similar functionality to its Internet Information System, although no chroot-esque functionality exists as part of the operating system itself. Basically, chroot lets a process change its concept of the system's root directory. For instance, because a Web server needs only the files under its installation directory—say, /usr/local/www/—the Web server process can chroot to /usr/local/www/, effectively restricting access to any files or directories above /usr/local/www/. This is not a security mechanism, per se, and there are some known ways to break out of a chroot "jail" once a user has access to the local system, but it can be an effective mechanism to locking down access to specific directories.

Mail Server Security

Mail servers are susceptible to all the normal vulnerabilities present in typical Internet servers. However, mail servers also must contend with the fact that they routinely receive and process content from unknown sources. This content can include malformed commands in the SMTP, IMAP, and POP3 protocols, or viruses in email attachments such as executables, scripting commands geared toward subverting mail client security, or a host of other nasty data. Because mail servers must accept unknown content, they are prime targets for attackers. Additionally, mail servers are in the uniquely dangerous positions of acting as data conduits to the internal network. To secure a typical mail server, you should consider the following:

- Mind the usual caveats about installing the latest supported software version and applicable security patches.

- Run virus-detection software on the mail server, both to protect it from viruses and to prevent it from propagating viruses to your system users through their mail clients.

- Use your firewall to block all but SMTP connections from the Internet. Block POP3 or IMAP except from your internal networks. Consider utilizing VPNs if you must allow POP3 or IMAP from the Internet (plain-text usernames and passwords will be passed over the Internet if you don't).

- Consider having the mail server block certain file attachment types that are the source of common attacks (executables, compressed files, scripts, and so on).

Spamming and Open Mail Relays

Although there are many mail-server exploits, the most common problem has nothing at all to do with subverting the security of the server. It has to do with mail relaying. A mail server can be used as a relay when it is configured to forward mail that does not come from its internal domain. For example, suppose that mail server A connects via SMTP to mail server B and sends a mail message in which neither the sender nor the recipient is in server B's domain. This simple relay function has had some disastrous consequences for unsuspecting relayers. For example, many organizations have "black lists," or sites from which they will not accept mail because they are known sources of spam mail. Knowing this, a spammer decides to send out 10,000 emails to a set of recipients but doesn't want to be blocked by the spam filters. If the spammer can find a company whose mail server is configured as an open relay, he can push the spam mail through that company and get past the anti-spam filters at his recipients' locations. What happens after this is that the mail relay is picked up as a source of spam mail and joins the black list recipients. The company will later find that nobody will accept any mail originating from its server, regardless of whether it comes from the spammer or its own employees.

Most new releases of mail applications include features that can be utilized to keep your mail server from becoming a mail relay or accepting spam mail. Among other things, these features will allow the administrator to do the following:

- Specify the hosts and domains that can use your server as a relay. Mail relaying is a useful function, as, for example, when many remote offices want to use the home office's mail server as a relay for sending mail from the company's domain (everyone coming from user@mycompany.com). Anyone not included in this list is not allowed to relay mail through the server.

- Reject mail from sources on a spam "black list," which can be compiled by the organization or procured from third-party vendors.

- Refuse to accept mail from a domain that doesn't exist. This prevents a spammer from sending mail in the format of username@phonydomain.com. If the mail server can't resolve the domain, it won't accept the mail.

Secure Mail Relays

A mail server occupies a unique location in the typical enterprise infrastructure, in that it is one of the few devices that talks to both the internal network (to allow users to send and retrieve email) and the Internet (to relay outgoing mail to its destination and to accept incoming mail so that it can be picked up by an internal user). Ignoring sound security practice, many organizations place their corporate mail servers on the corporate network, create trust relationships to other servers (such as by making them part of a Windows domain), and then open up a port in the firewall to allow inbound and outbound connections directly to and from the server. This makes the mail server a prime target for hackers because the hackers can connect to the server from the Internet; if they compromise the server, they have unfettered access to other hosts on the inside of the network. Even when a mail server is placed on a DMZ, it can connect to both Internet and internal network hosts.

Deploying a secure mail relay can solve the problem of allowing these direct connections to the mail server. A secure mail relay is, in effect, a stripped-down mail server deployed on a hardened operating system. The relay has only one job: to relay mail between the "real" mail server on the corporate network and the Internet. How is this more secure? Consider the network in Figure 7.3. The firewall must allow connections between the mail server on the internal network and the Internet. If an attacker is able to compromise the mail server, he is effectively part of the internal network.

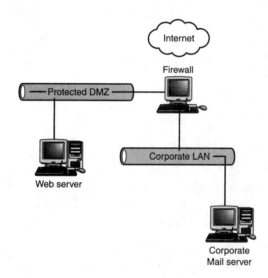

FIGURE 7.3

The firewall must allow connections between the mail server on the internal network and the Internet.

Now consider the setup in Figure 7.4. Here, a stripped-down server accepts mail from the Internet and is allowed to connect to only the internal network for SMTP. For an attacker to successfully compromise the internal mail server, he would have to first penetrate the mail relay and then go after the internal server. Because the secure mail relay does not have to perform any advanced mail functions, it can be configured extremely tightly from a security standpoint, further limiting its risk of compromise. Additionally, the use of a heterogeneous system is recommended here. If both the external relay and the internal server are running identical server software, a new vulnerability puts both systems at risk. By leveraging "hybrid vigor" in this way, the overall architecture becomes stronger.

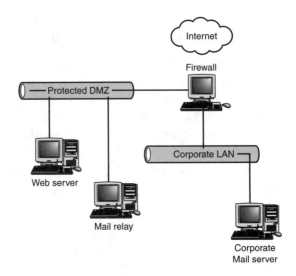

FIGURE 7.4

A stripped-down server accepts mail from the Internet and is allowed to connect to only the internal network for SMTP.

Name Server Security

For some reason, name servers traditionally have been rife with security holes, with the Berkeley Internet Name Daemon (BIND) being one of the most notorious. We often find DNS servers running in abominably insecure configurations, with the server software many times running on the same physical server as a mail server, Web server, and even the firewall!

This section does not address the many exploits against DNS server software—that alone would fill a volume, and enumerating every buffer overflow against BIND is hardly interesting reading. Instead, this section goes over attacks that are run against the name service that can result in the server delivering incorrect name to IP associations.

As before, let's first review some basic rules of running a secure name server:

- Name servers usually run as root in their out-of-the-box configuration. Make certain that you don't allow this. Run the server with the minimum user access necessary for it to do its job. For instance, BIND supports the -u option, which forces the name server to run as an arbitrary (and unprivileged) user.

- Consider running a split DNS configuration to keep from exposing the topology of your internal network (more on split DNS later).

- Limit zone transfers to authorized slave name servers (more on zone transfers later). Although this does not offer any direct level of security, it is our opinion that it's generally not a good idea to hand out maps of your network.

- If possible, run the DNS server software in a chroot'ed environment. Again, this does not offer a direct level of security, but it can limit the damage done after a successful penetration. BIND supports this internally by specifying the `-t` option at startup.

Zone Transfers

A zone transfer occurs when a client queries your name server for all of the information that it has about your domain. In effect, your name server "spills its guts" and lists all of the servers on your network for which it has records. This type of information can allow an attacker to immediately determine what hosts are on your network and deduce what service they are running (for example, `www.mydomain.com` is your Web server, `ftp.mydomain.com` is your ftp server, `gateway1.mydomain.com` is your firewall, and so on). In general, the only hosts that need this information are other slave name servers—that is, name servers that serve other portions of your network and get their domain name records from your server. This is the case if, for example, your company runs a name server at each of a number of remote offices. The master name server for your company is located at the main office, with slaves located at the remote offices to speed up DNS lookups for clients at those offices.

Split DNS

Often your organization will have hosts on the inside network that require name resolution but that are not accessible from the Internet. Consider Figure 7.5, in which a company is running a Web server, a mail server, and an ftp server that all are used only by internal users as part of the company intranet. At the same time, the company runs an external mail server and Web server that are accessible by both internal and Internet clients. If the company uses just a single name server, then the names and IP addresses of the intranet servers will be viewable by anyone on the Internet. Although the outside world won't be able to access the servers, it will know of their existence, and this could help an attacker target a specific internal system.

To hide the internal network topology, an administrator should set up a split DNS. In the simple example of Figure 7.6, the naming system has been split into two zones. The internal name server has entries for both internal and external servers, while the external name server has entries for only the Internet-accessible servers. This split functionality protects the internal infrastructure from being revealed to external entities. The specifics of how to implement split DNS are unique to various platforms and software vendors; however, the motivation for split DNS is common among them all.

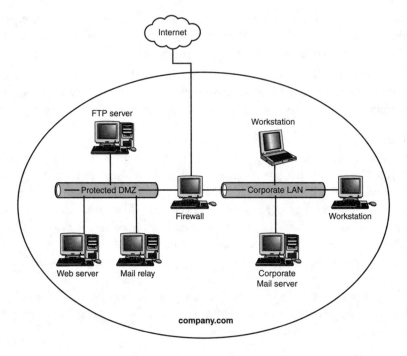

FIGURE 7.5

This network is vulnerable to attack.

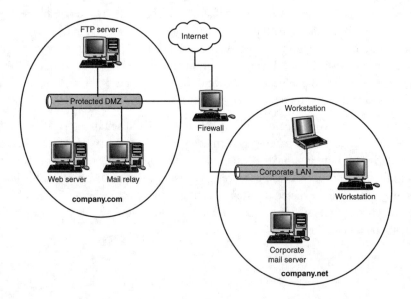

FIGURE 7.6

This split functionality protects the internal infrastructure from being revealed to external entities.

Cache Poisoning

One very common danger faced by name servers is called cache poisoning. In this attack, a name server is "fooled" into storing a false record, one that associates a true name with a bogus IP address, thereby causing anyone who queries that name server to resolve a name to the wrong address. This can be quite embarrassing if, for example, the record is for a Web server (www.mycompany.com) while the bogus IP address turns out to be that of a Web site of, shall we say, questionable moral content.

Cache poisoning is possible because name servers store (cache) records when a user queries them for a record that the user does not have. For example, a user at mycompany.com might point his browser at the www.acme.com Web server. His browser queries mycompany's name server, dns.mycompany.com for the IP address of www.acme.com. Because the DNS server for mycompany.com isn't authoritative for acme.com, it goes out and queries other name servers until it receives a reply that www.acme.com resolves to some address, such as 1.2.3.4. To save time on future lookups, dns.mycompany.com now caches the record that equates www.acme.com with IP address 1.2.3.4. The next time anyone queries dns.mycompany.com for this record, it will be returned out of the cache, and this entry could stay in cache for hours, days, or longer. This scenario can be created by an attacker via two main methods: recursive query responses and straight spoofing.

To illustrate how recursive query responses can be used to poison a DNS cache, suppose that an attacker runs a Web server called www.attacker.net and a name server called dns.attacker.net. The attacker's name server stores a record for www.attacker.net *and* a false record for www.acme.com, which resolve in the following manner:

```
www.attacker.net    2.3.4.5
www.acme.com        2.3.4.5
```

The attacker now issues a lookup request to dns.mycompany.com for www.attacker.net. In turn, dns.mycompany.com queries dns.attacker.net for that record. The attacker's DNS server replies with the normal response for www.attacker.net but *also* in the reply the attacker's name server includes the bogus entry for www.acme.com. Bingo—the cache of dns.mycompany.com has been poisoned. The next time that anyone queries dns.mycompany.com for the record for www.acme.com, 2.3.4.5 will be returned from the cache, and the user will be directed to the attacker's server instead of acme's! Fortunately, most modern name servers are protected against this type of attack, but older versions, such as BIND versions older than 4.9.6 and 8.1.1, are still vulnerable.

The second type of poisoning requires a bit more luck for the attacker. If an attacker is capable of spoofing a reply from a legitimate name server, the victim will cache the bogus record. In this scenario, the attacker would send a query to dns.mycompany.com for the address of www.acme.com. Again, if dns.mycompany.com did not already have the address in its cache, it would need to go find it. dns.mycompany.com would send a query to the dns.acme.com domain and wait for the answer. The attacker then would spoof a response, making it appear as if `dns.acme.com` has sent the response. The spoofed response would give the address of `www.acme.com` as being 2.3.4.5 (which is actually the IP address of `www.attacker.net`). `dns.mycompany.com` then would cache this response and thus would be poisoned.

Now, in implementation, this attack is not so straightforward. DNS queries contain an ID field that lets the DNS servers identify the query to which a response applies. So, the attacker needs to accurately guess this ID. If an attacker is able to sniff the traffic, this is fairly trivial. However, if the attacker is "blind," he might just send a lot of responses hoping to get the ID correct. This type of attack can be mitigated by configuring the name server to reject recursive queries from untrusted hosts and by ensuring that the name server software in use has a suitably hard-to-predict DNS query ID generator.

FTP Security

An ftp server can be considered similar to a mail server, in that they act as both sources and sinks for data over which they have little control. In the case of an ftp server, it is used as a place where files are uploaded to and downloaded from. Attacks against ftp servers, besides the usual remote exploits, are keyed to this inherent vulnerability. ftp servers are susceptible to similar attacks as Web servers, inasmuch as they might allow an attacker to traverse directories, read files that he's not supposed to be able to access, and write executable files to directories that later can be used to gain administrative control of the server. For these reasons, the "generic" list of ftp server security hints has common characteristics to those of the Web server and mail server. In short:

- The ftp process should not be run as the root account, or should be in the same administrative group as an administrator.
- Protecting the directory structure of the system with appropriate read/write/create/execute privileges is key to preventing an intruder from uploading and executing code on the system.
- Anonymous ftp is a necessary evil. Prevent abuses by limiting the number of writeable directories and limiting their access privileges. Once an anonymous file is written to a directory, limit others' ability to read the file until it has been inspected by an administrator.
- Audit and review ftp accesses, and log all usernames, source and destination IP addresses, file transfers, and command usage.
- When possible, make use of chroot to limit users' (including the anonymous user) access to their home directory and lower.
- Be aware that allowing anonymous uploads to your ftp server can set you up to become a repository for pirated software and other undesired content. Monitor the data that is uploaded to your server, and watch for the creation of hidden directories or large spikes in your site's usage.

Summary

We began this chapter by discussing the importance of securing operating systems and applications. At the same time, we made the statement that no single book could possibly cover this topic in its entirety. The mere fact that new vulnerabilities are discovered every day means that any attempt to cover every vulnerability will immediately obsolete the text. The title of this chapter specifically used the word *concepts* for just that reason. Although it is important to understand the risks associated with operating systems and software, it's more important to understand the security concepts that underlay each of these components.

For example, once you understand how access-control mechanisms work, you can tailor them to your specific environment in a way that makes both security sense *and* operational sense. Anyone who tells you that he has the ultimate checklist for locking down Windows NT is doing you a disservice because locking down a Windows NT Web server is different from locking down a file server, and locking down a file server in a domain that utilizes NetBIOS will be different than locking down the same server when NetBIOS (hopefully) is not required.

This chapter covered a lot of ground, beginning with Windows NT security concepts. From there, we moved on to the Linux operating system and discussed security fundamentals that are widely applicable to most other UNIX variants. We then discussed network services in general detail, including RPC, NFS, and the X11 protocol. Finally, we brazenly tackled the subject of application software security and outlined general best practices for security Web, DNS, mail, and ftp servers. It is our hope that this chapter will provide you with the fundamentals for further research into the specific methods to lock down your particular systems in their unique environments.

7

**SYSTEM AND
SERVER SOFTWARE
ISSUES**

---

[1] *This is not everything that an access token specifies. For the sake of this discussion, however, it is sufficient.*

[2] *This is another difference from Windows. No special privileges are necessary to listen on low ports on Windows NT or 2000.*

Attack Scenarios

IN THIS CHAPTER

This chapter provides an overview of attack scenarios from the attacker's point of view. It details the options available to an attacker, the manner in which reconnaissance is performed, and how the actual attacks are launched. Additionally, we present the common motivations of attackers and the effect that these motivations have on the way attacks are performed. While individuals operate on their own accords and for their own idiosyncratic purposes, the generic purpose behind intrusion attempts does affect how the attack is waged. This book does not claim to be a sociological or psychological dissertation, but the generic motivations presented here might help administrators better determine their threats.

We begin with a review of "denial-of-service" attacks and then describe the details of the activities commonly associated with "hacker attacks." Although the former is designed to rather blatantly degrade or eliminate a system's ability to perform its mission, the latter can be quite sophisticated and stealthy, with a compromised system remaining undiscovered for months while the attacker has unfettered access to information and other resources.

It should be noted that this chapter does not condone or encourage nefarious and illegal actions. It is simply a presentation of techniques, and information itself is neither malevolent nor benevolent. You cannot know defense without understanding offense. However, to put a finer point on it: Do not use the material presented here to access or disrupt systems for which you have not been given explicit authorization. That is both illegal and rude.

Denial-of-Service Attacks

We begin with denial-of-service (DoS) attacks, due to their prevalence and ease. DoS attacks are confounding because they can be devastating to the target yet are almost trivial to perform. DoS attacks can be performed simply to annoy or in retribution for an act that the attacker finds disagreeable, or they can be part of something larger and more nefarious. These attacks also can be used to draw attention away from an area of the network where a penetration attempt is being carried out or to disable access-control mechanisms.

Many of these attacks are done out of curiosity or by attackers who want to "flex their muscles and brains." Most of them just want to see what will happen and like to quietly giggle and brag to their friends when their actions have made the news. This does not change the fact that these attacks can have serious economic repercussions on companies that rely on their Internet presence for either direct revenue flow or their corporate reputation. On the other end of the motivation spectrum, we find attackers who have targeted specific sites for specific purposes. This could include cyberterrorists who want to interrupt service of or shake confidence in critical infrastructure systems such as power grids or financial systems.

One Shot, One Kill DoS Attacks

All software has bugs. These bugs can sometimes be leveraged by an attacker to gain system access or simply to cause the software to crash and deny its service to legitimate users. Examples of this type of DoS attack are the "ping of death" and "teardrop" attacks that wreaked havoc in the late 1990s. Both of these attacks exploited IP fragment-handling conditions that the TCP/IP stack developers never anticipated: fragments that reassembled into extraordinarily large IP datagrams and fragments whose payload spaces overlapped.

The programming mistakes that allowed these attacks were not due to a lack of technical skill, but they resulted from an assumption that received packets would obey the technical and customary rules as detailed in the protocol specifications. For example, unlike TCP segments, there is no reason that IP fragments ever should overlap, so most stack developers never thought to check for and handle this condition. As a result, the normal IP reassembly code ended up crashing the system when these overlaps occurred on some systems. The mind-set that created this opportunity was one of trust—in this case, programmers trusted all of the other developers to follow the rules of the protocol specifications.

By taking advantage of programmer error in critical software (in the case of the two previous examples, in the kernel TCP/IP code), an entire infrastructure can be taken out of service. DoS attacks are particularly maddening because, even if the attack itself is recorded, often very little can be done to trace its source. Attempting to find the origin of one or two packets with a spoofed source address on the Internet is a little like trying to find a particular needle in a stack of needles. The upside of these "one-time" DoS attacks is that once these bugs become publicly known, an administrator need only patch his systems with vendor-supplied fixes to prevent future DoS attacks from succeeding.

System Resource-Exhaustion DoS Attacks

If a sucker punch, in the form of a killer packet, cannot topple a system, it still might be possible to pummel the system with many less forceful packets until it simply falls to its knees. DoS attacks that do not rely on software bugs to create immediate system crashes can employ a variety of "resource-exhaustion" techniques to do the job over time. These attacks require a bit more effort from the attacking system because it must send out many packets, or they require coordination of multiple systems, but not much more effort is demanded for the attacker.

Resource-exhaustion attacks generally consist of a series of requests for legitimate services being sent to a system, but in a way designed to cause the target system to spend so much time and energy handling these requests that it is not capable of serving anything else. SYN floods are a good example of resource-consumption attacks. In a SYN flood, the attacking machine sends thousands of requests for a TCP connection to a targeted system. Because the victim system has been told explicitly that its job is to serve requests, it responds to the attacking system with a SYN/ACK saying, "Okay, great, let's talk." The victim system also allocates a portion of memory and a new file descriptor to handle the new connection. However, the attacking system never completes the third step in the TCP session establishment (the return ACK), so the victim system never frees up the allocated resources.

By creating hundreds or thousands of these half-open connections, an attacker can very quickly consume all available TCP connectivity resources on the victim system (not all available system resources, but the resources allocated for TCP connection setup). This attack also can affect ancillary systems, such as firewalls, intrusion-detection systems, and upper-layer switches. For instance, a stateful firewall will have to create a new state table entry for each connection request that passes by, or a proxy will have to create new proxy endpoints for each request. In effect, this puts the firewall in the same unfortunate position as the actual target of the attack.

Susceptibility to SYN floods is a direct consequence of trusting that other systems on the network (the Internet, for most IP systems) will play by the rules. These attacks do not exploit exception-handling errors as the teardrop and the ping of death did; they simply result from an attacker knowing the rules of the game and choosing not to play by them. As a result, SYN floods are pretty difficult to defend against. TCP/IP stacks will "time out" connection attempts that fail to complete; however, this takes time, and the attacker simply has to throw the session-initiating SYN packets at the target host faster than it can close out expired sessions. However, most modern operating systems have built-in algorithms designed to handle SYN-flood attacks; the efficiency of these algorithms varies by system.

In some other situations, resource exhaustion might be the fault of the programmer. Consider a Web-based application that takes input from a user, performs database lookups, and returns the results to the user. If the database query performed requires several joins, the creation of a few temporary tables and a number of locks, this query will be extremely resource-intensive and will tie up processor time and disk utilization on the server systems. Conversely, it requires very little in the way of resources from the attacker to submit a packet that initiates the database query. Thus, pounding the database with hundreds or thousands of complex queries will deny other users their clock cycles on the database, creating an effective DoS condition.

Once again, the administrator is faced with an attack that is due not so much to "bad programming" as it is to "bad security programming." Few Internet application developers are trained to even consider this kind of attack. So, although their code might be quite elegant and might function perfectly under normal conditions, it might turn out to be quire vulnerable to an attacker who wants to deny or severely limit the accessibility of the application to legitimate users.

To combat DoS attacks, some organizations perform their own testing to determine the susceptibility of their systems to DoS attacks. Recently, a well-known institution that maintains a critical enterprise network was so concerned about this type of attack that it commissioned a third party to study its systems and craft attacks that exploited DoS vulnerabilities in custom Web applications. After several rounds of these exercises, this particular company could identify potential sources of DoS attacks and tighten its systems—both through network configuration and application code modifications—to the point that its critical applications became highly resistant to many denial-of-service attacks.

Network Abuse

Another variation of the resource-exhaustion attack targets the network infrastructure instead of the servers or the applications that run on them. These attacks can be performed in a variety of ways, depending on the resources and relative cleverness of the attacker. Some of these attacks are designed to specifically consume network bandwidth, while others do it as a side effect. An example of the latter is a highly active SYN flood attack, perhaps originating from many attacking computers, which results in many thousands of packets per second being directed toward a target network. In this case, an attacker would be able to create bogus network traffic that overwhelms the bandwidth of the network infrastructure. This type of attack does not rely on software bugs or flaws in network protocols, but it uses merely brute force to accomplish its goals. There are few ways for a victim to prevent such an attack, although it might be possible to block such activity through the concerted efforts of ISPs.

This raises yet another complication with dealing with DoS attacks. Suppose that an attacker is relatively unsophisticated and crafts attack traffic that easily could be blocked by an access-control list (ACL) on a router. For example, an attack that targets a specific TCP/UDP port or that comes from a single source IP address easily could be blocked from a network with one or two changes to a router's packet-filtering configuration.

Even if this is successful and the attacking packets can't get past the router, all the DoS traffic still is flowing through (and filling up) the administrator's connection from the ISP. So, even though the traffic doesn't make it into the network, it clogs the pipe that supplies the network. If an organization has a relatively low-speed circuit, such as a T1 (1.5Mbps), the network's response to legitimate users could be quite sluggish, to the point of being nearly useless. This points to the fact that ISPs must be part of the overall solution to DoS attacks. This makes it a necessity to have your ISP's technical help number available at all times—it is often not possible for the victim to effectively deal with a sustained resource-exhaustion attack.

Even if it is possible to block the flood traffic "upstream," another complication exists. While stopping the spoofed source addresses to curb the attack, any legitimate traffic from these addresses also will be blocked. This can be devastating if the source addresses happen to be the same as the addresses of a group of proxy servers from the larger ISPs: In effect, by attempting to stop the flood, you're also explicitly denying legitimate access requests.

8

Amplification Attacks

When a single attacker possesses less bandwidth than the target or victim, the attacker cannot always carry out an effective DoS attack on his own and must find a way to even the playing field. For example, if the attacker connects to the Internet through a T1 (1.5Mbps) and the intended victim has an OC-3 (155Mbps), it is not possible for the attacker to consume enough of the victim's bandwidth to effect a DoS situation. Amplification attacks facilitate this by allowing each packet that the attacker sends to result in much more data being delivered to the target network. Amplification attacks employ techniques that the military might call "force multipliers." A classic example of this is the Smurf attack from early 1998.

In a Smurf attack, which is illustrated in Figure 8.1, the source address of an ICMP echo request[1] (ping) was spoofed to the IP address of the intended victim. This made it seem as though the victim was sending out an ICMP ECHO request and was waiting for ICMP REPLY packets. The destination address was the broadcast address somewhere on the victim's subnet. Thus, it seemed to surrounding computers that the victim wanted all computers within the broadcast domain to send reply packets. As a result, potentially hundreds of packets were sent to the victim as the result of one forged ping. It is interesting to note that the widespread success of these attacks was due in large part to poor administrative policies on routers: Gateway routers should not pass packets with a destination of the broadcast address.

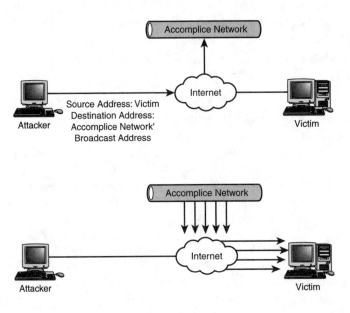

FIGURE 8.1

The Smurf attack.

This is the first time that we have explicitly mentioned spoofed, or forged, source IP addresses in this chapter. In normal network communications, the source address of the packet is set by the native TCP/IP stack running on a host computer or other network device. Many of the DoS attacks craft their packets, including the IP headers, allowing the attacker to set the source address to anything he wants. This is a common technique used in many denial-of-service attacks. In this case, the spoofed IP was key to the attack because it is the mechanism used to trick all of the hosts that received the broadcast "request" packet to "reply" to the victim. The same technique often is used to hide the identity of the true source of an attack.

Fragmentation Attacks

Packet fragmentation at the network (IP) or transport (TCP) layer can cause headaches for access-control devices, such as routers or firewalls, and network intrusion-detection sensors. These attacks generally are not aimed at specific servers because they are not terribly resource-intensive once they reach the host (unless the attacker has *a lot* of bandwidth). Instead, these attacks are designed to chew up time on a network's defensive systems. The basic theory is not complex:

- Fragment everything.
- Fragment the packets into the smallest pieces that will be processed (target-dependent).
- Send the fragments out of order.
- Have the fragments overlap.
- Resend the same fragment multiple times.
- Delay the sending of each fragment in a random fashion.
- Make use of IP or TCP options.
- Create a lot different connections.

The result is that defensive devices (router, firewall) spend a lot of time waiting and continually reassembling IP datagrams and TCP sessions, while still having to process all of the normal traffic or monitor and regulate the rest of the network activity. Many commercial network intrusion-detection systems designed to monitor networks for suspicious activity often can be overwhelmed by such an attack.

Distributed Denial-of-Service Attacks

Unless you're new to the planet, the term *distributed denial-of-service* (DDoS) should be all too familiar (it has even entered the vocabulary of one of our grandmothers). Although the Smurf attack can be considered a distributed technique, the specific mode of attack that is associated with the term *DDoS* did not appear until the summer of 1999. The day that many of the Internet's most prominent news and e-commerce sites ground to a halt in February 2000 marks the point that the public at large learned of these attacks. Fortunately, this is a lesson that will not soon be forgotten. Unfortunately, the issue does not have an easy solution.

DDoS Theory

The theory behind DDoS is by no means complex, and it has been used in warfare since the beginning of conflict: Overwhelm your opponent with sheer numbers. If an attacker controls a large number of systems, then many of the attacks described previously can be launched simultaneously, and a victim site can do very little to stop the traffic. With a little cleverness, even a few systems with limited bandwidth can clog a site's Internet connection.

The only new requirement for the DDoS attacker is to find a method to gain access to and then control many systems simultaneously from a central location. This hurdle has been solved by a wealth of software available from a number of hacker sites across the Internet. Such exploit software allows an attacker to install a program that allows the target machine (also referred to as a zombie) to receive simple commands that trigger sometimes complex actions on the part of the target machine. Furthermore, several DDoS attacks have employed existing communications infrastructures such as IRC chat by which to communicate with the troops (attack computers) in the field.

The generic model of a DDoS attack network is illustrated in Figure 8.2. Although the details vary from attack to attack, there is typically an attacker, his agents, and a target. The agents—also called 'bots or zombies—are almost always unwitting accomplices: They are computers that have been previously compromised by the attacker. When the "troops" are in place, the attacker simply issues a command to the attack software that has been secretly loaded onto the agents, and the agents begin attacking one or more target systems using all sorts of techniques, usually of the resource-exhaustion variety.

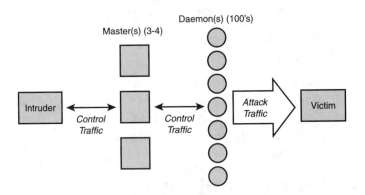

FIGURE 8.2
The DDoS model.

The command and control systems for DDoS vary with the specific attacks. The Trinoo code discovered in June 1999 employed TCP and UDP connections on fixed ports. Two months later, a system dubbed "Tribal Flood Network" was found that used ICMP echo replies with encrypted payloads for command and control, allowing the attacker to communicate with agents that sat behind loosely configured firewalls and router filters. Finally, in September 1999, the Stacheldraht (German for "Barbed Wire") DDoS agents were found, which added authentication and configuration encryption and also enabled attack agents to connect to a site and upgrade themselves.

Although firing packets at a target as fast as possible is effective, it lacks a certain elegance. This approach also might not be capable of the proper deluge necessary to disable the target's network. However, by employing a variation on the amplification attacks described previously, an attacker can very quickly tilt the scales in her favor. A simple example is that of abusing the HTTP protocol. The idea is to send small requests that result in large amounts of data being returned. By sending a 100-byte request—say, `GET /video/giant_movie.mpg`—an attacker can force a server to return 40MB of data. If 100 systems simultaneously made a request for giant_movie.mpg, 4GB of data suddenly would try to move out of the target network, thereby clogging the network with this bogus traffic.

In a relatively short period of time, DDoS agents and command and control techniques became quite sophisticated. The threat from DDoS attacks is quite serious. Fending off resource-exhaustion attacks from hundreds or thousands of computers, each using randomized source IP addresses, is problematic, at best. In this case, one of the most effective ways to reduce the threats of these attacks is to increase the security posture of Internet users. These attacks rely on compromised computers to do the dirty work. Security practices that reduce the likelihood of your systems being used in an attack, such as keeping operating systems and applications patched and implementing simple antispoofing packet filters on your border routers, help make the Internet a safer place to be. In addition, ISPs can filter out packets with spoofed IP addresses to limit the amount of bogus traffic that attackers can send.

System-Penetration Techniques

Although the techniques involved in denial-of-service attacks range from the relatively simple to the increasingly sophisticated, the damage of such an attack is almost always obvious: Networks or servers are rendered incapable of performing their intended tasks. Less obvious but equally (or even more) damaging results can be achieved through system penetration, where the intent is not to kill the target but to "own" it. "Owning" a computer in this sense, of course, has nothing to do with a receipt for the amount of purchase, but it describes the ability of the attacker to do anything he wants, whenever he wants, to or with the compromised system.

8

ATTACK
SCENARIOS

In some cases, these intrusions might be as unsophisticated as running a precompiled exploitation program or script. Other times, the methods contrived to break into a system can border on the sublime.

The reason *why* an attacker attempts to compromise a particular system might be impossible to determine, but a small number of core motivations are worthy of discussion:

- **Boredom/thrill**—This is usually an untargeted attack. Generally, an attacker just wants to get in somewhere and doesn't really care where.
- **Curiosity**—This can be a targeted or untargeted attack. For example, an attacker might just be trying out some new exploit against a random system, or perhaps she is targeting a specific operating system to learn more about it.
- **Use in DDoS attacks**—This is almost always an untargeted attack. The eventual target of the DDoS will be targeted; an attacker needs to put zombies on any and all available computers available to her and point them at a specific target.
- **Graffiti**—This can be a targeted or an untargeted attack.
  - *Untargeted*: Just painting your name on the wall for fun or notoriety.
  - *Targeted*: Defacing a site as an act of protest against the owners of the site.
- **Use as a hop point**—This can be a targeted or an untargeted attack.
  - *Untargeted*: Collecting systems through which an attacker later can be capable of hiding his tracks.
  - *Targeted*: Compromising a system trusted by the actual target of an attack.
- **Resource theft**—This attack involves using a company's servers as "warez" sites for sharing cracked programs or media files. This is typically a target of opportunity.
- **Information theft**—Any information asset can be a target; however, credit card numbers, personal information, and intellectual property are all common examples. This is almost always a targeted attack.

This list is presented in a rough order of increasing skill. The designation of targeted or untargeted indicates whether the attack is usually the result of an attacker taking particular interest in a particular system, or whether the attacker simply wants access to *any* system. Penetrating a particular system generally takes a higher level of skill, but this is system-dependent.

The personal motivation for information theft can vary greatly. As an example, consider the options open to an attacker who is able to obtain 20,000 credit card numbers from an e-commerce site:

- Simply charge some sum of money to each of the cards and hope to collect on most of the transactions.

- Post the credit card numbers on the Internet, embarrassing the owners of the compromised site.

- Contact the CEO and offer to "fix" the security holes that you used for a consulting fee of $500,000. This is also known as "blackmail."

The path to a successfully compromised system usually has several steps in it: reconnaissance, vulnerability research and development, and vulnerability exploitation.

Reconnaissance

Usually an attacker must gain a level of information about a network and its systems before he is capable of launching an actual attack. Reconnaissance can be either active or passive, and it can range from making use of public information to interrogating individual systems. Astute administrators are aware of reconnaissance methods and their signatures, so wary attackers must employ deception to keep from being noticed.

The scope of reconnaissance is really a function of the goals of the attacker. If a specific organization is selected as a target, with the goal of somehow acquiring specific information (such as the recipe for the secret sauce or all of the credit card numbers on a server), then the attacker can look for every possible way into the network. On the other hand, if the attacker intends to compromise as many systems as possible in an attempt to field an army of DDoS "agents" using a ready-to-run exploitation, then the reconnaissance might be tailored to look for any system with the specific vulnerability. Automated "scan and compromise" systems such as this are increasingly common with worms such as Code Red and Nimda, both of which ran rampant across the Internet for several weeks in the summer of 2001. As a final example, consider an ISP that wants to verify that its customers are not violating its "acceptable use policy" by running a news server. The ISP simply might perform regular reconnaissance of its own network, looking for such servers.

We will conduct this discussion from the standpoint of an attacker who is targeting an Internet presence to steal information. This attacker is very aware of the potential for raising suspicion with his actions. As we go through each step in reconnaissance, we will note the various methods that can be used to avoid detection.

Gathering Network Information

Here the attacker attempts to discover the architecture, location, and components of the network being attacked. Note that by "location," we mean logical location, not geographical location. Although the legal consequences of penetrating a system can vary with the geographical locations of the target and the attacker, it is rarely significant to the technical attacks themselves. There is a wealth of information out there ready for the taking, ranging from publicly available information to active sweeps of an address space, to active sweeps of individual systems.

Public and Anonymous Sources of Information

The various Network Information Centers (NICs) around the world have databases that contain information about every registered domain on the Internet. The information in these databases is supplied by the individual who initially registers the domain and, in some cases, might be false. However, three distinct fields must be valid for domain records: the primary DNS server for the domain, the secondary DNS server for the domain, and the email address of the administrative contact for the domain. Note that the contact email address must be a valid email address, but it does not necessarily need to be the administrator's primary email address. NICs can be queried for their information in a variety of methods, but the most common is via the whois utility. Data gathering of this nature is undetectable by the target network's administrator because the queries are made against systems not under their control (unless, of course, the target network happens to be a NIC).

The American Registry for Internet Numbers (ARIN) database contains information about the network addresses assigned to a particular company. This is important for the attack because it gives the breadth of an Internet presence. In some cases, the ARIN record might contain only information about the ISP that owns the network, not the company itself (this is generally the case for address spaces smaller than Class C addresses). As with the NIC queries, this information can be retrieved without the administrator's knowledge.

Although ARIN might be useful for gathering information about IP addresses assigned by registries in the Americas, the RIPE and APNIC databases would have to be consulted for registration information regarding IPs assigned by European and Asian Pacific registries. IP addresses *generally* are distributed to the various major registries (ARIN, RIPE, and APNIC) on a Class A network basis. The registration authority then is further delegated to other registries. For example, a recent search for information on a suspicious IP address resulted in a query to the APNIC whois database. Although some information was available, the query response included a reference to the Korean NIC (KRNIC), which maintained a more detailed database. Furthermore, some .gov and .mil information can be found in their own databases.

Accessing Public Information

With this information in hand, the attacker now can begin querying the target's DNS servers for information. The dig utility is quite flexible and easy to use, but its virtues over any other DNS utility come down to just a matter of personal taste. Issuing an ANY query (a request to return all of the records in the database) for the target domain returns the mail exchange and name server records. This gives a list of the systems responsible for receiving mail and handling DNS requests for the domain. In rare cases, host information (HINFO) queries will return (possibly false) configuration information (for example, hardware platform, OS type and version, and so on) about a particular system. Finally, a domain's zone file, which contains all name-to-address mappings that an administrator has defined, can be obtained by issuing DNS zone-transfer requests.

A bit of a religious war exists regarding whether zone transfers represent a security risk. If the DNS server includes records about internal systems that the public has no business accessing, then DNS information can be considered sensitive. On the other hand, if it simply contains records on things such as publicly accessible servers (for example, www, mail, and ftp), then it is no more sensitive than your listing in the phone book. Like all religious wars, no side will ever win, but attackers like zone transfers because they provide a list of targets that might not otherwise be accessible (or that might be more difficult to obtain).

It is possible for administrators to notice DNS queries, but, in most cases, they are considered normal traffic and will not likely send a red flag. The exceptions to this are zone transfers (which are not normal unless originating from a slave DNS server), HINFO queries, and lots of normal name-resolution queries from the same source over a short period of time.

Obtaining More Restricted Information

The various services that a site offers also can yield valuable information. For instance, most Web sites have a site map section that offers links to whatever resources the site has decided to offer. After grabbing this HTML file and putting it through a simple shell or Perl script, an attacker can obtain a fairly decent list of the Web server's directory structure and a list of other Web servers and application servers, including internal servers, that the main Web site needs to carry out its duties.

Finally, the robots.txt file is designed to tell Web-crawling robots not to crawl through specified directories. Obviously, this might contain a list of directories useful for an attacker. Nearly every IDS on the planet matches the GET /robots.txt string as an attack-detection signature, although it often is disabled due to the number of false positives that it generates.

Network Probes and Detection-Evasion Techniques

Although "normal" queries to servers can yield some interesting starting points, only so much information is available without active "probes." To gain a full understanding of network architecture and constituents, it is necessary to send more tailored reconnaissance network traffic and analyze the results returned by the target. Paranoid attackers aim to carry out this active reconnaissance while going unnoticed by the trained administrator's eye. Accomplishing this end falls into two categories: blending into normal traffic and spreading out the probes (in the sense of both source addresses and time), so as to "fly under the radar." In most attacks, the two are used in tandem.

To blend in with normal traffic, probes are sent that are in character with the type of service that a particular system offers, or they do not stray much from benign traffic. When there are only a few systems or services to probe, this is fairly straightforward and does not require too much cleverness. However, when a good number of probes are required to gather the desired intelligence about a network, it is often desirable to incorporate the dynamic of spread, or "slow" scans.

"Normal" requires that the structure, service, and frequency of the probes fall within the standard deviation of the average. So, rather than sending a host probe to all 253 addresses on a Class C from one host in a couple of seconds, one probe might be sent of each of 253 different source addresses over the course of a week. The downside to this approach is that the information gleaned might not be entirely accurate (hosts go up and down all the time), and it might still be detected by advanced event-correlation engines. Because the number of potential hosts is a constant, a maximum number of source addresses can be used. Thus, the only variable in the equation that can be modified to decrease the chance for detection is time.

Because any scan is just a snapshot in time of the target environment, the results of a slow scan are not necessarily any less valid than the results of a fast scan; however, attackers find it a good idea to verify that a specific host is still "up" if they want to revisit it later. This same formula holds for port scanning. Because the TCP port space provides 65,536 possible service "addresses," the potential number of source addresses now increases to the number of hosts to be scanned, multiplied by the product of ports and number of protocols to be scanned.

To summarize, avoiding evasion is the product of gathering as much information as possible with the fewest number of probes possible and then attempting to make those probes that are necessary appear as normal as possible. The next few sections concentrate on the different techniques that gather intelligence, weighing ostentatiousness and effectiveness.

Network Sweeps

Sweeping a network is simply the act of addressing a packet to each address on a network and analyzing the results. The most common form is using ICMP echo requests (pings) and waiting for results. This is naïve, for two reasons: ICMP often is blocked at gateways, and it's incredibly obvious to administrators. As we discussed before, the goal is to look as innocuous and normal as possible, and a slew of ICMP pings is hardly normal.

A more clandestine approach is to send pings that look like normal (if misdirected) traffic, such as HTTP. There are clever ways to accomplish this, such as sending TCP ACKs instead of SYNs. In most TCP/IP stacks, an RST ("reset") is returned for any unexpected or invalid ACK. However, if an attacker is concerned only with whether a host exists, this accomplishes the task quite nicely because any response indicates that the host exists. This technique also has the advantage of evading any NIDS that does not have a state table of all active connections, and it will slip past some router access control lists. On the negative side, these probes might not make it past a firewall that performs stateful inspection of the packet traffic.

Network Routing Information

Scanning for hosts results in a list of IP addresses that are remotely accessible from the Internet; however, it does not tell anything about the layout of the target network. Knowing the path that a packet takes from point A to point B can reveal a great deal about the topology of a network, access-control devices, and trusted systems. There are a few methods of gathering this information, each with its advantages and disadvantages.

The most common and well-known method is that used by tools such as traceroute. In this scenario, the Time to Live (TTL) field in the IP header is set to a small value, normally 1. The packet is sent with a destination address of the target. After the TTL expires at the first gateway, an ICMP "TTL expired in transit" message is returned, and the gateway drops the packet. A second packet is sent, with the TTL incremented usually by 1, and an ICMP error message is returned by the second gateway along the route. "Lather, rinse, repeat" until a response from the target is received. This is a fairly effective method, although it is common for ICMP unreachable messages to be blocked by a site's border gateway. It is also easily detected by NIDS. Regardless of what happens after the packet reaches the target network though, usually a decent path will be traced to the target's gateway. Note that the path of packets through the core of the Internet can vary over time; however, the topology of the edge networks usually does not provide much flexibility in routing.

The IP protocol specification provides support for the "Record Route" IP option, which instructs each gateway along a route to insert its IP address (and, optionally, a time stamp) into the Options section of the IP header. When the destination host responds, it includes these addresses in the response. This approach has varying levels of success and is fairly obvious. The IP header also has room to record only eight IP addresses (four, if time stamps are desired along with the gateway address), an increasingly aggravating limit as the Internet continues to expand.

It is also possible to request routing tables from a gateway directly. The effectiveness of this is based on the configuration of the router and the routing protocols in use. These queries go undetected more than they are caught, probably because many network administrators understand the details of configuring the routing service but are not familiar with the underlying details of the protocols themselves; they simply assume that routers talk to each other and don't worry about monitoring this activity.

Gathering Information About Individual Systems

When a decent concept of a network is established—that is, a list of available hosts and how the target network is connected to the Internet—it is necessary to gain insight into the individual constituents of the network. Much like a burglar needs to case the joint before developing a plan for entry, an attacker needs to find the doors and windows of a specific host.

Port Scans

Port scanning is a fairly straightforward act: Send packets to an arbitrary number of TCP or UDP ports and wait for responses. This approach provides a wealth of information, but is very, very loud. Sending TCP SYNs to 65,000 ports is rather likely to raise a few eyebrows. Thus, it is best for an attacker to send a few targeted probes and spread these probes over a few systems and a few days. Connection requests from untrusted hosts for some ports, such as TCP/139 (NetBIOS/Microsoft Networking) or TCP/111 (Sun Remote Procedure Calls) are evil by nature and will raise flags (more on this later).

TCP scanning can take many forms, based on which TCP flags are set. In a generic scan, a normal session-initiating TCP SYN is sent to each port; if the port is listening, a SYN/ACK is returned. A valid connection then is established and immediately ended. This is a very loud way to go about things, so clever people over the years have learned how to judge the responses elicited by more arcane and less suspicious TCP packets. A good treatment of the topic can be found in *The Art of Port Scanning* (Fyodor, 1997).

UDP scanning often is called "negative scanning," as an artifact of the way in which the UDP protocol works. Recall that UDP is a connectionless protocol. Thus, unless the UDP probe contains a properly formatted payload for the application layer of the service requested, no response will be returned. However, TCP/IP stacks are *supposed* to return an ICMP port unreachable message if the destination port of the packet does not correspond to a listening service. Thus, UDP scanning involves sending a UDP packet and waiting to see if an ICMP port unreachable message is returned. If so, the port is considered closed. If no response is received, the port in considered open.

UDP scanning is horribly imprecise because the unreachable messages might not be sent at all or could be blocked by a gateway router or firewall. Furthermore, because UDP is a "fire-and-forget" connectionless protocol, the packet might simply never make it to the intended host. Additionally, hosts are supposed to throttle the number of port unreachable messages that they send to reduce network traffic, so even if a host is configured properly, an attacker still might not get all of the responses expected.

Banner Grabbing

A good number of network services inform their clients of their type and version of software. This is ostensibly so that clients may speak in a compatible manner, but the ancillary effects make it incredibly useful for an attacker. By simply grabbing the "Server:" header from the reply to an HTTP request, an attacker knows the type and version of HTTP server software running on a target, and he has a fairly decent idea of the operating system. For example, the following "File Not Found" error message from a Web server reveals that the server is running Apache (with SSL) on a UNIX variant of some kind:

```
HTTP/1.1 404 Not Found{D}{A}
Date: Fri, 10 Aug 2001 00:13:34 GMT{D}{A}
Server: Apache/1.3.12 Ben-SSL/1.40 (Unix){D}{A}
Connection: close{D}{A}
Content-Type: text/html; charset=iso-8859-1{D}{A}
{D}{A}
< !DOCTYPE HTML PUBLIC "-//IETF//DTD HTML 2.0//EN" > {A}
< HTML > < HEAD > {A}
< TITLE > 404 Not Found < /TITLE > {A}
```

The same holds true of FTP, SMTP, POP/3, IMAP, SSH, telnet, and so on. As alluded to before, the fewer active probes are necessary to retrieve useful information, the less likely it is that the reconnaissance will be detected. Application banners provide a wealth of information with very little network traffic. The following example of a typical greeting from a telnet program is even more illuminating:

```
Red Hat Linux release 4.2 (Biltmore)
Kernel 2.0.35 on an i686
```

It is possible, although relatively rare, for an administrator to modify the data returned in these banners. This sometimes requires the modification and recompilation of the application's source code, but it can be as easy as just changing a field in a configuration file. If a change is obvious (for example, the SMTP daemon reports that it's running Microsoft Exchange, but the HTTP daemon reports that it's running Apache on UNIX), it might mean that the administrator has a clue or that the system is watched carefully. Of course, it also could be a trap.

OS Fingerprinting via TCP/IP

Due to idiosyncrasies in the implementation of the TCP/IP protocols, it is possible to remotely determine the operating system (and usually the operating system version) by, once again, violating or twisting the rules of the protocol. This technique works by analyzing a system's response to the various combinations of network and transport headers. This usually is performed using two techniques:

- Sending TCP/IP packets with an illegal TCP flag combination. For example, setting SYN and FIN at the same time is like calling and hanging up a phone in one move. Setting all of the TCP flags (the so-called "Christmas Tree" packet) is also not normal.

- Making several connection attempts in a row to gather statistics about how the target computer selects its initial TCP sequence number (ISN).

In the first technique, the probe takes advantage of the fact that different stack implementers have made different choices for explicitly or inadvertently handling the illegal packets. The second type of probe makes use of the observation that different developers employed different ISN algorithms. The science is astonishingly precise but is quite obvious. Additionally, fingerprinting through a proxy firewall usually returns information about only the firewall, not the protected host.

SNMP Queries

The Simple Network Management Protocol (SNMP) is indispensable for administrators on most large networks. It is designed to provide a standard interface for retrieving and setting configuration options on individual hosts, storing and retrieving statistics, and sending alerts in response to events. It is also an invaluable source of information for attackers. Information such as a system's user database, logged-in users, IP address (useful in NAT'ed environments), listening ports, OS type and version, hardware platform, and so on are free for the taking. A discussion of SNMP as a protocol is outside the scope of this chapter. Although there are currently three standard versions of SNMP, we will concentrate on Version 2 due to its prevalence.

Access control in SNMPv2 is based solely on community names. In general, there are two communities in an SNMP implementation: read-only and read-write. The default name for the read-only community is public, and the default for the read-write community is private. The "community strings" effectively act as passwords, so, unless the administrator has changed these names, it is possible to SET or GET any SNMP object identifier (OID) from the device's management information base (MIB) simply by supplying private or public, respectively. In cases when the community names have been changed, the names are often easy to guess. And because SNMPv2 runs on top of UDP, it is also trivial to spoof.

Being able to GET a record from a MIB can be very useful. For example, the MIB on an SNMP-equipped router will include details of every interface on the router, as well as statistics about the traffic it has passed. It is often very easy to GET the router's routing table as well, revealing significant information about the topology of the network. Usually, when an administrator fails to change the read community string, he also fails to change the read-write community string. This can be particularly disastrous, especially if an outsider is allowed to PUT the disabled value into a key router interface's Status field (for example, you remotely turn off the router's connection to the Internet).

SNMP provides an enormous amount of information, but it is also one of the most ostentatious reconnaissance methods available. Additionally, SNMP traffic often is blocked at the network's border interface to the Internet, rendering this reconnaissance technique useless.

SMB Information

Systems implementing LanManager-derived services (such as Windows, SAMBA, and OS/400) can provide an enormous amount of information for an attacker. In this section, we focus mostly on null sessions with Windows, but much of this also applies to other operating systems, depending on their configuration.

Null or anonymous sessions allow a remote user to log into a server providing SMB services without the trouble of supplying a username and password. There are valid reasons for this "feature" to exist (for example, system-management services and some back-up systems use it), but administrators have the option of disabling it. The Anonymous user, however, is severely restricted in what actions he may perform, and these actions do not stray outside the realm of requesting information. For an attacker's purposes, however, this is fantastic. The information returned includes the following:

- A list of all user and group accounts on the target
- Sundry information about the user accounts, such as last login date, whether the account is enabled, whether a password is required to access the account, the user's home directory, user ID, privilege level, and so on
- A list of all shares on the system
- System uptime, platform ID and version, the domain or workgroup of which the system is currently a member, the system's domain controller, and so on
- System policy information, including minimum password lengths, failed login lockout parameters, services supported, and so on
- A list of active sessions

The benefits of this information are probably fairly obvious. However, it is rarely possible to gather this information due to system configuration and choke-point access-control lists. It also requires the use of TCP port 139, which, as mentioned before, is a red-flag port that likely will set off bells and flashing lights.

RPC Services

Remote Procedure Calls (RPC) have a long and troubled history, from a security perspective. Both Sun and DCE RPC utilize a "portmapper" responsible for informing would-be clients of the TCP or UDP port on which the desired RPC service is running. Knowledge of which RPC services are enabled on a host can provide an obvious avenue of attack. Additionally, knowing which services are installed and running provides background information on the purpose of a system and what trust relationships might exist on the target network. For instance, if mountd is registered as an RPC service, that system is acting as an NFS server for other hosts. Issuing a showmount -e request will return a list of hosts allowed to mount its various exports (in some case, this list might include the attacker).

In both Sun and DCE RPC, requests to the portmapper (TCP port 111 for Sun RPC, and UDP port 135 for the Microsoft implementation of DCE RPC) normally are blocked by choke-point access-control lists. Given its history, external requests for RPC information immediately raise suspicion.

Vulnerability Determination and Choosing Targets

With the information gleaned during the reconnaissance phase of the attack, it is now possible to begin to determine the initial point of entry. When a particular system is the target of an attack, it is uncommon for it to be the first point of entry. This is because generally the target of attack is the most attractive and thus the most heavily guarded. Through reconnaissance effort, however, the attacker probably has been able to determine chinks in the armor and how he might be able to leverage the compromise of an ancillary system toward his ends.

Vulnerabilities can manifest themselves in numerous ways but can be classified in a few categories:

- System misconfigurations
- Software bugs
- Defaults/back doors
- Poor passwords

Discovering which vulnerabilities might or might not exist in a target network requires thorough knowledge of the operating system a software running on the target. Although a great number of vulnerability databases exist on the Internet, it is not always possible or convenient to search each for every potential vulnerability present on a target. Additionally, most are incomplete or out-of-date.

Automated vulnerability scanners exist, but their use likely will be severely limited in clandestine attacks because they are very obvious (even those who claim "stealth" capability). And like the vulnerability databases, they are often incomplete and out-of-date. It is critical that any user of a vulnerability scanner (offensive or defensive) know the current state of the tools and databases. Anyone using a security tool that was developed three years ago is likely going to leave many vulnerabilities undiscovered.

Choosing the first target is based on three factors taken together: the likelihood that an attack will succeed, the possibility that the intrusion will be detected, and how close the system will get an attacker to the ultimate target.

A host that can be compromised via an HTTP request (which could possibly be sent over HTTPS, making it undetectable by a network IDS) is highly attractive. Exploiting a buffer overrun in an SMTP server temporarily could disable mail and might set off IDS alarms, making it a less attractive target. Most of the time, however, attackers are not afforded the luxury of picking and choosing exactly *which* system and service will be the initial point of entry: They simply need a wedge from which they can leverage further access.

The vulnerability-determination phase overlaps quite a lot with the reconnaissance phase. When attempting to be stealthy, an attacker wants to reduce the amount of traffic sent to a host. Thus, as soon as a potential vulnerability is detected, the advantages and disadvantages of using that particular attack avenue are weighed. Remember, the more reconnaissance that is performed and the more information that is gleaned, the greater the chance of raising eyebrows is. The basic rule, unfortunately, is also a cliché: A bird in the hand is worth two in the bush. If a vulnerability is discovered early and it has a high probability of success, an attacker won't worry about waiting to see if a "better" way arises. Reconnaissance always can be continued once the initial wedge has been achieved.

It has been said that the majority of system intrusions originate from the inside. This is not so much because people inside a network are more motivated for mischief or are more skilled, but, rather, security is far more lax on internal systems. Even as of 2001, it is rare to find a corporate network with internal firewalls. This is presumably due to the unfortunate inverse needs that often are perceived between productivity and security; internal systems generally are left less secure to allow employees to perform their duties. Furthermore, many organizations tend to focus on the security of their public connection first and never seem to get around to locking down their internal architecture. It should be noted, however, that internal security policy enforcement is getting easier. We will cover this subject in depth in Chapter 6, "Example Network Architectures and Case Studies."

So, attackers generally need to compromise only one internal system before they have free reign of the typical corporate network. Getting to the internal network, however, is not generally as easy as compromising a Web server because most architectures segment Internet-accessible systems in a sort of quarantine zone where they have little, if any, contact with the internal network. Well, this is how the architecture is *supposed* to work anyway. In implementation, holes commonly are poked through access-control devices to allow developers to upload content to Web servers, to allow systems to talk to back-end databases, or to relay mail to internal servers. Attackers can make the most of these holes.

Compromising a System

How an attacker manages to compromise a system is based wholly on the vulnerabilities they have discovered. There are no magic bullets that will pop open an arbitrary system (although far too many lame exploits work far too often). An attacker could walk though the front door, hoping that it's unlocked, or he can find an open window. In this section, we will break down each of these approaches.

You're probably noticing that this section seems a little small for such an important topic. There is good reason for this: Most of the work is done discovering network architecture and determining where vulnerabilities exist, not actually exploiting them. Once an attacker finds a way in, all that's left is to exercise the avenue. And the exercise normally takes one of two forms: using a bug in software or pretending to be someone else.

./0wnit

The majority of system intrusions take place thanks to prewritten programs or scripts that exploit known vulnerabilities. As with denial-of-service attacks, running precanned software generally does not take an exceptional amount of skill, but exploit software is certainly valuable. That being said, a good portion of exploit code available on the Internet is inefficient, broken, and possibly a Trojan horse, compromising the would-be attacker in the course of committing nefarious deeds. Attackers must always be wary of any software run; when in doubt, they generally write their own. Although this is time-consuming, it's a fairly straightforward act once a vulnerability is known—if nothing else, it offers a modicum of self-respect, differentiating skill levels from those of a 15-year-old kid drunk on cough syrup running the latest "warez."

Additionally, a good number of NIDS signatures are exploit-specific, *not* vulnerability-specific, increasing the odds that a popular, ready-to-run exploit tool will be detected when it is aimed and fired at a network that has some level of security awareness.

Password Guessing

Repeated failed logins are a really good way for an attacker to get noticed. Not only will network-based and host-based IDS notice this, but firewall logs, router logs, and host logs also will faithfully record the insanity[2]. Furthermore, an attacker simply might be locked out on his third unsuccessful try. However, in some situations, such as dial-up servers, other options are not available. Knowing the risks and the fact that this likely will not be the most profitable approach, an attacker can help his cause by keeping a few considerations in mind.

For password guessing to be successful, an attacker must know the target. Passwords are often easy to guess once a user and a target have been researched. Additionally, remember that not everyone speaks English (or whatever your native tongue happens to be). If possible, an attacker might resort to the age-old reconnaissance technique known as "dumpster diving" and jump in a trashcan: Passwords are hard to remember, and people write them down.

Using Targeted Viruses and Trojans

If the target is on an internal system, it might be possible for someone to surreptitiously employ the service of an internal user's system to act as a hop point. If an attacker can convince this user to execute an application of his choosing, he can take control of that user's system remotely. Getting the user to execute the virus, however, is the stumbling block.

A good number of viruses presently spread via email. Email is ubiquitous, easy to forge, and targeted—and most end users feel comfortable using it. Having a user execute an email attachment on an attacker's behalf basically comes down to social engineering, and a user can be convinced to do an attacker's bidding in two main ways: positive action or negative action. A positive action occurs when the victim is curious and wants to, say, visit a Web site; a negative action occurs when the user is irritated and, say, wants to get off a spam mailing list. In both scenarios, the same end is accomplished: The user clicks on the attachment.

A fairly successful way to exploit a user is with applications ending in ".com" on Windows. Back in the DOS days, a .com file extension specified a small application (under 64k). In the 21st century, however, most people associate .com with an Internet site. Confusion and deception are a hacker's two best friends. The .com extension still signifies an application on all versions of Windows (and the 64k limit has been removed, in most versions), with the default action for clicking on something ending in .com being program execution. So, if an attacker sends mail to an internal user with a program attached called `www.winbigcash.com`, and a user clicks on what appears to be a link to a Web site, the application will execute.

A link such as this can be considered positive or negative: If the user really wants to win big cash, he will follow the link. If the user is annoyed by what appears to be spam, another "link" called `unsubscribe.winbigcash.com` can be provided. Furthermore, if the attacker were really clever, he could have the virus make the system open up a Web browser directed toward an Internet sweepstakes site, reducing the suspicion that "something didn't work right."

The goal here is still the same as in all other exploitation examples—simply to gain access to a system. However, rather than exploiting software bugs or guessing a password, an attacker is exploiting the weakest link in security, humans.

Extending the Reach

After initial access is gained, the initial point of entry becomes the base station from which all further operations will be launched. Penetrating a system on the same network is far simpler than attacking a system on a remote network. In this section, we cover a few of the options available once network access has been gained.

Sniffing the Wire

The obvious act once on a network is to take a look at what sort of data is being transmitted. All sorts of interesting data, such as system and application usernames and passwords, flies by every millisecond. Additionally, it is possible to gather a wealth of information about the other hosts on the network just by observing and analyzing the traffic that they emit. Even better for the attacker, sniffing a network is a passive act and leaves virtually no artifact on the network. We say "virtually" because methods do exist to determine whether a network interface is in promiscuous mode (which is required for network sniffing). These methods, however, are active and, for the most part, known, so it is possible to adjust sniffing software to recognize these attempts at discovery and adjust accordingly.

Of course, there must be a downside for the attacker. In this case, the downside is that most networks now are deployed using switches instead of hubs or coaxial cable, and sniffers do not work very effectively in switched environments. At the very least, however, the attacker will be able to capture any data sent to or from any host that has been compromised.

Exploiting Trust Relationships

Earlier we likened an attacker's activities to those of a physical burglar, but in some ways the attacker is luckier than a physical burglar. In this situation, he has an advantage: It is not uncommon for the keys to the house next door to have been left in house that was accessed. The concept of trust between systems might be loosely defined as an administrator making a policy that says, "If a user has been authenticated by system A, she's okay—let her in." Trust of this nature exists in the Berkley r* protocols (`rlogin`, `rcp`, `rsh`, and so on), NFS, the Windows NT domain authentication, and, to an extent, `ssh`.

If compromise of a trusted system is not possible, however, an attacker still has a few options. The most obvious is to spoof his address to appear as if he is the trusted host. Performing this task remotely (blind spoofing) is normally a fairly difficult task over TCP: The attacker must be capable of properly predicting TCP sequence numbers to complete the three-way hand-shake, and most modern TCP stacks employ at least a decent concept of randomness in their initial sequence-number generation. If the attacker is on the same network as the target system, he can attempt to take over the IP address, either by spoofing or simply by changing his inter-face's IP address. The complication here is the ARP tables: Other hosts on the network still will have the MAC address of the legitimate host. This issue usually can be solved simply via ARP poisoning. Refer to Chapter 4, "Network and Application Protocols," for more details on this subject.

Although session hijacking is not strictly within the domain of trust relationship exploitation, it deserves mention here. The idea itself is somewhat glamorous, but attackers probably will avoid it whenever possible. It's a fairly obvious act, and, generally, it is possible to avoid hijacking by simply being patient and waiting for the username and password strings to fly by on the network. In some cases, however, it is quite useful, most notably when host-based access control (such as TCPWrappers) are in use and spoofing is not possible.

Summary

This chapter discussed the threats and techniques that administrators must guard against. An attempt was made to provide a decent understanding of the most common methods in existence, but this chapter is by no means an exhaustive reference. About 99% of successful attacks use some variation of the methods presented here. So, being familiar with them puts you on par with the vast majority of your opponents. As for the other 2%, well, those are the dragons that you cannot know or stop. You can only hope to notice and have a recent backup.

---

[1] *Later variations made use of other protocols, such as UDP echo (port 9), but the theory remained that same.*

[2] *We're using Webster's Collegiate Dictionary's third definition in this situation: a: extreme folly or unreasonableness; b: something utterly foolish or unreasonable.*

Protecting Your Infrastructure

IN THIS CHAPTER

Ask most managers with responsibility for a network why their infrastructure is secure, and chances are good that the first thing they'll point to is their firewall. The fact that an organization has chosen to protect its network with a firewall is good, but, as a mathematician might say, the presence of a firewall is a necessary but not sufficient condition to demonstrate that a network is secure.

As we've tried to stress throughout this book, the security of an organization is dependent upon the sum of many different components: policy, implementation, monitoring, awareness, architecture, and the list goes on. By the same account, the effectiveness of a firewall is dependent upon a host of conditions. The reason for this is that effectiveness can be measured only with respect to business requirements. The Department of Defense maintains many "network high" information systems that are secure because they don't connect to any outside systems or because they don't allow any outside entities to access their systems. Obviously, this "perfect" level of security isn't an acceptable solution for an e-commerce retailer. This is perhaps the most important point that an IT professional should remember. *Secure* is a relative term, and the suitability of any firewall for a particular task is always a relative decision.

In this section, we will investigate the different types of firewall technologies prevalent in today's market, their relative benefits and drawbacks, and their overall capabilities and configurations. It's important to remember that, contrary to the claims of most manufacturers, there is not one "best" firewall. This is not to say that there are not market leaders or dominant technologies, but the suitability of any solution has to be measured against what your particular needs, budget, and capabilities are.

What Is a Firewall Supposed to Do?

Even before you start reading about how firewalls work, what their limitations are, and how to determine the best type for your network, it's important to first ask a simple question: What is it that you want a firewall to do? The short answer is, of course, to protect a network, but this is too simplistic to be of use and, in reality, is something that a firewall can't on its own accomplish. In many cases, the business needs of an organization are such that a firewall is almost superfluous: The organization requires so many "holes" to be poked in the firewall's rule set that its function is reduced to satisfying a check box on an auditor's checklist (Yes, the organization employs a firewall). The answer that we should be looking for is that the firewall is supposed to be a mechanism for implementing an organization's security policy. Given this definition, it's much easier to judge what constitutes a "good" firewall.

Let's take as an example a simple Web farm consisting of nothing but Web servers that serves up informational content for a big political campaign. The only real requirement is that the farm handle millions of hits a day. Let's assume that the group that deployed the farm did a great job of locking down the operating systems and configuring the Web server applications, and the group keeps them patched and up-to-date so that there are relatively few opportunities for compromising the systems. Let's also assume that there are relatively few services running on the servers besides HTTP and perhaps secure shell (ssh) for administering the operating systems. Now the question arises, "What's the best firewall to protect this network?" Without answering that question, let's consider another type of network, this one for a small office. This organization doesn't run any of its own Internet services, such as Web or mail servers; it has its email hosted by its ISP, and the only function that network users need with respect to the Internet is to be able to surf the Web and access their email accounts.

Now let's ask the same questions as before: What's the best firewall to protect this network? Does anyone believe that the answers to these two identical questions are going to be the same given the different circumstances and systems? Should the firewall product that can handle gigabit throughput be the same one that's deployed at a small office with a DSL line for the employees to check mail and surf the Web?

These types of scenarios lead us to a definition of a firewall as a function rather than a device. A router can provide a firewall function, as can an operating system, a proxy, or a load balancer. Often you hear an IT professional state that a firewall isn't practical for a network because of cost or performance constraints. These types of statements allude to the firewall as a device rather than a function. Turning this statement around allows us to say without qualification that all networks with untrusted connections need firewalls (a firewall function). The implementation of the firewall function is what the rest of this chapter will attempt to illuminate. It is exactly the definition of the firewall as a function rather than a device that dictates the need for the security professional to understand and weigh the capabilities and benefits of a firewall against the operational scenario in which it will be deployed. Phrases such as *considered the most secure* and *best of breed* make sense only in this context. Given these caveats, let's begin by reviewing the basic firewall types, features, and usages.

Firewall Functions

Because we're defining a firewall as a function rather than a device, let's begin by reviewing the basic attribute of a firewall. What most firewalls have in common is the way that they are programmed to limit or allow network traffic. This is done through the firewall rule set. Typical firewall rule sets consist of a source, destination, service, and rule. The source indicates the originator of the traffic. The destination indicates the intended recipient of the traffic. The service is the type of traffic (such as ICMP, TCP, or higher-level protocols such as telnet or HTTP). The diagram that follows gives the rule that allows a Web browser on the Internet to access the Web server on the network:

Source	Destination	Service	Rule
Anyone	Web server	HTTP	Allow

This says that anyone is allowed to access the Web server for Web browsing (HTTP). A rule that allows a site administrator to access the system via telnet from a remote workstation called Admin1 (let's not argue the advisability of that) might read as follows:

Source	Destination	Service	Rule
Admin1	Web server	telnet	Allow

A rule set that allows connections to a mail server from other mail servers or users on the Internet (again, let's not scrutinize the advisability of this) is:

Source	Destination	Service	Rule
Any	Mail server	SMTP/POP3	Allow

Now, you'll notice that there are no rules that allow the return connections for these services. These are implied in the syntax, so the rule that allows anyone to contact the Web server via HTTP implies that the Web server can reply back. As you will see in a few paragraphs, this might or might not be true when it comes to a particular firewall device (router, gateway, and so on), depending upon the type of firewall being used.

One very important point to remember about a firewall, and one major differentiator between a firewall and a router, is that the firewall's default condition should be to load a rule that states the following:

Source	Destination	Service	Rule
Any	Any	Any	Deny

That is, if none of the other rules applies, then deny any service from any source to any destination. A firewall should explicitly deny that which is not allowed, while a router is expected to allow anything that is not explicitly denied.

Firewall Ancillary Functions

The basic capabilities of a firewall should be, therefore, to filter traffic based upon source and destination addresses and service. Anyone who has surveyed commercial firewalls knows that this is only the beginning of a firewall's capabilities. Many firewalls have the capability to implement Network Address Translation (NAT), perform antispoofing functions, block some types of denial-of-service attacks, detect simple network scans, disallow attempts at subverting service protocols, encrypt communications, and authenticate users, as well as a host of others. As networking devices become more advanced, these firewall capabilities could be found on equipment that has not been traditionally associated with firewalling functions, such as switches and load balancers, and they even have been built into most popular operating systems.

Many firewalls also have the capability to interface with additional security devices such as virus scanners, intrusion-detection systems, active content scanners, and authentication servers. There are also firewall features that have nothing to do with the security of the firewall, per se, such as the capability to manage many firewalls from a single access point, or the capability to implement a firewall in a high-availability or load-balanced mode. Finally, you can look at the ways that firewalls have been implemented, such as the so-called "appliance" firewalls, software-based firewalls, and "personal" firewalls that run on end-user machines such as laptops and desktops. There are even firewalls for PDAs and cell phones.

Again, given our definition of the firewall as a function rather than a device, it's easy to talk about these additional features separately and then allow you, the IT professional, to determine what set of features is necessitated by your security policy. This also makes it very easy to debate the relative merits of a "traditional" firewall versus, say, a router that claims to also be a firewall, because you will be able to compare the functions that each implements rather than the name that it calls itself. For example, if you decide that your network requires a firewall with stateful inspection (discussed later) and the router that you have in place performs only packet filtering (also discussed later), then you have a good argument for purchasing a stateful-inspection firewall to augment the packet filter firewall function implemented in the router. By the same token, if you want to protect your Web farm with a stateful-inspection firewall and your load balancer already implements a stateful-inspection firewall function, then you might not be adding any additional security by introducing a standalone firewall to the mix.

The rest of this chapter is devoted to defining and investigating the following sets of firewall functions and capabilities, with the goal of allowing you to make informed decisions about the type of firewall your network requires:

- Packet filters
- Stateful inspection
- Application gateways
- Hybrids
- O/S–based

- Air Gap
- Use with 802.1b VLANs
- Virus scanning
- Content scanning
- IDS
- DoS protection
- NAT
- Antispoofing
- Firewall management
- Logging
- Administration
- Firewall appliances
- Authentication
- VPN
- High availability
- Load balancing

The Basic Firewall Types

Now that you know what the basic functions of the firewall are, it's time to look at how it carries out those functions. Three basic types of firewalls are in broad usage today:

- Packet-filtering firewalls
- Stateful-inspection firewalls
- Application proxy firewalls

Along with these "pure" firewall types, there are hybrid firewalls that allow a mixture of these methods to be utilized to balance speed, security, and scalability.

Packet-Filtering Firewall

The first type of firewall is the "classic" packet filter. A filter operates on individual IP packets and has no knowledge of the payload being carried. Packet filters typically make their go/no-go decisions based on the source and destination IP addresses in the packet header, as well as the source and destination TCP/UDP ports. The filter looks at only data at this network layer and ignores other layers of the OSI model. This means that a packet filter does not understand or process any of the details of Layer 4 protocols such as TCP, or Layer 7 protocols such as telnet, HTTP, or SMTP. Therefore, a packet filter doesn't know the difference between the start of a connection and the end of a connection; it simply examines the traffic packet by packet and applies its rules to them one at a time. An example of this is shown in Figure 9.1. Here, a TCP connection has been broken up into multiple packets, each of which is examined by the packet filter before being passed or stopped. Note that the packet filter doesn't care which order the packets arrive in. If, because of quirky Internet routing, the final (FIN) packet shows up before the initial (SYN) packet, the packet filter will forward it the source address, destination address, and port numbers that match its criteria.

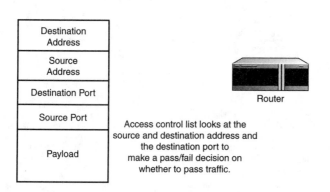

FIGURE 9.1

Packets arriving out of order.

In short, the packet filter doesn't look at anything past the first few bytes of the packet header. This makes a packet filter a poor choice for, say, preventing a denial-of-service attack perpetrated by sending a large number of packets with the SYN flag set and the source and destination addresses identical (see Figure 9.2). As far as the packet filter is concerned, all will meet its criteria and be passed along as valid traffic.

This same weakness allows an attacker to craft fragmented packets that will circumvent the logic of a packet filter. In the most basic example, an attacker crafts fragmented IP packets that look to the packet filter as if they are valid port 80 (HTTP) traffic but, when reconstructed by the destination machine, are really telnet traffic that was supposed to be screened out by the packet filter. This technique assumes that the simple packet filter will make a decision for all fragments associated with a specific IP datagram "identification" value based on the first fragment of the original IP datagram, which will have the Layer 4 (TCP, UDP, ICMP) header in it (see Figure 9.3).

9

**PROTECTING YOUR
INFRASTRUCTURE**

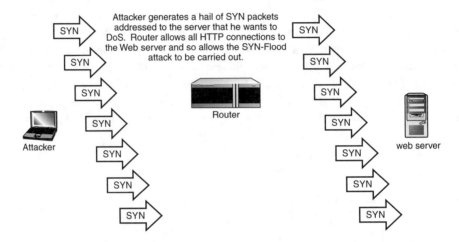

FIGURE 9.2

A SYN flood attack.

An attacker begins by sending a fragmented packet through the packet filter. Since Port 80 is allowed by the ACL, the filter passes this packet. When the next several fragments come through, the packet filter only checks the ID value in the IP header. The last fragment is set up to overwrite the initial fragment. When the fragment packet is finally reconstructed, the result is a TCP connection to Port 23.

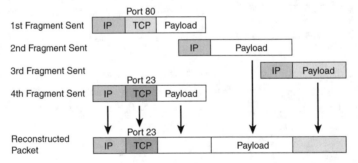

FIGURE 9.3

Fragmented packets that appear to be HTTP traffic are reconstructed as telnet.

Another drawback of packet filters is that the rules are applied to each packet in order; as soon as a match is found, no other rules are considered. This often is referred to as a "fall-through" rule list. This means that the order in which you place the rules can change the way that the packet filter screens traffic, sometimes to the dismay of the administrator. For example, let's say that an administrator has put a rule in the packet filter to block all telnet traffic from the Internet to the Web server, but he wants to allow telnet from a developer's network. The following rule set will implement this policy correctly:

Source	Destination	Service	Rule
Developer's net	Web server	telnet	Allow
Any	Web server	telnet	Deny

Conversely, the same rules put into a different order will have the effect of blocking all connections to the developers because, after the first rule is matched, the packet will be dropped by the firewall.

Source	Destination	Service	Rule
Any	Web server	telnet	Deny
Developer's net	Web server	telnet	Allow

By the same token, it is possible to inadvertently allow services that were thought to be blocked, simply because a previous rule allows the service through in an unexpected manner. The overall lesson here is that packet filters will do exactly what you tell them, however smart or stupid that might be.

Finally, it is often quite easy to circumvent the router ACL and fool it into believing that a connection is allowed. This is because checking a packet against an ACL takes up processor cycles of the router, so many routers automatically allow all previously established connections through, without checking the ACL. The logic is that for a connection to be established in the first place, it must have been checked against the ACL, so there should be no reason to recheck an already established connection. Unfortunately, many routers assume that any TCP packet with the ACK flag set is part of an already established connection. Therefore, an attacker can slip a packet past the router ACL simply by setting the packet's ACK flag, even though no TCP connection handshake took place!

This is not to say that packet filters are useless. In fact, implementing a packet filter (also called an access control list, or ACL) on an edge device such as a router can block a large amount of traffic and act as the first line of defense for your network perimeter. On their own, however, packet filters are easily fooled and provide only basic firewalling functions. Unless you are very sure that the devices behind a packet-filtering firewall are quite secure by themselves, this type of firewall is a poor choice for protecting a network. The big benefit of using a packet-filtering firewall is its speed. Because there is very little logic associated with making deny/allow decisions, a packet-filtering firewall can operate at very high speeds, which can be a deciding factor for extremely high-bandwidth applications. In many modern networks, a packet filter on a router often is used to implement basic "screening" rules, while the bulk of the security policy is enforced in a more advanced firewalling system that employs "stateful inspection" of the traffic.

Stateful-Inspection Firewall

The idea behind packet filtering is a good one: to filter out unwanted traffic based on where it's coming from, where it's going, and what it is. The implementation, as you've seen, is somewhat lacking. The downfall of packet filtering is that a packet filter doesn't know anything about the connection or protocol that it is managing. Stateful-inspection firewalls address this shortcoming by adding in logic that looks not just at the flow of traffic on a per-packet basis, but also at a protocol connection level, typically at the TCP or application layers. A stateful firewall still is driven by rules, just like a packet filter, but it interprets these rules based on this additional logic. Now, every firewall vendor has its own idea of what "stateful inspection" means. Depending upon the type of stateful inspection being implemented, the firewall might look at one or more of the OSI layers to make determinations about passing or dropping traffic.

The first place that stateful inspection differs from packet filters is in looking at the Layer 4 (TCP) data. In the previous section, you saw that a packet filter doesn't care whether a FIN packet precedes a SYN packet in the same connection. Stateful-inspection firewalls do. They look at not just source, destination, and port numbers, but also at the state of the connection—hence their name. That is, this more advanced firewall understands that a TCP connection has a beginning, middle, and end. This state information will include source, destination, and port, but it also will include the packet sequence number and TCP flags. This means that hacker tricks such as setting all the TCP flags to confuse or crash operating systems won't get past a stateful firewall because it "knows" that this is an invalid state.

The core of any stateful inspection firewall is, no surprise, its state table. The state table is where the firewall stores all of the information about each connection. The state table is consulted every time the firewall examines a packet and has to make a decision about what to do with it. The state table is updated whenever the state of a connection changes, such as when a session is started or terminated.

At Layers 3 and 4 (IP and TCP/UDP), a stateful-inspection firewall looks at and remembers each connection's protocol state. For example, a client initiates an ftp session by contacting ftp server A on destination port 21. To communicate back to the client, the server initiates a return connection on which data can be returned to the client. The client's port is typically a random port above port 1024, which, for our purposes, we will assume to be port 10,000. A stateful firewall monitors the outgoing ftp request from the client and "remembers" the port number for the return connection. When the ftp server attempts to connect back to the client (and, therefore, through the firewall) on port 10,000, the firewall checks that the ftp IP address and port numbers match the state information for the client that it is trying to contact (see Figure 9.4a). If it finds that the information in its state table is consistent with the request being made, it temporarily opens up a "hole" in the firewall for the server and client to talk through (see Figure 9.4b). If another ftp server—call it server B—with a different IP address attempts to connect to this client through the same port 10,000, the firewall will deny this connection. This is because even though this port is open for server A, the state table will show that it is not open to server B (see Figure 9.4c).

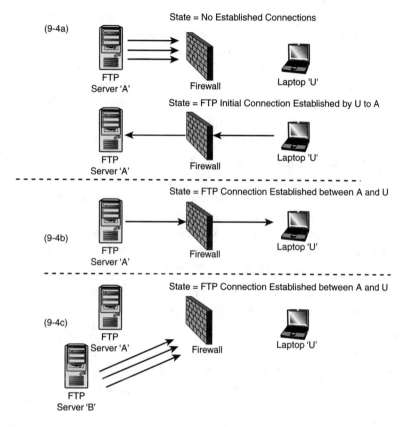

FIGURE 9.4A

A stateful-inspection firewall initially has all inbound ports blocked. An internal host initiates an ftp session by contacting the ftp server.

FIGURE 9.4B

The ftp server can create a return connection to the client because the firewall "remembers" the connection state.

FIGURE 9.4C

Another ftp server is blocked from making an inbound connection because it does not have an entry in the firewall's state table.

Because a stateful-inspection firewall can be application-aware, it also can be tuned to allow only certain types of protocol traffic to pass. Being application-aware means that the firewall understands how an application works. This application could be something complex, such as a videoconferencing application, or something simpler, such as the File Transfer Protocol (ftp). So, for example, you might want to allow the ftp PUT connection but not the ftp GET connection through the firewall. This would allow users inside the firewall to upload files to an external ftp server, but they would not be able to download files into the protected network. To accomplish this, the firewall needs to know not only that ftp occurs on a particular port, but that there are commands within ftp, some of which are allowed (the PUT) and some of which are prohibited (the GET). Again, this is beyond the capabilities of a packet-filtering firewall. The same holds true for connectionless protocols such as ICMP, when you might want to allow users within the firewall to ping servers outside the firewall but are yet to be determined.

In addition, the stateful-inspection firewall can add some level of security to even connection-less protocols such as ICMP in another way. In the following example, the host inside the fire-wall pings (ICMP Echo Request) a server on the Internet. The firewall notes this request and puts the server and host addresses in the state table. When the server replies to the host (with and ICMP Echo Reply), the firewall checks that the server was indeed contacted and then, if it finds this to be true, passes the ping reply. In this way, even a connectionless protocol such as ICMP can have some modicum of security applied to it.

Finally, stateful-inspection firewalls can look at additional information, such as whether a user has authenticated to the firewall, to make decisions about whether to pass or drop their connec-tions.

One drawback of stateful-inspection firewalls compared to packet filters is that they require additional processing power and memory to filter all of the incoming and outgoing traffic pass-ing through the firewall. Therefore, CPU cycle for cycle, they perform more poorly than packet filters. They also suffer from the same drawback of packet filters in that they are dependant upon the order in which their rules are evaluated. Given the fact that processor speeds over 1GHz are now commonplace, the performance argument has been made largely obsolete. In addition, stateful firewalls often can preprocess their user-entered rule sets to check for any conflicting rules, thereby alleviating the rule-ordering issue.

A potential vulnerability of stateful-inspection firewalls is that, just like any state machine, it is always possible that the developers of a stateful firewall can build in mistaken logic when it comes to making pass or drop decisions. After all, the security of a stateful-inspection firewall is only as good as the forethought of its developers. In the past, a number of vulnerabilities have been found with regard to stateful firewalls that allowed attackers to take advantage of anomalies in how the state information is applied or interpreted. To be fair, such examples have become increasingly rare in the newer generations of firewalls; however, the chance that an unreported bug is still out there waiting to be discovered is always present. This is another reason to make every component of your infrastructure as secure as practical rather than relying on a single device to protect your entire infrastructure.

Application Proxy Firewalls

Both packet-filtering firewalls and stateful-inspection firewalls allow direct connections between hosts on the inside and outside of a firewall. Although these connections are monitored and filtered, it seems that there is an inherent risk in allowing these direct connections to occur. Application proxy firewalls were developed to address this issue. An application proxy does not allow direct connections between hosts inside and outside the firewall. Instead, the firewall forces all of the connections to pass through an application (or daemon, in UNIX terms) called a *proxy*. The proxy intercepts any incoming or outgoing connections, checks them against its rule base to see if they are allowed, and then creates another connection between the firewall and the destination host. In essence, the proxy acts as a middleman between the two hosts. For example, to ftp to an external server, a client inside the firewall connects to the firewall's ftp proxy. This proxy then creates a separate connection to the server and receives the return connection from the server. The firewall then creates yet another connection to the client and passes along the server's information via this connection. In this way, no direct connection ever is created between the client and the server (see Figure 9.5).

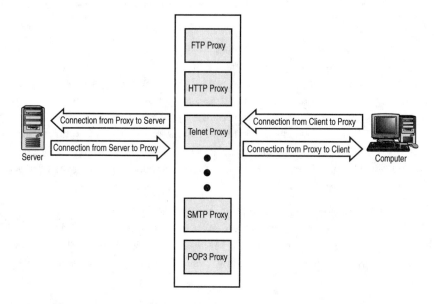

9

PROTECTING YOUR INFRASTRUCTURE

FIGURE 9.5

An application proxy firewall.

How is this more secure than a direct connection? The answer is that the proxy itself can understand and interpret the application-level protocols and, theoretically, has been written to disallow any dangerous components of these protocols. Let's say, for example, that an SMTP protocol is vulnerable to a buffer overflow that can occur when the Subject field of the message is extremely long. The proxy can check that the Subject field length is not greater than a certain amount and can disallow any fields longer than normal. In this way, the buffer overflow is prevented because the firewall's proxy screens it out before the data ever hits the mail server. This, of course, presupposes that the developers of the firewall's application proxy are smart enough to check for all of the nasty types of attacks that can be perpetrated via the application protocol. Essentially, this is the same problem that the developers of the stateful-inspection firewall face when they try to determine the correct logic for processing every combination of connection states. As with the stateful-inspection firewall, a number of vulnerabilities in firewall proxies have been uncovered over the years, leading to the subversion of the application proxy firewall's security.

The biggest complaint about firewall proxies is their speed and the amount of resources that they consume. A proxy must create two connections for every connection that it proxies. This is inherently slower than allowing direct connections between internal and external hosts because the firewall must always broker the connections. In addition, because each proxy is an application, it consumes processor resources such as memory and CPU cycles. Some application proxies create a new instance of the proxy for every connection, thereby increasing the processing burden on the firewall.

Finally, the firewall's application developers must create a new proxy (software application) for every service that needs it, and they must keep up with new revisions of these protocols. So, if a new version of a streaming audio program appears that uses different ports or behaves in a different manner than the previous version, the firewall manufacturer's development team might have to re-engineer the proxy and then send out updates to the user population. Even worse, if the firewall does not provide a proxy for a particular service that your organization needs, you often you must default to using a packet filter to pass this traffic. This means that the application firewall that is supposed to be very secure is reduced to using the least secure method of firewalling, the ACL.

Many proxies also require each client to be aware that the proxy exists. So, for example, rather than directly making an HTTP request to a Web site, the client must make the HTTP request to the proxy, knowing that the proxy will broker its request out to the Web site. This can cause additional administrative overhead to those fellows who must make such changes on the client devices.

It should be noted that some proxying capability is required in almost all modern stateful-inspection firewalls because of the proliferation of applications that employ dynamically assigned TCP or UDP connections. The long-lived FTP protocol is a classic example. The FTP-Control connection on TCP port 21 can include instructions for the server to call the client back on a different port with the data to be transferred. The firewall must be smart enough to understand the FTP control protocol and open up the correct "hole" for the FTP-Data connection. A more advanced example is the H.323 protocol, which is the foundation of many video-teleconferencing applications such as Microsoft's NetMeeting. In this case, an initial control channel on a well-known TCP port (1720, in this case) can lead to many dynamically assigned TCP and UDP connections for additional call control and media (audio, video, chat, whiteboarding, and so on) channels. If the firewall does not understand the H.323 control channels, it will not be capable of allowing the more interesting media streams through.

To sum up, then, the benefit of the application proxy firewall is that it does not allow direct connections between internal and external devices, and it can alleviate many of the vulnerabilities in poorly written protocols by disallowing the offensive behavior. Furthermore, an application proxy could be required to facilitate the transfer of applications that employ dynamically assigned connections. The drawbacks of such firewalls is that their performance is less than other firewalls, while the resources they require are greater. In addition, services for which no proxy exists must be either filtered using traditional packet filters or denied completely, and changes in a protocol sometimes can obsolete the utility of the proxy handling it.

Hybrid

As you can imagine, there is no reason that the previous technologies—packet filtering, stateful inspection, and application proxy—can't be mixed and matched in a single firewall device. This is exactly the tack that some manufacturers have taken, combining what they consider to be the best of each of the technologies. Such hybrids, for example, can initiate a session utilizing an application proxy to keep the client and server connections completely separate until the validity of the connection has been established. Then, once the session is in progress, they switch to stateful inspection to allow information to flow with less processing overhead and, therefore, at greater speed.

These firewalls also might give the administrator the option of installing packet-filtering rules for services or connections that are considered low-risk. For example, firewalls often separate not only the Internet from the internal network, but also internal network segments from each other. So, an organization might determine that ftp sessions between its internal corporate network and the Internet warrant the security of a proxy. However, other ftp connections, such as between the graphics department and the production server, which we assume to consist of large files that need to be transferred quickly, might be firewalled using only a packet filter.

As with most devices, the benefit of a hybrid firewall is its flexibility. Its drawbacks include its increased complexity and the chance that it can be misconfigured by an unwary administrator to open up unwanted holes in an organization's security posture. Given the previous example, an administrator could easily and accidentally set up a packet filter that is applied before the proxy even on the Internet connection, thereby inadvertently allow unproxied ftp connections to and from the Internet and usurping the overall security policy of the organization.

Air Gap

In the last few years, a few firewalls have been developed using a so-called "air gap" technology. *Air gap* is, to our knowledge, a term first used in the Department of Defense (DoD) to describe a physical separation between networks. A true air gap meant that no information could flow between networks because there were no physical connections between them. Many of our colleagues in the DoD like to say that a pair of wire cutters make the best firewall of all.

In the context of more useful firewalls, an air gap has come to describe a firewall that converts the native protocol of the Internet, TCP/IP, into a proprietary or hardware-based protocol before making pass/drop decisions on it. After the decision is made, the data flows through a data bus into a secondary processing engine that reconverts the data back into TCP/IP. The processor that handles the "dirty" (Internet) side of the connection is physically separate from the processor that handles the "clean" side. So, the logic of an air-gap firewall is that even if the Internet-side processor is somehow compromised, the Internal processor still cannot be touched and the security of the firewall will remain intact (see Figure 9.6). In this sense, an air-gap firewall can be likened to an application proxy firewall, in which the proxy is implemented in hardware rather than software. Because the data transfers are not completed utilizing TCP/IP, the air-gap proponents claim that normal hacker tricks can't be used to break through the firewall.

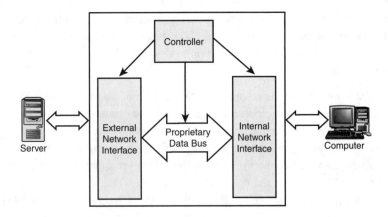

FIGURE 9.6

The air-gap firewall.

Whether air-gap technology is actually more secure than other advanced firewalls is something that can be argued. Certainly, the fact that the air gaps use a proprietary scheme for transferring information makes hacking them a harder problem than hacking TCP/IP. However, just like any computer system, the air-gap firewalls are dependant upon the action of software that might itself have hidden flaws or errors in logic. And, in the end, the action of the firewall is still to pass IP traffic. At this date, air-gap firewalls have not been time-tested in the same way that conventional firewalls have, so it is difficult to assess whether their proprietary architectures actually provide more security than their conventional counterparts.

Secondary Firewall Features

The primary function provided by a firewall is one of filtering—that is, allowing or disallowing specific services based on the source and destination IP addresses and other protocol information. Anyone who hasn't been living under a rock for the past decade can tell you that this is only the most basic function provided by modern firewalls. In the following sections, we will review some of the many secondary firewall features available. These range from specific security functions provided by the firewall itself, such as protection from denial-of-service attacks, to integrated features that work with other security devices, such as virus scanning and user authentication.

Address Translation

One of the most useful features of a firewall is its capability to perform address translation. Without translation, all devices on a network need to be assigned real IP addresses—that is, addresses that are routable via the Internet. Figure 9.7 shows a simple example of a network consisting of a few workstations and a mail server connected to the Internet. Because all the hosts have routable IP addresses, a would-be attacker can connect to them directly through the Internet. From a security perspective, this is not a good scenario because it allows attackers to map the topography of the internal network, as well as connect directly to any poorly configured system.

Network Address Translation

NAT addresses this issue in the following manner. The internal hosts are assigned nonroutable IP addresses. These addresses are defined in the IETF RFC 1918 (see this RFC for a full explanation of nonroutable addresses). For our purposes, we will assume that the address space uses the Class A network 10.0.0.0, resulting in the new network diagram in Figure 9.8. None of the 10.x.x.x addresses is routable, meaning that none can be passed by Internet routers; Therefore, they are not addressable from the public Internet. The internal workstations can still talk to each other, but nothing from the Internet can talk to them directly.

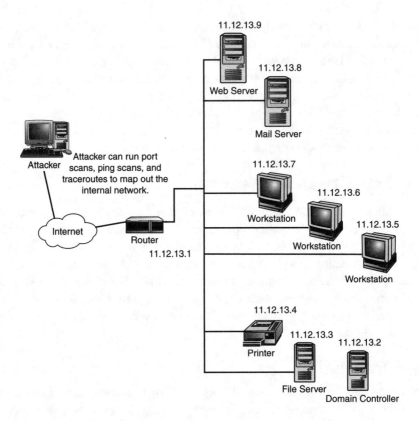

FIGURE 9.7

Mapping the topography of a network without NAT.

This is much more secure than the previous scenario, but now there's a problem because the mail server cannot send or receive mail. The firewall addresses this problem by translating the mail server address to a real address. Figure 9.9 shows how the source and destination IP addresses are translated for the mail server, allowing it to connect to the outside world. This form of NAT is often called static NAT because it provides a static, one-to-one correspondence between real and translated addresses.

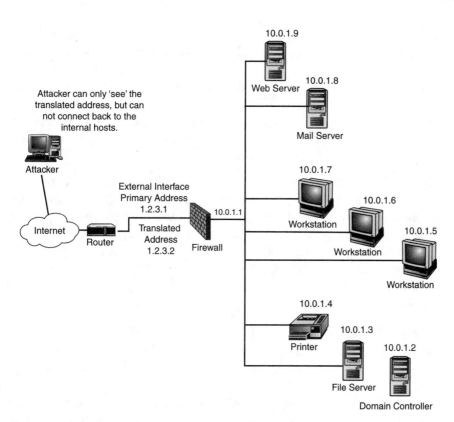

FIGURE 9.8

Network configuration using NAT.

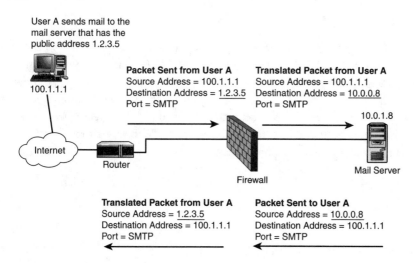

FIGURE 9.9

A statically NAT'ed mail server.

9

PROTECTING YOUR
INFRASTRUCTURE

A few common problems arise with static NAT through firewalls. The first is that devices such as routers often want to communicate using the MAC address of the device's Ethernet card directly, and this can cause a problem because the firewall is impersonating the IP address but not the MAC address. This is solved by most firewalls using a proxy-ARP function, which involves answering ARP requests to the translated devices address with the MAC address of the firewall interface. Be wary when setting up a firewall for the first time because routers often cache the MAC address of devices; it is often necessary to clear a router's ARP cache so that it can recognize the firewall ARP response.

A second issue with NAT is that some applications utilize their IP address as part of their own proprietary communications protocol. Because the outside world sees the translated (routable) address and the application is using the private RFC-1918 address, there could be problems in getting applications to work using NAT. This has been a long-standing problem in the Microsoft NetMeeting application, for example, in which NAT'ed hosts can't utilize NetMeeting for this reason. Similarly, file-sharing programs such as Gnutella clients suffer from this problem because they attempt to advertise a private IP address in their responses to file search queries.

Port Address Translation

Static NAT works well for devices that need to connect to the Internet, and also be connected from hosts on the Internet. This is the broad range of Web, mail, DNS, and ftp servers. However, the previous example left the internal workstations without any means of communicating with the Internet for Web surfing, sending email, or performing other functions. To remedy this, firewalls also can provide a secondary translation mechanism, often referred to as port address translation (PAT) or dynamic NAT. With PAT, an internal network is translated to a single outgoing IP address, with return connections made to any one of the 65,000 or so high ports.

For example, in Figure 9.10, workstation 10.0.0.2 wants to connect to a Web server on the Internet. Its address is translated to the PAT address 123.45.6.7, and the return connection is assigned to port 5000. When the Web server replies to 123.45.6.7 port 5000, the firewall "remembers" that this corresponds to 10.0.0.2 and makes the appropriate translation. When 10.0.0.3 wants to surf to the same Web server, the firewall translates its request to the same address, but a different port—in this case, 7001. When the Web server replies to 123.45.6.7 port 7001, the firewall translates the reply back to 10.0.0.3. In this way, many thousands of internal hosts can communicate utilizing only a single IP address.

Firewall Port Translation Table

Internal Server	Destination Server	Service	Port
10.0.02	Web Server	HTTP	5000

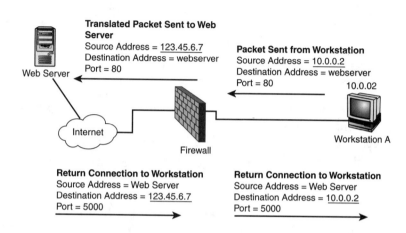

Translated Packet Sent to Web Server
Source Address = 123.45.6.7
Destination Address = webserver
Port = 80

Packet Sent from Workstation
Source Address = 10.0.0.2
Destination Address = webserver
Port = 80

10.0.02

Web Server

Internet

Firewall

Workstation A

Return Connection to Workstation
Source Address = Web Server
Destination Address = 123.45.6.7
Port = 5000

Return Connection to Workstation
Source Address = Web Server
Destination Address = 10.0.0.2
Port = 5000

FIGURE 9.10

Port address translation.

From a security standpoint, the benefit of PAT is that it is not possible for an arbitrary host on the Internet to connect to the internal systems because there is no pre-existing mapping. The port mappings occur only when requested by an internal host connecting to an external server, and then they are removed when this connection is complete. As far as an attacker is concerned, only a single IP address is associated with all of the internal network, so internal hosts cannot be arbitrarily addressed and connected to. One issue with using PAT is that if a service requires some specific ports to be used for return connections, multiple internal hosts cannot connect using that service. For example, if a particular videoconferencing application must use port 9000 for a connection, then, using PAT, only one host at a time can use the video connection because only one port 9000 connection is available at a time.

Both NAT and PAT provide extremely useful methods for protecting networks by preventing unwanted connections from external networks, and by making it much more difficult for attackers to determine the internal topology of a network or exploit it. Most firewalls can implement both NAT and PAT. By utilizing these two translation methods, it is possible to create secure networks that are difficult for an attacker to map or compromise.

9

PROTECTING YOUR INFRASTRUCTURE

Antispoofing

A common method for circumventing router ACLs or firewall rules is address spoofing. To illustrate this, let's assume that a firewall has a rule set that says something like this:

Source	Destination	Service	Rule
The Internet	Internal network	ANY	Deny
Internal network	The Internet	ANY	Allow

The intent of this rule set is to prevent anyone on the Internet from connecting to the internal network, while allowing anyone on the internal network to connect out to the Internet. Now let's create a very simple and contrived example to illustrate how spoofing works. Suppose that an attacker knows that there's a server inside the network that allows anonymous ftp access—perhaps it's used so that internal users can transfer and share large files. The attacker crafts a packet whose source and destination addresses are on the internal network and sends it to the firewall; let's say that it contains the ftp OPEN command. The firewall looks at the source address and sees that it falls within the Internal Network group, so it passes it to the ftp server. Now the attacker assumes that the open worked; knowing how ftp servers work, he sends another packet to log into the ftp server. He assumes that, because the logon is anonymous, the command executed; then he sends a command that transfers the contents of the default directory to his computer on the outside of the network. Because the firewall allows these external connections, the transfer goes through, and, voilà, the attacker has successfully compromised the firewall's security (see Figure 9.11).

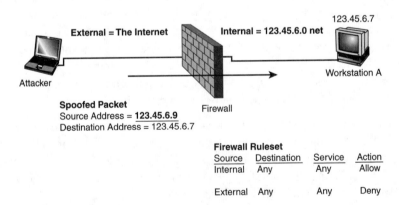

FIGURE 9.11

Spoofing a firewall.

The term for this type of attack is *spoofing*. To combat spoofing attacks, firewalls can institute an antispoofing feature. The features is used to "tell" the firewall which networks are behind which physical interfaces. In the previous example, the firewall knows that if the source address is on the internal network, that address is valid only if the packet is coming from the internal interface. If this address appears on another physical firewall interface, then the firewall assumes that the address has been spoofed and blocks the traffic (see Figure 9.12).

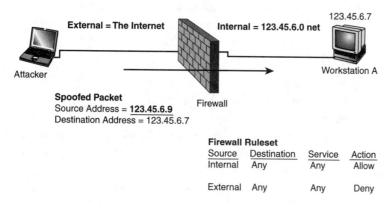

FIGURE 9.12

The antispoofing feature of a firewall prevents internal source addresses from being accepted by the external firewall interface.

This antispoofing feature is an extremely important one: Without it, an attacker can circumvent the firewall rule set and gain access to the internal network.

Utilization with VLANs

It is possible for the logical topology of a network to differ from the physical topology. The occurs in switched networks when virtual local area networks, or VLANs, are utilized. VLANs allow a LAN to be defined in a more logical manner than restricting it to a physical switch. In this scenario, the physical ports on a switch are grouped into logical segments that appear, at least from a routing standpoint, as separate LANs.

The 802.1Q specification defines how packets are tagged at Layer 2 so that they can be appropriately routed and associated with particular VLANs as they move from device to device. Firewalls that understand the 802.1Q specification can be utilized in switched environments to provide firewalling capabilities across multiple VLANs. This means that by connecting a single interface of a firewall to a switch that supports 802.1Q, *all* of the VLANs can be treated as if they were on different firewall interfaces, and firewall rule sets can be developed as if the VLANs were physically separate networks. This is a great feature for enterprises that utilize high-density switches and many VLANs, or for service providers that need to provide their clients with firewall capabilities but don't want to deploy a new physical firewall for each of their clients' networks.

From a security standpoint, using 802.1Q has one major drawback: A single firewall and switch become massive points of failure if they are compromised. Imagine a dense switch with many VLANs, all protected by a single firewall. If that firewall fails by going down or by being compromised from an administrative standpoint, the whole security infrastructure collapses. By the same token, if the switch's security is compromised by an attacker, the VLANs themselves can be collapsed or rerouted, or the firewall can be completely circumvented.

VPN Capabilities

Firewalls can be configured to encrypt and tunnel network traffic. This is very useful when an organization has a number of disparately located offices that want to communicate via the Internet. Using the VPN capability of the firewall, the enterprise can create encrypted connections between each of the offices' firewalls. Any traffic passing between the firewalls automatically is encrypted, with the added benefit that (because we hope that the offices are using RFC 1918 addressing schemes) all of the networks appear like they are on the same WAN rather than separated by the Internet. This can offer tremendous cost savings when compared to leasing a private line from a Telco provider or paying for a commercial WAN service (such as Frame Relay or ATM). It is also possible to create VPNs for remote users so that when someone uses a dial-up connection (or cable modem or DSL) to connect to the Internet, that person can access the internal network via a VPN. This is handy for traveling users when they need to access network services while away from the office.

Algorithms and Exportability

The key (no pun intended) to implementing a useful firewall VPN is that it is standards-based. A number of different symmetric-encryption algorithms are supported by firewalls, ranging from well-documented and tested algorithms such as DES, RC5, Blowfish, and IDEA to proprietary algorithms whose inner workings are known only to the firewall vendors, such as FWZ from Check Point Software. A general rule in cryptography is that any algorithm that hasn't been severely analyzed cannot be trusted, and most algorithms whose source code is not available for inspection can be expected to have unintended features (that is, vulnerabilities).

The main reason for choosing an encryption algorithm other than something mainstream such as DES, Triple-DES, or RC5 is to comply with export restrictions. Currently, there are restrictions on the type of cryptography that can be exported outside the United States, so organizations with global offices or worldwide remote users might opt for an algorithm that is not export-controlled. Beyond this, certain algorithms, such as RC5, were designed to execute in software and so are faster than other algorithms (such as DES) that originally were intended to be implemented in hardware. Because hardware accelerator cards are available for most firewalls, the speed consideration is considerably less than in previous years, and the major driver is now exportability.

With regard to VPN protocols, IPSec and L2TP are pretty much the protocols that you should see supported, and PPTP, which is Microsoft's predecessor of L2TP, is a de facto standard and also should be supported. All new Microsoft operating systems now support IPSEC, which should simplify the deployment of firewall-to-client VPNs in the future.

Regarding IPSec, it is important that the firewall supports the ISAKMP standard form of key exchange because this is the way that keys automatically are negotiated and updated between firewall-to-firewall and firewall-to-client endpoints. It is also possible to do manual IPSec key "exchanges," which means that each endpoint of the VPN must agree on a key in advance and then manually enter this key to accomplish the VPN. In case the explanation hasn't already alerted you, this is quite a pain for large deployments and also can be a security risk because those keys must be disseminated in a secure manner and protected very closely.

VPN Throughput

One characteristic of firewall VPNs is that they can be quite processor-intensive, so as the number of VPN users (or traffic through the office-to-office VPN) grows, the performance of the firewall suffers. This is especially true of the key exchange function (as opposed to symmetric encryption, which is employed for normal data exchange) because it is a numerically intensive function. For example, to conduct a key exchange with a 1024-bit key (a typical key length), the firewall must perform 1024×1024 bit multiplications repeatedly to develop a key. Given the fact that most processors can multiply numbers only in 32-bit chunks, getting the answer to this type of calculation can take a second or longer. Symmetric encryption (such as DES) isn't as processor-intensive because it doesn't require huge multiplications, but it still requires the processor to work overtime to encrypt and decrypt every connection. To solve this, many vendors integrate with VPN accelerator cards, which plug into the firewall chassis and offload the encryption and key exchange functions onto special-purpose hardware. This can significantly improve not only VPN performance, but also overall firewall performance because the non-VPN functions will be capable of utilizing more of the firewall platform's processing capability.

VPN Failover

An important capability for some organizations is high availability (HA). This feature was discussed previously, and we saw that one firewall can take over the operations of a failing firewall when the pair is configured in HA mode. VPN failover, however, is another story. Some firewalls will not fail over the VPN connections because the encryption keys that are used on the primary firewall are not transferred to the backup. This can cause all of your VPN users to

9

PROTECTING YOUR INFRASTRUCTURE

lose connectivity if the firewall fails over. In such a case, all the VPN users would have to reauthenticate to the firewall, essentially making them log in again, and users hate that! And unlike the normal login process, which occurs at different times during the day depending upon when people initially connect to the VPN, this reauthentication will take place all at once, with all of the users trying to log back in at the same time. Given the processing overhead associated with key exchange, this can cause a significant increase in the time that it takes for a user to reconnect. Although most dedicated VPN appliances will perform the failover function elegantly—that is, by transferring the encryption keys—not all firewalls do. If VPN HA is a concern, make sure that the VPN sessions are maintained during failover.

Management Capabilities

Although it's not really a firewall function, it is important to note that the management capabilities of firewalls vary. This can be a security feature, so it is worth noting. In general, you might find that is impractical to log onto the firewall system directly, either by connecting a keyboard and monitor or by remotely logging into the system. When an organization has many firewalls, this is especially true. For that reason, it is important for the firewall to have remote management capabilities. The most essential feature of remote management is employing encryption and authentication between the firewall and the remote client. Encryption is essential because anyone sniffing the management connection will be able to see the authentication information and then possibly gain administrative control of the firewall. In short, don't ever telnet to your firewall! Remote firewall GUIs should use strong encryption, and any command-line tools should be done over an encrypted channel (such as secure shell).

In many enterprise networks that employ VLAN-capable switching infrastructures, network-management functions often are encapsulated in dedicated "management VLANs." Depending on the make and model of the switches, these VLANs can be defined by physical ports, such as the management interfaces of routers and firewalls, and logical UDP/TCP ports, such as SNMP (ports 161 and 162) or a particular vendor's firewall-management protocol.

Authentication

Firewalls are, by nature, access-control mechanisms. To make a decision about whether to grant access (pass a packet or make a connection), the firewall needs some type of information about the identity of an entity. In the most basic case, this is accomplished by checking the source IP address and then determining whether this address is allowed access to the destination IP address for the specified service. Firewalls, however, are not necessarily limited to checking source addresses to determine whether a connection should be allowed. Many firewalls first can authenticate the source before granting it access to resources. Figure 9.13 shows the process. For example, a user outside the firewall might try to log onto an ftp server that is on the firewall's DMZ. If the firewall supports authentication, it can request that the user first enter a username and password before granting the user access to the server. The rule for this type of authentication might look as follows:

Source	Destination	Service	Action
Internet	FTP server	FTP	Password authentication

This assumes that the firewall has a local database of valid users and their passwords. This is a somewhat clumsy arrangement because the firewall administrator must, along with taking care of the firewall, also administer the user database.

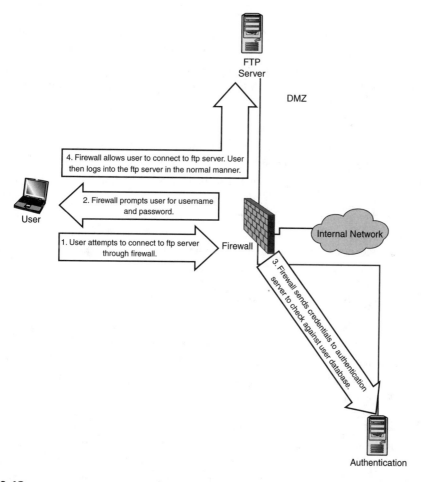

FIGURE 9.13

Logging into an ftp server on a DMZ, and authenticating to a firewall before being allowed to log into an ftp server on a DMZ.

For this reason, many firewalls can interface to external authentication mechanisms. Some of the more popular mechanisms include Windows Domain Authentication, RADIUS or TACACS, and digital certificates. Let's assume that a user on the Internet wants to access a share on a Windows File server protected by the firewall (let's also temporarily suspend reality and assume that this isn't a security nightmare). The user attempts to connect to the firewall using NetBIOS (ports 137–139), and the firewall sees that this service requires RADIUS authentication.

Source	Destination	Service	Action
Internet	File server	NetBIOS	RADIUS authenticate

The firewall then queries the user's RADIUS client and sends its response to the RADIUS server. The server reviews the credentials and gives a pass or fail message to the firewall. If the RADIUS server successfully authenticates the client, the firewall allows the connection to go through. The same basic mechanism is used for other types of authentication, whereby the firewall "outsources" authentication to a third party and abides by the go/no-go response of the authenticating mechanism.

The benefit of using a third-party authentication mechanism is that the administration of the user database can be offloaded, so that the firewall administrator does not have to handle the day-to-day user issues that crop up, such as issuing credentials, reinitializing lost passwords, and adding and deleting users from the database. Another benefit of authentication is that it can allow the firewall to conduct much more granular access control and can identify a particular user rather than simply an IP address. Given the fact that dial-in Internet connections, as well as most DSL connections, utilize dynamic addressing, strong user authentication is really the only secure solution for allowing remote access to critical systems.

High Availability

Given that a firewall is typically an enterprise's gateway to the Internet, its customers, and its partners, it is fairly important not only for the firewall to perform a protective function, but also for it to not fail and cut off access to the outside world. A single firewall is a single point of failure; if for any reason the hardware, software, or operating system goes south, so can an organization's connectivity.

High Reliability

To address this issue, many firewalls can be configured in a high availability (HA) mode. This HA can be accomplished in a number of ways. The most basic way is to implement HA internal to the firewall, such as by incorporating redundant hard drives, power supplies, and network interface cards (NICs) into the firewall's design. Although this does provide a higher level of availability than a nonredundant internal architecture and sometimes is called HA by manufacturers, it is actually a form of high reliability rather than high availability.

Cold Spares

The next form of HA is the cold spare. A *cold spare* is a complete, ready-to-go firewall that is not plugged into the network but that can be swapped in if the primary firewall fails. Obviously, this does not provide an immediate failover capability because the network connection will be down until the new firewall can be put in place. It also can be difficult to kept the software version and rule set of a cold spare perfectly synchronized to that of the primary firewall. Recent rule changes can be lost if the cold spare isn't updated on a regular basis. In addition, encryption keys used by the firewall sometimes can change over time, and these keys might need to be regenerated when the cold spare comes online. If the firewall is integrated with a third-party application such as a virus scanner, IDS, content filter, or authentication mechanism, it can take a considerable amount of effort to get these systems "talking" even when the cold spare is an apparent duplicate of the primary firewall.

You also should remember that the MAC address of the cold spare's NICs will differ from those of the primary firewall, and this can be an issue with devices such as routers that cache their ARP entries and expect a specific mapping between IP address and MAC address. If an organization wants to use a cold spare as part of its HA plan, it is imperative that it have a written procedure for keeping the cold spare up-to-date and that the swapping procedure be tested periodically to ensure that everything will run smoothly. Never assume that identically configured firewalls will work identically; experience shows that they seldom do.

Hot Spare

True HA requires a completely redundant backup firewall that can take over the function of the primary if it goes down. This is accomplished by a "heartbeat" connection between the two firewalls. The secondary firewall constantly monitors the primary firewall through a heartbeat connection that can be implemented with a dedicated cable or a normal Ethernet network connection. Most manufacturers employ the IETF standard Virtual Router Redundancy Protocol (VRRP) for the heartbeat messages. If the primary firewall's heartbeat stops, the backup firewall takes over. Until the backup firewall is needed, its network interfaces are downed so that they do not appear on the network. When the backup must take over, its interfaces are turned on and it takes over the IP addresses of the primary firewall's interfaces. The better class of HA firewalls also makes sure that the backup firewall takes over the MAC address of the primary to ensure that there are no routing issues during the switchover (see Figure 9.14).

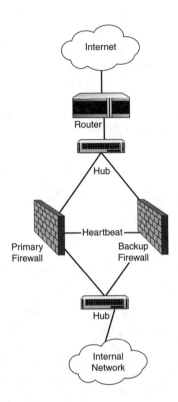

FIGURE 9.14

A firewall pair set up in a hot failover mode.

If the firewall utilizes stateful inspection, then not only the rule set but also the state table must be maintained between firewalls for there to be a seamless handoff when the primary fails. If state is not maintained between firewalls, all connections will be broken when the backup firewall takes over from the primary, and it will have to be re-established when the backup is in control. If the firewall is an application proxy, the proxy state must be maintained and transferred between firewalls for there to be a seamless failover.

Obviously, the backup firewall's rule set also must be kept current so that whenever a new rule is added to the primary, it automatically is propagated to the backup.

If the firewall is capable of encryption (VPNs and so on), the encryption keys must be maintained between the primary and the backup, and VPN state information and session keys must be synchronized between the two firewalls if the VPNs are to be maintained during the cutover between primary and backup. Note that *very few firewalls* do a very good job of maintaining VPN state during failover, so this can be a differentiator for those organizations that cannot tolerate a disruption in service for its remote users or point-to-point VPNs.

Firewall Platforms

Historically, the first commercial firewalls were not much more than router ACLs. The software that really kicked off the firewall as we know it today was Marcus Rannum's Firewall Toolkit package (FWTK), which ran on top of a UNIX operating system. The commercial Gauntlet firewall is an evolution of this original effort. Today, there are a range of implementations of the firewall function, which run from such freeware options as IPChains (which runs on platforms such as Linux or BSD) to $100,000 firewall devices (which run their algorithms in special-purpose computing hardware). In the past several years, these "appliance" firewall devices have become much more popular. Let's investigate the major types of firewall platforms and look at the advantages and disadvantages of each. In no particular order, they are listed here:

- OS-based
- OS-based appliances
- Traditional OS plus commercial firewall software
- "Appliance" plus commercial firewall software
- Full hardware appliance

OS-Based Firewalls (IPChains)

The operating system–based firewalls typically rely on the capability of the operating system itself to perform firewall functions. This can range from simple port filtering, such as can be done on Windows NT–based and UNIX-based operating systems, to add-on freeware packages such as IPChains (or IPFW or IPFWADMIN, depending on which flavor of UNIX you are running). These incorporate such firewall features as NAT, antispoofing, VPN (sometimes), and others.

This sounds great, so why doesn't everyone just use IPChains? There are three major reasons for this. The first is that the OS-based firewalls do not do stateful inspection; they are more like packet filters, so they inherit all of the vulnerabilities of the latter. The second is administration/support. For a small shop with a very savvy administrator, setting up and patching a Linux box running IPChains could be a reasonable solution, as could be getting technical support from user or news groups. For a large enterprise, this is probably not the way to go. The third reason for not going with an OS-based firewall is manageability: These firewalls are administered from the command line, making the rule set somewhat difficult to interpret. In addition, there is no concept of an enterprise-management system that would allow all of the firewalls to be centrally administered and monitored. For a large enterprise with many firewalls, the lack of a formal support structure and management features are reasons enough not to consider unsupported firewalls.

Recently, many new "personal firewalls" have been marketed for the Windows desktop. In fact, Microsoft's latest operating system, Windows XP, provides its own native firewall. These products typically integrate with the TCP/IP stack software on a workstation and perform basic firewalling functions such as stateful TCP inspection. In some cases, the user must tell the personal firewall which applications running on the computer are allowed to talk to the Internet. You usually get a "Don't ask me anymore" option when you allow a common application, such as your Web browser, to access the network. These programs also alert you when a remote computer attempts to connect to your computer. This can become quite distracting given the amount of routine scanning that occurs on the Internet today.

OS-Based Appliances

The next step up from a pure OS-based firewall is the basic firewall appliance. These devices are typically a somewhat disguised, but still standard, Intel-based PC running a hardened version of Linux (or BSD) with IPChains, with a user interface that "pretties up" the IPChains command-line interface and makes it more user-accessible. Different vendors go to different lengths in modifying IPChains, the OS, or the Intel platform, to improve the reliability and manageability of their products. For example, some vendors store the operating system kernel in a flashable RAM so that a hard drive (which is the least reliable component of most computers) isn't necessary, and so that the system can be quickly reloaded in the event of a crash or power failure. This also makes it easy to upgrade the system with a new version. Vendors can add stateful inspection to the firewall capabilities and can provide VPN client software (to allow VPNs for remote users) and extensions for third-party authentication (such as digital certificates). These firewalls are good solutions for small to medium-size enterprises (the SME market, as the sales guys like to call it) because they offer firewall functionality with a supported infrastructure and good management capabilities at a reasonably low cost. Often, however, their performance, in terms of throughput and number of connections that can be handled, does not match that offered by high-end firewall vendors.

Traditional OS Plus Commercial Firewall Software

The next step in firewalling is to use a fully custom firewall implementation. These can run on either a firewall appliance or a standard operating system. There is a long list of vendors that produce such products. The software typically is installed on a hardened operating system, such as a UNIX or NT platform that has had unnecessary services disabled. The software then implements stateful inspection, proxy, or hybrid firewall features. These packages might allow the operating system to perform the low-level routing functions or might perform the routing themselves, but in all cases they force the network traffic through their firewall engines before letting them pass from interface to interface. The nice thing about these packages is that it is possible to scale their performance by running them on different platforms. For example, running a package on a gigahertz-speed dual-Pentium system will provide significantly better performance than running it on a 600MHz single-processor system.

It would be impossible to review all of the features and foibles of commercial firewall software, but a few concerns are worth noting. First, these systems do run on top of a standard operating system that *must* be hardened to be truly secure. This is because many operating system services are vulnerable to either DoS or compromise leading to administrative privileges for the attacker. In theory, the firewall should block any such connections to vulnerable services, but, in practice, this is not always the case.

The next issue is that, depending upon the particular implementation of the firewall, if it crashes, the firewall could fail open, meaning that when the firewall daemon, dies the operating system continues to route. This is very bad! For example, one popular package requires that routing be turned on when it is implemented on Windows NT so that it will fail open on that platform. The same package running on Solaris does not require routing to be turned on, so it fails closed.

Finally, any package that runs on a standard computing platform runs the risk of disk crashes and kernel malfunctions, meaning that the firewall is no more reliable than the hardware/OS that it runs on. This actually can be a strength rather than a weakness because it is relatively easy (although expensive) to build a high-reliability hardware platform for the firewall to run on.

Firewall Appliances

The term *firewall appliance* is used somewhat loosely in the industry. It is applied to anything from a standard firewall software package running on a rack-mountable PC to an all-hardware firewall with its functionality implemented in customized ASICs. The major advantages of an appliance over a standard OS-plus-software firewall are listed here:

- **Hardened OS**—The operating system of a firewall appliance has been prehardened by the manufacturer, so no vulnerable services should exist.

- **Easy to deploy**—Typically the firewall comes preloaded with software, so it does not require anyone to load the OS or the firewall software.

- **Low maintenance**—Appliances *should* come back up automatically after a reboot and should be less sensitive to unexpected shutdowns (such as a power outage). Depending upon the implementation, this is not always the case, however.

- **Higher performance**—In theory, a stripped-down OS should perform better than a standard OS-plus-firewall software combo. Because many appliances are really no more than slightly customized PCs, this is not always the case.

We should note that there is a huge difference between an appliance that sports a hardened OS and firewall software running on a general-purpose processor (such as a Pentium), and an

9

PROTECTING YOUR
INFRASTRUCTURE

appliance that utilizes custom ASICs (Application Specific Integrated Circuit, a special-purpose chip that incorporates key firewall functions into hardware rather than relying on a general-purpose processor and software to carry out the function). The latter is much more likely to enjoy the dual benefits of higher performance and higher reliability that is inherent in the hardware-only design. When shopping for appliances, it is very important to look under the hood to see what you are really getting. Is it a PC in a neat package, or is it truly a high-reliability high-performance appliance?

Third-Party Integration

As firewall vendors compete, they strive to incorporate more features into their products. Many vendors now integrate with third-party applications such as virus scanning, active content scanning (Java, ActiveX, and so on), intrusion detection, and URL filtering. In general, the firewall provides "hooks" through which it communicates with the third-party applications. In general, the firewall sends specific content to the third-party application, which then examines it and tells the firewall whether to allow or block the data. A good number of third-party applications are available for firewalls, and we will discuss only a few here.

- **URL filtering**—This allows the firewall to block certain types of URLs, such as pornographic sites or gambling sites. The firewall reviews the URL and matches it against a database of objectionable sites, which it updates regularly from the filtering engine. Objectionable sites are blocked. This can cause a problem when the blocking is done by Web server IP address because often perfectly benign sites share the same physical Web server as a more objectionable site. This can lead to the unwanted condition of the benign site being blocked by virtue of its IP address rather than its content.

- **Content scanning**—Some attacks are carried out when a user surfs to a Web site that attempts to download code or execute functions through the Web browser. For such traffic, the firewall will send the content to a content scanner that will review the data and give the firewall a pass/drop decision.

- **Virus scanning**—The firewall sends all email traffic to a virus-scanning server that looks for viruses and then either drops or modifies the email before sending it to its destination, or signals the firewall to block any further traffic from this user or server.

- **Intrusion detection**—The IDS system can look at the firewall log traffic or state information and make decisions about whether an attack has occurred. The IDS then signals the firewall to drop the connection if it is determined to be suspect.

One feature that is common to many third-party applications is the capability to modify the firewall rule set. For example, an IDS can modify the firewall rules to block a site that is attempting DoS attacks against a Web server. Although on the surface this sounds like a good way to automatically block attackers, in reality we recommend that this feature never be used.

The reason for this is threefold. First, it is possible that a false alarm will create an anomalous rule. Second, an attacker can send many attacks against the firewall with a spoofed address (for example, by using the IP address of one of your business partners as the source of a DoS attack), thereby causing your firewall to add a rule that blocks a legitimate set of IPs. This is a great way to have your firewall carry out a new form of DoS attack! Finally, fundamentally we believe that it is a bad idea to give control of your firewall rule set to anyone but your firewall administrator and that any firewall change should be done under a strict change-control process. Allowing automatic changes to a firewall rule set effectively turns over control of your security policy to entities outside of your network and eliminates your ability to control the change process. Because the firewall is the gateway to your enterprise, it should not be allowed to modify itself based on the inputs that it receives from a third-party software package.

DoS Prevention Features

Firewalls can provide some denial-of-service prevention features; however, this is very dependant upon the type of DoS attack being performed. As new DoS attacks are formulated, the anti-DoS capabilities of the firewall might not suffice.

The most common form of DoS prevention using firewalls is preventing the SYN-flood attack. This is, of course, only one variant of a DoS attack, although at one time it and its variants were the predominant form. To prevent a SYN-flood attack (discussed elsewhere in this book) the firewall acts as "SYN proxy" and accepts an incoming SYN packet from a connecting host. This SYN is cached by the firewall and is not transmitted to the internal host. The firewall responds to the originator with a SYN-ACK and then waits a period of time for the corresponding ACK from the originator. If this is received, the firewall assumes that the connection is not a denial-of-service attack and conducts the three-way SYN, SYN-ACK, ACK handshake with the internal host to initiate the connect on the inside of the firewall. If the ACK is not received from the external host, however (indicating a SYN-flood attack), the firewall either drops the connection or sends a FIN packet to the external host to close out the connection. The timeout period while the firewall waits for the SYN-ACK from the external host is configurable and generally is shorter than the amount of time that a normal operating system would wait (see Figure 9.15).

The logic is that because the firewall utilizes fewer resources while waiting for the SYN-ACK and has a shorter timeout period, this form of DoS attack will be less successful against the firewall than against a normal operating system. In essence, this shifts the burden of dealing with the SYN-flood attack from the host operating system to the firewall. Of course, firewall resources also are consumed in this scenario, and eventually even the resources of the firewall will be consumed by a heavy enough SYN-flood attack.

9

PROTECTING YOUR
INFRASTRUCTURE

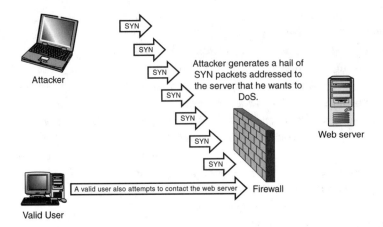

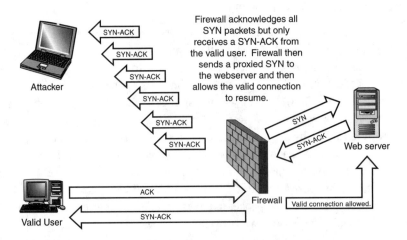

FIGURE 9.15

SYN-flood protection.

Realistically, firewalls can be utilized to prevent DoS attacks by configuring them to block common sources of DoS, such as unnecessary ICMP or SNMP traffic coming into or going out of the network. This has the dual function of preventing a large portion of DoS attacks from entering your network and disabling your servers, and it also prevents any server of yours that might be compromised from being used to carry out a DoS attack against another target. Note that, in this respect, packet filters (on routers or other networking gear) are an equally good way to prevent a large number of DoS attacks, both incoming and outgoing.

Performance

This is a tough area to pin down to firewall manufacturers because so many different variables come into play when evaluating the sheer speed of a firewall. The major factors that drive performance are listed here:

- The number of simultaneous connections supported
- Packet throughput
- Number and type of rules
- Volume of logging
- VPN loading

All of these factors can be dependant upon the hardware platform being utilized, the operating system (if applicable), available memory, and often even the brand of network card being used. This makes it extremely difficult to make blanket statements about firewall performance. One manufacturer might claim that its firewall is faster than a competitor's, and this could be true if the competitor's firewall is run on a 600MHz Windows 2000 server with 128MB of RAM. But what if you're deploying on a dual-processor Sun platform with 512MB of RAM? What if you switch from a 3COM network card to an Intel card? For this reason, manufacturers' claims and even independent test results can be judged only in the context of the test bed and specific firewall configurations used.

To be absolutely blunt, for those businesses whose Internet access is in the T1 or less category (1.544MB), just about any firewall from the leading manufacturers will probably suffice, be it a stateful-inspection or proxy firewall. Even many of the firewalls that cost less than $1,000 will handle this level of traffic, assuming that you are not doing a large amount of VPN'ing. The limiting factor on firewall performance at this bandwidth is also seldom the number of simultaneous connections that it can handle because, after you get more than about 25 users on a T1, you effectively have reduced everyone to a 56K connection anyway. In this arena, firewalls typically are deployed with just two or three active interfaces—inside, outside, and sometimes DMZ—so few complex routing concerns can degrade performance.

When you begin to graduate to higher-bandwidth connections or you start adding network interfaces, factors such as the number of simultaneous connections supported, the rate at which connections can be created or broken down, and routing efficiency become more significant. If your connections are less than about 10Mbps of throughput, it is safe to trust the figures that are quoted by most leading manufacturers as far as performance and throughput go. Above this level, and especially as you approach T3 levels and range into 100Mbps or greater, things really get fuzzy. If you are planning on deploying a firewall to handle this level of throughput, you probably also will be deploying a mission-critical application and will be spending a large sum of money. In these scenarios, it makes sense for you to either talk to colleagues that have had similar experiences to yours and see what worked for them, search through credible reviews conducted by independent third parties (if there are really any of those out there), or, after narrowing your selection to a few firewalls based on their capabilities and claimed performance, bring them in-house and evaluate them yourself.

Implementation Issues and Tips

Like any tool, a firewall is only as good as the hand that wields it, or, in our case, the hand that deploys and manages it. Too often, clients purchase the best, most expensive firewall on the market; deploy it on a high-end hardware platform (if it isn't an appliance); and then totally botch the firewall's rule set, deploy a nonsensical architecture, or circumvent its security features through poor planning or implementation. In the years that we have been deploying security systems, we have seen such configuration mistakes as this:

- Firewalls configured to fail-open (when the firewall software fails, the operating system routes all traffic without applying any rules)
- Firewalls with blank or default administrator passwords
- Firewalls with rule sets that allow the Internet at large to connect directly to critical (supposedly protected) systems inside of a corporate network
- Firewalls with so many ancient rules still installed that no administrator can tell what services are allowed or disallowed

The biggest mistake that organizations make—and please remember this—is to believe that the mere presence of a firewall is some type of guarantee of security. Just the reverse is sometimes true. The presence of a firewall often is a false symbol of security, and the sheer number of configurable parameters on a modern firewall make it easy for an unwary or uncaring administrator to completely obfuscate the benefits that the firewall presents. In this section, we will take a look at just what a firewall can and cannot do, how firewalls should be configured and deployed, and what some common pitfalls are when deploying them.

Firewall Architecture

With secure architectures in mind, realize that firewalls can be used as the gatekeeper between network segments.

One note that we must make is that *firewalls alone don't protect a network*. A poorly configured mail server will be hacked regardless of whether it is firewalled. That DNS server that nobody has looked at for two years will be compromised even though your $50,000 firewall cluster has it on a protected DMZ. Someone will be able to log into your domain server if your firewall rule set allows it. Enough said on that topic.

Intrusion Detection

The intrusion-detection capabilities of firewalls when compared to those of a dedicated intrusion-detection system are extremely limited. Those firewalls that do a form of intrusion detection usually concentrate on either of these:

- Port scan activity
- Event thresholds

Port scans already have been fully discussed, but, given the large number of port scans that any network is subjected to, the value of detecting such a scan by itself is of little value. Event thresholds are of somewhat more interest because some firewalls can alert you to when a particular event occurs (for example, 10 failed connection attempts to a server in a certain time period). Operationally, the number of false alarms generated by firewall IDS is high enough that it is more of an annoyance than a help to the networking professional.

There is a way that firewalls can be very helpful when it comes to IDS, however, and this is through the propitious use of the firewall log information. A typical firewall can log a large amount of information regarding accepted and dropped connections, and this information often can be processed by a secondary IDS system. In this respect, firewalls can be a very useful IDS and forensics tool. The utility of firewall logs in IDS processing is discussed more fully in the IDS section of this book.

Translation Issues

The value of Network Address Translation (NAT) has been discussed elsewhere in this book. NAT is well regarded as a mechanism for protecting internal hosts from being directly accessible via the Internet, as well as expanding the address space available for building large networks. Firewalls implement NAT in two ways: static NAT and hide-mode NAT (the terminology for these two modes varies among manufacturers).

One issue that we do find with many firewalls is that they can get a bit confused when it comes to translation. In Figure 9.16, a Web server is statically NAT'ed to an external IP address. When an internal host tries to access the real IP address of that Web server, the firewall sometimes gets into a routing loop. This has to do more with the firewall software implementation than any real routing issues. The way things *should* work is that the firewall sees the real IP address and routes it to the external interface, which recognizes that this is a translated address, rewrites the translated address to the Web server's internal address, and sends it back to the Web server. However, remember that the user is also utilizing NAT (actually, PAT), so the user's address might get translated as well. You can see the problem. Now the internal Web server is trying to talk to an internal client via translation of both of their addresses, and things go downhill from there. And if you're having trouble understanding this discussion, then you have a pretty good idea of why the firewall has trouble with this. Often the only solution is to have the internal client send requests to the internal IP address to access the server. We have found this to be a problem without a good solution for many scenarios.

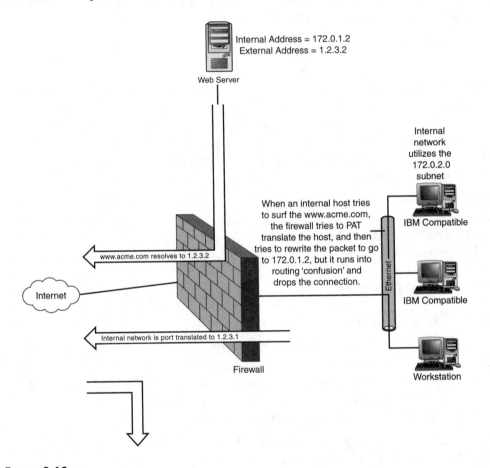

FIGURE 9.16

Routing and translation problems can make it difficult for internal hosts to communication when both utilize some type of translation.

Complex Rule Sets

If the firewall is a pot holding all of your assets, then a complex rule set will quickly turn it into a colander. The biggest challenge that a firewall administrator faces is in balancing security requirements against the business needs of the organization. Too often, we have seen firewall's reduced to near uselessness because of a complex and overly abundant rule set. Having a lot of rules on your firewall is bad, for a few reasons. First, a large number of rules will slow down the operation of the firewall because many rules might need to be evaluated before there is a hit. One good trick to speed up the operation of a firewall for stateful inspection firewalls is to put the most often used rules at the top because they will match most often and the rest won't need to be evaluated.

Next, as your firewall rule set grows, it becomes increasingly difficult to determine just what's being allowed or denied and why. In one large organization, we noted *more than 300 rules* on a single firewall. Many of these were legacies left over from administrators past, and these included some rules that allowed telnet in from the Internet, administrative connections to specific servers, and other horrors. Nobody would revamp the rule set because nobody knew why each of the rules actually was needed! When it came time to move to a new firewall architecture, they had to spend several months tracking down the requestor of each firewall rule, determining whether it was still needed, and then figuring out whether it conflicted with the existing security policy. Comedy, as Steve Martin once said, is not pretty.

Finally, every service that is allowed through the firewall represents a potential security exposure, so it is just common sense to keep the number of firewall rules to a minimum. The most elegant solutions are often the simplest, and the same holds true for firewall rule sets. If you need to poke dozens of holes through your firewall to accomplish your business, then you probably need a better architecture to address how your business functions. In a large enterprise environment, it is often very worthwhile to define a standard "Internet application" architecture that developers must adhere to. Components such as Web servers, databases, and authentication servers should be placed in standard locations so that firewall rule set proliferation does not get out of control. This has the added benefit of educating application developers, who often do not have any significant formal training in secure application architectures or coding techniques.

Logging, Monitoring, and Auditing

Firewalls often are set up and then forgotten. That's a shame because, as the gatekeeper to your network, firewalls produce a plethora of information about what's going into and out of your environment. Firewall logs should be reviewed on a regular basis. This can be a chore, especially for high-volume sites, but there are plenty of good log-analysis tools out there, both commercial and freeware packages. Because, in theory, your firewall should implement your security policy, auditing the firewall rules and logs is a good way to determine whether your policy is being adhered to. If your policy prohibits telnet but your firewall logs show telnet connections, then you've got a clear policy violation. The same can be said of Web-surfing traffic or any other service.

Firewall logs also can show you what types of things are being tried but are failing. For example, is someone trying to telnet to your domain server from the Internet? Why is that? What else might this person be trying? The firewall will show these failed connections. Or, perhaps an internal host on your network has been infected with a Trojan horse virus and now is connected to a hacker's computer on the Internet. Your firewall logs will show this. If your firewall prohibits this connection, it still will show the failed attempts that will tip you off that one of your hosts has been hacked. The convenience store has cameras to watch for shoplifters or robbers. Firewall logs should be reviewed to look for unusual activity, and they also can be used for forensics if some unusual event is detected.

What to Log?

One problem regarding firewall log files themselves is just what to log. If you are running a Web farm, logging every successful HTTP connection will bog down your firewall and product huge daily logs. Also, your Web servers most likely are maintaining URL access logs so that you can perform business analysis of your site. For security purposes, we generally recommend that you always log failed or denied events on your firewalls (and other network devices) because these can tip you off to attempts to thwart your firewall's security. You also should log any connection that allows significant access to a resource. So, for example, if you have to allow just one of your administrators to telnet to a router, you should log both the accepted connections and the denied connections. The same holds true when your CEO wants all of Microsoft Networking, or any other high-risk connection, opened up for his cable modem at home. Depending upon your configuration, you also might want to log successful remote access events, such as a successful VPN connection from a remote user. Really, any low-volume but high-risk event should be logged and reviewed on a regular basis.

Dedicated Log Servers

An important firewall feature is its capability to send its log information to a dedicated log server. By utilizing a dedicated server, it is possible to significantly increase the performance of a firewall because it will not need to execute the lengthy disk writes for every log entry. It is also nice to be able to aggregate all of the logs from multiple firewalls onto a single servers, especially if you need to archive the log files for long periods of time to meet either a policy or a regulatory requirement. If your firewall can put out log information in a standard format such as syslog, then all the better. If not, check that the firewall can export its proprietary format to something more common, such as comma- or tab-delimited formats, so that they can be parsed by third-party applications. Note that log parsing can be done offline for periodic reporting or in real time by software agents that integrate with an intrusion-detection system.

Firewall Vulnerabilities

Much has been written, and even more conjecture has been circulated, about how secure the firewall itself is. For example, we've heard urban legends about back doors in particular firewalls or secret vulnerabilities known only to a select few. In general, the greatest vulnerability that a firewall presents is its capability to be poorly configured by the administrator. In one example, we found that a particular firewall allowed unfettered access to a company's critical internal server to every host on the Internet and didn't log any of the connections. With this type of misconfiguration, it matters very little whether there is some secret hack against the firewall's operating system or administrative interface.

Covert Channels

Besides misconfiguration, firewalls are susceptible to covert channel attacks. For example, let's say that a firewall is locked down very tightly, allowing only email to the mail server on the inside network and outbound Web browsing. Now suppose that one of the internal users gets an email with a Trojan horse in it and has his machine compromised. You might think that because almost every outbound port is blocked, nothing can be done. But, wait—what if the attacker wrote the Trojan to communicate using HTTP and set up a server that is listening for HTTP traffic. The attacker then can use port 80 to have the Trojan'ed host create an outbound connection, and the firewall will allow the reverse connection. Presto, the firewall has been "compromised."

This scenario is called a *covert channel*, meaning that a prohibited communication channel (Trojan horse to attacker) is created using an allowed protocol. If the attacker is smart, he can write the Trojan horse so that it communicates over multiple methods that usually are allowed through firewalls—these could be ICMP, HTTP, and even Trojans that communicate by sending email back and forth, unbeknownst to the user! It is worth noting that legitimate application developers have used this technique so that their applications are not hindered by firewalls. For example, several VPN vendors have implemented "firewall bypass" modes that encapsulate the encrypted IP packets over HTTP (port 80) connections.

Other attacks abound, such as the ftp bounce attack, which uses allowed connections to internal ftp server to gain access to other hosts that supposedly are blocked through the firewall. In all, these are less firewall vulnerabilities than they are firewall limitations.

Firewall Bugs

Sometimes firewalls do have bona-fide vulnerabilities because of bugs in their management interfaces or protocol-handing methods that allow an attacker to create a denial-of-service condition, in the implementation of their proxies if a proxying firewall, or in the way that they handle packets that allow an attacker to circumvent the correct operation of a firewall. Earlier in the chapter, we described a scenario in which an attacker could set a bit in the TCP header that fooled a router ACL into thinking that the connection already was established, thereby letting the packet through. It would be fruitless to try to list all of the vulnerabilities of every firewall in existence. Refer to any of the many sites listed at the end of this book to review specific vulnerabilities.

Summary

We've covered a lot of ground in this chapter, from the types of firewalls—including packet-filtering, stateful-inspection, and proxy—to their basic and advanced features, how they integrate with third-party applications, and some of their implementation issues and vulnerabilities.

You've seen that the word *firewall* really describes a function rather than a particular implementation. A router can perform a firewalling function, as can a load balancer, a switch, or even an operating system. The main characteristic of a firewall is its capability to differentiate and filter traffic into and out of its interfaces. Some firewalls, such as packet filters, perform only a rudimentary filtering function that is based on the source and destination IP addresses of each packet that traverses it. Stateful-inspection firewalls look at information dealing with the history of the connection, as well as the protocol information within the packets. Finally, there is the application proxy (and, to some extent, the air-gap or hardware proxy), which breaks the direct connection between client and server.

Each firewall trades speed and complexity against security and available features. You saw that beyond the simple function of filtering packets and connections, firewalls can offer some very advanced ancillary functions. These included the capability to create VPN connections, authenticate users, stop denial-of-service attacks, perform intrusion detection, operate with VLANs, and integrate with third-party applications, as well as a host of others.

Given the definition of a firewall as a conglomerate of functions rather than a single device, it becomes much simpler to determine what type of firewall is appropriate for your organization. By consulting your security policy, you should be able to determine what functions must be supported by the firewall. By weighing the risks posed by threats to your network against the protective functions that a firewall can offer, you should be able to choose a firewall with appropriate features and performance that fits the budgetary and administrative constraints of your organization. As we said early on, there is no "best" firewall—there are only best choices given your organization's constraints and needs. Happy firewalling!

Watching the Wire: Intrusion-Detection Systems

IN THIS CHAPTER

What Is IDS?

So far, we have described the threats to a modern IT infrastructure, the components of the network and their vulnerabilities, and a large selection of procedural and technical means for limiting your exposure to these threats. Just as any prudent enterprise, organization, or homeowner would put a lock on its doors, we have described how to "lock" servers, applications, and network chokepoints through the proper configurations of operating systems and the deployment of security devices such as firewalls. However, just as any locked door can be opened or bypassed, either by picking the lock, breaking down the door, or running in behind a careless person with a key ("tailgating"), there is no way to guarantee that an unwanted intruder will not gain access to your network. Anyone who claims to sell something that guarantees perfect security has probably got a large portfolio of other things to sell you, including snake oil and the Golden Gate Bridge.

In the world of physical security, this eventuality almost always is planned for by installing video cameras, motion sensors, infrared detectors, and door and window alarms. So, certainly the equivalent intruder-detection mechanisms must exist in the world of computer networks. As it turns out, they certainly do, and the collection of hardware and software components that make up these mechanisms collectively are referred to as *intrusion-detection systems*, or IDS.

Today, IDSs consist of a variety of functions that can provide alerts of suspicious or malicious network activity. Common IDS functions include these:

- Monitoring packets on network segments
- Monitoring file attributes (such as permissions, ownership, and modification times)
- Monitoring for gross file changes (such as file checksums)
- Monitoring system and application log files for security-related events (such as router logs, UNIX system logs, and Web server access logs)
- Monitoring key system configuration files (such as the Windows Registry)
- Monitoring system process creation
- Monitoring traffic for known attack signatures and behavior patterns that do not coincide with the normal traffic baseline and activities

The key word here is *monitoring*. This chapter describes the types of IDS sensors that are available, discusses considerations in their deployment and operation, and introduces some new management issues that commonly arise with the installation of an IDS architecture. By the end of this chapter, you should have a lot of food for thought about what capabilities to look for in IDS products and where and how to deploy an IDS.

How Internet Sites Utilize IDS

Intrusion-detection systems really are analogous to alarms and video cameras. Although they do not stop anyone from entering your network, they can tell you a lot about who is "casing the joint," alert you if someone tries to or succeeds in breaking through your front-line security, and also tell you whether the intruder got into any really sensitive places. Note that this does not just cover outsiders. In many cases, the most successful and damaging thefts and sabotage are committed by insiders, including disgruntled or former employees and contractors.

And, just as a video tape often will reveal everything that a burglar or wayward employee does when no one is looking, an IDS often can provide detailed records of malicious or suspicious activity that can be used to drive an investigation or pursue some other form of resolution. For example, we have worked with several companies that have used IDS data to bring a dispute to an advantageously negotiated settlement, thereby avoiding costly court battles. Indeed, although IDS data and system logs have been used in courts of law, they often can provide enough strong evidence to bring a dispute to closure quickly. Think about it this way: How many cases in which there is video tape of the suspect committing the crime make it all the way to trial before the suspect pleads guilty?

On a more day-to-day basis, IDS data is used to routinely perform trend analysis on attempted network break-ins and to maintain watch over network activity. Many IDS products also provide robust detection of activity that an employer might consider to be resource misuse. Examples include online chat, gambling, pornography, and music or video file trading.

The Different Types of IDS

Intrusion-detection systems consist of several components, including sensors, monitoring servers, historical event databases, and analysis tools. Intrusion-detection sensors can be placed in many locations within a network's infrastructure, and they typically report back to a common server. Two basic types of sensors commonly are deployed in the IT infrastructure: network sensors and host/OS sensors.

Network Sensors

Network sensors, or network IDS (NIDS), are used to monitor raw packet data on a network segment. The vast majority of these sensors are designed to monitor ethernet links, although it is often possible to watch ATM, FDDI, or token ring with the appropriate network adapter and driver. Typically implemented as dedicated "appliances," network sensors usually are connected to a LAN segment via a hub or switch, as shown in Figure 10.1. NIDS sensors perform all sorts of tests that examine network traffic at almost every layer of the OSI stack. We will discuss the specifics of these tests later in this chapter.

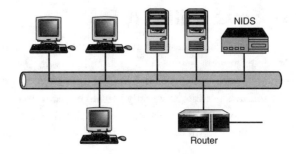

FIGURE 10.1

Network IDS sensor.

Historically, network IDS sensors have monitored an entire network or subnetwork segment; however, a new type of NIDS recently has emerged, which we will refer to as a host-based network IDS (H-NIDS). These sensors are loaded and run on workstations or servers, and they perform essentially the same function as a traditional NIDS, except that they are designed to monitor the inbound and outbound packet traffic on that workstation or server's network interface, as illustrated in Figure 10.2. Even though they run on end-user host machines, we will consider these devices to be "network sensors" because they perform the same basic function as traditional network IDS. These sensors have enjoyed most of their success in the consumer market, where they usually are combined with a "personal firewall" and are used to protect a single computer.

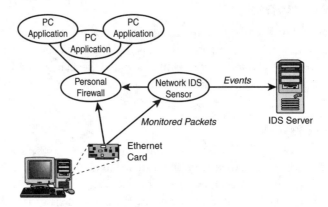

FIGURE 10.2

Host-based NIDS.

Host/OS Sensors

An alternative to monitoring packet traffic is to monitor the processes and file systems of host computers. This is accomplished through the use of a host intrusion-detection system (HIDS). For example, a security administrator might want to know when a specific program is executed on a server, or if the user password file is modified or changes permissions. Indications of Trojan horse or worm activity also can be detected by looking for gross changes in executable files. For example, the Qaz virus usually was copied into the NOTEPAD.EXE executable on Windows systems.

Furthermore, many operating systems and applications typically generate log files with a large volume of status, diagnostic, and error information. However, a network or server administrator rarely has the time to review every log file in her network. A number of products that we would classify as "host sensors" are capable of scanning these logs for security-related information and alerting an operator or administrator of events that warrant further investigation. Examples of these types of events include failed "su to root" attempts on UNIX systems, or client-side or server-side error messages on a Web server.

One other feature of host sensors that perform file content monitoring is that they can be used to monitor dedicated hardware appliances. Most medium- to high-end network devices, such as routers, switches, load balancers, and firewall appliances, generate "syslog" data that can be exported to another computer for processing and reporting purposes. For example, a router will make note of access control list (ACL) violations (which result in packet filtering) as well as any failed attempts to log into the management port in its syslog file. A host IDS that resides on a log server can monitor those files as well as the files that are native to the server itself.

IDS Servers

Almost all commercial products marketed toward enterprise networks include a capability to monitor and manage multiple sensors from one location. Event data is forwarded to a central server, usually over an encrypted channel, where an aggregate view of all the sensors can be obtained, allowing a single console to monitor the activity of many sensors. The server platforms typically provide a method of configuring individual sensors or groups of sensors remotely. So, if you have sensors at three sites around the world, you could monitor and configure all your network and host sensors from a central facility (see Figure 10.3).

Analysis Tools

The output of all the sensor types that we have described includes both *events* and *evidence data*. Security events are "fact of" records, indicating that something happened. Security events can include these:

- A packet was detected with a source IP equal to the destination IP.
- A call to the phf CGI was detected in Web traffic.
- A root login attempt failed.
- A DNS zone transfer was detected.

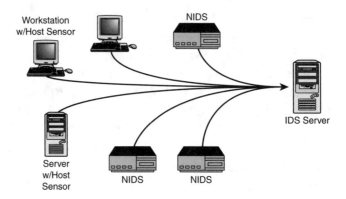

FIGURE 10.3

IDS sensors and servers.

These events, in and of themselves, can be interesting; however, a security analyst always starts asking questions:

- "Have I seen this source IP address before?"
- "What else did the intruder do after he got into my system?"
- "What domain name or netblock does this IP address resolve to?"

This is where evidence data comes into play. Good IDSs always provide data capture support. A network sensor should at least capture the event-causing packet. Really good sensors capture follow-on packets, providing the analyst with an opportunity to get a glimpse at what else the suspected intruder might have done. For example, an IDS might tell you that an attacker has successfully performed a buffer overflow attack and has obtained a command-line shell with root privileges on a server. That alone is useful knowledge, but it is far more useful to see what the attacker did once he could enter commands into the compromised system. Follow-up packets to or from the attacker would contain the command-line traffic, indicating whether the attacked modified or transferred any files, created a new user account, or performed some other action. Similarly, host-based log processors often capture the log entry that gave rise to the security event, saving the analyst from having to find the original log and look for the relevant data by hand.

Finally, the IDS operator should have high-quality analysis and reporting tools that are capable of summarizing recent events and supporting investigations into potential misuse or intrusions. These tools should provide automated correlation of event data, name resolution, trend analysis, and captured data display, including packet decodes and reconstructed TCP session views.

IDS Capabilities

So, what exactly does an IDS do? In short, an IDS monitors network traffic, operating system parameters, or file systems to look for indicators of suspicious activity. The word *suspicious* is important: Although many network attacks have obvious indicators that an IDS can detect and report with a high degree of certainty that something malicious has happened, many real-world intrusions are more subtle. Many IDSs detect and report on a wide range of network events that merit further investigation; however, in many cases, the security analyst will discover that the IDS has detected something fairly benign. This is normal and introduces the classic IDS configuration trade-off: Making the sensor sensitive enough to detect real intrusions, but not so sensitive that it will continuously issue false alarms. As you will discover later in this chapter, the process of "tuning" a sensor in the early stages of an IDS deployment is a critical step in deploying an effective intrusion detection architecture.

We described in previous chapters many of the fundamental network principles and exploitations that an IDS is based on. Given that knowledge, we are ready to look under the hood of an IDS and see how an effective system actually works.

An ideal IDS will be capable of alerting you to any malicious activities on your network. There are two schools of thought on how to accomplish this task. The first is to design a system that can look for all of the known "bad" things that can happen and to report whenever any of these events occur. This approach often is referred to as *signature-based IDS*. On the other end of the IDS spectrum is the philosophy that the best way to detect the meaningful events is to design a system that understands the normal behavior of a network and reports anything out of the ordinary that happens. This commonly is referred to as *anomaly detection*. Anomaly detection is indeed a powerful concept because it is difficult to catalog and develop signatures for every possible variation of every exploit that has been dreamed up by every hacker/cracker in the world. On the other hand, anyone who has managed a network knows that the "normal" behavior of the network can evolve quite rapidly and, at the very least, can be highly cyclical. For example, traffic loads and mixes can change throughout a day.

The reality is that both approaches have their strengths and weaknesses. The first-generation IDSs leaned heavily toward the signature-based techniques, while more recent offerings employ more of a hybrid approach. They combine lists of known bad or suspicious patterns with techniques for describing normal behavior of common application-layer protocols. We will cover this in more detail when we discuss signatures and how they can be used to look for both known and anomalous events.

Observation Points

The best way to understand the tests that are performed by most modern IDS implementations is to remember the basic operation of the TCP/IP protocol family:

- An application generates data that must be transferred from a client to a server. For example, the World Wide Web consists of Hypertext Markup Language (HTML) documents, embedded images (GIFs and JPEGs), Java applets, and so on. To view a Web page, the client (a Web browser) must request these objects from the Web server, and the server must deliver the requested objects back to the client.

- An application-layer protocol is used to facilitate the data exchange between the client and the server. In the case of WWW traffic, the Hypertext Transfer Protocol (HTTP) is used to request and deliver the HTML documents and other components of a Web page.

- The TCP protocol breaks the HTTP and its payloads into manageable blocks, or "segments," of data and works with its peer on the other computer to ensure that all the blocks of data arrive and are delivered to the remote HTTP module in the correct order.

- IP acts very much like the post office. It takes each of the TCP blocks and tries its best to get the packets across the network, through a series of routers, to its final destination. If a packet gets lost along the way, it is assumed that TCP will notice this and handle any requests for retransmissions.

As we have previously illustrated, clever attackers who understand exactly how these protocols are supposed to work spend a lot of time looking for ways to take advantage of things that the protocol developers or implementers might have forgotten to address. For example, we discussed the operations of the TCP flags and how normal combinations of those flags are used to control TCP sessions. We also showed you that you might be able to get past some firewalls or finger-print an operating system by transmitting packets with illegal flag combinations into a network. Going higher up the protocol stack, we also discussed how an application developer might forget to check all the data that a remote user can provide as input, leading to buffer overflow vulnerabilities and unanticipated access to file systems.

So, a good IDS examines the protocol and payload data at each of these layers described, looking for illegal or unusual behavior at each point.

Signatures and Tests

The tests that an IDS performs commonly are referred to as *signatures*. Many people think of signatures as sets of text or binary patterns that are loaded into an IDS. Indeed, this is how the majority of vendors describe their products. They often talk about the number of signatures that they provide and how often they deliver updates to their signature set. In many ways, this is just like virus-detection programs.

In practice, the more effective intrusion-detection systems use a combination of these loadable signature lists and hard-coded tests that are performed on the captured data. For example, you might not have to "write a signature" to look for IP packets that have a source IP address equal to the destination IP address (the classic "land attack"); this test might be built into the sensor, and you simply would have to enable it. Some routers and firewalls perform these kinds of basic packet-header security tests. You also will find that similar hard-coded tests can be performed on higher-layer protocols, such as HTTP, DNS, and FTP.

The point of all of this is that IDSs work in several ways, and the exact techniques employed by a product will vary from vendor to vendor. The terms *signatures*, *tests*, *anomaly detection*, and *protocol analysis* all get thrown around by the various vendors, and you should invest some time and ask enough hard questions, such as the following, to find out exactly what a specific product actually does and does not do:

- Is the IDS strictly a pattern matcher?
- Does it decode or analyze higher-layer protocols?
- Does it perform any kind of anomaly detection? If so, what kind?
- Are the tests/signatures updated by the vendor on a regular basis?
- Can an end user develop his own tests or signatures?

Some vendors provide users with the opportunity to develop their own signatures. In some cases, the product's signature might simply look like a string of text or binary patterns that you add to a list of things that the IDS should look for in captured traffic. In other cases, the signature is more of a programming language that can be used to describe complex sequences of tests and pattern matching. Writing IDS signatures might or might not appeal to you. Some IDS users want their system to act very much like a virus detector, coming out of the box ready to go and regularly updated via downloaded "updates" from the manufacturer. They feel that they might have neither the resources nor the expertise required to customize an IDS and would prefer to rely on the vendor for this. Other users have strong requirements for an open signature set that they can modify. Users who desire to write their own signatures are usually interested in either "tuning" the IDS to work optimally in their specific network or focusing in on specific activity once a suspected intruder has been identified.

The shrink-wrapped IDS that you deploy and forget about really offers only a basic detection capability. Yes, it will detect many known exploits and script-kiddie activity; however, it will not provide the more robust detection capabilities and operational options that we will explore in depth later in this chapter. An IDS that provides the end user with the capability to develop his own signatures provides a powerful means for tuning a sensor to a particular network and conducting focused technical investigations.

Now that we have a general concept for how an IDS implements its basic function, let's take a deeper look at a representative set of intrusion-detection tests that a good system would perform.

Packet Header Tests

Network IDS systems are designed to "sniff" packets on a network segment, so the most logical place to begin looking for suspicious activity is to examine the lower-layer packet headers. Two types of tests usually are performed:

- **Per-packet header tests**—Tests that examine a specific header field (such as the IP Time to Live [TTL] value or TCP flag combinations) for a specific value of set of values.

- **Header statistical tests**—Tests that gather statistical information over time. These can be used to detect resource exhaustion–based denial-of-service attacks and some scanning activity.

TCP/IP Tests

IP-related protocol headers, which include IP, ICMP, TCP, and UDP, are the first place that an IDS typically looks for unusual behavior. A large number of tests can be performed on these protocol headers. The following list provides a feel for the kinds of header tests that can indicate suspicious or malicious activity:

- Source IP equal to destination IP and source port equal to destination port (the "land attack")
- Misused "reserved bit" in the IP header (an old router ACL bypass trick)
- TCP or UDP ports set to 0
- Unusual TCP control flag settings (OS fingerprinting and firewall bypass)

The previous tests would be performed on each packet as it is "sniffed" from the network. Statistical tests over many packets often are used to detect network reconnaissance and denial-of-service attacks. Examples of these kinds of tests include the following:

- Looking for one-to-many patterns from one IP address to many IP addresses (a potential scan for active hosts)
- Looking for one-to-many patterns from one IP address to many TCP ports (a potential scan for active services)
- Looking for many incomplete connections from one IP address to a single port (a potential SYN flood)

As you might imagine, these statistical tests can get fairly complicated and can become a drain on IDS system resources. For example, it can take a fair amount of memory and CPU time to maintain the state of all active TCP sessions on a big Web server farm and to continuously compute session connection statistics.

It is important to remember that an IDS also can be used for more generic network monitoring. For example, some IDSs allow for the simple detection of specific protocol values, such as these:

- IP addresses
- IP protocols
- TCP/UDP ports
- ICMP types or codes

Not all IDSs provide this capability. It can be quite useful when you want to dig a little deeper into suspected intrusions or misuse. For example, if a specific IP address keeps coming up in your IDS event data, you might decide to start monitoring everything from that IP address to see what that host is really up to. Although it is certainly possible to do the same thing with a network analyzer or sniffer (such as TCPdump), you might not have any additional monitoring tap points in your network. In this case, having a monitoring capability integrated into your IDS could be a big plus.

Monitoring for specific ports can be a great anomaly-detection mechanism. For example, we tune our network sensor to alert on and record any IP packets that do not carry ICMP, TCP, or UDP payloads. Furthermore, in our DMZ, we configure our IDS to alert on and record non-Web (port 80) or SSH (port 22) traffic because we should not see anything other than those two services on that network segment.

NetBIOS over TCP/IP (NBT)

After TCP/IP, Microsoft Networking has become the most popular network- and session-level protocol family in use in many enterprise networks. Microsoft Networking is supported by protocols that handle NetBIOS session establishment, datagram transport, and name resolution services, as well as the server message block (SMB) headers that are used to implement Microsoft's file- and print-sharing services. These protocols are built into all of Microsoft's operating systems and other OSes, and they are very popular in Windows $9x$ and NT networks. Windows 2000 has introduced new networking technology; however, the NetBIOS-based protocols still are supported for backward compatibility.

It is now very common to find the NetBIOS protocols running over TCP/IP, using an encapsulation known as NBT. This allows Microsoft networks to run in conjunction with common Internet applications and to interoperate with UNIX systems. Similarly, it is also possible for a UNIX platform to interoperate with Microsoft network services, such as file and printer sharing, through the use of Samba.

Some IDSs understand the function of the NBT and SMB protocols and can look for suspicious activity within those protocols. Examples of NBT/SMB tests include these:

- Monitoring for suspicious administrative logins
- Monitoring for suspicious Null account logins
- NetBIOS name service queries

Unless you are running in a pure TCP/IP environment, with no chance that any Windows networking services may be turned on, either intentionally or accidentally, you should be sure that your IDS is capable of detecting these types of events.

Other Networking Protocols

In practice, it is certainly possible to run Microsoft networks without using TCP/IP. The NetBIOS Frames protocol can be encapsulated in IEEE 802.3 frames and is capable of carrying SMB traffic, allowing things such as the Network Neighborhood Browser Protocol and file and print sharing to work without ever introducing an IP header. This is becoming less popular as many Microsoft networks have some connectivity to the Internet. Because just about every IDS vendor has focused on IP, the NetBIOS tests described usually work only if they are transported over TCP/IP.

Similarly, none of the mainstream IDS vendors supports IPX or AppleTalk intrusion detection. The more recent versions of the Novell products run the higher-layer protocols that usually are associated with IPX, such as the Netware Core Protocol (NCP), over TCP/IP. So, just as a number of NetBIOS tests currently are performed by some IDSs, we might see new tests for the higher-layer Novell protocols as well.

Ethernet and Other Data-Link–Layer Headers

We have not discussed data-link layers such as ethernet or 802.3 frame headers yet. Most IDSs do not spend much time examining these headers, mainly because they have only local significance. When a packet gets to a router or bridge, the next hop may use an entirely different transport and data link layer (such as PPP, Cisco's HDLC encapsulation, or Frame Relay). As a general rule, data-link–layer manipulation really is available only to someone who resides on the same network segment.

This is not to say that there are not very interesting things that can be done with crafted data-link–layer packets. For example, the L0pht Anti-Sniff program uses specially created ethernet packets to actively probe for network adapters running in promiscuous mode. One way that it does this is to send out packets with fictitious ethernet destination addresses. Under normal circumstances, this packet will not be "heard" by normal network adapters; however, an ethernet card that is "sniffing" the network will pick it up and deliver it to whatever packet analysis program is running (such as TCPdump or even an IDS). This, in itself, does nothing to detect the "sniffing" card; however, if the analysis program is configured to look for IP addresses and perform reverse DNS lookups, it will transmit a DNS query packet. If the computer running Anti-Sniff sees that packet go by, it will know that some computer has seen a packet that it normally should not have received.

In reality, Anti-Sniff detected the analysis program, not the promiscuous network card; however the effect is the same, and it used a crafted ethernet packet header to do the job. For an IDS to have detected this, it probably would need to be keeping track of normal ethernet addresses on the local segment and would generate an alert whenever an IP address was observed in association with a second ethernet address, or if it detected that an ethernet address was only ever used as a destination and that no data ever originated from that address.

Another example of potential ethernet abuse is to create a pseudocovert channel. This might work by taking advantage of the fact that the minimum size of an ethernet payload is 46 bytes and the minimum size of a TCP/IP header is 40 bytes. So, a normal TCP "acknowledgement" packet would result in 6 padded bytes in the ethernet frame. At a minimum, this space could be used to move data between two local hosts in a mildly stealthy way because many protocol analyzers simply might ignore the pad bytes. No easy test for an IDS to perform is evident here because there is no normal way to pad the ethernet payload. We have seen some NICs that simply use whatever is left sitting in the transmit buffer from the previous packet as the pad data.

The point of both of these examples is that data-link layers *can* be abused, often to achieve some objective involving other local computers. However, most IDSs do not spend much time examining these headers. The reason for this is that ethernet is a *local* area network protocol and that only insiders on the same LAN (or VLAN) could even attempt to perform some of these acts. Furthermore, these kinds of attacks are fairly rare and do not represent a serious danger to most networks.

Application-Layer Protocols

Many of the most common vulnerabilities in modern IT infrastructures revolve around application-layer protocols. If the 1980s was the decade of TCP/IP, with its formal introduction into the ARPANET and the rise of the routing and network infrastructure vendors, the 1990s was the decade of the application-layer protocol. Although the classic SMTP, telnet, and FTP protocols were used heavily in the 1980s, the arrival of HTTP was the turning point in the commercialization of the Internet.

The tremendous popularity of Web applications in the mid- to late 1990s gave rise to an entire industry of software developers who were charged with creating huge numbers of e-commerce and Web-enabled database applications. In almost all cases, these applications were associated with projects with very aggressive development and deployment schedules, and with little real emphasis on secure software architectures or coding guidelines. The result is that many of the applications and Web servers were delivered with serious security vulnerabilities that are exploited on a daily basis.

For this reason, modern intrusion-detection systems must have some understanding of the proper function of popular application-layer protocols. Several approaches to this exist. One way is to build in tests that have defined checks for application-layer validity or misuse. Let's take a look at the File Transfer Protocol (FTP) for some examples of tests that can be performed.

FTP uses at least two TCP connections to transfer files from one machine to another, as illustrated in Figure 10.4. A "control" channel is established by the client to the server and is used to pass a user's name and password, as well as commands for traversing the remote file system and copying files back and forth. Each actual file transfer is performed over "data" connections. So, how can this protocol be abused?

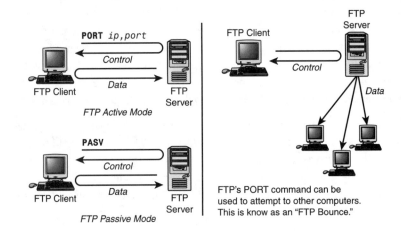

FIGURE 10.4

FTP protocol operation.

- Typically, the FTP server decides which port it will use for the data connection and informs the client via the control channel. Alternatively, the PORT command can be used by the client to tell the server which IP address and port to use for the data exchange. There are valid reasons for this; however, the PORT command can be misused in several ways. In one example, a mildly clever individual could establish a normal control channel to an FTP server and then attempt to copy a file to a bunch of machines in another network by specifying a series of data channel IP addresses in repeated PORT commands.

These transfers most likely will not succeed; however, based on the error messages that are returned over the control channel, the first stage of network reconnaissance could be performed in this way. The advantage of this approach is that the actual probe is performed by someone else's computer. Furthermore, if you were able to find the right FTP server that the target network has some level of trust in, you might be able to get through a firewall.

- Another potential vulnerability involves older FTP servers running code that is vulnerable to buffer overflow attacks in the user-provided password field. It would be nice to be able to look for buffer overflow data in the password field of the FTP control channel. Most IDSs have a collection of tests that look for obvious indicators of buffer overflows, such as strings of Intel or Sparc "no-ops" (microprocessor-specific machine language codes that often are found at the beginning of buffer overflow code segments). Unfortunately, buffer overflow developers have gotten pretty tricky, and there are some clever techniques to evade the traditional buffer overflow "no-op" signatures. However, one thing hasn't changed: Buffer overflows still require at least several dozen bytes of data to get enough functionality in them to do their job. So, instead of updating your IDS with every new potential sign of a buffer overflow, maybe you would do better by looking for unusually long passwords in FTP. Have you ever used a 20-character password? If your answer is "no," you are the same as the other 99.9999% of us.

So, you can see that you can look for many things if you have an IDS that understands these higher-layer protocols. In this case, we have come up with two simple tests that would catch lots of misuse:

- Checking for PORT commands with an IP address other than the source IP of the packet
- Checking for PASS commands (the way FTP encodes user passwords) that are longer than a specified size

In both cases, these tests could generate false-alarm events from valid traffic; however, those circumstances would be rare in most modern networks, and any observations of them would merit further investigation.

NOTE

The current trend in IDS development is to build more hard-coded tests for misuse of application layer protocols. Other examples of such tests include these:

- **DNS**—Monitoring for zone transfers from unusual IP addresses (this is a common early step in network reconnaissance).

- **SNMP**—Monitoring for SETs or GETs from external IP addresses. SNMPv2 has very weak security, and it is often possible to extract or modify system-configuration information using default passwords.
- **RPC**—Many serious vulnerabilities are associated with remote procedure calls. Some IDSs monitor for suspicious or dangerous RPC packet activity, especially from external IP addresses.

Of course, many of these attacks should be blocked by proper firewall policy sets; however, people make mistakes, and it is not always possible to block all undesired traffic from getting into your network. Remember our lock and alarm analogy: You install alarms to catch those cases when the lock fails.

Application Data

Finally, application-layer data, the information that modern commercial and enterprise networks are designed to transport from point A to point B, is the most challenging place for an IDS to monitor, mainly because it is harder to characterize what is "proper" in this data. In general, signatures can be written to look for anything that is carried by the various applications. It is here that a sensor can look for inappropriate content, signs of some viruses, or anything that you care to look for. Some vendors provide "employee misuse" signature libraries that include tests for online gambling and pornographic Web sites. This is also where things such as Trojan horse commands and control channel data can be identified. For example, some Trojan horses use Internet Relay Chat (IRC) channels for this purpose, and keywords associated with specific attack programs are provided as IDS signatures.

Investigative Monitoring

We recently were asked to work with a client who suspected that a former employee was working with current employees to transfer proprietary data to a competitor. We set up an IDS to monitor the company's mail servers, and we wrote several dozen custom signatures that looked for both user email names and proprietary subject matter keywords that might appear in the documents in question. The IDS also was configured to collect all packets from TCP ports 25 and 110, guaranteeing that we could provide all the email transactions that contained information relevant to the investigation.

Using the IDS's native analysis tools, along with a few scripts developed by our company, we were able to deliver fully reassembled email traffic, indexed by the desired keywords, to the company's legal team. This information, in concert with other "deleted" data recovered from several suspect computers, was key to providing a favorable resolution to our client when this case was arbitrated out of court.

The IDS's custom signature support proved useful in two ways. First, it allowed the client's attorneys to zero in on the relevant traffic very quickly. It also provided the benefit of minimizing the exposure of other users' communications, an issue that both we and our client were sensitive to.

File Integrity

File integrity checking is a function performed by a number of host-resident sensors. These sensors watch for changes in files that could be indicative of malicious activity. For example, it is fairly common for a hacker who "owns" a computer to cover his tracks by modifying log files. This might mean opening a file and deleting a few lines, deleting the log file, or replacing the log file. Similarly, the hacker could add new information to a file, providing back doors for later access. Examples of this include adding addresses to the .rhosts file in a UNIX system, creating a new user account, and modifying the Windows Registry so that a Trojan is run every time a workstation is started.

File-integrity sensors can monitor for this type of activity by watching certain attributes of a file (or files) for changes. Attributes can include operating system parameters such as these:

- File size. (Has it gotten bigger or smaller?)
- File ownership. (Who does the file belong to?)
- File permissions. (Who can read/write/execute?)
- UNIX inode. (This is a technical file system parameter.)

One other attribute that often is created by the file-integrity sensor is a file checksum. This is typically a cryptographic hash, such as MD5, that is computed for the file when the sensor begins to monitor it. After that, it periodically recalculates the checksum to see whether the value has changed. If it has, then the file content has changed in some way. This does not tell you what changed within the file; it tells you just that something changed. Although it might be theoretically possible to modify a file and retain the same checksum, this is extraordinarily difficult to do using the modern cryptographic techniques that are employed in things such as MD5 or other digital signature types of algorithms.

A HIDS that performs these kinds of tests will report "events" back to an IDS server, just like the traditional network sensors. In this case, the event will indicate something like "Permissions changed on /etc/passwd."

Log Processing

A number of IDS and other security vendors have begun to offer automated log-processing products. These products are designed to monitor log files from all sorts of devices and applications and to look for activity that could be a sign of security problems. Examples include these:

- Router logs (such as ACL violations or failed telnet attempts to the router's management interface)
- Firewall logs (for example, security policy violations such as "denied traffic")
- Windows event logs (such as failed user logins)
- UNIX "Message" files (such as failed superuser logins or a network card going into promiscuous mode)
- Web server logs (such as error messages with 400 or 500 codes, indicating client- or server-side problems)

An example of log processing, combined with file-integrity checking, is illustrated in Figure 10.5.

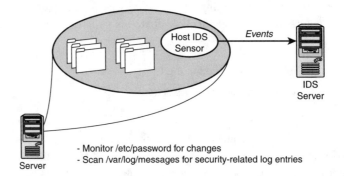

FIGURE 10.5

File monitoring on a UNIX system.

Although it is not a log file, the Windows Registry is a well-defined file that also can be monitored for changes. Some of the host IDS products watch certain Registry hives and keys for changes.

Sensor Integration

We have worked with several clients on large network IDS and log-processing integration efforts. We have seen two approaches to these efforts. In some cases, a network IDS infrastructure already exists, sometimes consisting of several vendors' products. In these cases, a product that is primarily a log processor is used to integrate the various IDS sensor events into one database. To accomplish this, each IDS is configured to generate log files containing records of their respective security events, and then a host sensor is used to convert the different vendors' logged events into a common format.

The other approach deals with the fact that several traditional network IDS vendors recently added new products that perform the same function as file integrity checkers and log processors. These sensors generate events just like the network sensors and forward their data back to the same security server. This allows an enterprise or other organization to supplement its network IDS system with new "host agents" that work within the vendor's IDS architecture.

Counter-IDS Techniques

Now that you have an understanding of the types of tests that an IDS must routinely perform to do its job effectively, it is time to look at some of the challenges that IDS developers are faced with and how these challenges can be overcome. Some of these challenges are based on the difficulty of actually performing all the tests that we have described in an effective manner. Many of the others arise from the fact that determined crackers have worked hard to circumvent any IDS that might be watching for their activity.

The primary challenges to IDSs involve the network sensors. Many counter-IDS techniques have been either demonstrated or proposed over the past several years.

Volume, Volume, Volume

The first challenge for real-world network IDSs is that they must perform fairly complex processing of all the packets that they observe. Many network devices must look at many packets: Routers and switches are the obvious examples, but these devices usually perform relatively simple operations (such as switching) or a single mildly complex function (such as routing) that can be optimized either in clever software implementations or with hardware acceleration.

To do its job effectively, an IDS typically must perform several dozen protocol header tests and hundreds (or thousands) of signature comparisons on every packet that it receives. Because of the complexity of the problem, just about all IDSs are implemented in software and are run on dedicated server-class host computers. It will be interesting to see what strides are made toward accelerating some of the IDS functionality in hardware in the coming years.

IP Fragmentation and TCP Segmenting

The next challenge comes from the fact that application-layer protocols and application data are cut up into different packets by the TCP and IP protocols.

- TCP's primary function is to "segment" data into manageable blocks and hand them over to IP for delivery to the destination computer. If the receiving TCP module determines that it is missing data, it effectively requests that the sender repeat the missing segments (this is really an implicit request, not an explicit request). Because of the way this works, the transmitting TCP module might send more bytes than what the receiver is missing. It is up to the receiver to take these possibly overlapping blocks of data and pass a resequenced, deduped stream of bytes to the application layer (see Figure 10.6).

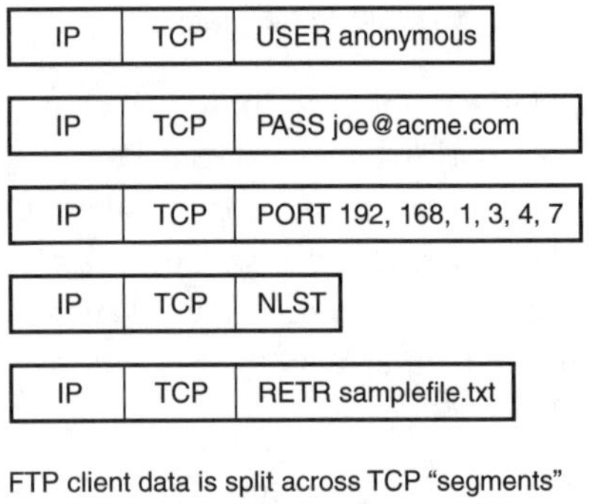

IP	TCP	USER anonymous

IP	TCP	PASS joe@acme.com

IP	TCP	PORT 192, 168, 1, 3, 4, 7

IP	TCP	NLST

IP	TCP	RETR samplefile.txt

FTP client data is split across TCP "segments"

FIGURE 10.6
TCP segmenting.

- IP adds the source and destination IP addresses to these segments and sends the packet into the network. Along the way, routers receive the packet, look at the destination IP address in the header, figure out which of its interfaces to push the packet to, and then send the packet on its way to the next stop in the network. However, each router must handle the problem that can arise if the next link along the path to the destination supports only a maximum packet size that is smaller than the incoming packet. This can happen if the packet comes from an ethernet network with a maximum size of 1500 bytes and needs to be forwarded on a point-to-point link that supports only 512 bytes.

In this case, IP uses its fragmenting mechanism to chop up the packet into two (or more) pieces, attach IP headers to all the pieces, and then send each on as standalone IP datagrams. When the packet gets to its destination, the receiving IP module gathers the pieces and puts them back together before handing them up to the TCP module (see Figure 10.7). Of course, if one of the pieces doesn't make it, the IP module simply discards all the pieces. Remember, IP does not make any promises about getting data anywhere.

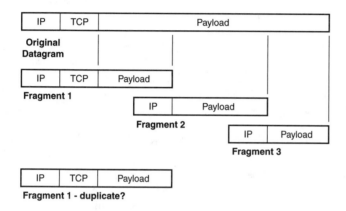

FIGURE 10.7

IP fragmenting.

So, what does all of this have to do with an IDS? Well, if it is to do its job well, it must do its best to reassemble these fragments and TCP segments so that it can look for the data patterns of interest at the application protocol and application data layers. Early IDSs totally ignored these problems, and the clever hackers knew it.

So, what if someone wants to attack a computer that is "protected" by one of these less-capable IDSs? The attacker simply crafts the attack packets so that the signature that normally would give him away is split between two packets. The IDS will look for the signature in one packet and then the other, will come up empty-handed, and totally will ignore the attack pattern that eventually will be reconstructed at the target computer.

This can be quite a challenge to an IDS. Although IP fragments are fairly rare "in the wild," TCP segmenting is a very normal, routine function on an IP network. So, to really do its job well, IDS simply has to keep track of all the packets coming into it, buffer them in memory, reassemble the application-layer session, and apply its signatures to the various streams of data for each session. Simple, right? The function itself is simple because every computer on the Internet does it. The problem for the IDS is that it has to do it for every computer on its local network. So, if your IDS is monitoring the traffic coming into a network with 10 Web servers, it must essentially do the work of all 10 servers just to look at the data in an effective method.

The problem only gets worse. What rules should the IDS use to reassemble this traffic? Remember that many of the vulnerabilities in networks and applications come from implementation decisions made by software developers. Sometimes there is no wrong decision, but a decision has to be made. For example, a TCP stream reassembler might receive overlapping TCP segments because of normal retransmissions. Which copy of the overlapping data should be passed up to the next layer? Under normal conditions, if the TCP protocol is used as it was designed, it really shouldn't matter. You could use the first copy that you got or the last copy that you got because the data should be the same.

The same is true for IP fragments. In fact, under normal circumstances, you should never get overlapping data in IP fragments. IP doesn't support retransmissions (remember, that is TCP's job); it simply breaks packets into pieces if it needs to so that they "fit" on a specific data link. So, the developer who was given the job of writing the IP fragment-handling software probably never even though about this.

As it turns out, developers for different IP stacks made different choices. Again, none of these was a bad choice; each was just different. Unfortunately, the diligent hacker will take note of this and, if he understand his target well enough (especially if he knows what IDS is in use), he can craft packets so that their key "giveaway" attack strings are contained in packets that the IDS will ignore but that their target will not. This concept is illustrated in Figure 10.8.

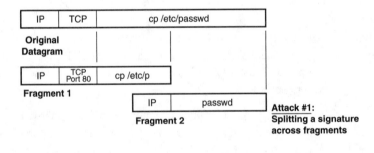

The first attack splits the suspect command line "cp /etc/password" so that a simple IDS will not "see" it when it performs its signature pattern matching. The second attack could be used to bypass the ruleset in a simple firewall, where the firewall uses the first fragment's TCP port to allow the packet through and the target host uses the duplicate fragment's TCP port to call the Telnet service on the host.

FIGURE 10.8

Avoiding an IDS with IP fragments.

So, although it is definitely a good thing (it is really a requirement) that an IDS makes reasonable efforts to defragment IP datagrams and reassemble TCP data streams before applying signature, it is not quite enough.

- The IDS should look for overlapping IP datagrams and issue security events if any are observed.
- The IDS should look for overlapping TCP segments in which apparently valid data differs in value.

One of the more advanced commercial IDSs not only detects overlapping fragments, but it also provides the capability to set the fragment processing to mimic operating systems that employ different defragmenting rules. This allows the user to "tune" the sensors to act like the workstations or servers that it is protecting. So, if the IDS was watching a Web server farm based on Microsoft NT/IIS, it would be configured to use the first overlapping fragment. On the other hand, if the Web servers were Linux/Apache configurations, the defragmenter would use the most recent packet.

Finally, given the basic processing issues that must be addressed to ensure that the most accurate signature matching is performed, the IDS further is challenged by the fact that it must do this for many computers at one time. This challenges the IDS designer to perform aggressive memory management while still maintaining the raw processing speed required to "keep up" with the monitored network segment.

Evasion via Application-Layer Encoding

We already have discussed the need for a robust IDS to understand the application-layer protocols to detect basic misuse of the protocol functions. Another aspect of this is the capability to compensate for various encoding options that might be used either innocently or with the intent of evading the IDS. To do the best job possible, the IDS has to "look at" the traffic the same way as the potential victim machines. This issue is best illustrated by two examples: the encoding used by the HTTP and telnet protocols.

HTTP URL Encoding

You probably are familiar with the HTTP uniform resource locator, or URL. This is the line that you type at the top of your Web browser to get to a site, such as `http://www.coolsite.com`.

Your Web browsers also generate these URLs based on what links or buttons you click on. As we described in some detail in Chapter 8, "Attack Scenarios," all sorts of clever things can be done either to execute very vulnerable code on a Web server or to navigate through a server's file system.

In the case of executing code on the server, let's look at the classic PHF attack, in which an attacker could execute system commands through a "demo" CGI program included in the early releases of the Apache Web server. You might hope that not many servers are providing access to this vulnerable code anymore; however, just to make sure, the IDS should look for URLs that include patterns such as this one:

```
GET /cgi-bin/phf
```

When this is in your signature database, you can be confident that anytime someone tries to execute this code, you will know about it, right? Unfortunately, the answer is "no." As it turns out, HTTP is pretty forgiving about exactly how you submit this URL. For instance, you could do one of several things to change this a little:

- Use some character encoding on the slashes, replacing those characters with their hexidecimal ASCII code (0x2F):

  ```
  GET /2fcgi-bin/2fphf
  ```

- Use some file system encoding to achieve the same thing:

  ```
  GET /cgi-bin/./phf
  ```

As you can imagine, many variations on this theme end up producing countless strings of characters that mean the same thing to the Web server running the HTTP protocol. Unfortunately, many early IDS systems would look for the exact string `GET /cgi-bin/phf` and come up empty on the previous two examples. Of course, a clever intruder knows all about this and just takes care to always do something to obfuscate the URL so that a simple pattern-matching IDS never will detect it.

So, how should you handle this from an intrusion-detection perspective? You can pursue two obvious strategies. First, you could try to guess every variation of the suspect string that someone might use to sneak something by and write a signature for each one. Of course, you would have to do the same thing for every other known CGI vulnerability. Or, you could use an IDS that is aware of the HTTP protocol and its encoding flexibility, and that attempts to normalize the data back to its "true meaning" before applying any of the CGI signatures that it has.

Telnet Encoding

The telnet protocol, as described in RFC 854, is a terminal-emulation protocol that allows users to log into one computer from another. Note that telnet servers usually are configured to listen on the well-known TCP port 23, and they often are left running in default installations of many UNIX systems. If an intruder can gain access to a telnet server, he might want to "cover his tracks" by obfuscating some of the common operating system commands that an IDS might be looking for. This can be done relatively easily if the attacker remembers that the telnet protocol does more than simply pass text from one computer to another.

Telnet uses the Network Virtual Terminal (NVT) protocol when it exchanges data between two computers. One of the features of this protocol is that it contains control characters that can be inserted into the data stream. These characters are not obvious to the user who is typing at the command console, but they are in the data stream. The telnet server knows how to handle these characters, and they will be removed before the user's commands are passed on to the operating system. Knowing this, a clever attacker can insert control characters in the middle of patterns that he suspects an IDS might be looking for.

Yet another option for inserting signature-evading characters into a telnet session is simply to insert "mistake" characters followed by backspaces, as shown in Figure 10.9. The extra characters will be transmitted over the network; however, the telnet server will strip the terminal keystrokes before passing the user command strings up to the operating system shell.

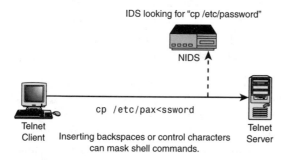

FIGURE 10.9
IDS evasion using telnet encoding.

These examples illustrate once again that one of the primary challenges for an IDS is not just to "keep up" with the network, but to examine the traffic in the same manner as the potential targets in the network.

Other IDS Avoidance Techniques

By now, you should have a pretty good appreciation for what an IDS has to go through to look at traffic the same way that targeted IP stacks and applications do. We have discussed fragment handling, TCP reconstruction, and application-layer encoding issues. On top of the complexity of this processing, the IDS is challenged with doing this for all the traffic on its network.

It turns out that still more tricks can be used to confuse an IDS. We will give one more example, just to give you a feel for the amount of thought and cleverness that can go into a directed attack against a network.

Suppose that you are running your IDS at the front end of your network, just behind your main gateway router. Through some reconnaissance, a hacker has found a server that is interesting. During the reconnaissance phase, the hacker also was able to download the routing tables from your router via an SNMP walk through the router's MIB. So, the attacker knows which server to attack and where it is in your network. Knowing that you are running an IDS out toward the Internet, and having a good feel for the distance (in router hops) between him, your IDS, and the target server, the attacker crafts several packets with IP TTL values set to expire between the IDS and the target server. This means that the IDS will see packets that will never make it to the server. It is now possible to inject data into the IDS to desynchronize any TCP session reassembly that it might be doing. For example, a FIN or RST packet normally would indicate that the session is closing. If a TCP session terminating packet was sent with an appropriately low-valued TTL, then the IDS would see this packet, but the target system would not because it would "die" after it passed by the IDS but before it reached its legitimate destination. The IDS now would be out of step with the legitimate TCP session because it would think that the session was over, even though the intended recipient was still waiting for more data. This can result in the IDS flushing buffers that contained partial attacks.

This would be a pretty sophisticated attack, and there might be nothing that an IDS can do to correct for this; however, some of the more industrial-strength systems can look for activity that hints that someone might be trying to play these kinds of games. For example, if the IDS sees IP packets with extremely low-valued TTL values, this might be something that you should know about because this is the number in an IP datagram that indicates that the packet is about to "die." It might be innocent enough, but it is not typical; this is something that is probably worth taking a quick look at.

If you want to join the ranks of IDS developers, or if you just want to know more about this subject, we recommend the paper "Insertion, Evasion, and Denial of Service: Eluding Network Intrusion Detection," written by Tom Ptacek and Timothy Newsham, which can be found on the Internet (because specific URLs often change, we recommend a query of your favorite search engine).

DoS'ing an IDS

A relatively new set of tools has begun to emerge within the security/hacker community, marking the next round in the continuing IDS/anti-IDS battle. The tactic with these tools is to change from a mind-set of sneaking past an IDS, using many of the techniques described previously, to overwhelming an IDS. The basic concept is quite simple. If an attacker can acquire the set of signatures that the IDS uses to monitor for suspicious activity, why not simply transmit a storm of packets at the IDS that contain those signatures? Such a "signature flood" can result in several disastrous consequences for an IDS:

- Thousands of false security events will be generated in a short amount of time, resulting in significant slowing of the sensor.
- Operator displays will be filled with these events, resulting in operator confusion.
- Alerting mechanisms will be overwhelmed. If an IDS is set up to page or email a security analyst or system administrator, the sensor or server system can be slowed down by repeated calls to the mail programs. Furthermore, the unfortunate pager wearer will find that his pager is constantly going off, filling up with potentially hundreds of messages.
- Disk systems might fill, resulting in a crash of the IDS.

In effect, the IDS system can be "DoS'ed" ("denial of serviced") with a signature storm. The outcome of this is that an intruder might attempt to insert a real attack in the middle of the storm, with the hope that his actual intentions will not be detected amid all the noise. Alternatively, the plan could be to maintain the signature storm long enough to feel reasonably certain that an IDS has been knocked offline, and then to perform the attack. In either case, any indication of a signature storm should be taken seriously and should be anticipated and planned for in IDS response guidelines (these are discussed at the end of this chapter). At a minimum, such an event should be treated as any other DoS attack. Your network has been specifically targeted, and you need to know why.

Note that the IDSs that are most easily affected by these tools are the ones with open signature sets. We believe that this is no reason to shy away from these products, and we think that the advantages of a customizable signature set far outweigh the higher susceptibility to these tools. In the end, even "closed" signature sets are vulnerable to this technique because many of the basic signature contents will be the same whether they are published or not. And, of course, several IDS vendors are beginning to release versions of their products that they claim have some resistance to these attacks.

The point of all of this is not to scare you away from IDS, but to give you an appreciation for the things that a good IDS can do. Several IDS vendors have taken many of these issues into account and do an admirable job of detecting sophisticated attacks that employ all sorts of evasion and obfuscation techniques. An industrial-strength IDS can perform quite well and offer many operational and security advantages to you.

Practical IDS Implementation Issues

An intrusion-detection system obviously can be a powerful tool; however, some challenges must be considered in planning an IDS rollout.

Switched Networks

Monitoring a network five years ago was much easier than it is today. Any modern network of significant size will be built on a switching infrastructure, not the broadcast hubs that were popular in the early 1990s. Their primary feature, that they send packets only to their destination node or collision domains, is their primary drawback for any kind of monitoring, whether day-to-day network analysis or intrusion detection. Because the monitoring device is not an intended receiver, it will never see the packets (see Figure 10.10).

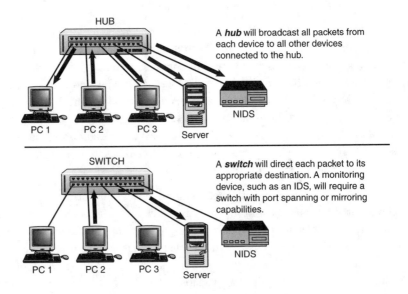

FIGURE 10.10

Network monitoring in a switched environment.

All is not lost, however! Most enterprise-quality switches provide "spanning" or "mirroring" capabilities, which allow duplicate copies of packets to be forwarded to designated monitoring ports on the switch. You usually can copy a specific interface, set of interfaces, or VLAN to a monitoring port. Higher-end switches perform this function in hardware and do a good job of getting all the packets copied. So, using this switch feature, you could monitor a network chokepoint (the interface that connects to your gateway router), or you could monitor a collection of devices by copying all the interfaces connected to user workstations.

Of course, you can run into problems if you try to copy ten 100Mb ethernet interfaces to a single 100Mb interface. If you are monitoring the traffic between user workstations in an internal network, this could be your only viable option; however, it is likely that few of those users really are using all the bandwidth available to them, and this solution could work just fine. As with all real-world network designs, you just have to look at what applications you are supporting and architect appropriately. In this case, if all the users are doing a lot of streaming media work, the 10-to-1 traffic copy might not work very well.

A few other options for monitoring single ethernet segments can work well if you are looking at a network chokepoint or a single server. You always can grab one of your old hubs and use it to "tap" a 10/100 twisted pair. The disadvantage to this is that you have introduced one new device which will fail in your network. An alternative is to purchase a dedicated ethernet tap. One current vendor of such a device is Shomiti. These devices are designed to separate the traffic from each direction of a 10/100 link and output them to a network analyzer. They also have the reliability feature that they "fail closed," meaning that if the tap fails for some reason, the network traffic still will be passed.

Switched networks are one of the primary reasons that host-based network IDS (H-NIDS) has been developed. Along with providing an IDS capability to home and mobile users, these network sensors provide a partial solution to the switching problem. In an enterprise configuration, the IDS function is distributed across the infrastructure. Like everything, this has its advantages and disadvantages. Host-based NIDS can provide good detection at each computer, but this does not provide a global view of the network. This is particularly a problem for detecting certain reconnaissance activity.

Encryption

Many networks are beginning to employ encryption technology at one or multiple levels within the protocol stacks. Application data can be encrypted using tools such as Pretty Good Privacy (PGP) or S/MIME. Application-layer protocol data can be encrypted using the Secure Socket Layer (SSL/TLS). Although implementations of SSL have been defined for several of the Internet application protocols, it most commonly is used to encrypt HTTP in Web applications. HTTPS, the secure version of HTTP, typically is transported over TCP port 443. Similarly, secure telnet and file-transfer sessions are implemented using the Secure Shell (SSH) applications, typically on TCP port 22. Packet traffic, down to IP and TCP headers, can be encrypted using virtual private network (VPN) technology protocols such as IP Security (IPSec), Microsoft's Point-to-Point Tunneling Protocol (PPTP), or the IETF's Layer 2 Tunneling Protocol (L2TP).

There has been quite a bit of debate about the long-term value of network-based intrusion-detection sensors in the face of all of this encryption technology. Indeed, in some circumstances, encryption significantly can limit an IDS's capability to detect suspicious activity. However, all is not lost.

One of the key tenets of this book is that information security is not achieved through one device, but through a cohesive policy and technical architecture. Similarly, intrusion detection can play a significant role in a security architecture with the appropriate planning and sensor combinations. Let's address each of the previously described encryption challenges.

Encrypted application data is probably the biggest challenge to traditional IDS sensors. However, if you consider virus detection to be a part of the intrusion-detection architecture, then there are many solutions in place to monitor email for malicious content, including virus and Trojan-bearing attachments. Many administrators implement virus scanning much sooner than traditional IDS; however, we suggest that the two perform very complementary functions—they both are looking for suspicious activity that might indicate an attack on a system.

SSL/TLS can be handled in one of several ways. As previously mentioned, SSL/TLS is most commonly used in conjunction with HTTP traffic, and it is employed to impart a sense of security to the client. Given this, the network and server engineers have a fair amount of flexibility regarding where the decryption process takes place. One option is to use an "SSL accelerator" appliance, which handles the bulk encryption and decryption on the server side of the HTTPS traffic. This option offloads CPU-intensive cryptographic algorithms from the Web servers and provides a monitoring point between the accelerator and the servers from which to perform IDS monitoring. Of course, the decision to perform encryption and decryption off the Web servers will be influenced by operational security needs (for example, is it acceptable to have "plain-text" traffic anywhere on the network?).

A second option that can work quite well with HTTPS is to use a host-based sensor to monitor the Web server access logs. These logs contain detailed records of all the client requests and URLs, and they often are used for business analysis purposes, using tools such as WebTrends to gather statistics on content popularity, referrer sites, and so on. A log-monitoring sensor can be used to look for the same types of suspicious strings contained in URLs in the log file as would be seen in the packet traffic.

VPNs are becoming increasingly popular for organizations that want to enable mobile connectivity with their internal networks. Although they provide privacy (that is, encryption) and authentication mechanisms and often dramatically reduce the cost of remote access, VPNs also can open significant holes in your security architecture. For example, you might trust the business ethics of a partner organization with whom you share a VPN connection, but you might not have any input into or control over their information security practices. A tunnel that ends inside your firewall perimeter could have a remote endpoint with no meaningful security measures. This also can be true with remote users, especially telecommuters and "road warriors" who often connect to the Internet when away from the corporate network. This vulnerability is illustrated in Figure 10.11.

In cases when one or more VPN tunnels terminate within your secure perimeter, an IDS can provide valuable monitoring of potentially dangerous traffic that is not filtered by your normal router ACLs or firewall policies.

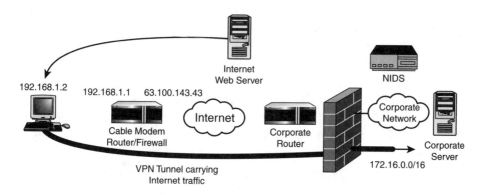

FIGURE 10.11

Vulnerabilities with VPNs.

Tuning Your IDS Sensors

After an IDS has been installed, you must invest a little bit of time in initially tuning the sensor. Our experience is that most sensors come "out of the box" configured to detect either nothing or everything. In the case of the former, the sensor obviously is not very useful; in the latter case, it is likely to generate a great number of false alarms. Remember that the output of an IDS is events that represent some condition on the network that you want to know about. Until you determine what you want to know about, the IDS will generate many events that you don't care about. This applies to both network and host sensors, although the network sensors tend to be more susceptible to generating false alarms.

> ## IDS Tuning and Your Sleep Habits
>
> We did some work with a major telecommunications service provider that was in the process of deploying an extensive IDS system. During the pilot program, the network engineers were responsible for managing and monitoring the sensors. Because few network engineers can work 24 hours a day, at least on a regular basis, they decided to turn on the email and paging features of the system. The lead engineer reported that his pager's battery was drained by the IDS the very first night of operation. Needless to say, he began tuning his sensors the next morning.

What kinds of events could be false alarms? That really depends on your configuration and what you care about. Let's look at a couple examples of IDS events.

- **Ping sweeps**—Many network reconnaissance tools (such as the free and very popular nmap) use ICMP Echo Request, commonly known as *pings*, to look for active workstations and servers. Many IDSs look for one-to-many patterns of pings to detect reconnaissance attempts on a network. On the other hand, many network-management tools (such as HP OpenView) perform similar "discovery" operations. How does an IDS know that this is a network-management tool instead of a network-reconnaissance tool?

- **Application content events**—Some IDSs contain signatures that look for application-layer content. For example, IRC (chat) traffic contains telltale indicators within the application-layer protocol. Maybe you care about your employees chatting online, and maybe you don't. How does your IDS know whether to report these events to you?

The answer to both questions is that you have to tell it. This is what IDS tuning is all about. In the first case, you simply might be able to configure the IDS to ignore all ICMP traffic from your network-management server. In the latter case, you simply would enable or disable that signature or tell the IDS to block those events from being forwarded (it all depends on how the particular IDS works).

Some commercial products have very crude tuning capabilities. For example, your only option for eliminating a recurring false alarm could be to turn off the test or signature that generates the events. In other cases, you get more flexibility; you might configure your IDS either to totally ignore all traffic from a specific IP address, to ignore certain ports, or to ignore a combination of IP addresses and ports. Or, instead of filtering packets up front, an IDS might allow you to filter specific events from specific source IP addresses. The capability to perform this kind of granular tuning is an important consideration when selecting an IDS.

Network Monitoring and Quantum Physics

One humorous story about the need to tune an IDS involves the changes to a network that an IDS can create. Werner Heisenberg is the physicist who is famous for his "Uncertainty Principle," which essentially says that it is impossible to measure something without affecting it. Although his theory revolved around his work in quantum mechanics, a loose analogy can be made to network sensors.

An IDS sensor was installed on a network segment (we won't say by whom) and was configured to report its event data to a management server running on another computer. That sensor also was configured to collect all the network traffic as a test. So, the sensor dutifully captured each and every packet, packaged them up as events, and sent them on their way to the management server. Of course, when the event hit the network, it was collected just like any other packet and was forwarded to the server. This captured event data then was detected, packaged as yet another event, and forwarded to the server. Obviously, a problem was developing.

The next morning, this unnamed inquisitive security engineer came in to find that his normally very stable IDS server had stopped running. A quick look at the logs revealed that the hard drive filled up with captured event data a few hours after he went home. A quick modification of the IDS configuration was made so that the sensor would ignore any traffic between the sensor and the server on the IDS management TCP port, and the problem went away. To this day, the engineer in question wonders what happened to the network load during those couple of hours.

NOTE

Although it is important to plan on a tuning phase as you install any IDS architecture, it is also important to remember that tuning is something that you will always be doing.

New applications will go online that suddenly will result in a burst of IDS event notifications. This can be caused by new internal applications or by the latest popular application on the Internet. After an investigation, you will discover the cause of these events and can tune your IDS as you see fit.

As with any data-filtering exercise, you must balance the needs of reducing false alarms with maintaining a good chance of catching actual suspicious traffic. It is certainly possible to inadvertently blind your IDS to malicious traffic in the process of tuning out undesired events. Just as you do with your cell phone, you should accept the fact that you will always have a little bit of noise in your IDS system. If you get to the point that you never see any false alarms, you most likely have tuned your IDS too much.

One other advantage to having your IDS is that it often will detect misconfigured network devices and servers. These devices typically generate a fair amount of ICMP traffic. Because most IDSs take a hard look at ICMP packets, examining them for signs of network reconnaissance and covert channels, these often appear on your IDS monitoring tools. In these cases, the fix will be in the configuration of the network device, not in the IDS. For example, our company recently detected some unusual IP traffic coming in off the Internet. After a little bit of investigation, we quickly determined that there was a routing table problem with our ISP's gateway router.

One networking technology that really can cause some interesting IDS activity is VPNs. Our company uses an IDS that pays special attention to ICMP packets. This IDS tends to detect a number of unusual IP error messages that are the result of maximum segment size problems between ethernet and the remote VPN client programs.

IDS Tuning and VPNs

Another interesting issue likely will come up the first time that you run a VPN with your IDS. Although the names have been changed, this is a true story involving several telecommuters.

Consider an employee named Sally who telecommutes using a VPN. She has a cable modem connection to her house and is running an internal network (192.168.1.0/24) behind a firewall/router, as shown in Figure 10.12. When Sally comes home, she plugs her laptop into her private network and is assigned an IP address by her internal DHCP server, which is built into her firewall. She then establishes a VPN tunnel between her laptop and her employer's VPN gateway, and she begins to work. Everything seems fine. Back at the corporate network, Sally's traffic emerges from the encrypted tunnel and is dropped onto the company's internal private network (172.16.0.0/16). The IDS sees this traffic and generates a few events of the type described previously.

At about the same time, Sally's co-worker, Bob, does the same thing. Because Sally and Bob both work for a high-tech company, they have compared notes and built themselves similar home networks. Bob's laptop is assigned an IP address from his 192.168.1.0/24 network.

How does the security analyst know which computer is sending the packets that are generating these events? In this case, his VPN server logs were capable of connecting the IP addresses to a remote user authentication.

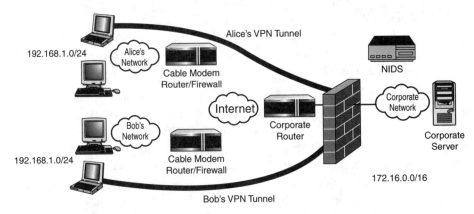

Alice and Bob are co-workers who telecommute via a VPN connection from their laptops to their corporate network. How does a security analyst monitoring the IDS know which private IP network is which?

FIGURE 10.12

IDS analysis complications with VPNs.

The point of all of this is that an IDS is not a passive device that you can deploy and forget about. If you care enough about your network's security to invest in intrusion detection, the odds are good that you are going to take the time to watch what it is telling you, investigate anything that you don't understand, and resolve any problems that might be discovered. Plus, in the end, you will know your network a lot better than you ever thought you would!

IDS Management

As you have seen, intrusion-detection systems can provide valuable early warnings, attack and misuse detection, and investigative data. We also have explored the technical challenges and solutions that must be considered to successfully deploy a meaningful IDS capability. One final set of challenges includes management issues that invariably must be addressed along the course of an IDS deployment.

Security Responsibility

We have worked with many companies on IDS selection and deployments, and one question that has come up repeatedly is, "Who has operational responsibility for network security?" This is especially true of larger corporations and organizations.

The question is not about who should install and maintain an IDS architecture; that responsibility always falls on the IT staff or its contractors. However, typically several sets of "players" are involved in IDS rollouts including these:

- **Corporate security**—Facilities and personnel security management and staff
- **IT management**—CIO and subordinate management team
- **Network administration**—Providers of day-by-day support to network infrastructure (routers, switches, VLAN configuration, authentication servers, DNS servers, load balancers, and so on)
- **Server administration**—Providers of day-by-day support for information servers (mail, Web, databases, and so on)

In many cases, the corporate security staff has almost no interaction with the IT folks until the first time something happens that involves serious monetary loss or corporate embarrassment. It is also not uncommon to find that the people who run the network infrastructure are not very well connected to the people who run the servers. And, in some instances, the IT staff that manages the Internet-exposed resources (the DMZ) is different than the IT staff responsible for the internal enterprise network infrastructure.

Although the specific duties are sometimes different, the situation often arises that several different groups feel that they "own" IDS, at least operationally. In larger organizations, it is common to find that different departments will argue about who should select and deploy the IDS, who should look at OS and application logs, who is responsible for reviewing security events, who should monitor trends in reconnaissance and penetration attempts, and who should receive summary reports.

This is an example of where the rubber hits the road in information security policy development. Policy developers should be clear about who has ownership of information security and what key roles are assigned to the various management and IT staff.

A Case Study in Information Security Policy Ownership

We recently worked with several clients on investigations involving possible wrong-doings by their IT staffs. In one case, the network manager was leaving for another company and was under suspicion of stealing confidential client lists and Web infrastructure. In the other case, several members of the IT staff were suspected of manipulating data with the goal of embezzling money from the company. In both cases, corporate management and security officers quickly became aware that they did not have much input or exposure to the information security problems at their company. Although we were able to assist these companies in their technical investigations, it was clear that little thought had been put into information security issues from a corporate perspective. Unfortunately, it often takes a costly internal problem to force corporate management to take the leadership role that they should on these issues.

This story is not intended to cast suspicion on (very) hardworking IT professionals, the vast majority of whom are honest employees. The point of this is that, in much of the corporate world, information is the key asset that the company holds. Protecting that asset requires that management set clear operational priorities and responsibilities.

Staffing

Operating a robust intrusion-detection architecture can require many resources. Just as many companies monitor their physical security on a 24/7 basis, you might decide that you want to monitor your network security on a continuous basis. This makes even more sense if you consider that much of the "hacker" activity tends to occur late at night or very early in the morning.

One final consideration is that IDS operators often have access to sensitive data. More powerful intrusion-detection systems—the kind that are capable of collecting extensive evidence data—can capture usernames and passwords, email traffic, and other data that normally would be kept private.

Taking Care to Protect Sensitive Information

Our company deployed a new IDS system last year. Given our professional belief that an IDS should be capable of collecting detailed evidence data, we decided to turn on the "full packet capture" option on the sensors to see if it could keep up with our network traffic and still perform its normal IDS functions. After letting the sensor run for a day in that mode, we went back to review the collected data. We were happy to see that the device performed as advertised and that the analysis tools were quite good at displaying reconstructed network sessions. We also discovered that many of our employees, including several executives, have configured their Outlook clients to check their personal email accounts at their various ISPs. So, right there in the logs were many Post Office Protocol (POP) negotiations, including usernames and passwords.

Monitoring an IDS can be similar to monitoring a network-management system (NMS). Both generate real-time alerts that are routed to status screens monitored by "Tier 1" operators on a continuous basis. In fact, we have worked with several companies and service providers that have added IDS monitoring to their normal NOC staff duties.

Staffing a 24/7 network operations center with qualified personnel is never an easy job, and much of the Tier 1 staff often is composed of younger, entry-level persons who have less professional maturity than the higher-tiered staff. Depending on the amount of information that these operators are exposed to or have easy access to, special emphasis should be placed on training them to the sensitivity that should be used in their day-to-day duties and any specific procedures or policies that relate to the disclosure of personal information.

Privacy Issues

We have shown that an IDS can provide valuable information regarding unauthorized access to proprietary information and evidence of employee misuse of network resources. In the latter case, more companies are using this information as a basis for punitive action, including termination of employment. This can be a tricky business. There is a general belief that a private enterprise or organization can monitor anything that its employees do, without limit. The accuracy of that belief varies from state to state and regularly is tested in courts of law. We have heard stories that illustrate both ends of the spectrum on this issues. In one case, a state determined that an employee successfully won a wrongful-termination lawsuit because the employer fired her based on information gathered from monitoring her email without her knowledge. On the other hand, another state's courts held that an employer may monitor whatever it wants in any manner, even if it tells its employees that it won't do it. As with all matters of law, the case history and precedents in each jurisdiction will drive what an employer can and can't do.

One easy first step in dealing with this issue is to always remind people who will have access to the network that they are using private property that is provided for official or business purposes, and to notify them that they should have no expectation of privacy and that they are subject to monitoring. This information should be included in any policy agreement documents that users are required to sign (for example, when they apply for their computer account); they also should be included in logon "banners" that appear on the computer screen as they sign onto the network.

Specific wording of employee agreements and logon banners should be based on any guidelines or laws that apply to your company or organization. It is a good idea to have these documents reviewed by your legal counsel.

Incident Response and Recovery

If you haven't thought about it before, deploying an IDS usually forces you to deal with developing an incident response plan (an IRP, for those who like three-letter acronyms, or TLAs). IRPs can be quite involved, and their exact form can be influenced by corporate culture and resources.

Severity of IDS Events

We have discussed quite a number of IDS events. Modern commercial IDSs can generate thousands of different events. For response planning purposes, we have found that it is useful to think about these events in categories, with varying levels of severity within each category. This concept is illustrated in Figure 10.13.

Severity / Class	Normal (Tune out/Ignore)	Suspicious (Analyze/Trend)	Critical (incident Response)
Network Recon	Scan from NMS	RPC Scans	Host scan behind firewall
Denial of Service	N/A	N/A	SYN Flood Bandwidth Fill
Exploitation Attempt	N/A	Buffer Overfflows	Buffer Overfflows
Successful Exploitation	N/A	N/A	Web Defacement Hiport Shell
Misuse	N/A	Chat Gambling	N/A
Authenticate Failure	N/A	"su to root" RADIUS failure	N/A

FIGURE 10.13

Categorizing IDS events by class and severity.

We commonly discuss three severity levels: normal, suspicious, and critical. For our purposes, "normal" events are things that you might either filter out through tuning or simply ignore. Suspicious events are things that you want to retain, perhaps for trending purposes. Finally, critical events are indicators that something serious could be happening and requires immediate action.

For example, network reconnaissance events come in many flavors. Depending on which events you see and where you see them, your reactions probably will be quite different. Microsoft SMB probes detected outside your firewall are pretty common and can be considered Internet noise. However, if your firewall is supposed to be blocking the NetBIOS ports (137–139), and you see these probes from the Internet on your internal network, you have a problem that needs to be investigated immediately.

Automated Response

Many IDSs provide mechanisms for automatically responding to certain events. In these cases, the IDS takes a slightly more active role and actually injects packets into the network, usually at the computer with the source IP address of the suspicious event. Examples of automated responses include these:

- Terminating TCP sessions by injecting a "reset" (RST) packet
- Sending many packets back to the source to confuse the suspected aggressor
- Rewriting router ACLs or firewall policies to block any traffic from the suspect source IP

As a general rule, these "features" should not be used. Although they offer some protection, they can have several unforeseen consequences. The biggest danger comes from attacks that use spoofed source IP addresses. If you enable the response "features" that your IDS provides, you could end up doing some undesired things:

- Revealing to an attacker that you are using an IDS, as well as the make or model of the IDS
- Turning your IDS into a DoS amplifier—for every one spoofed packet sent to you, your IDS sends several packets back to the unsuspecting computers that really own the source IP address
- Blocking valid data from the legitimate host that the attacker spoofed from getting through your router or firewall

That last issue can be quite serious and has a significant impact if you have deployed the host-based NIDS that we discussed earlier. Although blocking valid targets from one host might not be too serious of a problem, especially for home users, at least one vendor uses a messaging protocol to tell all other H-NIDS hosts in an enterprise environment to also block the suspect traffic. The point here is that you should seriously consider the impacts of active responses from your IDS before enabling these types of functions.

Tier 1 Response

On the simple side of things, you probably will end up training your Tier 1 operators some basic investigative techniques so that they can perform some triage on the events that they observe. This can save you some valuable sleep time and provide some data to support initial responses. Here are some basic tools that Tier 1 operators should have at their disposal:

- **NMS**—If you have one, use your network-management system to check the health of your network. How are your bandwidth utilization, CPU loads, and so on? The answers to these questions might help determine whether your network is under a denial-of-service attack.

- **nslookup**—This is a common command-line tool for resolving IP addresses into domain names, and it can be used to identify what company or ISP an IP address "belongs to."

- **whois**—If IPs will not resolve into a meaningful name via DNS, a whois query often can tell you whose netblock the address is from. whois databases often contain points of contact for security problems as well.

- **Web browser**—If you suspect that you are being DoS'ed, check out your Web site. Is it up? Is it defaced? A slightly more aggressive step on the investigative side is to simply attempt to browse whatever default Web page is running on a suspect source address to see if that reveals anything about the attacker (or the network they are using).

If the command-line tools are not available to your operators, many utility applications and Web sites provide some of the same DNS and netblock lookup capabilities.

Responding to Real Incidents

When you or your first-Tier 1 operators have determined that a real incident has happened or is in progress, you should be able to respond in a well-thought-out way. We have found that a handful of general response plans can be used to provide good guidance for many different classes of incidents. For example, there are many ways that someone can "DoS" your network. However, no matter how this is being done, you usually must follow some basic steps. Some of the incident classes that we have found to be quite useful include these:

- Network reconnaissance
- Denial-of-service attacks
- Web defacement
- Exploitation attempts (for example, inbound buffer overflow)
- Exploitation success (for example, shell traffic on an unusual port)
- Access failures (for example, superuser logon failure)

Each of these classes of events likely will be handled differently. If you are being DoS'ed, you probably will be trying to block the traffic with your router ACLs or contacting your upstream ISP. If you think that someone has "owned" one of your servers, you will be acting to isolate the server as soon as possible and will be preserving any evidence on the compromised machine's file system. Finally, if your Web site has been defaced, you probably will be suspicious of any affected servers, and you will implement your plan to restore your Web site on a backup server. Of course, in this case, you will need to remember that there is a good chance that any new server that you bring online will have the same vulnerabilities that the defaced server had.

Because incident response plans can be quite involved and are affected by organizational structure and management considerations, this chapter is not intended to provide deep coverage of all the different response strategies; however, it is intended to make you start to think about your needs.

Hacking Back: Just Say No!

As network engineers and administrators get more knowledgeable about the network security and exploitation tools that are available, there is more of a temptation to counterattack people believed to be "hacking" them. Although it is one thing to cautiously probe the suspected IP addresses, it is another thing entirely to attempt to gain root or administrative privileges on another system and delete files or launch your own denial-of-service attack. You easily could end up violating the law or attacking the wrong person.

If you suspect that something serious is happening—that you actually are suffering a loss or that people are being threatened or endangered—then the appropriate step is to contact law enforcement. As with any other injustice that is done to you, it is best not to take the law into your own hands.

Do It Yourself or Outsource?

By now you probably will agree that an IDS can be a powerful asset in your inventory of information security tools. However, you also might be feeling a bit overwhelmed by what an IDS could force you to deal with. Most network and system administrators have a strong background in the normal behavior of the IP protocol suite and the applications that they use and support; however, not everyone knows just how to determine whether things such as TCP SYN packets with data payloads should be something to worry about. Or, even if they do know that, they might not have the time to investigate it or keep track of the latest trends in network exploitations.

Just as many companies outsource their physical security monitoring, some are starting to consider the same option for their network security. This decision often is made for a combination of business and practical matters. For example, a company might not be too thrilled about the idea of giving a service provider access to internal servers with sensitive data; however, they simply do not have the budget or access to enough qualified information security specialists to provide 24/7 coverage.

Some companies have taken a hybrid approach to this, contracting with managed security providers (MSPs) to lock down and monitor their front-line resources that provide their connectivity to the Internet, while giving their own staff responsibility for the security of internal IT infrastructure. This can be effective because it allows the company to leverage the security expertise and 24/7 coverage provided by the MSP while retaining control of internal security matters.

Depending on your organization, outsourcing might or might not make sense. If you are a small company with limited IT staff but you have business-critical Internet applications, then an MSP could very well be for you. Larger enterprises likely will take their budget, expertise, and corporate culture into account when making this decision.

If in the process of deploying a network intrusion-detection capability you decide to consider outsourcing, you should be careful to ask several key questions of potential MSPs:

- Is 24/7 manned coverage provided?
- How are signature upgrades performed?
- Are custom signatures provided?
- What is the professional background of the MSP's staff?
- Are any background checks performed on the MSP's staff?
- Does the MSP have robust access to the Internet?
- What are the MSP's facilities like?
- Is backup power available?
- What are the incident response procedures?
- Will you have access to the raw IDS data?
- What kind of reporting is provided?
- What is the SLA?
- How fast can the MSP respond to an incident?
- What will the MSP actually do if an attack occurs?
- Will the MSP tune the software for the customer?

Summary

Our focus in this chapter was to describe the technical and managerial issues involved in selecting and deploying an intrusion-detection capability within an IT infrastructure. We described how a combination of passive network sensors, host-based file integrity monitoring, and log processing can be employed to implement the "monitor and detect" component of your information security architecture.

When selecting an IDS, it is critical to consider factors such as raw data throughput, application-level protocol awareness, IDS evasion detection and compensation capabilities, the capability to tune a sensor to work optimally in your network and support investigative efforts, and the quality of the evidence data provided by the sensors. The deployment of these sensors then must be architected to provide a robust detection capability within a network that more than likely employs high-speed switching and encryption technologies such as VPNs and SSL/TLS.

Management issues are just as important to an effective intrusion-detection capability as the technical issues that we have discussed. To remain effective, a staff of qualified network security specialists should be available for event analysis, sensor tuning, and incident response. Furthermore, management should ensure that monitoring and reporting activities support established corporate information and personnel security policies, and that the appropriate legal issues regarding the monitoring of employee communications have been addressed.

Incident Response and Forensics

IN THIS CHAPTER

What Constitutes Incident Response?

No matter how good of a job you do securing your network, eventually you will have a security incident. The difference between this incident becoming something major or remaining only minor often is determined by your level of preparedness.

The biggest mistake that most organizations make when it comes to incident response is not having a predetermined incident response policy and procedures to back it up. The time to determine what to do about an incident is not when the incident occurs. If you wait until your Web server gets hacked to determine how to respond to it, chances are good that you won't have the optimal response. In many cases, the initial response to a security incident will set the tone for what can be done going forward.

For example, let's say that your company's Web page is defaced. If your first instinct is to delete the defaced page and replace it with the original page, or to just completely rebuild the Web server to get rid of any possible Trojans that might have been installed by the hacker, then you've completely blown any chance of prosecuting the offender. Plus, chances are good that you'll never figure out how he got in and how to avert it in the future. Of course, taking a hacker to court might not be important to your organization; on the other hand, it might be. The time to determine this is not at the time of the hack; it's before the hack ever happens, and it should be driven by your incident response policy.

The term *incident response* has different meaning to different people. To the administrator, it might mean how to recover from a security incident and get network services back online. To your legal council, it might have to do with how to follow up with law enforcement or make a decision about whether to prosecute the perpetrator. In this chapter, we approach incident response from two directions. The first is incident response as it applies to the IT staff. That is, what policies and procedures should be in place, what should these address, how should operators be trained, and what type of escalation procedures should be in place? The second approach looks at incident response from the forensics standpoint—that is, how should you go about investigating a security incident in a manner that will allow you to present your findings in an evidentiary procedure? These are two very different types of incident response. In the first, you are concerned with identifying the source or type of incident and then remediating the problem. In the second, you are concerned not necessarily with remediating the problem, but rather with tracking down its source.

As part of this chapter, we will look at how an organization can build out its incident response capabilities, what the legal considerations are when responding to an incident, and some specific methods for data gathering and forensics. We will also look at how and when to bring law enforcement into the picture and what the ramifications of engaging law enforcement can be.

Preparing for an Incident

As stated before, the most important step in response is preparation. In many cases, we have found that a forensics investigation or incident investigation could have been made infinitely easier with just a small amount of preparation. For example, companies sometimes let their employees go (okay, fire them) because of a breach of conduct, which could be anything from visiting Internet gambling or pornography sites while at work to running their own businesses on company equipment. If the basis for firing an employee is computer conduct, you would think that it makes sense to keep a trail of evidence to prove that the employee is really guilty of such wrongdoing.

In one case, we were called in to investigate an employee who had been doing the latter, running his own business on company equipment, including his desktop and laptop. After informing the employee that he was being fired, the company let the employee go back to his desk to "clean out" his personal effects. In fact, the employee cleaned out not only his drawers, but also his browser cache, cookies, and network files, and then walked out of the company with his laptop. The laptop was later returned to the company after it had been purged of all information. In effect, the company let the employee wipe out the trail of information that led to its decision to fire him. Had the employee decided to sue the company for the dismissal, the company's position would have been severely weakened because of this lack of evidence. Had the company had a simple policy to prevent the employee from accessing his systems or taking home equipment, the evidence on his computers could have been archived in case they were needed in future legal proceedings, not to mention that his actions stood in direct violation of the stated company policy.

Companies can do a few things as part of their normal activities to make forensics and incident response much easier to perform, when necessary. These come under the following categories, which are discussed in the following sections:

- Maintaining log files
- Maintaining user account information
- Timestamping
- System and account banners
- Creating cryptographic checksums of system or other files

Maintaining Log Files

System log files are a rich source of forensic information. In the previous chapters, we discussed what type of information should be logged for various operating systems and applications. Such information should be logged and archived on a regular basis. The requirement for log archiving and retention, including the retention period, should be part of the organizational security policy and should be augmented by written procedures. This is crucial to having such information admitted as evidence in any proceeding.

When properly maintained, log files can be used to determine who was doing what and when. For example, Web server log files can be used to determine who was browsing which site and when. They also can be used to determine whether someone was using a Web-based email site to send or receive information. When investigating a Web site hack, Web server logs can show the time that the hack occurred, how it was perpetrated, the source address of the attacker, and other useful information.

Firewall, router, remote access, and authentication logs also might show the source and destination addresses of connections, user account information, and timestamp information that can be correlated to other events. For example, a dial-in server can be set up to show the phone number of the caller and the ID that it authenticated with. This could be correlated against the event log of a domain controller to determine which files the user accessed or attempted to access. These might then be cross-referenced to an anonymous ftp event picked up by the firewall that indicated that some files were transferred to an external ftp server, the IP address of which might be found in the firewall, router, or ftp server's logs.

Maintaining User Accounts

The fate of employee data should not be left up to the whims of the IT administration team! Given the choice, most administrators will reclaim any resource that is made available when an employee leaves the company. This includes deleting that 1GB of email that the user has been saving for the last several years, or getting rid of all the files in the user's personal drive. Again, the company's security policy should detail whether employee information should be archived and for how long, but, in general, the best practice is to keep (but deactivate) the user account and to archive the user's email for an appropriate period. In no case should an employee be allowed to log onto the network or have access to computing equipment, including laptops and desktops, after they have been terminated.

Timestamping

The time that a certain event occurred is obviously of worth when investigating security incidents or correlating events between different systems. For this reason, it can be worthwhile to utilize a time-synchronization service such as ntp.

Creating Banners

Most systems allow some type of banner to be presented to a user when that user attempts to access the system. By utilizing such banners, you are doing two things. First, you are warning

Incident Response and Forensics

CHAPTER 11

347

11

INCIDENT
RESPONSE AND
FORENSICS

a would-be intruder that his actions are prohibited. Second, you are letting users know that their actions are being monitored and are subject to a written policy. Banners serve as the "No Trespassing" sign of the Internet. By posting a banner, you explicitly inform any user of your system of the existence of a security policy and a limitation on what they may be allowed to do on the system.

The existence of a banner also can make it easier on you if it ever becomes necessary to take a case to court. A banner lets a user know that the improper usage of a computing resource is, indeed, prohibited, and that the user is subject to monitoring. When possible, the portion of the security policy that relates to acceptable usage should be made electronically available. This allows you to post a very succinct banner that references an online policy.

Creating Checksums

Often an important file is modified or replaced by an intruder, such as when a Trojan horse program is installed on the system. Checksums can be used to determine whether a system (or any) file has been modified by an intruder. For each critical system, the administrator creates a checksum (which can be a CRC, MD5 hash, or other) on each critical file and stores these checksums in a secure location such as an off-network server or write-only media such as CD-ROM. After an incident occurs, new checksums are generated on the same critical files, and these checksums are compared to the original. If the checksums for a file don't match, that file has been modified and should be examined during the forensics portion of the incident response. The most popular type of checksum is the cryptographic checksum created by an MD5 hash. Utilities for creating such checksums abound for all popular operating systems.

Real-Time Incident Response

Now that you've done the basic preparation by maintaining log files, user accounts, and time-stamps and have posted the appropriate banners, it's time to look at the steps that you should take to prepare your IT team for an incident. The best way to prepare for an incident is to create an incident-response team that is trained to handle events. This team does not have to consist of dedicated individuals; instead, it is made up of representatives from appropriate organizations that fill critical roles. For the purposes of this book, we will review the basic steps of creating an effective incident response team and then will focus on specific methods and concerns regarding incident response and forensics.

Response Policy

Incident response needs to be driven by policy. This policy should address response not just at the IT and administrator levels, but also at the management level. For example, what organizations need to be included as part of the response mechanism? IT does of course, but what about human resources, public relations, or the office of the president or CEO? If a prominent company's Web site is hacked, you can bet that the CEO will be getting calls from newspapers and investors expecting him to *know* that the defacement occurred and what is being done to correct it. These types of considerations can be driven only by high-level policy and will rarely, if ever, be addressed if you begin by writing incident-response procedures that deal mainly with IT.

Another thing that you should consider in your policy is whether incidents should be investigated so that they can later be prosecuted, if that route is chosen. In addition, you will want to define the roles and responsibilities of your company's organizations with respect to incident response, how responses will be escalated within the organization, what training and drills are considered necessary, the types of assets that are being protected, and what requirements will be levied upon the intrusion-detection systems and the monitoring staff, facilities, and support organizations. The response policy answers the question "What should be done?" with respect to incident response. The next document, the response procedures document, answers the "How is it done?" question.

Response Procedures

When you know what needs to be done, you need to document how it is going to be done. Response procedures capture the details of how operators are going to monitor your IDS as well as report, escalate, investigate, and remediate security incidents. The response procedures will include such things as the following:

- What constitutes an incident?
- How incidents are classified
- The escalation procedures for responding to an incident
- How to collect and preserve evidence of the incident
- What specific actions can and should be taken as a result of an incident (such as blocking addresses and changing ACLs)?
- How incident-handling mechanisms will be tested

Organizational Roles and Responsibilities

Where more than one organization within the enterprise has responsibilities that will impact incident response, it is imperative that the organizational roles and responsibilities be clearly defined, preferably in the policy document. For example, in most large organizations, different sections manage the network infrastructure (routers, firewalls, and so on), the external application infrastructure (Web servers, database servers, and so on), internal application infrastructure (domain controllers, email, and so on), and the IDS function. The function and interaction of

Incident Response and Forensics

CHAPTER 11

349

11

INCIDENT
RESPONSE AND
FORENSICS

all of the components must be fully defined because the group with responsibility for IDS might, in fact, have no ability to change router ACLs or recommend patches to Web servers. The company's legal counsel also might have a voice in how incidents are handled and escalated, and, in many cases, the legal counsel can direct the operations of a forensics investigation to keep under attorney-client privilege any information that is discovered during the course of the incident response. Incident response is probably not limited to just the IDS group because those individuals who handle virus scanning, active content scanning and blocking, and other functions also might have a component of incident response that is included in their job functions. All of these organizations must have a coordinated plan for responding to incidents within the framework of their responsibilities.

Training

Organizations must maintain training plans for the personnel involved in incident response. This can range from the creation of internal user groups that monitor newsgroups and vendor-notification mechanisms, to ongoing training in exploit techniques, to brown-bag seminars, conferences, and external training opportunities. Remember that your incident detection and response can be only as good as the people that are driving it. Without ongoing training, your people will lag behind the "state of the hack."

Remediation

A clear mechanism must exist for remediating any shortcomings that are illuminated during the course of incident response. For example, how does the IDS group make recommendations to the firewall group or the Web server administrators? Unless the concerns that are discovered during incident monitoring and response can be brought up to the appropriate level within the organization, it is possible and probable that the same incident will happen again without being corrected.

What Constitutes an Electronic Crime?

Not all investigations are in response to crimes. Often an organization needs to determine the amount of "damage" done by an event, whether that is a hack or an insider incident. Other times an investigation will turn up evidence that will persuade a company to pursue legal action when it otherwise wouldn't have expected to. One important question that you should be able to answer is, "Does what happened constitute a crime?" There are a number of criteria for determining when something actually constitutes a crime. To begin, a number of federal laws are applicable to electronic crimes. The most important of these statutes are listed here (and are available on the Department of Justice Web site at www.usdoj.gov):

- The Digital Millennium Copyright Act
- The Computer Fraud and Abuse Act

- The Privacy Act 5 U.S.C. Section 522
- Title 18 United States Code, Section 1030

In general, for an incident to be something that law enforcement will take on for investigation, it must involve accessing a system with intention and knowledge without authorization. In general, however, you should be aware that there are generally limitations on the minimum dollar amount of damages before state and federal agencies will look at a crime, unless it has other ramifications, such as hate crimes, terrorism, pornography, or other such societal issues.

If you are performing an investigation geared toward pursuing civil litigation rather than criminal proceedings, any violation of civil or criminal statutes can be used to provide the basis for a suit. This includes violations of your posted security banners or policy to infiltrate or deface your systems, unacceptable usage by employees, theft of proprietary information, or the enforcement of the covenants of noncompete clauses in contracts (such as taking proprietary information to a competitor).

The techniques detailed in the following sections are intended to provide the foundation for admissibility of electronic evidence for either criminal or civil litigation. Note that even if you are not planning to pursue any type of litigation, the evidence gathered during an investigation also can be used as leverage in mediation, especially when dealing with corporate officers, managers, or employees. This can help you avoid litigation and its associated headaches and costs by giving you a persuasive bargaining chip.

Admissibility of Digital Evidence

The real evidence that you're going to find during an investigation really exists on electronic media such as hard drives, tapes, CDs, and the like. As an investigator, you need to preserve that evidence in its original state while duplicating it in a manner that allows you to review it. Ultimately, you will have to provide the foundation to have the original form of the evidence admitted *as evidence* at trial. You then use a variety of forms to outline what you found in the evidence, such as log file entries, file fragments, recovered email, and other such information. If you fail in the early steps of an investigation in preserving that evidence in its original form, the valuable information that you find in any stage of the investigation might not even be heard by the judge or jury.

To help ensure the admissibility of electronic evidence, it is crucial to have a policy in place to have email and other electronic evidence stored as a part of the normal business practice. Collecting this information regularly will allow such data to be admitted into evidence as a "business record" rather than being dismissed (and, therefore, inadmissible) as hearsay.

Chain of Custody and Documentation

Chain of custody refers to tracking a piece of evidence from the scene of the crime until it is admitted into evidence at trial. Whether evidence is admissible at trial might depend on whether the chain of custody has been broken. Evidence takes different forms—some are fungible items such a drugs and electronic evidence, which can be altered—so maintaining the chain of custody is essential for admissibility. Other items, such as a gun, a knife, or a paper check, are not easily altered and can be physically marked with the investigator's initials at the crime scene for future identification. The chain of custody for these types of items goes only to consideration of the evidence and not the admissibility of the evidence. That is, evidence such as a gun will be admitted because it can't easily be altered, while a hard drive might not be admitted at all because it can easily be altered. Thus, it is extremely important to document the chain of electronic evidence for electronic investigations.

To maintain the chain of custody of evidence, it is imperative that the investigator document everything that he does. It is imperative to ensure that evidence has not been tampered with during the course of the investigation. The documentation produced as part of the investigation, even if it is not admissible in an evidentiary proceeding, can be used by the investigator during testimony to refresh his memory and thus is invaluable, considering that it could be months or years before a case actually comes to trial. In the following sections, we detail the steps that you should follow to build a solid foundation that will allow your findings to be admitted as evidence.

Taking Notes

The investigator should keep diligent notes on everything that he does, from the time and date that he begins the investigation to the people whom he worked with and interviewed, and the addresses and room numbers of the equipment visited. These notes also should reference any additional documentation that is produced, such as photographs of the scene or chain-of-evidence documents produced.

Computing Equipment Information

The investigator must keep track of all the model and serial number information of any devices examined or used. This means copying down the model and serial number on the chassis of desktops, laptops, and servers, as well as noting the model and serial number of any disk drives that are part of the investigation, including any drives that are used to image (make copies of) a target drive. It's also worthwhile to keep notes on the hardware configuration of a system. For example, if you are going to examine the swap file of a UNIX system (the file that is used to copy data that is kept in memory), it is important to note the amount of RAM that is in the system under investigation. Depending upon what else is being investigated, it might be important to note the following data as well:

- Serial numbers and MAC addresses of Ethernet gear
- BIOS revision
- Hard drive serial and model numbers
- Chassis model and serial number
- Installed RAM
- Processor type, speed, and serial number (if applicable)
- Hard drive(s) size location, master/slave configuration, or SCSI ID
- Peripherals such as CD-ROM, tape drive, or ZIP drive
- Operating system version numbers

Photographs

When possible, it is worthwhile to take photographs of the area where the investigation is being done, including the positioning of equipment, the computer screen, and the external and internal configuration of equipment that is being investigated. This can both serve as evidence that a particular system was in a particular place and help refresh the memory of the investigator when it comes time to testify. In some cases, it can be difficult to tell which of the many strings of numbers printed on equipment are the serial number, the product ID, and so on. In such cases, we have found it useful to photograph the equipment at close range to show all of the pertinent information in the frame.

Keystroke Logging

When performing an operation such as making a copy of a hard drive, it is important that every step of the process be closely documented. This is important because it is the task of the investigator to show that no data was modified or introduced during the investigation process. Most software that is suitable for use in forensic investigation has the ability to log every keystroke performed by the investigator. This allows the investigator to show the exact sequence of commands that were given in order to, say, copy a disk drive or dump an area of memory. Many forensics devices such as drive duplicators have a built-in capability for printing or otherwise logging the physical parameters of the devices that they are working on. If such a capability is not built into the software or device that is used, the investigator should take notes that detail each keystroke or action taken during the course of the investigation. Although this is without question a tedious operation, it is an essential part of maintaining the chain of evidence. It's also one reason that forensic investigators take so long to do their job, as opposed to the average system administrator, who might accomplish the same job in a much shorter time. The difference, of course, is that the investigator's results will stand up in court, while the administrator's results most likely will not.

Importance of Licensed Software

Many tools can be used to perform forensic investigations, ranging from free utilities such as dd, which can be used to copy hard drives, to multithousand-dollar software packages that are very effective at searching for keywords or reconstructing deleted files. It is imperative that any software tool that is used in the investigation be licensed, not just because we are all good Internet citizens and don't use pirated software, but because not just the results, but the method by which data is gathered, can and will be scrutinized by a defense lawyer. Your reputation as an investigator is sure to be diminished if you are found to be using pirated, unlicensed, or license-expired software. In the same manner, the evidence that is gathered using illicit software is sure to be discounted if the illegality of the software comes to light.

Investigator Credentials

Because of the changeable nature of the information that is gathered by an investigator (electronic logs, files, recovered file fragments, and so on), the credentials of that investigator are of the utmost importance. The believability of their testimony is the key to the weight given to—and, indeed, the admissibility of—the evidence found. Because of this, it is critical that you scrutinize the credentials of the investigator you choose to conduct your forensics. Credentials should include the following:

- Background, training, and previous experience in computer forensics
- An understanding of the concept of chain of custody
- Previous experience as an expert witness in similar investigations
- A list of tools utilized during the investigation
- Expertise in the particular systems being investigated (Windows NT and 2000 experts don't necessarily make good UNIX expert witnesses)
- A knowledge of the rules of evidence
- A clear and documented process and procedures for investigation and evidence handling

The time to verify these credentials is before you engage an investigator, not just before trial!

Liability and Right to Privacy Issues

In certain states, if you are going to monitor someone's electronic activities, you need to notify the users. So, before putting an IDS on a network, you need to notify the users of that network. If you don't do that, you might violate a state privacy provision, which could have potential criminal and civil liability. This situation can be averted by posting the appropriate notification banners on the systems (this is discussed later). You should check your local and state laws pertaining to audio and visual monitoring of employees whenever you are performing an investigation, so as not to violate these statutes. This is especially important in a situation in which you might be monitoring keystroke activity and using a video cameras to document user activity.

Investigation Techniques

Every electronic investigation has its own peculiarities, and the experience and knowledge of the investigator is always a key aspect of a successful investigation. That said, some basic techniques, as well as do's and don'ts, are essential in conducting an investigation, determining how and by whom the event was perpetrated, and avoiding invalidating the evidence because of poor procedures. In this section, we visit many of these techniques and procedures.

Before that, though, you need to ask yourself one question before you take on the job of electronic private eye: "Do I really want to do this?" The second you touch a compromised system, you bring your suitability as an investigator into the realm of evidence. Did you do something to invalidate the evidence? Could you have changed some data inadvertently? Are you unfamiliar with some aspect of the application, operating system, or hardware that could cast doubt on your expertise when you are cross-examined? Do your credentials really support the idea that you are an expert in the field? If the answer to any of these questions is "no," and if you are investigating an IIS hack and wouldn't feel comfortable fielding advanced Windows Registry questions, then you're probably better off not performing an investigation *if you plan to take the legal route*. You must weigh the cost of hiring a professional against the value of the case that you might plan to bring. In general, however, if you haven't conducted an electronic investigation before, the courtroom isn't the place for the do-it-yourselfer.

Securing the Crime Scene

One of the problems with electronic evidence is that it is so easy to modify. File contents and timestamps are almost trivially easy to change without detection. Unless you can show that it is unreasonable to believe that someone could have modified data, it will be very hard to have it believed. As mentioned earlier, the concept of chain of evidence is the key to a successful investigation, and this begins with securing the "crime scene." Physical access to any equipment that is under investigation should be limited to those who are investigating the event. The investigator should take photos of the system placement and configuration and, when useful, the screens of the effected equipment.

Next, the investigator should document the configuration of the systems and network under scrutiny, as detailed in the previous sections. If you're going to disconnect the equipment and then rebuild the configuration at another location, you should also label all cables before disconnecting them and take liberal photographs to make sure that you get everything back to the way it was at the time of the incident.

Shutting Down Equipment

The next thing that you must evaluate is whether to turn off the equipment before performing any additional investigations. Shutting down the equipment by performing orderly procedures (such as `shutdown` on UNIX systems or the Ctrl+Alt+Del–style shutdown on Windows systems) is almost never recommended because it will allow the system to overwrite or delete any temporary files that could be stored on the disk drive. However, simply yanking the power cord will cause you to lose any information in memory, including which processes are running, which users are logged onto the machine, and so on. It's generally up to the investigator to determine the best plan of action.

If the type of incident leads you to believe that there is value in the "live" information on the system, you might want to run a few commands before turning off the system. Be advised that intruders often plant Trojan'ed versions of commands when they compromise a system, so issuing a seemingly innocuous command such as `who` on a UNIX system might do something other than show you who is logged in. To reduce the chance of using a Trojan'ed utility, investigators should always use statically linked binaries that are mounted from read-only media (such as CD-ROM) when investigating a compromised system, rather than relying on the binaries that are available on the system. If you do decide to run such commands, you should consider taking photographs of the results on the screen to document the results of your queries.

If you believe that the file system or swap file holds important information, pulling the plug could be the way to go. This is one decision that only experience can help you with.

Copying Hard Drives and Floppies

If you will be parsing through and reconstructing deleted files, traversing directories, or otherwise looking at a compromised hard drive or floppy, you must do this on a copy (or image) of the drive rather than the original. The best way to create a copy of a disk is to do a byte-for-byte copy. You should never boot the original computer and then do a file copy; this invalidates the original drive and, worse, doesn't give you access to the raw data. Doing anything other than a byte-for-byte (or binary) copy of the drive will not preserve slack space, deleted files, file fragments, or hidden files.

Plenty of good utilities are out there for performing disk imaging—some free, some commercial. When using any utility, it is important that it have some legal history behind it. That is, the utility should have been used and accepted in a previous legal proceeding so that the suitability of the tool itself is already established. There are many good tools out there; if your goal is to take the legal route, it might be best to spend the money on a commercial package. For the most part, we have found that the Linux dd utility is quite cost-effective (it's free) and, when combined with a well-documented procedure, does the trick. In a typical scenario, the investigator creates a boot disk that is used to boot the target system and then mount the target disk in read-only mode. For most PC-based investigations, the source (original) and image (copy) drives are placed in a PC chassis, and the system is booted using the floppy drive. The source drive is mounted read-only, and then dd is used to perform a sector-for-sector copy to the destination. For example, issuing this command will copy all data from the source drive to the destination drive in blocks of 512 bytes:

```
dd if=/dev/hda of=/dev/hdb -bs 512
```

It's important to get the source and destination drives correct. When the system boots up, you can note which drive model is associated with had and hdb, and then triple-check your syntax before you hit Enter. (Working in two-person teams and having your partner double-check your commands can help you build up the confidence to hit that Enter key.) All keystrokes should be logged, and the number of blocks copied is noted as part of the documentation. You then create a checksum utilizing an MD5 hash. This creates a "fingerprint" of the original data, which later can be relied upon in court to show that the original data was not modified during the investigation. Note that the destination (image) drive should either be new, out of the box, or wiped of all information before being used. This can be done through any number of accepted freeware, shareware, or commercial utilities that perform low-level formatting of the drive and also overwrite the drive's data to erase any existing data.

When the copy is complete, the original disk should be labeled and stored in a secure location so that it cannot be either intentionally or unintentionally modified at a later time.

Searching Hard Drives

After you have made a copy of the hard drive, it's time to search it for evidence. This can be a tedious process. Those who have performed such investigations probably are laughing at that sentence because the truth is that it is almost always a tedious process until you find some "good stuff." Although we have written and used our own utilities to perform disk searches, by far the fastest and most powerful utilities tend to be found in commercial packages. In addition, such packages have already been through their "trial by fire" in courts of law, and the information produced by them is widely accepted in legal circles.

Besides having a workable utility, you also must compile a reasonable list of keywords to search for. This is the area in which you must work with your client to limit the scope of the search. In one case, a client wanted to include words such as *Internet*, *www*, *email*, and *job* in the list of keywords to search for. These obviously would have produced a massive list of hits that would have been impossible to search through. Limit your initial list of key words to those that are the least common and that will produce the most useful hits. You can always open up your search list later.

Deleted Files

Just because a file has been deleted from the file system doesn't mean that the data is gone as well. Complete files or file fragments will live on until they are overwritten by other files or until they are erased intentionally. Recovering these deleted files can reveal a wealth of information. Note that from a legal standpoint, the fact that data has been deleted can be used to establish the intent of the owner. That is, if you get back a laptop or desktop that has been completely wiped of data, then just the fact that it has been wiped indicates that the owner was trying to hide something. If you are looking for deleted files and find nothing but 0s or 1s or 0101 patterns, there's a pretty good chance that the former owner purposefully wiped out the data.

Now, let's assume that you're not dealing with that sophisticated a user and look at how to recover deleted files on a PC. Basically, a number of utilities will look for files that have been deleted from the file system but are still fairly intact.

If you're working on a Windows machine, then the job of undeleting files is not that difficult. There are a number of commercial and freeware utilities to do this. Recovering Windows files isn't too difficult. This is because Windows keeps track of the location of all the clusters that belong to a file in the file allocation table (FAT) and keeps track of the filename by writing it into the directory tree.

Things are a bit different for FAT32 and NTFS (used in NT-based OSes), but they're similar enough that this explanation will suffice. The directory entry has space for the filename and extension, file attributes, the change date, the file size, and a link to the starting cluster. When a file is deleted, all that Windows really does is to "hide" the filename by overwriting the first byte in the name field of its directory entry with 0x5h. All the other data remains until that directory entry is reused or until the file space is overwritten by another file. Undelete utilities take advantage of this to restore deleted files by doing things such as combing the directory looking for deleted filenames or piecing together file fragments from entries in the FAT. Some good undelete programs are put out by commercial vendors such as McAffee, Norton, and Symantec. Many such tools do run into a problem when many of the program blocks are missing, and you might have to fall back to piecing together files manually if this is the case. (As you will see in the next paragraph, this same problem occurs for UNIX systems.)

On the UNIX side, things are a bit tougher. Filenames are listed in the directory, which is itself a file. UNIX's version of a FAT is the inode, which stores information about a single file's owner and group ID, permissions, and location, and contains a list of the blocks where the file chunks are stored on the disk. When you delete a file, you free up the inode; in fact, some of the key information, such as the list of block numbers, is actually zeroed out, kind of like wiping out the FAT entries for the file, in Windows-speak. In addition, the file's entry in the directory (itself a file, remember) is marked as unused but, luckily for you, is not zeroed out. So, it appears that all of the really useful information about the file is essentially gone. What you do find is that the filename itself is not wiped out of the directory; in some systems (such as Linux), the inode is marked as unused, but *some* of the block information (which tells where the file lives) is still there. As in Windows, there are both commercial and freeware packages to take advantage of these and other little eccentricities to recover deleted files. The best known of these is called The Coroner's Toolkit, which contains the utility unrm that is used to recover chunks of lost files, and Lazarus, which is used to piece together those chunks into the original (or close to it) file.

Temporary Files

Temporary files are created when an application opens a file and creates a temporary working copy. For example, when you open an attachment using Microsoft Outlook, a temporary copy is created in the Windows \tmp directory for that user. The same is true for applications such as Microsoft Word and others that create temporary files. These temporary files might or might not be deleted when the application exits, and they can include the full text of email messages, attachments, or other files.

File Slack and Unallocated Space

Let's suppose that a data file, such as a document or spreadsheet, is sized at 29,121 bytes. When this file is written to disk, the operating system does not write exactly the same number of bytes; it rounds up to the nearest cluster size. Clusters typically are written on multiples of sectors, which usually are 512 bytes in length. So, for example, the cluster size of a 4.1GB hard drive might be 128 sectors, or 65,536 bytes long. Operating systems do this because writing and reading on sector boundaries is more efficient in terms of speed. But what about the 29,121-byte-long file? It's written into a 65,536-byte-long cluster, which leaves 36,415 bytes to fill.

This unfilled space is called file slack, and it occurs on the tail end of files. The Windows operating system fills file slack in two ways: either by writing whatever data happens to be in RAM into the slack space or by writing whatever data is on hand on the disk into the slack space. From a forensics standpoint, this is a bonanza because you will get little slices of RAM and assorted files padding all of the data files on the drive. By investigating slack space, you can turn up fragments of previously deleted files, usernames and passwords, Web sites that were visited, fragments of email, or other delightful information.

When a file is deleted, both the file itself and the slack space are freed up to be utilized again by another file. However, the information is not actually erased unless the space happens to be overwritten by another file. This type of space is called unallocated space, and it is another boon for investigators because it contains files, file fragments, and slack space.

Incident Response and Forensics

CHAPTER 11

359

11

INCIDENT
RESPONSE AND
FORENSICS

Swap File

Whenever a computer runs out of physical memory (RAM), it writes out a block of memory to disk to free up the resources. This disk area is called the swap file because portions of RAM continuously are swapped in and out of disk. The swap file, for all you Scooby Doo fans out there, is a great place to look for and find clues. What type of clues? Well, imagine that you're a ruthless insider and you want to copy a proprietary client list to sell to a competitor. You copy the file from the fileserver onto a floppy and open it to view the contents on your local workstation. It's possible that the contents of the file that you were viewing will end up in the swap file of the workstation, so even though the file was never physically copied onto that machine's hard drive, evidence of it still remains. The swap file is a good place to find evidence of recent activities that were carried out on the computer. This can include fragments of recent email, Web sites, files, or passwords. It also can show the filenames of recently executed programs, dlls, or other programs that can be associated with a site hack.

Core Files

When a system crashes, it produces a core file that includes a dump of memory at the time of the crash. If an intruder causes the system to crash, this core file will contain that same type of information as the swap file does.

Conducting a System Audit

Whenever a system is compromised, there is a chance that the attacker installed a Trojan horse program or has otherwise modified your system. Trojans can replace often-used utilities such as directory listings, service listings, copy functions, and others, or they can be secreted away in hidden or disguised directories. Attackers also can create user accounts for themselves, modify the permissions of existing accounts to give them administrative privileges, or modify directory or file permissions to give them a back door into the system. When you are performing an investigation of a system, you must be aware of the potential for Trojan'ed programs and modified system settings. Such changes can cause damage to your investigation (imagine that the UNIX directory listing command `ls` is replaced with a program that deletes the directory rather than listing it) and must be fixed if you decide to repair rather than rebuild the system.

An attacker can modify or booby-trap a system in an almost endless number of ways. Tracking down these changes is something that can be learned only by doing, and it is part of the challenge of conducting a forensic investigation. Nevertheless, we will attempt to go through some of the basic areas to check for both UNIX- and NT-based operation systems.

File Integrity

To detect whether an executable, dll, or other system file has been modified by an intruder, you need one of two things: either a clean copy of that file to compare it to or a checksum of the original file. In the previous section on incident preparedness, we described how checksums can be used to test the integrity of a file. If you didn't take the time to create and store file checksums for your system, you also can do a comparison against known good (or "clean") copies of the files. You can either do a binary comparison or do checksums on both the current and clean copies to determine whether any have been changed. Remember, all system binary files should be checked.

On Windows systems, any binary, whether it is a dll, an exe, or a com file, is a possible hiding place for a Trojan, and all such binary files should be checked.

Cron Jobs

It is possible for an attacker to schedule a job to execute at a future time through the UNIX cron or Windows At, Startup, or Task Scheduler services. Such jobs can do anything from erasing your hard drive to enabling a login account for the intruder, to popping up a harmless message letting you know that you were hacked. You can check for cron jobs using the following syntax:

- **For Windows systems**—Type **AT** at the command prompt, or view the scheduled tasks in the Control Panel\Scheduled Tasks folder, or use the Task Scheduler user interface that is part of the Internet SDK client at http://www.microsoft.com/workshop/prog/inetsdk. In addition, you should search the Windows Registry for Run and Run Once keys that will include the full path to any executable that will be run by the system.

- **For UNIX systems**—Type **crontab –e** to view all cron jobs, and look for the scripts themselves in /var/cron/tabs.

Startup Scripts

Another area where an intruder can leave a back door is in the startup scripts. If you clean up the system but don't check for this, you could be reinfected when the system is rebooted. You can check that no new startup scripts have been added to your system by reviewing the following files and locations:

- **For Windows systems**—Check all the \Startup directories, including Administrator\Startup, All Users\Startup, and each user's \Startup directory. Also, check the Registry keys Run and Run Once, as mentioned previously.

- **For UNIX systems**—On operating systems such as Solaris Red Hat Linux, you should check all of the RCx.d directories. On BSD systems, you should check in /etc/rc.d and /usr/local/etc/rc.d. You also should check inetd.conf for any network services that might be starting.

Trojans, Sniffers, and Other Unexpected Services

You already checked for Trojans by using file integrity checkers, you looked for any unusual listening ports or connections, and you checked the daemons or services that were running. You also should check whether someone has installed a password sniffer by determining whether any of the network cards are configured in promiscuous mode, meaning that they will be listed for any traffic on the network, not just that which is bound for their destination IP address. This can be done by running a "sniffer detector," a different system that is connected to the same network as the compromised system. Two tools that do this quite well are cpm and ifstatus, which are available from COAST (www.coast.org). You also should check the system for any new or unusual listening ports or running services. Trojans often use high ports to communicate, and although there are certain "standard" ports that Trojans such as NetBus, BackOrifice, and Strecheldracht utilize, they are easily reconfigured and so should not be assumed.

You also can check for this on the compromised system in the following manner:

- **For Windows systems**—You can use `netstat -a` to see all the services that are listening and the ports they're on, as well as all established connections. You can't really tell whether the interface is set in promiscuous mode, however, using ipconfig, which is the Windows version of `ifconfig`.

- **For UNIX systems**—Use `ifconfig -a` to display the interface statistics. An interface in promiscuous mode is shown here:

```
fxp0: flags=8943<UP,BROADCAST,RUNNING,PROMISC,SIMPLEX,MULTICAST> mtu 1500
        inet 192.168.1.5 netmask 0xffffff00 broadcast 192.168.1.255
        ether 00:a0:c9:60:7e:58
        media: autoselect (10baseT/UTP) status: active
        supported media: autoselect 100baseTX <full-duplex> 100baseTX
10baseT/UT
```

Hidden Files and Directories

As an investigator, you also must check for hidden files or directories that might have been created by the intruder to store rootkits or other files or executables.

It is possible to hide files and directories in a number of ways. For example, a classic way to hide a file in UNIX is to name it . (period). You probably are accustomed to seeing . and .. in directory listings to connote the current directory and the parent directory, respectively, so the "hidden" file looks like ..., which is easy to miss. A good way to hide a directory is to name it . or .. —that is, "dot-space" or "dot-dot-space-space," respectively. When you do a directory listing, this looks like it's supposed to be there because you can't really see the trailing spaces. Intruders use hidden directories to store copies of rootkits (used to install Trojan horse software) or other nefarious software. Knowing this, how can you find such hidden directories?

The only good solution is to do an `ls -a` at the root directory to list all of the directories on the system, and then be observant or write some scripts to look for typical hidden directory tricks.

Hiding files and directories in Windows is even easier because all you need to do is mark them as hidden in their properties tab and, whoosh, they're gone! Of course, it's just as easy to find them, but these are just steps to make the investigator's job harder, not impossible. A freeware tool such as dumpACL is handy for checking the access control lists in windows to audit file and directory permissions.

While you are looking at the file and directory structure, it's worthwhile to review the file and directory permissions to make sure that they haven't been modified by the intruder. For example, suppose that your ftp server has a location where anonymous users can deposit files (an ftp drop-box). This directory normally would not allow users to execute files, which would prevent someone from uploading an executable and then running it on your system. Suppose, however, that an intruder modifies the directory permissions on this directory. This would allow him to come in at a later date, drop a file on the system, and reinfect it. The same would be true for a directory on a file server that is accessible by an insider.

Altered Account Settings

An attacker can alter the account settings of an existing user to make it easier for him to break back into the system at a later date. For example, adding a regular Windows user to the Domain Administrators account will allow that user full access to the Windows domain, rather than his normal, limited access. It is also possible to alter the privileges that a group of users has. For example, an intruder might give the Windows Everyone group the ability to log on to the computer as a Service, thereby giving even anonymous users the ability to gain future administrative access to the system. You should check all user and group settings to ensure that no such modification have been made.

You also should check that no new accounts have been created. This is accomplished easily on Windows systems by reviewing the user accounts, or on UNIX systems by checking the /etc/password file.

Registry Modifications

The Windows Registry is a file that is used to store all kinds of important system and program information. For example, the Registry can store the name of the default directory that a program will read and write files to. Information is stored in different Registry directories, which include ROOT for file associations, SYSTEM for operating system parameters, SOFTWARE for application stuff, and CURRENT_USER for, you guessed it, information that is specific to particular users. The entries within these directories are called *keys*, with keys holding multiple types of data called *values*. Sometimes the ROOT keys are called hives—don't ask why. If someone accesses your Registry, it should show up in the security event log for NT-based systems, assuming that you have set up auditing. If you suspect the veracity of your audit logs, the only way to go is to compare your Registry to the last good backup, just to be sure. A freeware utility such as dumpreg is handy for converting Registry entries to text for easy comparison.

For any changes to the Registry data to show up in the system event logs, the administrator will need to choose the particular Registry hives that he wants to audit and turn auditing on or off using regedt32.

UNIX-Only: Setuid and Setgid Files

You should check a few more UNIX-specific things when doing your investigation.

The file permissions attribute of a UNIX file has a bit that is the Set User Identification bit. It basically says that when this file is executed, it can get access to system privileges based on the permissions of the owner. So, for example, if root owns a file, and the permissions on that file allow it to be executed by any old user, then that file still can operate with root-level permissions even when Joe User executes it. So, if Joe User mucks with the file, he can operate with root-level privileges. This is not a good thing. Most files should not have this bit set. Intruders will create such files so that they can come in later and elevate their privileges to root.

Setgid operates the same way, except that it looks at the permissions of the group rather than the owner of the file. Again, this can allow someone with very few user privileges to execute a file owned by a group with root privileges and thereby elevate himself to the power of root. In general, you should search for and scrutinize any file with the setuid or setgid bit set. These are prime targets for Trojans.

Reviewing Log Files

After all of the sleuthing that you've done, tracking down lost clusters, re-creating inodes, and parsing through Registry keys, let's not forget the easy stuff, the log files! Any good hacker should cover his tracks by deleting all pertinent log files, but, to be truthful, many either forget to or miss a few. Here are some log files worth looking at for both UNIX and Windows systems:

- **Windows event logs**—The security, application, and system event logs will supply a host of information, depending on the level of auditing that is enabled on system objects. We covered how to set up logging in previous chapters, but all important events such as successful and failed logging attempts, object accesses, and change of file, user, and group privileges (to name just a few) will be recorded in these logs. A utility such as DumpEVT is useful for turning Windows log files into flat text files for easier parsing.

- **UNIX system logs**—Quite a few different UNIX system logs are worth reviewing, which largely will depend on the particular processes running on the machine and the logging that has been enabled. A good place to start is the syslog, where most processes will log events of interest, such as failed login attempts and other anomalous behavior.!

Tracking the Intruder

The job of tracking down an intruder after you have detected him usually takes one of two forms, either nearly impossible or surprisingly easy. That is, most attackers are either very clever or not very smart. Luckily, experience shows that the latter is more regularly the case. Tracking an intruder is really an exercise in applied logic. You see something unusual and check it out, which leads you to something else, and so on. The following sections outline some of the things that you should be on the lookout for when tracking an intruder

Source IP Address or Machine Name

Obviously, finding the *true* source IP address of a machine is akin to getting the intruder's home phone number. It's possible that you can find the IP address through careful examination of the compromised system or by analysis of the logs of dial-in servers, domain servers, routers, firewalls, load balancers, Web servers, mail headers, or IDS equipment. It is also possible that you will see signs of the intruder in other, less obvious areas. For example, an intruder might try to perform a zone transfer from your DNS server (either successfully or unsuccessfully) before attacking your network and then might switch to a more stealthy mode when performing the actual attack. You also might see some denied traffic in your firewall or router logs, again, possibly indicating the precursor of an attack. We have found clues ranging from failed attempts at accessing Web server directories to rejected router packets to a directory traversal of a Web server. You should be able to track the intruder at least one hop outside your network if you keep good logs on your networking equipment, assuming that you're not dealing with an insider. The fact that there isn't any information in your networking gear might, in fact, point to an inside job. You often might find source addresses in core files or swap files, as well as the usual search locations mentioned previously.

If you are dealing with a denial-of-service attack, there's not much chance that the intruder used the true IP address of his machine. In the case of a DDos attack, you must track the attacker through the zombies all the way to the master machine to get at the source of the problem.

Contacting the Source

In many cases, you will track the intruder to a machine that doesn't resolve to anything in particular because it is not registered with the InterNIC. In this case, you can at least determine which network it is a part of, who owns that network, and who the administrative contact is.

Incident Response and Forensics

365

CHAPTER 11

11

INCIDENT
RESPONSE AND
FORENSICS

You then can make the decision whether to call or email this contact to pursue the problem. Often you will find that you have tracked the intruder to yet another compromised system, in which case that system administrator will need to start the forensics process on that end.

Even when you can determine the administrative contact for the actual host rather than just the network, it is sometimes still a good idea to contact the network administrator. The reason for this is that if the host itself is compromised, then any email that you send to the host might be read or redirected by or to the intruder, in which case you've tipped your hand to him. Note that unless you are serious and persistent in your desire to track down the intruder, you might find that you don't get much of a response from the network administrator.

You can determine which network a particular host is a part of by querying the American Registry for Internet Numbers (ARIN) through the whois command. For non–U.S. entities, you can check RIPE (www.ripe.net) for Europe or APNIC (www.apnic.net) for Asia Pacific. For example, querying ARIN using whois whitehouse.gov returns the following information:

```
Executive Office of the President USA (WHITEHOUSE-HST)
   Room NEOB 4208
   725 17th Street NW
   Washington, D.C. 20503

   Hostname: WHITEHOUSE.GOV
   Address: 198.137.241.30
   System: SUN running SUNOS

   Record last updated on 19-Oct-1995.
   Database last updated on 16-Oct-2001 23:24:55 EDT.
```

This is handy if you know a machine or domain name and you need to get the contact information. On the other hand, if you use whois to submit a query based on an IP address, such as 198.137.241.1, you'll get this information:

```
Executive Office Of The President USA (NETBLK-EOPNET-C)
   725 17th Street, NW
   Washington, DC 20503
   US

   Netname: NETBLK-EOPNET-C
   Netblock: 198.137.240.0 - 198.137.241.255
   Maintainer: EXOP

   Coordinator:
      Reynolds, William  (WDR1-ARIN)  william_d._reynolds@oa.eop.gov
```

```
    202 395 6975 (FAX) 202 395 3209

Domain System inverse mapping provided by:

DNSAUTH1.SYS.GTEI.NET    4.2.49.2
DNSAUTH2.SYS.GTEI.NET    4.2.49.3
DNSAUTH3.SYS.GTEI.NET    4.2.49.4

Record last updated on 27-Dec-2000.
Database last updated on 16-Oct-2001 23:24:55 EDT.
```

So, if you want to know who owns the domain that an intruder came from, you can query the ARIN servers using whois to find out. This tells you that if you find that you're getting hacked by someone in the 198.137.240.0 network, you should give William Reynolds a call to let him know!

Getting a Subpoena

Occasionally, you will end up with an IP address that is linked to a dial-up account. These addresses typically resolve to names such as 111.22.33.44dialupIspNetwork.com, which is basically the temporary IP address assigned to the dial-in user prepended to some information about the type of connection and ISP that is providing the dial-in service. Because dial-up addresses are assigned dynamically and at the time of dial-up, the only way to further resolve this address is by contacting the ISP. The ISP keeps phone logs that can be used to determine which user ID was dialed in at the time, the dial-up number used, and (sometimes) the number that was calling. This can be correlated to the information that you have to determine who the user was (unless he used a bogus credit card to create the account). Unless you are a member of law enforcement, the only way to persuade an ISP to give out this information is by presenting it with a subpoena for the information. Before getting the subpoena, you should contact the ISP and let it know that it will be receiving the document. Most ISPs know the drill and will preserve the appropriate log information so that it won't have been deleted by the time the subpoena comes through.

Case Studies

The following case studies are taken from actual cases worked by our associates and us. We've taken some liberties to change the specifics of the events so that they don't exactly match the actual incidents, and, in some cases, we have combined aspects of several incidents to round out an example.

Web Site Hack

11

In this case, a high-profile informational Web site was hacked and its home page was defaced. The administrators at the client site were quite competent and did the right things from the beginning. They locked out the intruders by unplugging the Ethernet cable, brought down the system by manually powering it off rather than by going through the shutdown process, and then made an image of the hard drive and stored the original system in a secure location. All investigation was then performed on the image and always in read-only mode.

Because this was a Web-page defacement, the attackers weren't terribly concerned about hiding their tracks—in fact, "tagging" this site was considered quite an achievement. They did go to the trouble of deleting all log files, and a number of random files were created all over the file system with messages that taunted the client's system administrators. The log files, consisting of everything in /var/adm and /var/log, were deleted just by using rm, indicating that the attackers weren't overly sophisticated. Although the process was not trivial, it was possible to recover the deleted log files. These files were restored and transferred to CD-ROM, ensuring that they could not be modified. An MD5 checksum of each log file also was generated by the investigator who restored the log files.

In addition to deleting the log files, the attackers also replaced several system binaries with Trojans. Most interesting was that the binary file that was used initially to gain access to the system was also Trojan'ed. It's unclear why an attacker would Trojan an application that was already vulnerable to compromise, and it's possible that the attackers, who didn't seem overly sophisticated, simply installed a generic rootkit.

Most of the investigation centered on examination of the log files of the compromised system and the firewall logs. Although the compromised system itself was in a traditional DMZ in front of the firewall, some of the initial reconnaissance performed by the attackers (notably host sweeps and port scans) "spilled over" to systems behind the firewall. This allowed the investigation team to correlate the source IP addresses from the initial reconnaissance to those discovered in the recovered log files. The log files revealed the initial manner of compromise (as it turns out, the exploit failed the first few times it was attempted, creating error messages in syslog) was a known but unpatched bug in one of the default operating system binaries. The bug allowed the execution of arbitrary shell commands, and the attackers chose to execute an xterm that displayed on their attacking machine. Because of this exact method of exploitation, it was obvious who the source of the attack was (that is, the system on which the xterm was displayed).

This information was correlated with the firewall logs to chart the actions of the attackers from initial reconnaissance to exploitation. This trail of evidence was not easily disputed in court. These findings were turned over to law enforcement and subsequently were used in the prosecution of the perpetrators.

The Unstable IT Employee

This case involved an employee in the IT department whom the company suspected was misusing company resources to run his own business. This alone probably would not have been reason for them to dismiss him; more likely, he would have been told to cease his actions, if not for the fact that he had openly told other employees that he would set off a code bomb if he ever were fired! Management had a problem. First, they needed to gather proof that he had been misusing resources. Second, they needed a way to fire him and make certain that he couldn't keep good on his promise. Third, they had to prepare for this without tipping him off to what they were doing.

This case required a combination of techniques. Determining that he was using company resources was fairly easy. A quick whois query showed that his private business site was hosted within the network address spaced owned by the company. Some surreptitious traceroutes proved conclusively that the servers were routed through the company's Internet connection. The next phase, planning for his dismissal without the help of the IT department, was a bit trickier. Luckily, the IT department was small, and our team was able to go in after hours and visually inspect all of the critical systems. There were two Internet connections, one used for corporate browsing and the other was used for an informational Web site and email, DNS, and ftp. We also found that the company used a dial-up remote access server for traveling users. Based on interviews with management, we learned that the company was running a Windows NT domain, with most of its critical business functions and databases hosted on a mainframe.

When all of the servers and services were identified, management dismissed the employee and our team "took over" the IT department temporarily. The employee was dismissed just before the start of a long weekend, so our team temporarily shut down the Internet connections and dial-up server to prevent the employee from getting back into the system. Next began an extensive forensics investigation of all of the corporate servers, during which we checked assiduously for Trojans and possible system back doors. We found that one of the company's NT Web servers had BackOrifice installed on it, and the DNS server had a Trojan'ed version of Telnet installed. After completing the rest of the audit, we decided to turn on a full complement of logging on the Web and DNS server, as well as the firewalls and RAS system. Sure enough, during the weekend we found that several connections were attempted to both BackOrifice and the DNS server from a connection that resolved to the employee's DSL account.

A few days later, we received the employee's laptop for forensic investigation. He had returned it to the company at the end of the weekend. We found that the entire contents of the drive had been zeroized, presumably by running a utility to wipe the drive of all information. Although this would seem to be a dead end, in actuality it supported the supposition the employee was, indeed, hiding something. The fact that such an unusual step had been taken created a legal precedence for making the assumption that the employee had knowingly destroyed evidence,

Incident Response and Forensics

CHAPTER 11

369

11

INCIDENT
RESPONSE AND
FORENSICS

possibly of his wrongdoing. If he had just wiped the unallocated space or perhaps defragmented the drive and then wiped it, this wouldn't have been the case. This, combined with the log information that was collected on the firewall and servers, created a convincing case against this fellow. Interestingly enough, the servers that he was using to run his own applications were never found, apparently having been removed before his dismissal.

Employee Misuse of Company Resources

In this case, a financial institution suspected that one of its employees was utilizing company time to run his own competing financial business and was using company resources to research his endeavors before conducting the transactions. In this case, the suspect was fairly knowledgeable of Windows networking and, in fact, had Local Administrator privileges on his workstation. Because the employee's normal duties involved querying the same systems that the employer believed that he was misusing, it was not immediately apparent how to proceed. In addition, the organization did not have much logging enabled on the routers and firewalls, and management was concerned that because the employee was "in" with some of the IT staff, they might tip him off if management requested that additional logging be enabled or even asked for log files to be provided to management. Basically, getting help from the IT staff to investigate the employee wasn't considered a prudent idea.

The goal became to gather information about where the employee was browsing, emailing, and trading during the day through the normal corporate Internet connection, as well as to monitor the specific queries that he was doing and reports that he was generating from the internal systems. We considered a number of means, all of which had to be "invisible" both to the employee and to the IT department. We looked at the possibility of installing a keystroke logger on his system, but because he had administrator privileges, this was ill advised. We also considered a hardware version of a keystroke logger installed inside his computer, but the employee always left his system on; shutting it down and restarting it would have left a trail in the event log. We even thought about placing a hidden camera in the ceiling above his workstation to videotape his keystrokes and capture the contents of the screen, but the logistics of the setup were untenable.

Finally, we settled on placing an IDS in an unobtrusive location in the wiring closet for the floor on which the employee worked. The IDS was installed on a small laptop that was plugged into the main hub for the floor (luckily, it was not a switched network), and the IDS was configured to gather all data going to and from the employee's workstation. After a few days of data gathering, we were able to replay several transactions and data queries and reports that proved management's suspicions, and the employee subsequently was dismissed.

A Few Words on Anonymous Postings

One particularly irksome kind of incident, and one that is the hardest to trace, is when someone posts an inflammatory or misleading message on a newsgroup. This often happens on newsgroups that are dedicated to a particular company or stock. Often a disgruntled individual will post misleading information about the company's health, misinformation about the goals of the board of directors, new initiatives, and even the CEO's personal life or supposedly "actual" meeting minutes. In some cases, the information is actual (although confidential) rather than manufactured, which can cause an even bigger stink! In numerous such investigations, we have found that it can be exceedingly difficult to track these individuals, even when they are not particularly sophisticated. The reason for this is the abundance of Web-based email services that require no real user information to create an email account. Because most message boards require no more than a valid email address to post, users can create bogus email accounts and then post with anonymity. The most fruitful methods have proved to be the following:

- If the posting is done during business hours, you can check your own company's firewall, router, dial-up, VPN, IDS, or proxy logs to determine whether an internal user was logged in to the message service or received email that matched the username on the posting. This assumes that the offender is dumb enough to post from a work account, which people sometimes are.

- If the posting is after hours, you still can check the same log sources, plus you can check who was accessing any corporate service such as email during the posting time. This could indicate who in the company was online during the posting and narrow the list of possibilities.

The only other way to find the identity of the offender is to attempt to correlate the posting activity and the "style" of the offender with other newsgroup and email activity available to you, or to engage in social engineering, the techniques of which are beyond the scope of this book.

Working with Law Enforcement

An important consideration in making the decision to bring law enforcement into an electronic investigation is whether you are willing to give up control of the investigation, including the electronic assets that could become part of it. When a criminal investigation is launched and grand jury subpoenas are issued by law enforcement, the investigators are precluded by law from sharing any information about the progress of the investigation, even with the company that brought them into it (the victim). This can be a serious source of heartache for an organization because such investigations can take months or years to resolve. In addition, civil litigation and potential remedies will be hindered by the parallel criminal investigation and might, in

Incident Response and Forensics

CHAPTER 11

371

11

INCIDENT
RESPONSE AND
FORENSICS

fact, have to wait until the criminal investigation has been completed. After evidence is turned over to law enforcement (such as your hard drives, servers, or anything else that could be deemed evidence), that evidence will not be shared, even with you. Therefore, you should maintain copies of any evidence that you might want to investigate, either to determine how to remediate the problem or to assist you in a civil proceeding.

We've heard of horror stories in which law enforcement has been brought into an investigation and seized assets that included networking equipment and servers, and then refused or delayed providing copies of the necessary data to the victim. The equipment itself sometimes can be held for months *before even being reviewed,* let alone returned.

The lesson here is that if you decide to bring law enforcement into your investigation, you should be prepared to lose control over the investigation and any equipment that might be seized. More importantly, any court documents will become part of the public record, so your company and its security incident could show up on the five o'clock news. Unless you are intent on pursuing criminal charges or have a strong motivation for bringing the event into the public forum, you should strongly consider how and when to involve law enforcement.

Summary

In this chapter, we investigated the exciting world of incident response and electronic forensics. Probably no other field challenges the expertise of the IT professional more than detecting an incident, responding to it, and investigating its cause.

We began this chapter by discussing some of the preparation that needs to be done before you have to respond to your first incident. This included some tactical components, such as calculating cryptographic checksums on files, establishing regular logging schedules, and putting up banners on your equipment, as well as some more strategic concerns such as incident response policies and procedures, training, and organizational requirements. We then looked at some of the legal requirements that come into play with regard to security, such as what constitutes an electronic crime, the admissibility of evidence, and how to document your investigations and findings so that they are legally admissible in court.

After preparing for an incident, you learned about how to respond to one. Here we focused mainly on system-level incident-response and investigation techniques—that is, how to secure, search, and audit UNIX and NT systems. You saw that a host of hidden and deleted information can be resurrected during a forensics investigation, and we also noted how to perform a complete system audit to turn up any additional clues on how the system was compromised and how its vulnerabilities can be remediated.

After investigating the system, we took a stab at tracking down the intruder, and we gave some examples of near-actual cases that we have investigated in recent years. Finally, we wrote about how and when to interface with law enforcement.

Overall, it's important to stress that incident response, especially the forensic flavor, requires a specific set of keen and proven skills. However, it also can be the most challenging and rewarding type of work, and one that requires the security professional to focus all of his knowledge, skills, and processes to nab that bad guy.

References

"Basic Steps in Forensic Analysis of UNIX Systems." http://staff.washington.edu/dittrich/misc/forensics.

CERT Coordination Center. *Steps for Recovering from a UNIX or NT System Compromise.*

Smith, Danny. *Forming an Incident Response Team.* Australian Computer Emergency Response Team.

Willer, Lori. *Computer Forensics.* May 4, 2001.

CERT Coordination Center. *Windows NT Intruder Detection Checklist.*

New Technologies, Inc. *Computer Evidence Processing Steps.*

Staggs, Jimmy. *Computer Security and the Law.* December 1, 2000.

"Forensic Procedures." http://www.cops.org.

Carnegie Mellon University. *Using the Coroner's Toolkit.*

DiCarlo, Vincent. "A Summary of the Rules of Evidence: The Essential Tools for Survival in the Courtroom." http://www.dicarlolaw.com/RulesofEvidenceSummary.htm. April 21, 2001.

Veritect, Inc. "What Lawyers and Managers Should Know About Computer Forensics." http://www.veritect.com/about_veritect/comp_forensics.pdf. April 22, 2001.

Wheeler, David A. "Secure Programming for Linux and UNIX HOWTO." http://www.linux-doc.org/HOWTO/Secure-Programs-HOWTO/.

"Hard Disk Drives, The PC Guide." http://www.PCGuide.com.

Developing Secure Internet Applications

IN THIS CHAPTER

A great deal of this book has dealt with how to implement security using different flavors of standard components, whether they are operating systems, network devices, or protocols. This chapter is a bit different because it deals with custom components—specifically, Web applications.

Most organizations that are serious about electronic commerce or other Web applications tend to write some or part of the applications themselves, or have them developed by third parties. For example, your average Internet banking application isn't something that has been purchased off the shelf and loaded onto a couple of servers. It actually has been custom-designed and coded, most often by a group of people (developers are people, after all) whose main focus is not, unfortunately, security.

You can't really fault developers for not making security a priority. They're typically driven by deadlines and functionality, with launch dates for their Web products set by folks in marketing or sales or management. What's important from our perspective is not the developers' motivations, but rather, the resulting vulnerabilities that they can inadvertently introduce into their code and, therefore, the overall applications. These vulnerabilities can create an opportunity for an attacker to circumvent the security of the overall Web application without ever touching an operating system, spoofing a router, or hopping past a firewall.

Coders can make mistakes that can introduce vulnerabilities in many ways. For example, suppose that an electronic banking customer logs onto a banking application. To keep track of the customer, the coder embeds the bank account number into a cookie stored on the client side. When the customer checks his balance, the coder reads the value from the cookie to get the customer's account number so that it can query the database. The customer, guessing how this works, changes the account number and, whoosh, is now able to access a different customer's account information. This actually used to be a common mistake made by developers, and it illustrates how a system that is extremely secure from the standpoint of policy, operating systems, firewalls, routers, and other infrastructure can be rendered functionally insecure if application security isn't taken into account.

Internet application development is often the place where major insecurities are introduced. Many headline-grabbing security incidents have been the direct consequence of poor application security. This chapter discusses best practices for developing Internet applications. Although many secure programming topics are necessarily operating system–specific, and although a thorough list of these topics far exceeds a single volume (let alone a single chapter), we plan to arm you with enough knowledge to know *how* the general topics of programming errors impact security. By doing this, we hope to bring together the most common coding and development mistakes and present the best-practice solutions to these mistakes.

Developing Secure Internet Applications

CHAPTER 12

375

12

DEVELOPING
SECURE INTERNET
APPLICATIONS

Common Sources of Programming Mistakes

Software developers make mistakes in several broad categories when developing Internet applications. As a general rule, almost all of these can be boiled down to not exercising enough care when handling user-provided data. The simple example of an account number being stored in a cookie on the client side is this type of error. Poor handling of user-provided data can happen at all layers of the protocol stack, not just at the application layer. An analogous example of poor data handling at the protocol layer is the land attack, in which an attacker (user) crafts TCP packets with their IP addresses and ports set to identical values, thereby causing systems to crash or slow down. This problem has affected products from several major vendors, including Microsoft, Cisco Systems, and Sun Microsystems, and it was a problem only because the applications (really, TCP/IP stacks) that accepted this user data (TCP packets) didn't handle it appropriately (basically and infinite loop occurred).

The same type of problem can occur at the application layer. For this reason, user-provided data always must be treated suspiciously. This is not a philosophy that many software developers are taught, although the level of awareness among developers has increased over the last several years. This is probably because of the number of well-publicized events that involved manipulations of user supplied data, such as users changing electronic shopping card information and buying appliances and the like for a few cents, or transferring funds from bank accounts that weren't their own. This chapter details several of the most important best practices that can go a long way toward securing an application exposed to the Internet. Although the details of specific implementations might vary between different environments and programming languages, the core concept remains the same: Any software module or system that handles user-provided data must be written with extreme care to ensure that the user has followed the expected rules of the game.

In a sense, Web applications are unique because part of the application is not really under the coder's control. For example, if the Internet application employs HTTP and Web browsers for the client interface, something that is most often the case, the developer's ability to affect client-side security is severely limited because the client environment is largely out of the developer's control. In this case, all user data must be checked on the server side to ensure that the client has not fooled with anything. On the other hand, if a custom interface is provided to the client so that it can access the application, it is equally important to ensure that this application does not adversely affect the security of the client's system. In the former case, the developer is concerned with only how the security of the client environment affects the server environment; in the latter case, the developer must ensure that he does not adversely affect the security of the client environment.

Overall, this chapter discusses six major topics that form the basis of secure Web application development:

- Metacharacter usage
- Buffer overrun conditions
- String formatting
- Session management
- Credential checking
- Client-side data cleansing

In addition, we'll discuss the importance of coding standards and code review in the development process. By understanding the security implications of each of these topics and how to code their applications appropriately, the Web application developer will have a solid basis for creating safe and secure code.

Metacharacters

It is difficult to assign the title of Most Prevalent Security-Related Bug to any one type of coding shortcoming, but a strong challenger for the title would be poor handling of metacharacters. First, some definitions are in order. *Metacharacters* are characters that have special meaning to certain applications. For instance, in the generic UNIX Bourne shell, the semicolon character (;) can be used to separate multiple commands. In standard SQL, the asterisk character (*) acts as a wildcard to match anything, just as it does in DOS commands such as `find *.doc`. These metacharacters are a problem for developers because they can allow users to manipulate applications in ways that subvert the security of the system.

Danger of Metacharacters

The way in which metacharacters can cause problems can be illustrated by considering the single-quote character ('). In SQL, the single quote is used to delimit strings in queries and thus acts as a metacharacter. However, the single quote is also entirely legal in a lot of user-supplied data, notably names. For instance, let's say that a Web application prompts a user for his name, perhaps as part of a registration procedure. This name then is put into a SQL database by the application. Remembering that the single quote is a delimiter used by SQL, let's look at what happens if the user's name is Jane O'Smith. If the application tries to put this name directly into the database, the SQL statement will look something like this:

```
UPDATE Customers SET Name = 'Jane O'Smith'
```

This statement won't be interpreted in the way that we would like (adding Jane O'Smith into the database) because SQL will think that the data is "Jane O" because the ' character is a delimiter (metacharacter). Worse yet, there's a trailing `Smith'` that throws a monkey wrench into the database and might very well crash the application with it.

Because the characters that can act as special metacharacters vary widely based on the application that is evaluating them, there is significant overlap between those characters that constitute "normal" characters and those that constitute metacharacters.

The special nature of metacharacters doesn't really seem like a security concern yet, but consider what someone clever might do using metacharacters. Suppose that, instead of just inputting their name as Jane O'Smith, a sneaky user decides to enter a complete set of database commands when prompted for his username. This user enters his name as `Jane O' UPDATE Admins SET Name= 'gubb', Privilege = 'Administrator'`. The application, expecting that what the input supplied is the user's name, creates the following string, which is sent to the back-end database server as a command, thereby turning the previous innocent SQL statement into this:

```
UPDATE Customers SET Name = 'Jane O' UPDATE Admins SET Name = 'gubb', Privilege
➥= 'Administrator'
```

The result of this statement is to add a new account called gubb with administrator privileges. Now you can begin to see the danger of metacharacters. In Microsoft JetSQL, this statement is completely legitimate; it's a technique called "batching" queries, in which a program is allowed to submit multiple statements as in single database request. The Jet engine will happily execute all valid SQL statements within this request. In effect, the unwary application programmer has given a sneaky user a way to submit commands directly to the back-end database!

Working Safely with Metacharacters

One solution to the previously illustrated metacharacter problem is to write an application that is aware of the way Jet operates and to screen all the input for any attempts at using Jet-specific metacharacters in the username. This is fine, but what about the myriad of other types of databases or back-end services that the programmer will come up against? Because of the myriad of applications and the fact that each has the opportunity to define its own metacharacters, it's largely futile to try to envision every possible metacharacter attack scenario and screen for it in the code. For this reason, we recommend a more generic approach to tackling the metacharacter problem. To protect an application from attacks that utilize metacharacters, the developer must be aware of three issues:

- What does "normal" input for each user-supplied value look like?
- For each user-supplied value, what about the data supplied that is considered "significant"?
- Which characters do back-end applications treat as "special"?

When approached in this order, a developer's job of adequately handling these funny characters is eased dramatically. When the developer understands these three issues, metacharacters can be addressed by removing their ability to cause special actions. This is accomplished by "escaping" the metacharacters.

Identifying Normal Input

First, the developer asks, what does *normal* input look like? Consider a phone number. For all intents and purposes, a phone number consists of some numbers and possibly a few punctuation characters. Depending on where in the world you are, phone numbers can take the form of (123)456-7890, 123.456.7890, 01-23-45-6-78, or maybe 12 3 456 78. Given these four formats, you can dramatically restrict the possible characters that you allow. So, instead of 127 possible characters (the base ASCII set), you have 16 characters (digits, the parenthesis, the period, the dash, and the space). Anything outside of this set can be rejected as invalid. This allows a developer to write a script to "clean" the input of any characters that fall outside of this range, or to simply reject any input that includes characters other than these 16.

Determining Character Significance

Second, the developer should consider what is *significant* about these characters. The punctuation is just there because it's easier to read for humans. In fact, when you dial a number, you never use these punctuation marks or spaces. When you're storing and handling this data inside of a program, the punctuation just gets in the way. Therefore, when a user submits the phone number, you can strip out these unnecessary characters and put them back in when presenting the data. Thus, the only significant characters are the digits, 0123456789. So, you've reduced your allowed character set to only 10. Now when you clean the input data, you can get rid of everything except these 10 digits.

Identifying Special Characters

Finally, you must think about which, if any, of these characters the back-end application considers *special*. In the case of the phone number, you would not expect any of this set of 10 digits to be a metacharacter. However, you saw that in the case of someone's name, this is not the case (the single quote was indeed a special character). In some cases, you might determine that some of the allowed characters in the input can be considered metacharacters by the application. For example, $50.01 requires the characters $ and ., which could very well be considered metacharacters by the back-end application. If you have to leave in characters that might be considered metacharacters, there are two main ways to deal with them: Escape them or delete them. Deletion is the most straightforward method; if a character doesn't belong or is potentially hazardous, just get rid of it. This is what we did in the first two steps described previously. Unfortunately, this not always can be done if the character is necessary, for example, if a license key for a software product can include $, #, @, &, or other characters. In this case, you must escape the characters.

Escaping Metacharacters

Escaping metacharacters means that you strip them of their special meaning. This is done by placing an "escape character" before the metacharacter. This is where things get a bit tough to explain. Basically, you choose a character that will represent your escape. This character is placed before any potential metacharacter to say, "Treat this next character, which looks like a metacharacter, as just a plain old normal character." An example is warranted here.

Some UNIX programs, such as grep, make use of the asterisk (*) inside the program itself. Now, like SQL, most UNIX shells treat the asterisk as a wildcard. So, for example, you can issue the UNIX command grep c* myfile to look for every word that starts with a *c* in the file myfile. The developers who wrote grep knew that the asterisk would be used as an input to the command, so they supplied mechanisms for users to say, "Hey, I know that this next character is special, but just treat it as normal."

For example, how do you grep for anything in myfile that starts with an asterisk? You can't say, grep * myfile because * is a metacharacter and that command would return everything in myfile. You need a way to tell the program that the next character isn't a metacharacter. Aha! This is where the escape comes in. The most common of these escape mechanisms is the backslash (\). Whenever an application encounters a backslash, it treats the character that follows as a literal (normal character), not as special character. Astute readers probably are noticing that this \ character is just another metacharacter. You're right, it is. And to specify the "real" backslash, you precede a backslash with a backslash. The backlash can be used in SQL just the same as in the Bourne shell—that is, SQL recognizes that the \ character is a metacharacter. What must you do with it? Well, the former application that accepted any data that the user gave must now do some data cleaning first. You still will be handling the data supplied by Ms. Jane O'Smith, but you will code in some steps that will escape the single quotes before submitting the data to the database. The first example that we gave (the "good" example) will look like this:

```
UPDATE Users SET Name = 'Jane O\'Smith'
```

This is entirely valid and will be accepted by the database without a problem. In this case, the developer has written code that looks for any metacharacters in the string (in this case, it finds the single quote) and adds an escape character before it. When this is passed to the database, the database "understands" that the data has been escaped and treats it as a normal character, not a metacharacter.

Now, let's take a look at what the "evil" data will look like:

```
UPDATE Users SET Name = 'Jane O\' UPDATE Admins SET Name = \'gubb\', Privilege
➥= \'Administrator\''.
```

This command will add a very silly name into the database, but it won't execute any commands, which is what you want. Although it's silly, this value potentially could be handled incorrectly by another application down the line. So, just because hazardous data is handled properly on the way in, don't assume that everything is okay. The same vigilance must be part of *all* applications, whether they directly handle user input or whether they handle it on the way back, when it's coming from a trusted system.

In the world of metacharacters, the most common offenders that you, as a programmer, need to look for are these:

- ASCII 0xa (newline)
- ASCII 0xd (carriage return)
- % (percent)
- ; (semicolon)
- * (asterisk)
- ! (exclamation point)
- # (pound sign)
- $ (dollar sign)
- & (ampersand)
- (and) (parentheses)
- { and } (curly braces)
- [and] (square brackets)
- " (double quotes)
- ' (single quote)
- | (pipe)
- ? (question mark)
- < and > (greater than, less than symbols)
- ` (backtick)

Again, this is not an all-inclusive list, but it is a good start.

Client-Side Data Cleansing

Note that many sites make use of client-side JavaScript to validate user input before it is sent to the server. This is a nice feature for the user because he won't have to wait for the server response to find out whether some of the submissions were incorrect or incomplete. For instance, if a user doesn't fill out a required phone number field, a JavaScript routine can catch this and alert the user before the form is submitted to the server. Input validation of this sort, however, is not sufficient when attempting to ensure that user input is safe from a security standpoint. It is trivial to evade client-side JavaScript, either by simply disabling it in the browser or by submitting the request directly to the server. If data is not also stripped of invalid characters on the server, the potential for batched SQL queries, escape characters, and so on exists. All data cleansing should occur in the back-end application (either in addition to or in lieu of cleansing on the client side).

Exploiting Executable Code

Executable code exploits are in strong contention with metacharacters for the title of Most Prevalent Security-Related Bug out there. As with metacharacters, most developers have encountered executable code problems when debugging their code without realizing the security implications involved. Examples of this are the ever-popular Microsoft Blue Screen of Death or the more generic segmentation fault. These are both examples of what happens when a program changes data that is outside the bounds of the memory space that it has been assigned.

The C programming language is especially susceptible to this problem because it allows programmers to write to memory directly with pointers, without performing any bounds checking. Contrast this with other languages such as Java that perform more rigorous bounds checking to explicitly prevent this type of problem. Executable code exploits, such as buffer overflows, might allow an attacker to introduce and run his own executable code rather than simply issuing commands to pre-existing applications or system calls. This means that an attacker can upload his own applications and subvert the security of the existing application, all at the same time. In this section, we examine two of the most prevalent types of executable code exploits: buffer overruns and format string bugs.

Buffer Overruns

A buffer overrun occurs whenever an application allocates a specific amount of memory (a "buffer") and then later copies more data into this buffer than there is room for. For instance, suppose that a programmer reserves 256 bytes in memory for the name of a file, thinking that no filename ever could be longer than 256 bytes. Then later it turns out that a file is 40 directories deep, and the name of each one of these directories is about 8 characters (not to mention the name of the file itself). So, when the program tries to copy the more than 320 bytes of the name into a buffer that was designed to hold only 256 bytes, something's got to give. What normally occurs is that the data that directly follows the buffer in memory is overwritten. In this case, it turns out that computers are fairly stupid; they are capable of doing only what users tell them to and they don't really think about the consequences. So, when a programmer says, "Take this stuff and copy it over that buffer," the computer just does it. Whether "over there" is capable of holding whatever happens to be "over here" is left up to the programmer. And that's where the problems start.

Buffer overruns manifest themselves often when dealing with strings in the C programming language. Most C libraries have a set of functions designed specifically to deal with strings, and they handle strings by treating them as an array of characters terminated by the NULL (ASCII value 0x0) character. One of the most rudimentary of these functions is strcpy() (string copy, in case you couldn't guess), which copies a string from one location in memory to another.

strcpy() takes two parameters: the address of the location in memory where the strings are to be copied to and a pointer to where in memory the string should be copied from (the destination and the source locations). strcpy() does its job by copying the contents of memory at the source location into the destination location, doing this byte for byte. strcpy() keeps doing this until it finds a NULL character in the source string, which it takes to mean that the end of the string has been reached. If it turns out that the source string is longer than the amount of memory that has been reserved by the destination pointer, something is going to get overwritten. strcpy() is dumb and has no idea how big the buffers are. It just copies data. So, if the programmer does not make certain that enough room has been allocated to take the entire string being copied, a buffer overrun occurs. The result? Whatever happened to be in memory *next* to the allocated buffer gets overwritten. This is probably better explained by Figures 12.1, 12.2, and 12.3.

FIGURE 12.1
Destination buffer before copy.

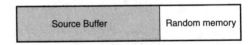

FIGURE 12.2
Source address before copy.

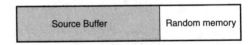

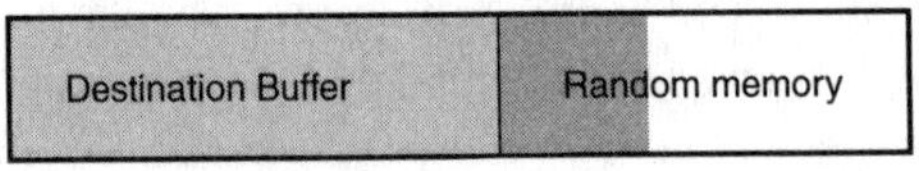

FIGURE 12.3
Destination address after copy.

When a buffer has been overwritten, all sorts of nasty things can happen. For instance, the capability to change the value of variables in memory can have serious repercussions. For instance, what if a filename was stored next to the destination string buffer? If you, as an attacker, knew how the filenames and permissions were set up in memory, you could utilize a buffer overflow to change the name of that file and possibly its permissions to gain access to a protected file that you couldn't normally access.

Here's a simpler example: Let's say that the next value in memory is the bank account number that the application is going to transfer money to in conducting a transaction. If you can create an overflow condition that changes the bank account number from your own to, say, Bill Gates's, you can transfer funds from his bank account to pay for that new big-screen TV.

A wider class of buffer overflow attacks utilizes the fact that computer subroutines often store information about the next program line to execute in memory. In layman's terms, when a routine executes, it looks into memory for where to go next (what to execute next). If you can create a buffer overflow that overwrites this area of memory, called the stack, you can redirect the subroutine. The best type of buffer overflow happens when you not only put a redirection into memory, but also put new program code into memory using the same overflow. So, for example, you can create some code that gives you root privileges and then use a buffer overflow to place that code into memory and redirect the computer to execute that code.

An Example: String Functions in C

To illustrate how difficult it can be to protect against buffer overflows, let's look at a widely used class of functions and delve into some detail on how they can be used, both inadvertently and purposefully, to create buffer overflow conditions.

"Dumb" functions such as strcpy() aren't the only way to trigger a buffer overflow. *Any* code that copies data from one area of memory into another can overrun an allocated buffer. For instance, consider the following fragment of C code:

```
for(i = 0; i < length; i++)
    buf1[i] = buf2[i];
```

This code fragment copies length number of data from buf1 into buf2. If the variable buf1 isn't at least length + 1 characters long (remember, you need the NULL terminator), you will get an overflow. The following is a list of commonly found C library functions that can cause overflows:

- strcpy(), strncpy()
- sprintf(), snprintf()
- strcat(), strncat()
- memcpy(), memmove()
- fgets(), read(), fread()

Note that some of the functions listed (strncpy(), strncat(), and snprintf())specifically were developed to help protect against buffer overruns. Each of these functions is a modified version of its generic counterpart (strcpy(), strcat(), and snprintf(), respectively) that accept an additional parameter: the size of the destination buffer. However, it is *still* up to the programmer to provide the correct value for this parameter. Consider the following:

```
strncpy(dst, src, strlen(src));
```

The previous function uses the strlen() function to calculate the length of the source string (src), and this becomes an input to the strnpy() function. The problem here is that the strncpy() function just looks for a null terminator to figure out the length of the source string. This is a common technique used by programmers, but it will have the exact same effect as just calling strcpy() because it's still possible for the source string to be longer than the destination buffer! The correct way to call strncpy() is to specify the length parameter as the size allocated for the dst parameter, *minus 1*. Remember, you have to leave room for the NULL terminator at the end of the string.

Most implementations of strncpy()copy *exactly* the number of bytes specified by length. The result is that the destination will not include the NULL terminator, and dst will be what is called an unterminated string. If someone later uses the strlen() function to find the length of this string, strlen() will keep searching in memory until it finds a NULL character and so will return the wrong value. This, in itself, could result in a buffer overflow or cause data to be handled in an insecure way. To cause additional headache for programmers, the way that strncpy() copies data is not standard among all strn functions. In fact, there really is no standard behavior. For example, most implementations of snprint() *will* add a NULL character to the end of dst[1]. Because it might not always be possible for a programmer to know exactly how a function will be implemented given any operating system, it is recommended that the programmers manually terminate all strings, just to be safe.

How Buffer Overflows Are Utilized by Hackers

This previous example illustrates how much care must be taken by software developers when writing code. You might ask, "How does this turn into a security problem?" The problem occurs whenever a function accepts user-provided data and that function has been written so that a buffer overflow can be created by a crafty user. This data can come from two basic sources. The first source is client data that is provided to an application. The second is remote procedure calls (RPC) in which one machine can execute procedures on a second machine by passing it data, having the remote system process the call and have the result returned to it.

A good example of the former case is the Microsoft ISAPI overflow that was utilized by the well-publicized Code Red attack that occurred in the summer of 2001. In this case, the vulnerable code was a dynamic link library (DLL) called idq.dll that resided in the Microsoft

Indexing Service; it was loaded by default with the Internet Information Server (IIS) Web server. This allowed anyone on the Internet to access the vulnerable code through a hand-crafted URL sent to the server.

The URL contains a large amount of bogus data (the XXXXs) that are used to create the overflow condition, along with a block of starter code that points to a much larger block of executable code. In this particular case, the goal of the code was to install a program on the target system that then would go out and scan for other vulnerable servers and attempt to infect them. Keep in mind that somewhere in the ISAPI DLL was a function written by a developer who assumed that the function always would be given "clean" data to process, a mind-set that all developers now should be getting over.

Just as a user can provide data to a function that can create overflow conditions, applications that employ RPC architectures can create the same condition by sending function arguments across a network to a target machine running a vulnerable application. For example, UNIX RPC has been a notorious source of many buffer overflows. A procedure such as statd, which provides system statistic, and nfsd, which is part of the Network File System, have allowed a generation of hackers to successfully "own" legions of UNIX systems.

Format String Bugs

Format string bugs have traits similar to both buffer overruns and incorrect metacharacter handling. Format string errors manifest themselves when a function that takes a variable number of arguments inadvertently is given *too few* arguments. To illustrate how format string bugs can occur, let's look at another C language class of functions, the lib C printf() functions. As a reminder to all of you out there who aren't up on your printf trivia, this function expects arguments in the following form:

```
printf(formatstr, var, ...)
```

For example, printf("Hello %s", *name*) would print "Hello Bob," assuming that the variable *name* = "Bob" and the %s are formatting variables that say, "Insert a string here."

Now consider the following fragment of C code:

```
void my_function(char *somestring)
{
    printf(somestring);
}
```

In this perfectly valid code, the programmer has assumed that somestring will be a literal value that needs to be printed. If my_function() is called as follows, everything is fine:

```
my_function("hello, world");
```

In this case, the string `"hello, world"` would simply be printed to standard output. Note that, in this example, no formatting string is used and none is assumed to be present in the argument passed to the function. However, if `my_function()` is called in the following manner, problems creep in:

```
my_function("hello, %s");
```

When `printf()` is invoked by `my_function`, it sees `printf("hello, %s")` and expects that a second argument to the function would be substituted for the `%s` formatting code (as in the "Hello Bob" example). However, there is no second argument, so what will `printf` do? It looks for this second parameter, which typically is stored on the stack. Because no second parameter was pushed onto the stack by the calling function (in this case, `my_function`), `printf` actually will pull some other data resident on the stack.

How can this type of bug be turned into a security hole? Well, imagine that an attacker has access to the source code or is able to reverse-engineer the executable code and so knows that this bug occurs. He might be able to learn that a filename, password, or encryption key is sitting in a local variable on the stack. Knowing this, he can cause this sensitive data to be printed using the `printf` function. This is, of course, a simple and contrived example, but it should be obvious that other, more complex examples could yield similar results. One of these complex examples can be found in a little-known format character specification in the `printf()` functions: `%n`. Let's take a look at how this can be exploited to create bigger and better buffer overflows.

The `%n` specification instructs the `printf()` function to place a number of characters into a variable in the function call. So, a call such as this would place the value 5 in the variable `someint`:

```
printf("hello%n", &someint);
```

Now let's combine this with the previous example (yes, we *are* trying to stretch the bounds of your resolve). Suppose that you call `my_function` in the following manner:

```
my_function("sdaffkdlfjhdfkjhsdkfhdfjsdfjkfk %n").
```

The `printf` function that is called by `my_function` gets this:

```
printf("sdaffkdlfjhdfkjhsdkfhdfjsdfjkfk %n").
```

It then counts the number of characters before the `%n`, which, in this case, is 32, and assumes that a pointer exists on the stack pointing to the location in memory where the 32 will be stored. In this case, there is no pointer, so `printf()` treats the next 4 bytes on the stack as the pointer and stores 32 at that location. So, this particular oddity has allowed the attacker to put an arbitrary value (32) into a location in memory. Without going any further on the technical front, let's suppose that the memory value that the attacker overwrote is a seed to a pseudorandom number generator. If the attacker knows the seed, he can predict what the pseudorandom

Developing Secure Internet Applications

CHAPTER 12

387

12

DEVELOPING
SECURE INTERNET
APPLICATIONS

number generator will output (that's why it's called *pseudo*random). If this is used to create a session for an HTTP session, the attacker might be able to hijack a seemingly secure Web application.

A Final Word on Executable Code Exploits

It should be obvious that attacks such as buffer overruns and format bugs require an in-depth understanding of programming languages, memory utilization, and program execution on the specific platforms that the attack is designed to exploit. Typically, the attacker has access to either source code (for open-source systems) or the tools required to reverse-engineer executable code (for systems whose source code is not publicly available). Given the level of sophistication required to create such an exploit, it would seem odd that so many executable code exploits have been used by attackers; however, when an exploit is written, it requires only a moderate level of expertise to utilize the exploit against a vulnerable system. The Code Red exploit is an example of how the utilization of a well-documented buffer overrun was automated so that no expertise was required for it to propagate to new systems.

Application-Level Security

Thus far, we have concentrated our discussion on ways in which unsafe coding practices can have ramifications on other applications or operating systems. However, additional considerations must be made to protect the application from itself. This is particularly true in browser-based applications that function over the Internet, usually making use of HTTP as the communication protocol.

Although HTTP generally runs on top of the session-oriented TCP, it is woefully void of any concept of state. By this, we mean that each HTTP command is not dependant upon the previous command, and the server generally does not keep track of the order in which commands are presented to it. Because the HTTP connections are not persistent and each request takes place independently (from a connection standpoint), application designers are presented with a special problem of somehow correctly correlating these requests and defining some sort of an idea of "user session." This is much different than, say, a TCP connection, which is marked by a start or SYN and end or FIN. It would be nice if, when a user starts to browse to a Web site, he could signal, "Hey, I'm user XYZ and I'm starting to browse," and then could signal that he was leaving the site when he moved on. This is not, however, the way HTTP works. Every request is a start and finish unto itself.

Cookies

Cookies were created to aid in this effort and to create a rudimentary implementation of state at the application layer. To review, when a user makes an HTTP request, the server returns the appropriate response as well as a unique value, a cookie, that positively identifies the user.

Subsequent requests from the user contain this unique value that is read from the cookie stored by the user's browser, allowing the server to keep track of the session. Cookies make it easy for developers to keep track of state because most of the work is done by the Web server software itself. However, cookies are insufficient from a security standpoint. That is, using cookies on their own as an authentication mechanism is terribly ineffective (and was explicitly *not* their intended use when originally developed).

Cookies are often deterministic, meaning that they are constructed using very simple rules that can be guessed by an adversary. For example, suppose that you're at a hotel and you log on to your banking site using your username and password. You then get a cookie that is formed by concatenating your first name with your account number. Now, in the room next to you is a wily hacker (let's say that you're in Vegas and the Defcon conference is in town) who decides that he's going to steal your session. Because your first name and account number are easily obtained, he forges a cookie and then browses to your bank site. The bank's server sees the cookie and assumes that the hacker is you—voilà, your session has been hijacked.

This attack is simplified because cookies persist through user sessions and are stored in the clear on the client's system. They also have no challenge mechanisms built into them and are easily forged by an adversary. So, let's say that you log into your bank site from a kiosk in the lobby of the hotel (now you really deserve what you get). When you're finished, your cookie is most likely still on the computer! The next user might easily utilize the cookie, either to try to hijack your session or to study how the particular site creates cookies to forge an attack at a later time. Cookies can be used to track user sessions without any negative security impact, but they most certainly cannot be relied upon for authentication.

Source IP Addresses

You might be tempted to make use of the source IP address to correlate user sessions. This seems like a good idea on the surface because the source IP would seem to be something that identifies a specific user's machine, at least for the duration of the session. However, this is ineffective for multiple reasons. First and foremost, using a source IP won't work if you have multiple clients coming from the same source IP address, as is the case when clients are behind a firewall using hide-mode network address translation or a proxy. Along these lines, many hide-mode address-translation implementations operate from a pool of source IP addresses, so a client might have a different address every time he makes a request.

Additionally, by making use of a proxy, it is trivial for a user to pretend to be someone else. Therefore, no stock can be placed in IP addresses as a form of identification. It can be worthwhile to keep track of client IP addresses for audit purposes when developing applications that run on top of HTTP; however, you should never use them for identification or authentication purposes.

Effective Session Management

The best way to enable session authentication when hampered by HTTP is to augment the cookie with something that is more dynamic and that can't easily be forged. We call this a multifaceted authentication token. The idea behind this type of token is to create a set of variables, at least one of which is constantly changing. For instance, when creating browser-based applications, each request coming from the client should contain at least two credentials: a *client ID* that uniquely identifies the client's account (such as username, account number, and so on) and a constantly changing *session ID*. Every time the client makes a request, the server checks the client ID and the session ID to verify that the session is valid and belongs to the client.

For example, let's say that you log back into your banking application. The server returns to you a client ID that is JOHNPUBLIC and a session ID that is 14589 (right now, let's not worry about how the session ID is created). The next time the browser makes a request to the server (such as when you start to perform a funds transfer), it sends both the client ID and the session ID. The server checks the session ID and sees that it's the same one that it just gave you, so it carries out the browser's request. When the server returns the information to your browser (such as your new account balance), it hands the browser a new, randomly generated session ID—say, 83245. The next time your browser makes a request to the server, it presents `ClientID = JOHNPUBLIC` and `SessionID=83245`. Thus, the session ID is constantly changing. Again, the server checks the session ID against the last one that it sent to you. If someone gets hold of an old session ID, it's useless because the server "knows" that it already has been used and, therefore, is expired. This type of mechanism can cut down on session hijacking because the session ID is constantly changing.

Now, in introducing the session ID, you have to be careful: If an attacker can predict the session ID, he can indeed steal the session from the valid user. For example, if each session ID is created by incrementing the previous session ID by 50, it's not going to be hard for an attacker to forge a session ID. In addition, it's going to be easy for an attacker who can steal a few session IDs to figure out the ID creation mechanism (let's see, you steal one session ID that is 18543, the next one you steal is 18593, and then you miss a few but catch one later that is 18643—hmmm, how are they being generated?).

A good way of creating a new session ID is by utilizing a random number–generation program and a one-way function such as a cryptographic hash function (such as MD5). Why, you might ask, don't we just use the operating system–supplied RAND function to generate a random number? Why use the hash? There are a few reasons. The first is paranoia: You can go from about 4 billion possible values for a session ID (using a 32-bit number produced by RAND) to 18,446,744,073,709,551,615 possible values (using a 64-bit hash output) with very little performance impact. Second, by using a function in the creation of the session ID, you have an effective "stub" in case you decide to move to a challenge-response mechanism, such as some kind of digital certificate–based authentication scheme. Finally, it turns out that most random number generators that are provided as operating system calls aren't so random after all; by utilizing the combination hash function, you can get an additional layer of protection.

Replay Attacks and Session Security

As previously stated, the session key value is constantly changed, normally after each request. This prevents replay attacks in which an attacker tries to use an old session of the client to talk to the server. Changing the session key in this way limits the use to which a compromised session key can be put. For instance, if an attacker is capable of intercepting a session key (by either sniffing the network or reading it from the client's machine), that session key will be valid for one only client-to-server request.

In addition, the session ID can be used only if the attacker reads it as it comes from the server (if the key was intercepted when sent by the client, it would become useless to the attacker because the server "nullifies" if after processing the request). Changing the session key with every request limits the amount of damage that can be done by an attacker to one request only (because the next session ID will be different). In addition, this scheme is a fail-closed mechanism. For example, in the scenario in which a key successfully is compromised and the attacker successfully issues a request to the server, the real client's session will be desynchronized. The next time the valid user sends a request, he will find that this session ID has expired. This is easier to understand by looking at Figure 12.4.

When this desynchronization takes place, two things happen. First, the client is forced to establish a new session. Although this will be an annoyance for the user, it also will shut down the attacker's ability to make use of the compromised session. Second, the server will be aware that the session became desynchronized and can record this for audit purposes or can take additional steps. For instance, if the server application notices that the sessions from a specific client become desynchronized at a higher rate than normal, this could indicate that there is something wrong on the client side or that perhaps something more insidious is occurring.

Credential Checks Within the Application

Although being able to verify that a request is generated by a valid client with a valid session is important, this by no means is all there is to Web application security. Within the application, attempted client actions must be compared to access control lists that define what actions the clients are allowed to take. Take, for example, help-desk software. Usually clear roles are defined within the context of the application, the role of a manager, the role of an administrator, the role of a help-desk operator, and so on. Each of these roles will need to perform different actions and, more importantly, should be restricted from performing other actions. For instance, the operator should require access to only the trouble tickets currently open and assigned to him. A manager, however, would need access to all open tickets.

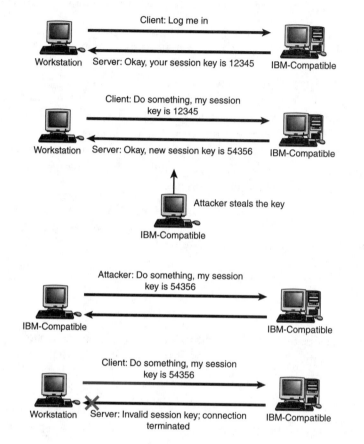

FIGURE 12.4

Desynchronization of client session.

When developing role-based security of this type, a great deal of planning must take place to properly define roles, assets, and the interaction between the two. This might seem obvious, but without sufficient planning and also room for further expansion, a credential system easily could turn into something insufficient and unusable.

Example: Access Control for a Trouble-Ticketing System

As an example, let's look at a problem that confronts many Web application developers: user access control. The intent of this example is to show that a Web application developer must plan ahead during the design process to determine *exactly* what a user will be able to do. The decisions that the developer makes at this stage of the application design will carry through the entire coding phase and have a significant effect on the overall security of the final software system.

One way of creating effective access controls within an application is to utilize a model based on a slimmed-down version of the Windows Discretionary Access Control List methodology. In this paradigm, each user object has a list of credentials associated with it, and these credentials either can be explicitly granted (user-level credentials) or can be inherited based on the type of user (role-based security). In addition, each object or asset has a list of credentials (usually read, modify, delete, and execute) associated with it. Whenever a user object attempts to perform some action on some asset object, the user's credentials are checked to see whether the action should be allowed. A paradigm such as this is sufficient for moderately complex systems, is easy to implement, and is quite extensible.

Let's take a look at a rudimentary implementation of this. Using the help-desk software example from before and our three roles (operator, manager, and administrator), let's apply the credential-checking methodology for three assets:

- Trouble tickets
- User accounts
- Client records

First, you need to define the structure used by all assets. This consists of a description of the asset, an ID that specifies the owner of the asset, a unique identifier (ID) for the asset, and so on.

```
/* structure to define an asset */
struct asset{
    u_char description[MAXDESCSIZ + 1]; /* internal description of asset */
    u_int owner;              /* ID of object owner */
    u_int asset_id;           /* unique ID of object */
    ...                       /* sundry other asset info */
};
```

Next, define the permissions that can be applied to the asset:

```
/*
 * type of permissions. we implement the permissions as a list of
 * explicit permissions or'd together as an unsigned integer
 *
 */
#define PERM_READ      0x00000001
#define PERM_CHANGE    0x00000010
```

```
#define PERM_DELETE      0x00000100
#define PERM_EXECUTE     0x00001000
#define PERM_CREATE      0x00010000

/*
 * structure to define an asset
 */
struct privilege{
    u_char description[MAXDESCSIZE + 1];    /* description of privilege */
    u_int   privid;                     /* unique privilege id */
    u_int   asset_id;                  /* ID of asset this privilege applies to */
    u_int priv_types;                /* types of privilege, e.g. read, write,
etc. */
    ...                      /* sundry other privilege info */
};

/*
 * linked list of privileges
 */
struct privlist{
    struct privilege *priv;
    struct privlist *next;
};

#define ROLE_OPERATOR       1
#define ROLE_MANAGER        2
#define ROLE_ADMIN          3

/*
 * structure to define a user
 */
struct user{
    u_char description[MAXDESCSIZ + 1];    /* description of user */
    u_int userid;                      /* unique user id */
    struct privlist *privs;          /* all privileges assigned to a user */
    u_int role;                     /* type of user, e.g. operator, admin, etc.
*/
    ...                      /* sundry other user info */
};
```

Although this code is not exactly ready for cut-and-paste use, it gives the general architecture for how to implement this type of system quite easily. Each user has a list of privileges. Each of these privileges links to a specific asset object and enumerates a list of permissions that the user has. Each object simply has an ID and an owner. With just these small structures, you can offer a relatively granular privilege system that can control the following:

- Whether the user is allowed to read, modify, delete, or execute an that object he owns
- Whether the user is allowed to create new objects of a specific type
- Whether the user is allowed to read, modify, delete, or execute an object owned by someone else

You also can define assets and users of nearly any type. To put a finer point on it, you can create privilege objects for more abstract assets, such as, "Can this user access objects that it does not own?" and "During what hours may this user be logged in?"

Again, the point is to create a system that offers flexibility and extensibility both in granularity of permissions and in the definition of its various objects: roles, assets, privileges, and users. The system presented here is by no means complete, and it is not intended to present the "best" solution; it is offered mainly as an example of the various constituents of what an application requires for internal credential checking.

Coding Standards and Code Reviews

Many times in this book we have stressed the importance of policy, and with application development this is no different. Besides heeding all of the technical matters discussed in this chapter, it's important that application-development teams have a baseline understanding of what's expected from when it comes to writing code. For example, do you expect coders to write their functions so that they check the length and number of the parameters passed to them? Do you expect coders to include a default condition in every IF ... THEN or CASE statement so that if any of the expected conditions aren't encountered, the code does not "fall through" into some unanticipated state?

Questions like these are best addressed in a coding standards document. Many good examples of such documents are freely available, making it easy to mix and match to come up with a document that fits your development environment. Some of the topics that should be addressed are listed here:

- What programming and scripting should be used
- How error messages should be formatted and how errors should be handled
- Function calling and return format
- Bounds checking
- Memory utilization
- Format and readability of code

Developing Secure Internet Applications

CHAPTER 12

395

12

DEVELOPING
SECURE INTERNET
APPLICATIONS

- Function and variable naming
- Documentation (always a sore spot for developers)
- Configuration management
- How and what to test

We have found that most developers are eager to build the best code they can, but they are sometimes ignorant of simple practices, such as metacharacter cleaning, that can help them develop better and more secure applications. By creating a coding standards document and keeping it brief, you not only create a framework for security, but you also tip off developers to practices that they might never have guessed are insecure.

Having a coding standard also sets up your team for an important step in developing secure code: code review. Code review has a bad rep, perhaps because coders don't like anyone criticizing their work or perhaps because it often is carried out by people who are more interested in how code is formatted than what it does. During a code review, the source code or an application is read by someone other than its developer to look for bugs or deviations from the coding standard. Like anything else, having a second set of eyes look at your work often uncovers problems that you, as its creator, are blind to. In our experience, code review often has uncovered bugs such as insufficient bounds checking, unanticipated or unchecked error conditions, or opportunities for the introduction of buffer overflow conditions that otherwise would have gone unnoticed.

Code review can be done by having developers "swap code" with their peers (a peer review, if you want the formal term) or by having a third party conduct the review. In all cases, the development team needs to be a part of the review process. In addition, the overall application architecture should be part of the code review process and should be available during that process, to allow the reviewers to see how pieces of the application fit into the overall system architecture.

By developing coding standards in implementing code reviews, development teams can help ensure that their members follow good coding practices and don't inadvertently (or even purposefully) introduce security flaws into otherwise well-performing applications.

Summary

Security must be a consideration in the development of *all* software. What might not be considered critical to security now someday could be expanded or reused in a way that directly relates to security. Software bugs and shortcomings are arguably the source of *more* vulnerabilities than anything else. Many developers are not security engineers, and many security engineers are not developers. Thus, it is the responsibility of both parties to work together to educate themselves and educate each other. Security engineers need to become aware of more than just the fact that buffer overruns exist and are bad, but also of the ways in which overflows manifest themselves in code and the proper way to guard against them. Likewise, programmers need to be very aware of the ramifications on the inner workings of what might appear to be perfectly benign function calls. How many programmers do you know who know what the return value from `sprintf()` is? How many more actually make use of it?

Good code comes from hard work, structured programming, extensive knowledge, and constant review. Development teams must design their coding standards not just from a readability and grammatical viewpoint, but also from a security viewpoint. Likewise, source code review and audits must be part of the development process not just to ferret out benign bugs, but also to check for security-related issues.

---

[1] *Well, more precisely, it will insert a NULL character of length bytes from whatever* `dst` *points to.*

INDEX

SYMBOLS

A